Intellectual Property and Cannabis

Intellectual Property and Cannabis

Edited by

Natalie Corthésy

Senior Lecturer, Faculty of Law, The University of the West Indies, Mona, Jamaica

Enrico Bonadio

Professor of Intellectual Property Law, The City Law School, City St George's, University of London, UK

Yentyl Williams

Research Assistant to the Dean, Faculty of Law, The University of the West Indies, Mona, Jamaica

Edward Elgar PUBLISHING

Cheltenham, UK • Northampton, MA, USA

Published by
Edward Elgar Publishing Limited
The Lypiatts
15 Lansdown Road
Cheltenham
Glos GL50 2JA
UK

Edward Elgar Publishing, Inc.
William Pratt House
9 Dewey Court
Northampton
Massachusetts 01060
USA

Authorised representative in the EU for GPSR queries only: Easy Access System Europe – Mustamäe tee 50, 10621 Tallinn, Estonia, gpsr.requests@easproject.com

A catalogue record for this book
is available from the British Library

Library of Congress Control Number: 2025933184

This book is available electronically in the **Elgar**online
Law subject collection
https://doi.org/10.4337/9781035329397

MIX
Paper | Supporting responsible forestry
FSC® C013056

ISBN 978 1 0353 2938 0 (cased)
ISBN 978 1 0353 2939 7 (eBook)

Printed and bound in Great Britain by
TJ Books, Padstow, Cornwall

Contents

Figures

Tables

Contributors

Lotte Anemaet is Assistant Professor in Intellectual Property Law at the Faculty of Law of the Vrije Universiteit Amsterdam. She holds a Master's in Dutch Language and Culture (Speech Communication specialisation), a Master's Talent Programme (Graduate School), and an LLM in Civil Law and in Corporate Law/Intellectual Property (Leiden University). After graduating in 2012, she worked as a lecturer and researcher in intellectual property law at the Vrije Universiteit Amsterdam (2013–17) and later as a PhD Candidate (2017–21). Part of her research was conducted at the Max Planck Institute for Innovation and Competition in Munich. On 25 October 2021, she successfully defended her dissertation entitled *Trademark Rights and Consumer Perception: The Tension Between a Normative and an Empirical Assessment of Consumer Perception in EU Trademark Law* at the Vrije Universiteit Amsterdam.

Enrico Bonadio is Professor of Intellectual Property (IP) Law at City St George's, University of London. His research agenda is wide-ranging, having focussed recently on international trade aspects of IP, the intersection between IP and new technologies such as artificial intelligence, and IP protection of non-conventional forms of creativity, amongst other areas. Enrico has attracted funding from a variety of bodies, including the European Commission, UK Research and Innovation, UK Economic and Social Research Council, and the UK Higher Education Innovation Funding. He is Deputy Editor in Chief of the *European Journal of Risk Regulation* and a member of the editorial boards of the *European Intellectual Property Review* and the *NUART Journal.*

Cristiano Cantore has been a Full Professor of Economics at Sapienza University of Rome since 2023. Before this, he worked as a Research Advisor at the Bank of England and Reader in Economics at the University of Surrey. He holds a BA from Bocconi University, an MSc from Universitat Pompeu Fabra, and a PhD from the University of Kent. He also worked at the OECD and the ECB as a trainee, visited the Bank of Spain as a research fellow, and the University of California at San Diego as a visiting professor.

Natalie Corthésy is a graduate of the University of the West Indies (UWI) Faculty of Law Cave Hill. She obtained an LLM from University College London, a PhD from CCLS Queen Mary University of London, and is qualified as an attorney-at-law in Jamaica. She is Senior Lecturer at UWI Faculty of Law Mona. In 2019 and 2022, she received the UWI Mona Principal's Award for the research project with the Greatest Business/Economic Development Impact for her scholarship on *International Intellectual Property Protection of Country Names*. Natalie is the recipient of the 2017 International Trademark Association's Ladas Memorial Award for her paper *Trademarks, Country Names and Misappropriation of National Identity*. She has served as a member of the advisory board of the Jamaica Intellectual Property Office, the Jamaica Cultural Development Commission, and is a member of the National Technical Working Group on Brand Jamaica.

Marcus Goffe is Attorney-at-Law and Lecturer at the Faculty of Law, University of the West Indies, Mona, Jamaica. Prior to joining the faculty, Marcus was Deputy Director of the Jamaica Intellectual Property Office (JIPO) and held the portfolio responsible for the Trade Marks, Designs, and Geographical Indications Directorate. Marcus has an LLB from the University of the West Indies and an LLM in Intellectual Property Law from Queen Mary, University of London. He is a member of the Rastafari community and has provided legal advice to the Rastafari and Maroon communities in Jamaica. He has also lectured in Intellectual Property Law at the University of Technology, Jamaica, and at the University of the West Indies, Mona. He has been a regular participant at the WIPO IGC and, as TK Consultant, is a member of the Caribbean Traditional Knowledge Working Group, working on the development of a Caribbean regional framework for the protection of genetic resources (GRs), traditional knowledge (TK), and traditional cultural expressions (TCEs). Marcus is in the final stages of completing his PhD at Queen Mary, University of London, focussing on the protection of the rights of Indigenous Peoples and Local Communities in the Caribbean Community (CARICOM) in relation to their lands, GRs, TK, and TCEs.

Cameron Hutchison is Law Professor at the University of Alberta Faculty of Law, where he has taught and published on intellectual property law for 20 years. He is the author of *Digital Copyright Law* (2016, Irwin Law) as well as Co-editor of *Canadian Intellectual Property Law Cases and Materials* (2022, Emond), now in its third edition. He is also the author of *The Modern Principle of Statutory Interpretation* (2nd edn., 2022, LexisNexis). Hutchison is the author of multiple law journal publications on various topics, including intellectual property law, most of which can be accessed on SSRN. He offers courses in musicians and the law, statutory interpretation, freedom of expression and the law, and the graduate seminar.

Bryan Khan is a lecturer and researcher specialising in economic development and intellectual property policy. He is Assistant Director of the WIPO-Turin LLM in Intellectual Property programme, and a senior legal researcher at the University of Turin. He holds a number of adjunct teaching positions at various institutions, including with the World Intellectual Property Organization Academy, and holds a PhD in Law and Economics from Erasmus University Rotterdam. His research focusses are trade secret protection, telecommunications regulation, creative industry social norms, political economy, and Caribbean economic development.

Justin Koo is Tenured Senior Lecturer at the Faculty of Law, University of the West Indies, St Augustine. Justin obtained his LLB from the University of Kent in 2011. He then completed his LLM in Intellectual Property Law at King's College London in 2012, with his PhD following in 2016. Resulting from his thesis was the book *The Right of Communication to the Public in EU Copyright Law*, which was subsequently cited by the Court of Justice of the European Union in the Advocate General's Opinion on the *YouTube* case.

Maximiliano Marzetti is Assistant Professor and the head of the Law Track at IÉSEG School of Management in Paris, France. He is also a research scholar at the *Lille Économie Management* Laboratory (LEM) at IÉSEG School of Management and Lille University, Joint Research Unit no. 221, affiliated with the French National Centre for Scientific Research (CNRS). Additionally, he serves as visiting faculty at various European and Latin American universities, a teaching fellow at Harvard University Law School's *CopyrightX*, and a tutor for distance learning courses at the World Intellectual Property Organization (WIPO). He holds an LLB from the Catholic University of Argentina, an LLM in Intellectual Property from Turin University, a European Master in Law & Economics from Hamburg and Bologna Universities (double degree), and a PhD from Erasmus University Rotterdam.

Marc Mimler is Senior Lecturer in Law at City St George's, University of London. Marc's research interests cover intellectual property law in general, and its interfaces with human rights and international trade law, information technology law, and competition law. He was involved in research projects for the EU Commission, the EU Intellectual Property Office, and the UK Intellectual Property Office, and has presented widely on IP topics on four continents. His work was also cited by the Advocate General of the Court of Justice of the European Union. He also used to be the founding General Editor of the *Queen Mary Journal of Intellectual Property* and the *Interactive Entertainment Law Review* published by Edward Elgar and currently acts as Editorial Advisor for the bi-monthly Japanese IP journal *Patents & Licensing*.

Toby Leon Moorsom is Adjunct Professor at the Institute of African Studies, Carleton University. During this research, Toby was a Social Sciences and Humanities Research Council postdoctoral fellow in the Department of Anthropology at the University of New Brunswick. He has a PhD in History from Queen's University, Canada, an MA in Political Science (York), and a BA in International Development Studies and Political Science (Dalhousie). He was formerly Lecturer in the Department of International Relations at Lancaster University Ghana (2017–19) and Senior Lecturer and Department Head from 2019 to 2020. From 2019 to 2022, he was Research Affiliate at the Institute of African Studies, University of Ghana, while Country Lead in an Arts and Humanities Research Council (UK) Global Challenges Research Fund study on "*Farmers' Perspectives on Challenges in the Food System: A Collaborative Research Partnership*", with Leeds University's Sustainability Research Institute and the Peasant Farmers Association of Ghana. Toby has edited multiple issues of the *Nokoko Interdisciplinary Journal of African Studies* at the Institute of African Studies at Carleton and published in *Review of African Political Economy*, *Canadian Journal of African Studies*, *Socialist Studies*, *Pambazuka*, *and Al Jazeera English*, among others. He has previously taught at Queen's University, the University of Toronto, Scarborough Campus, Nottingham Trent University, and Carleton University.

Emma Perot is Lecturer in Law at the University of the West Indies, St Augustine. Emma began her career at UWI in 2019. Her first book, *Commercialising Celebrity Persona: Intellectual Property Law and Practice* was published in September 2023 by Hart Publishing. Emma's expertise in the field of intellectual property has yielded publications on the impact of AI on performers, regulation of deepfakes, and the intersection between the right of publicity and celebrities and the copyright of paparazzi. She was awarded 'Most Outstanding Faculty Researcher' for Law at the Principal's Research Awards 2023.

Akshita Rohatgi is a student and legal researcher at the Guru Gobind Singh Indraprastha University, India. She is currently a research assistant specialising in intellectual property law at City St George's, University of London, as well as AI and platform governance at the Korea Advanced Institute of Science & Technology, South Korea.

Larry Sandell is a registered patent attorney, litigator, and cannabis IP strategist with Mei & Mark LLP in Washington, D.C., and heads the firm's cannabis practice. He focusses his practice on counseling clients on strategic intellectual property matters; drafting and prosecuting patent applications; litigating patent infringement and other matters in federal district courts and the International Trade Commission; arguing federal appeals; and handling patent-related Amazon.com take-down disputes. Mr Sandell has a passion for advising start-ups and other innovative companies on IP matters, with a focus on cannabis, consumer electronics, medical devices, food science, generative AI, and software technology areas. He has argued in the US Courts of Appeal for the Federal Circuit, the Ninth Circuit, and D.C. Circuit. Larry earned his JD, with high honours, from the George Washington School of Law, where he was Order of the Coif. Larry earned a BSE, with distinction, from Duke University with a double major in biomedical and electrical engineering.

Yentyl Williams is Research Assistant to the Dean (Faculty of Law, UWI Mona), Tutor of IP Law (UWI, Mona), and serves as Editor for the *Journal of Law, Governance and Society*, as well as *MonaLaw Student Law Review*. She obtained her PhD from the University of Bristol's School of Law on *Geographical Indications in the Caribbean: A Third World Perspective* (2019–24). Yentyl's academic interests also include International Economic Law, WTO Law, EU Law, Globalisation and Food Policies, and Caribbean, Indigenous and Marginalised Methodologies. Yentyl is a graduate of King's College London, Sciences Po Paris, and post-graduate of the College of Europe, Bruges. Yentyl has a decade of experience working on EU relations with the African, Caribbean, and Pacific (ACP) group of states, in the public (European Commission, CTA, European Economic and Social Committee (EESC), UN ITC) and private sector (consulting), as well as in academia (Ghent University). She has researched, published, worked, and travelled widely in Europe, Africa, the Caribbean, Asia, and South America.

Luke Sebastian Zimmerman is an attorney and has a law firm based in San Francisco, California. He started his legal practice with cannabis trademarks in 2013 and, in 2018, registered the first California state trademarks for cannabis in California's history. He has lectured extensively about cannabis trademarks throughout the world. He was identified by the California Department of Food and Agriculture as a specialist in his field and was invited to participate in a working group to create legal standards for the California Appellations Program.

Foreword

Intellectual Property and Cannabis is a volume that offers much more than the title promises. The editors, Corthésy, Bonadio, and Williams, like masters of weaving, combine four distinct threads to create a fascinating tapestry on cannabis.

Evidence of the approach ethos of the editors and contributing authors is that the reader can start anywhere in the volume, following a particular interest or an interest heading, but will continue reading it as one whole book. The authors have read each other's chapters; there are cross-references; social and economic considerations are raised in the more practical chapters, and practical points are highlighted where the focus is historical, social, or economic. The approach is interdisciplinary and comparative, and the diversity of topics and authors comes together as a rich tapestry to be thoroughly enjoyed by practising lawyers, academics, intellectual property students, and a broader audience that will be attracted by the currency of the topic.

The first thread is on the theme of branding, examining potential trademark protection in the United States and the European Union and under the regime of geographical indications. The authors dive deep into each topic; there is a lot of detail, but also enough context for the uninitiated in intellectual property to engage with the legal issues and the fascinating case law.

Part II, the second thread, covers moral rights, image rights, packaging, and plant varieties. The authors look at the challenges that a link with marijuana could bring to a work protected by copyright or to the image of an established personality. There is also a thorough, comparative analysis of the packaging of cannabis issues and a chapter on the protection of cannabis cultivars in the United States.

The third thread, Part III, builds on the detailed analysis of the first half of the book and offers four contemporary jurisdictional case studies on Jamaica, Canada, Uruguay, and the Netherlands. The intricate challenges and contradictions between positive intellectual property protection and the regulation of cannabis are themes that recur in this part of the book.

The fourth thread adds a new dimension, a thoughtful, rounded overview of the concept and social and economic aspects of cannabis. Part IV looks at the social origins of Jamaican cannabis, considers the topic from a critical development theory perspective, introduces an economic angle of cannabis, and links cannabis with traditional knowledge and Indigenous rights.

The clear, critical analysis, the lucid writing, the demystification of cannabis and intellectual property by the authors is well worth the reader's journey from Introduction to Epilogue, wherever the journey starts!

Professor Spyros Maniatis
Director, British Institute of International and Comparative Law

Acknowledgements

Reviews: Daenia Ashpole (Former Director, Cannabis Licensing Authority, Jamaica); Dr Machel Emmanuel (Principal Investigator, Life Science Cannabis Research Group, University of the West Indies and Cannabis Consultant, the Commonwealth of Dominica); Jeremy de Beer (Professor of Law, University of Ottawa, Canada).

Introduction to *Intellectual Property and Cannabis*

Natalie Corthésy, Enrico Bonadio and Yentyl Williams

This book provides the first interdisciplinary discussion on *Intellectual Property and Cannabis*. As one of humankind's oldest cultivated crops, cannabis is as controversial as it is misunderstood. Whether it is referred to as cannabis, ganja, weed, or with other terminologies, the legal and policy landscapes are shifting globally with regard to its regulation. This dynamic edited collection provides an informative overview of the key issues impacting the intersection of intellectual property (IP) and cannabis.

Cannabis has been a food, a medicine, a fibre, and a religious sacrament,[1] as well as a medicinal and psychoactive agent,[2] and an aid to divination and in ceremonies honouring the dead,[3] for thousands of years. Since 2015, Jamaica has become the first country globally to explicitly legalise the product for religious purposes, in relation to the Rastafari community's sacramental usage of the herb, and its consumption plays an important role in Jamaica's public image, being linked to cultural phenomena like reggae music and the Rastafari movement.[4] Today, more than 50 jurisdictions in the world have legalised or

[1] DT Brown (ed), *Cannabis, The Genus Cannabis* (CRC Press 1998); Geoffrey Guy, Brian Whittle, and Philip Robson, *The Medicinal Uses of Cannabis and Cannabinoids* (Le Pharmacien Hospitalier, March 2008).

[2] EB Russo, GW Guy, PJ Robson, "Cannabis, Pain, and Sleep: Lessons from Therapeutic Clinical Trials of Sativex, a Cannabis-based Medicine" (2007) 4(8) Chemistry & Biodiversity, 1729–1743.

[3] S Gray (ed), *Cannabis and Spirituality: An Explorer's Guide to an Ancient Plant Spirit Ally* (Simon & Schuster 2006); C Graindorge, "Les Oignons de Sokar" (1992) 43 Revue de l'Egyptologie 87 <https://doi.org/10.2143/RE.43.0.2011272> accessed 1 September 2022.

[4] MA Emanuel, A Klein, M Rychert, "Towards Social Justice And Economic Empowerment? Exploring Jamaica's Progress with Implementing Cannabis Law Reform" (2022) 43(11)Third World Quarterly, 2693–2711.

tolerate its production, sale, and consumption for recreational and/or medical purposes. This is the case for Jamaica, Canada, several states in the United States, Uruguay, and the Netherlands, amongst others discussed in this book. New markets and innovative business models have therefore emerged.

The legalisation of cannabis leads to major economic implications. In the US, the cannabis market is projected to reach $72 billion annually by 2030, according to industry research group New Frontier Data,[5] and as often happens with emerging markets, IP rights become important tools to support the growth of such burgeoning sectors. For example, cannabis-related trademarks are becoming popular, with registrations being granted that protect not only corporate names but also signs including the names of specific cannabis varieties. Likewise, patenting cannabis genes and cells, as well as new methods of breeding cannabis, gives producers a legal tool to recoup investments and invest in further research and development. Additionally, choosing and protecting a distinctive brand that links the product (including cannabis) with the relevant geographical area and provides consumers with relevant information is considered crucial.[6]

Yet, using IP to protect innovation in the cannabis industry also presents challenges. Several cannabis-related trademarks may turn out to lack the required level of distinctiveness and thus fail to obtain registration. Examples include "Bavarian Weed", "Well Weed", or "Mango Kush" in the EU context.[7] Likewise, trademark offices in more prohibitionist jurisdictions have already refused to register some cannabis brands because the product is considered immoral or illegal, which inevitably raises free speech issues.[8] The use of brands on the packaging is also restricted in many countries, thus reducing the

---

5 New Frontier Data, "New Frontier Data Projects Annual U.S. Cannabis Sales to More Than Double to $72B by 2030" (*New Frontier Data*, 20 March 2022), <https://newfrontierdata.com/cannabis-insights/new-frontier-data-projects-annual-u-s-cannabis-sales-to-more-than-double-to-72b-by-2030/> accessed 15 September 2024.

6 NGS Corthésy, "Brand New IP: Country Name Designation – From France with Love", in D Gervais (ed) *The Future of Intellectual Property* (Edward Elgar Publishing, 2021), 322–345.

7 Case T-178/20 *Bavaria Weed v EUIPO* (BavariaWeed), Judgment of the General Court (Tenth Chamber) of 12 May 2021. [21]–[23]. See, Case R 213/2021-5 *WELL WEED,* Decision of the Fifth Board of Appeal of 04 March 2021 [3]. For further insight, see Chapter 2 by Marc Milmer, "A Bridge Too Far? Trade Mark Protection for Cannabis-related Products and Services in the European Union. See also Chapter 1 by Luke Zimmerman on "Budding Opportunities: Cannabis Trademarks in the United States".

8 R Greenberg, "Recent Supreme Court Trademark Decisions and Cannabis Registrations" (2020) Cannabis Law Journal.

ability of cannabis producers and distributors to reach and communicate with consumers. Moreover, patents protecting cannabis may tend to have broad claims, with commentators fearing that the patent scope may cover 50 to 70 per cent of all cannabis strains on the market today, thus creating and consolidating monopolistic or oligopolistic scenarios.[9]

New cannabis cultivars can also be protected via plant variety rights (PVRs), which aim to protect new varieties developed through breeding for equitable return on their investments. Current estimates predict that over 300 new cannabis-related varieties which have fulfilled the criteria for registration have recently been protected via PVRs (as well as patents).[10] Yet, the availability of IP monopolies in this field may also lead to a few multinational companies accumulating PVRs and carrying out anti-competitive behaviours, which may damage small farmers, especially in developing countries, undermining the situation of local and Indigenous farmers who have been growing and breeding cannabis for a long time.[11] A consideration of this book is therefore about the intersection of the cannabis markets' growth and social equity, which is explored in the final section.

The book thus delves into the legal as well as socio-economic and cultural development potential of the cannabis plant and its intersection with IP rights. It is divided into four parts. Part I considers branding of cannabis with insights from trademark and geographical indications (GIs) analyses. Part II expands with chapters on copyright, image rights, packaging, as well as patents and PVRs. Part III is then dedicated to practical case studies covering the Jamaican, Canadian, Dutch, and Uruguayan scenarios. The concluding Part IV broadens the focus of the book to consider developmental, economic, historical, and sociological aspects.

In Part I on *Branding*, Chapter 1 by Luke Sebastian Zimmerman on "Budding opportunities: cannabis trademarks in the United States", highlights the unique relationship between trademark law and the legal status of cannabis due to the tension between federal and state laws. With references to the US Patent and Trademark Office, the Lanham Act of 1946, and relevant

---

9 A Maxfield, *Intellectual Property Survey: Cannabis Plant Types, Methods of Extraction, IP Protection, and One Patent That Could Ruin It All* (Ohio State Public Law Working Paper No. 480) (2019), Drug Enforcement and Policy Center, No. 3.

10 J Wyse and L Gilad, "Trends in Intellectual Property Rights Protection for Medical Cannabis and Related Products" (2021) 3 Journal of Cannabis Research.

11 S Title, *Bigger is Not Better: Preventing Monopolies in the National Cannabis Market* (Ohio State Legal Studies Research Paper No. 678) (2022) <https://papers.ssrn.com/sol3/papers.cfm?abstract_id=4018493> accessed 8 September 2022.

case law, this chapter shows the evolution of trademark protection from the era of prohibition. It also sheds light on the legal developments that followed the 2018 Farm Bill, which legalised hemp-derived products in the US and its implications for the future of the industry. The chapter concludes that with the growth of cannabis businesses and considerations of re-scheduling, cannabis trademarks will become more important, especially when considering issues of consumer safety. The second chapter, "'A bridge too far?': trade mark protection for cannabis-related products and services in the European Union" is provided by Marc Mimler. It assesses the legal questions surrounding trademarks for cannabis-related brands in the EU and sets out the EU system of obtaining and enforcing trademarks for cannabis. It also explains the balance that is being struck between questions of morality and innovation. With reference to the EUIPO and relevant case law, it outlines the divergences between the EU and its member states' laws on the one hand, and industry trends and legal and regulatory regimes on the other. Chapter 3, "Geographical indications and cannabis" by Yentyl Williams, explores the potential for protecting cannabis via GIs laws and draws on the case study of Jamaica Cannabis, Jamaica Ganja, and Jamaica Hemp, as well as other regional options for GIs, including Westmoreland cannabis or Orange Hill cannabis, among others. The exploration herein demonstrates how an inclusive GIs framework can be established between cannabis producers and government institutions. It sets out how the Small Island Developing State (SIDS) territory of Jamaica can be a forerunner in registering and implementing an inclusive GIs framework for cannabis nationally, presenting a model for other countries globally.

Part II begins with Justin Koo's Chapter 4, "Copyright, the moral right of integrity and marijuana." The chapter considers the open question of whether copyright works can be used in relation to marijuana without the permission of the author, given the absence of any case law. It explores the moral right of integrity as applied to examples of marijuana scenarios across the jurisdictions of France, the UK, Canada, Jamaica, and the US. Koo suggests that potential mischief can be avoided by contract in the copyright countries where moral rights are waivable and even in *droit d'auteur* countries where the author has expressly agreed to certain uses. "Marijuana and image rights" is then the focus of Emma Perot's Chapter 5. The legal landscape surrounding the use of image rights is considered in connection with the promotion and sale of marijuana, drawing on the relevant laws of the US, Canada, Jamaica, and the UK. Perot explains how celebrities' images should generally not be used without permission as claims can be made for unauthorised commercial uses of persona. Subsequently, in Chapter 6, Enrico Bonadio and Akshita Rohatgi consider "Packaging of cannabis", and explain how national rules (from jurisdictions such as the US, Canada, Uruguay and the Netherlands) have mandated, with different degrees of intensity, neutral packaging. The authors note how public health measures, such as removing eye-catching and colourful elements from the packaging, aim to discourage the consumption of a harmful product while keeping it legal. While similar measures were first implemented in some countries for tobacco products, this chapter extends the analysis of literature in this field to consider how it is now being applied to cannabis in those jurisdictions that have legalised this product. This section of the volume is closed by Larry Sandell's Chapter 7, "Protecting cannabis cultivars in the United States: utility patents, plant patents, and plant variety protection certificates". The chapter provides an overview of the regulatory frameworks for patents and plant varieties relating to cannabis by drawing on the approaches to protection via the USPTO and the Plant Variety Protection Office. It explains how cannabis breeders and genetic scientists seeking IP protections for their new strains can draw on the three distinct and overlapping forms of IP protection to protect cannabis cultivars and related genetic technologies – utility patents, plant patents, and plant variety protection certificates.

Part III is then dedicated to *Case Studies.* In Chapter 8, Natalie Corthésy provides an overview of "The development of an IP protection strategy for Jamaican cannabis". Corthésy considers the ongoing efforts to devise a strategy for the sector through public and private sector partnerships. Jamaica's current legislative IP framework is analysed to determine whether existing IP provisions for the protection of cannabis are adequate and considers what laws and/or regulations need to be adopted to bolster the policy framework and propel the nascent local industry forward as a competitive contender in the global cannabis market, balancing economic growth and market sustainability. "The Canadian scenario" by Cameron Hutchison is the focus of Chapter 9. This chapter considers how cannabis growers and distributors can protect and increase their businesses in Canada via IP rights, including trademarks, patents, and PVRs. It looks at the growing Canadian case law on IP rights related to cannabis products. The Canadian scenario provides an informative case study as this country legalised and regulated cannabis production, distribution, and consumption in 2018. Chapter 10, authored by Maximiliano Marzetti, then zooms in on "Cannabis regulation and IP rights in Uruguay". In 2014, Uruguay legalised and regulated cannabis production, distribution and consumption. Marzetti considers the evolution of Uruguay's legalisation of recreational, medical, and industrial cannabis. He emphasises how the state monopoly on recreational cannabis use does not benefit from IP since the market is not dynamic enough to generate commercial benefits in a free market, compared to the potential available to the medicinal and industrial industries that can more readily benefit from economic incentives and IP rights. "The Dutch scenario" is assessed by Lotte Anemaet in Chapter 11. It considers how the Netherlands regulates and protects IP rights associated with cannabis, particularly in relation to trademarks and plant varieties. This analysis is crucial for at least two reasons. First, the Netherlands has tolerated the production, distribution, and consumption of cannabis for several decades. Second, the Dutch courts have developed case law on how trademarks apply to this product. The chapter also considers the government's current considerations of further legalisation and acceptance of cannabis, which will have implications for IP protections of the cannabis.

The final section of the book, Part IV, is entitled *Developmental, Economic, and Sociological Analysis.* It begins with Chapter 12 by Marcus Goffe, "Traditional knowledge, traditional cultural expressions, and cannabis: an Indigenous rights-based access and benefit sharing framework". Goffe explores the cannabis-related rights of Indigenous Peoples and Local Communities, including the rights of communities to their genetic resources (GRs), traditional knowledge (TK), and traditional cultural expressions (TCEs), with particular emphasis on the global Rastafari community. The chapter examines the cultural appropriation of Rastafari TCEs in cannabis-related goods and services globally within an Indigenous rights framework and, in that respect, assesses the intersection of Rastafari cannabis TK/TCEs and IP laws related to trademarks, passing off, copyright, designs, GIs, and PVRs. Goffe explains that these communities, the bedrock of ancient cannabis culture and contemporary cannabis genetics, must be empowered to obtain the legal recognition, protection, and enforcement of community rights, including moral and economic rights, over their cannabis-related GRs, TK, and TCEs. Subsequently, Cristiano Cantore's Chapter 13 focusses on "The economics of intellectual property protection for cannabis: challenges, opportunities, and the evolution of patents". Cantore highlights the unique challenges and significant opportunities for leveraging IP to drive innovation, enhance market differentiation, and increase profitability. It also examines the evolution of cannabis-related patent filings and grants across different countries and time periods, revealing trends in market concentration and competitive dynamics. Practical recommendations encompassing branding, market differentiation, and product development are provided to optimise profit generation and successfully capitalise on the value offered by the cannabis IP portfolio. Bryan Khan's Chapter 14, "Postcolonial justice in the post-prohibitionist market: a political economy view on IP and cannabis", then explores the parallels between cannabis regulation and IP law from a political economy and postcolonial perspective. It also exposes the inherent coloniality in the international drug regulation system, and how, alongside IP, this is linked to a larger matrix of colonial power in international law. Khan notes that industrialised economies in the Global North have first-mover advantages in the production of cannabis-related IP assets in the post-reform market, which can also reinforce colonial injustices. Through an exposé of how legal frameworks are rooted in social control over marginalised peoples, a misrepresentation of scientific evidence, and even racist ideologies, this chapter outlines how the IP system can be strategically utilised by countries in the Global South. The final chapter of this section, and book, is Toby Leon Morsoom's Chapter 15, entitled "A history and social anthropology of the African origins of Jamaica's cannabis". This chapter challenges the dominant mythology tying the plant's Jamaican history with the arrival of East Indians post-emancipation in 1848. It presents evidence of its hidden history, linking cannabis culturally and materially to Africa to explain how the intellectual content of Jamaica's original cannabis strains derives from the African continent and the labour of Maroon peoples of Jamaica. It exposes how the processes of decriminalisation of cannabis have accelerated the dispossession of Maroon and Rastafarian peoples of the IP of their forebears, whereby subsequent laws served to entrench the structural inequalities of the slave-plantation economy beyond the age of empire.

Finally, an epistemological and ontological insight into the three co-editors reveals their shared love of the island of Jamaica, where they were united through an initial project considering GI protection for Jamaican products, of which cannabis was a specific case study. Corthésy's research on nation-branding links Jamaican iconography to key signifiers in global consciousness: reggae, rasta, and Ganja.[12] As the legal landscape shifts, the elegies of Bob Marley's "Kaya", Black Uhuru's "Sensimilia", Peter Tosh's ode to "Legalize It" or Lee "Scratch" Perry's plea to "Free Up The Weed", call to mind the long-felt want for epochal change in social attitudes and political reactiveness to the exploitation of cannabis. This book elucidates the key issues raised globally as a result of increased regulatory and environmental changes in the commercialisation of cannabis and cannabis-derived products and services. It gives insights into how IP can be leveraged, in particular by emerging economies formerly disadvantaged by prohibition and prosecution strategies, to provide a springboard for innovation and increased competitiveness in international trade.

---

[12] NGS Corthésy, *International IP Protection of Country Names: Balancing Nation Brands and Geographic Commons in a Competitive Global Market Place* (Ian Randle Publishers Ltd, 2023).

PART I

Branding

1. Budding opportunities: cannabis trademarks in the United States

Luke Sebastian Zimmerman

1.1 INTRODUCTION[1]

The history of trademark protection for cannabis is intertwined with the start of the United States' (US) legal cannabis industry,[2] which can be traced back to California's Compassionate Use Act of 1996 (CUA).[3] California's CUA was the first instance of a state allowing limited marijuana use for medical purposes.[4] In the 28 years since California implemented the CUA, 38 states have

1 Thank you to Enrico Bonadio, Yentyl Williams, Bryan Khan, Sean Clancy, Rachael Dickson, Hannah Stitt, Mary Shapiro, David Branfman, Lara Pearson, and Jessica Gonzalez for sharing their cannabis-related trademark wisdom with me. Thank you to my family for their constant support of my research and work. Lastly, thank you to my amazing girlfriend, Leilani Speer, for supporting my interest in researching the niche intersection between trademarks and cannabis for the past ten years.

2 In this chapter, the word "cannabis" is broadly used to refer to the plant *Cannabis sativa L.* I will differentiate between the words "cannabis," "marijuana," "marihuana," and "hemp" later in the chapter. The use of the word "cannabis" is intentional, as this is how the plant is generally identified internationally. In the US, marijuana is defined as any part of a *Cannabis sativa L* plant (except fibrous stalks) that is not hemp (21 U.S.C. § 802(16)). Hemp is defined as cannabis with ≤ 0.3 percent THC by dry weight (7 U.S.C. § 1639o (1)).

3 Compassionate Use Act of 1996, CAL. HEALTH & SAFETY CODE § 11362.5.

4 1 U.S.C. §§ 841, 844. Marijuana is defined as "[c]annabis" plants and any products made therefrom that contain more than trace amounts of the psychoactive chemical Delta-9-THC.

created laws allowing the medical use of cannabis,[5] and 24 states,[6] including California, have enacted laws legalizing non-medical cannabis use.[7] The progress of states legalizing cannabis contrasts with federal laws that still consider cannabis, also defined in federal law as marijuana, a controlled substance.[8] The tension between state and federal law creates a unique challenge for obtaining protection for cannabis trademarks; in most cases, enforcement of trademark rights is even more problematic. The irony of this is that the US cannabis industry is arguably the largest in the world, and the most well-known cannabis trademarks and largest cannabis companies are from the US.[9]

As of 2023, the US cannabis industry is estimated to have a value of US$33.88 billion,[10] with projections that it could reach US$97.16 billion by 2028.[11] By comparison, as of 2023, Canada's federally legalized cannabis industry is estimated to be worth US$3.90 billion, with a growth forecast of US$7.98 billion in 2028. If the US amends its federal cannabis laws, the US forecast could be even greater by 2028.

As this emerging industry continues to grow, there is an increased need for consumer safety for cannabis goods. One way to ensure consumers can consume cannabis safely is to ensure cannabis goods have been tested for pesticides, heavy metals, and other contaminants by allowing companies to access trademark protection under federal law. Unfortunately, this protection cannot be granted while marijuana is federally illegal.[12] Federal trademark protection, however, is generally not available to cannabis businesses because marijuana is federally illegal in the US. It is in the federal government's best

---

5 "National Conference of State Legislatures Medical-Use Update" <https://www.ncsl.org/health/state-medical-cannabis-laws#:~:text=Medical%2DUse%20Update,medical%20use%20of%20cannabis%20products> accessed 29 December, 2023, archived at <https://perma.cc/XK6T-A2JH>.

6 ibid. Non-Medical/Adult-Use Update.

7 Non-medical use of cannabis is referred to as "recreational use" or "adult use." There is an ongoing debate about which term is more appropriate for non-medical cannabis use. A more detailed explanation can be found at J Wilhelm, "Understanding Medical vs. Adult-Use Cannabis Dispensaries" (*Leafly*) <https://www.leafly.com/news/cannabis-101/what-is-a-marijuana-dispensary> accessed 19 April 2022.

8 21 U.S.C. § 802.

9 "Largest Companies by Market Cap" <https://companiesmarketcap.com/cannabis/largest-cannabis-companies-by-market-cap/> accessed 15 February 2024.

10 Statista, "Cannabis- Cannabis- United States" (*Statista*) <https://www.statista.com/outlook/hmo/cannabis/united-states> accessed 29 December 2023.

11 ibid.

12 21 U.S.C. § 816(16).

interest to protect citizens who choose to consume cannabis by ensuring cannabis products are safely produced and that there are comprehensive consumer protection laws for cannabis goods.[13] Instead, the federal government has maintained an extended prohibition of marijuana, which has its origins dating back to the early 1900s.

Against this background, the chapter is structured as follows. Section 1.2 provides a short overview of the history of cannabis prohibition and the evolution of trademark law in the US. Section 1.3 explores how the 1946 Lanham Act applies to cannabis-related trademarks. Section 1.4 highlights the confusion around descriptiveness and cultivar names for cannabis. Section 1.5 addresses the benefits and limitations of state trademark protection, while Section 1.6 touches on trade dress, celebrity brands, and geographic indicators. Section 1.7 then focuses on how the rescheduling of marijuana might impact trademark rights. Section 1.8 finally concludes.

1.2 A BRIEF HISTORY OF CANNABIS PROHIBITION AND TRADEMARK LAW IN THE UNITED STATES

There is no way to do justice to the history of cannabis prohibition without dedicating at least some amount of time to its origins in the US. This chapter explains how trademark law has been, and currently is, applied to cannabis in the US. To understand how trademarks apply to marijuana, hemp, and cannabis, a brief introduction provides an insight into the history of the US's complex relationship with *Cannabis sativa L.*

Ironically, the US has maintained cannabis prohibition for over 80 years despite the fact that hemp was present in the American Colonies as early as 1606,[14] well before the US declared its independence from the British.[15] Hemp was so important that the Jamestown Colony charter had a contractual obligation requiring colonists to cultivate hemp.[16] This was not unique to the British, as hemp was considered necessary to settle the Americas. The French and Spanish also promoted hemp cultivation because it was versatile and used for food, fiber, and types of medicine.

---

13 DJ Kochan, "The Regulatabilization of Cannabis" (2022) 49 Fordham Urb. L.J. 519 <https://ir.lawnet.fordham.edu/ulj/vol49/iss3/2>.

14 R Stoa, *Craft Weed: Family Farming, and the Future of the Marijuana Industry* (2018) The MIT Press 27.

15 ibid. Some drafts of the Declaration of Independence were written on hemp parchment.

16 ibid.

Hemp was an important agricultural crop in the early years of the US, and many colonial presidents cultivated it on their private estates.[17] The colonies were also producing an abundance of tobacco at this time. This gave rise to the popularity of combining hemp with tobacco, which is a tradition that is still prevalent internationally today,[18] although it has fallen out of fashion with cannabis users in the US.

The early 1900s saw the creation of federal laws addressing prohibition and temperance, which impacted not just alcohol but also various narcotics.[19] The ban in the US started with the federal government's enactment of the 1914 Harrison Act, one of the first narcotics laws in the US. This act made the distribution of certain substances federally illegal.

In 1919, the 18th Amendment of the Constitution was ratified,[20] which enacted alcohol prohibition in the US. Between 1914 and 1930, many states began making marijuana use illegal. The concern was, in part, due to worries that people would shift their focus from alcohol to marijuana use.[21] The ban on alcohol lasted until it was repealed by ratifying the 21st Amendment of the Constitution in 1933.[22]

On the heels of alcohol prohibition ending, a new series of cannabis laws were enacted that formed the origins of the US war on cannabis. In 1930, Congress created the Federal Bureau of Narcotics (FBN), of which Harry J. Anslinger was its first commissioner.[23] Anslinger is credited as the reason the Spanish word "marihuana," and not "cannabis," was included in federal criminal law.[24] There is ample supporting evidence to indicate that Anslinger's

---

[17] BM Adam, "Seven Founding Fathers Who Framed Hemp and Advocated for It", *High Times* (July 4, 2023) <https://hightimes.com/culture/seven-founding-fathers-who-farmed-hemp-and-advocated-for-it/>.

[18] ibid 29.

[19] ibid. The Harrison Act imposed "a special tax on all persons who produce, import, manufacture, compound, deal in, dispense, sell, distribute, or give away opium or coca leaves, their salts, derivatives, or preparations, and for other purposes." Notably, the act did not mention *Cannabis sativa L.*

[20] J Wexler, *Weed Rules: Blazing The Way to A Just & Joyful Marijuana Policy* (2023) University of California Press 16.

[21] ibid.

[22] U.S. Const. amend. XXI.

[23] Supra 20 at 17.

[24] Both spellings – marijuana and marihuana – are acceptable. To avoid confusion, many in the industry refer to the botanical plant cannabis. Cannabis Regulatory Agency <https://www.michigan.gov/cra/faq/licensing-list/additional-new/why-is-marijuana-sometimes-spelled-with-an-h-and-other-times-spelled-with-a-j#:~:text=The%20Cannabis%20Regulatory%20Agency%20(CRA,to%20the%20botanical%20plant%20%E2%80%94%20cannabis> accessed 21 January

choice of the word "marihuana" was based, at least in part, on xenophobic views towards Mexican immigrants who,[25] at that time, were coming into the southwest US to flee the Mexican Civil War.[26] The ramifications of using the word "marihuana" to differentiate between hemp and cannabis created an issue of semantics for the *Cannabis sativa L* that is still relevant today, and this is especially relevant as it applies to the nuances of trademark law.

The Marihuana Tax Act of 1937 was passed, which did not outlaw the consumption, sale, or possession of marijuana. Instead, it levied a US$100 per ounce tax on each transaction, creating a de facto ban on selling marijuana, as the tax was so expensive.[27] The government required a stamp to be acquired from the government to show that taxes had been paid. The Marihuana Tax Act was the primary federal law for marijuana until 1970, when the Supreme Court found it to be unconstitutional under the Fifth Amendment.[28] The response to this was for Congress to pass the Controlled Substances Act (CSA) later that year, which made marijuana[29] a Schedule I drug, defined as a drug with no approved medical use and a potential for abuse.[30] To date, marijuana exists

---

2024. See also R Solomon, *Racism and Its Effect on Cannabis Research* (2020) 5 Cannabis Cannabinoid Res. 2.

[25] Harry J. Anslinger is cited in quotes such as, "No one knows, when he places a marijuana cigarette to his lips, whether he will become a joyous reveler in a musical heaven, a mad insensate, a calm philosopher, or a murderer," and the following quote, which is at times disputed but is widely attributed to Anslinger: "There are 100,000 total marijuana smokers in the US, and most are Negroes, Hispanics, Filipinos, and entertainers. Their Satanic music, jazz and swing, results from marijuana use. This marijuana causes white women to seek sexual relations with Negroes, entertainers, and others." See, A Halpering, "Marijuana: Is It Time to Stop Using a Word with Racist Roots?" *The Guardian* (January 2018) <https://www.theguardian.com/society/2018/jan/29/marijuana-name-cannabis-racism>.

[26] MA Lee, *Smoke Signals: A Social History of Marijuana – Medical, Recreational and Scientific* (2012) Scribner.

[27] Based on the inflation rate, US$100 in 1937 is the equivalent of US$2,115.99 in 2023. "US Inflation Calculator" (*A Coin News Media Group Company*) <https://www.usinflationcalculator.com/> accessed 20 January 2024.

[28] U.S. Supreme Court. *Leary v United States*, 395 U.S. 6 (1969).

[29] (n 18).

[30] 21 U.S.C. § 812(b)(1) (2012) defines Schedule I drugs as having a high potential for abuse and no currently accepted medical use.

as a Schedule I drug, which is in the same class as heroin, LSD,[31] MDMA,[32] and Psilocybin.[33] Other than heroin, each of the listed substances is now being explored for its potential medicinal or therapeutic uses.

The CSA was the body of law that drove the "War on Drugs" during the 1980s. During this time, the penalties for possessing large quantities of cannabis, and trafficking or cultivating it could result in millions of dollars in fines and potentially even a sentence of life in prison.[34] In 1996, there was a campaign to legalize medical marijuana in the state of California called Proposition 215. Proposition 215 granted people a limited defense for possessing, cultivating, and making donations to others for medical marijuana use. Although the intent of Proposition 215 was for the medical use of marijuana,[35] the result was the start of a paradigm shift that grew into legalizing cannabis for recreational use.

What the end of prohibition would mean for cannabis trademarks can be seen in the impact that the Farm Bill of 2018 had on legalizing hemp in the US, making hemp legal for the first time since 1970. The differentiation

---

31 JJ Fuentes, F Foseca, M Elices, M Farré, M Torrens, "Therapeutic Use of LSD in Psychiatry: A Systematic Review of Randomized-controlled Clinical Trials" (2020) 10 Front. Psychiatry 943. LSD use for anxiety, depression, and addiction treatment is currently being explored.

32 JM Mitchell, GM Ot'alora, B van der Kolk, et al. "MDMA-assisted Therapy for Moderate to Severe PTSD: A Randomized, Placebo-controlled Phase 3 Trial" (2023) 29 Nat Med 2473 <https://doi.org/10.1038/s41591-023-02565-4> accessed 21 January 2024. MDMA is currently being studied for its therapeutic use for post-traumatic stress disorder therapy (PTSD) and may be approved by the Food and Drug Administration (FDA) in 2024.

33 K Foden-Vencil, "Oregon Now Offers Psilocybin Therapy. Here's What One of the First Patients Experienced" *Oregon Public Broadcasting* (August 23, 2023) <https://www.opb.org/article/2023/08/23/psilocybin-mushroom-therapy-oregon-psychedelic-bendable-bend-ptsd-ocd-mental-health/>. The state of Oregon has legalized psilocybin use for some forms of therapy.

34 21 U.S.C. § 841(b)(1)(A). For example, trafficking of 1,000 kilograms or more of a mixture or substance containing a detectable amount of marijuana or 1,000 or more marijuana plants, regardless of weight, would carry this sentence.

35 C Beale, "'Acts of Great Love': How the Marijuana Minister of the Castro Helped His Flock Endure the AIDS Epidemic" *The California Report Magazine, KQED* (28 January 2022) <https://www.kqed.org/news/11902998/the-marijuana-minister-of-the-castro>. The intent of Proposition 215 was to provide compassionate medical care, which gay men dying from the AIDS epidemic in San Francisco especially needed. The history of cannabis legalization started with the opening of some of the first medical marijuana dispensaries in the Castro District of San Francisco.

between marijuana and hemp is that hemp contains a concentration of 0.3 percent Delta-THC or less on a dry-weight basis.[36] The impact of the Farm Bill legalizing hemp affected numerous federal laws, including the Lanham Act. Legalizing hemp allowed the rapid expansion of a new agricultural industry in the US. Hemp was grown in many states that had already legalized cannabis for recreational use. This caused a considerable amount of confusion for state law enforcement as marijuana and hemp at times look identical (they are both the *Cannabis sativa L* plant but with different amounts of THC). Hemp legalization also stimulated the innovation of hemp products, resulting in products composed of novel cannabinoids that are still intoxicating but federally legal.

On January 23, 2023, HR 610 Bill, also known as the Marijuana 1-to-3 Act of 2023,[37] was tabled by Congress, which would cause marijuana to be rescheduled to a Schedule III Controlled Substance by the end of 2024. The text of the HR 610 is incredibly short, with two sections, but the implications of this rescheduling will radically impact the cannabis industry. Cannabis businesses will be exempt from 280(e) taxation,[38] be granted more access to traditional banking, and possibly allow for interstate commerce between states that have legalized cannabis. The DEA has indicated the agency will support the proposed rescheduling,[39] but marijuana will remain a federally controlled substance on the CSA. If the rescheduling occurs, there will be an additional impact on US treaty obligations, but the full implication cannot be known at this time.[40] Some members of the cannabis industry are frustrated that marijuana was not removed from the CSA, thus fully ending cannabis prohibition, and they worry that rescheduling will continue prohibition with laws that are more confusing[41] than they were when marijuana had a Schedule I status.

The history of goods made from *Cannabis sativa L* being denied federal trademark protection dates to 1791 when a sailcloth manufacturer named

---

36 Pub. L. No. 115-334, 132 Stat. 4490.

37 GovTrack.us "H.R. 610 – 118th Congress: Marijuana 1-to-3 Act of 2023" (2024) <https://www.govtrack.us/congress/bills/118/hr610>.

38 D Charnas, "Paid or Incurred: Marijauna Rescheduling. Taxes, and Section 280E" (JDSUPRA, 6 June 2024) <https://www.jdsupra.com/legalnews/paid-or-incurred-marijuana-rescheduling-3776358/>.

39 Z Miller, J Goodman, J Mustian, L Whitehurst, "US Poised to Ease Restrictions on Marijuana in Historic Shift, but It'll Remain Controlled Substance" *Associated Press New* (30 April 2024) <https://apnews.com/article/marijuana-biden-dea-criminal-justice-pot-f833a8dae6ceb31a8658a5d65832a3b8>.

40 ibid.

41 J Snider, CM Smith, "Cannabis Rescheduling: Winning the Battle, but Not the War" (*R Street*, 13 May 2024). <https://www.rstreet.org/commentary/cannabis-rescheduling-winning-the-battle-but-not-the-war/>.

Samuel Breck petitioned Thomas Jefferson, the then-Secretary of State, for a set of laws to protect his company's exclusive use of a trademark to designate the sailcloth's origin and quality. This would have been the first federal law to defend trademarks. The third US President, Thomas Jefferson, recommended this to the House, but the request was ignored, and a federal law for trademarks was not pursued until almost a decade later when the Patent, Copyright, and Trademark Act of 1870 was passed.

While the sailcloth material was not the reason for the federal government denying trademark protection, it is ironic that trademark rights and cannabis have such an interwoven history in the US. The Patent, Copyright, and Trademark Act of 1870 was finally passed because the US entered international treaties to protect trademarks, creating a need for federal involvement in trademark protection. The treaty obligations created the need to register and record trademarks, which the United States Patent Office (USPTO) managed. This meant state laws were primarily responsible for protecting trademarks; this worked to some extent but fell short of protecting trademarks used in interstate commerce and trademarks from foreign nations.[42] This prompted Congress to pass a bill in 1881 that protected trademarks used in commerce with foreign nations and Native American tribes.[43] While this was an improvement, it still failed to protect trademarks used in interstate commerce, which was frustrating for businesses operating in multiple states. The development of federal trademark law between 1881 and 1925 was patchwork at best,[44] and not a good framework for comprehensive trademark protection.[45] The Trademark Act of 1946, also known as the Lanham Act, eventually replaced these laws.

Congress created a comprehensive scheme for trademark protection by passing the Lanham Act. The Lanham Act addresses a wide range of trademark issues, ranging from common trademark law to the requirements for granting a registration for federal trademarks. The Lanham Act is the "foundation of current federal trademark law."[46] The Lanham Act is administered by the United States Patent and Trademark Office (USPTO).

---

[42] (n 19).

[43] ibid.

[44] Lanham Act, ch. 540, 60 Stat. 427 (1946) (codified as amended at 15 U.S.C. §§ 1051–1141n). Statutes passed in 1867, 1870, 1881, 1905, 1920, and 1925 established a system for registration of trademarks with the Patent Office.

[45] Multi-state operators in the cannabis industry are currently navigating a similar issue in registering state trademarks.

[46] *Matal v Tam*, 137 S. Ct. 1744, 198 L. Ed. 2d 366 (2017).

1.3 1946 LANHAM ACT APPLIED TO CANNABIS TRADEMARKS

Section 1 of the Lanham Act explains what is required to grant a trademark applicant registration[47] by the USPTO on the principal register. This includes the following: a "specimen or facsimile of the mark" and a "drawing of the mark," "specification of applicant's domicile and citizenship," a description of the "goods in connection with which the mark is used," a verified statement that the applicant is "the owner of the mark," a verified statement indicating that no other person has the right to use the mark in commerce in either identical form or a similar form that might cause consumer confusion, cause mistake, or be deceptive. Lastly, the applicant must declare that the applied-for mark "is in use in commerce" along with the date the applied-for mark was first used in commerce.[48]

Section 1(b) of the Lanham Act allows for the USPTO to accept trademark applications to be filed as 1(b) Applications for bona fide intention to use the trademark (ITU) for goods and services which are currently not in use, so long as the applicant has a "bona fide intention to use the mark."[49] The bona fide intent required to file an ITU application requires a "showing of the good faith of such person, to use the trademark in commerce." Filing a trademark application as a 1(b) application allows for an applicant to start the registration process without having used the trademark in commerce.[50]

While the benefits of a registered trademark are significant, the Lanham Act will not grant registration or protect trademarks associated with illegal goods or services. This is known as the "lawful use" requirement and is a significant problem for cannabis-related trademarks.[51] The USPTO is empowered to inquire whether the goods or services listed in the description are regulated under an Act of Congress.[52] The USPTO may then ask whether the goods and services comply with a specific Act,[53] to determine the trademark's lawfulness.[54] There is an argument to be made that the USPTO inconsistently applies the lawful use requirement. For example, the pharmaceutical industry regularly files trademark applications for drugs not approved by the Food and Drug

47 15 U.S.C. § 1057(a).

48 ibid § 1051(a)–(d).

49 ibid § 1051(b).

50 ibid.

51 *See* 37 C.F.R. § 2.69 (1989).

52 ibid.

53 For cannabis, or marijuana, this is the Controlled Substances Act (CSA). For hemp or CBD products, it is the Food, Drug & Cosmetics Act (FDCA).

54 37 C.F.R. (n 51).

Administration (FDA).[55] The USPTO's explanation for allowing intent-to-use (ITU) pharmaceutical trademark applications for unapproved drugs is that the FDA has a legal process for approving the drugs for medical use, so applicants can have a bona fide intent to use the trademarks in commerce.

In contrast, cannabis trademark applicants cannot have bona fide intent because marijuana is a Schedule I substance; there is no way for it to be legally sold in commerce. The Trademark Trial and Appeal Board (TTAB) upheld the USPTO's refusal to register the trademark JOY TEA because the applicant could not have bona fide intent when it filed an ITU application since the tea included the cannabinoid CBD as an ingredient. CBD currently has not been approved as a food additive.[56] Since CBD is not approved for inclusion in food, the TTAB held that the JOY TEA trademark application cannot be filed with bona fide intent.

Showing a lack of bona fide intent is grounds for a court to grant relief in a lawsuit by canceling pending intent-to-use trademark applications that have not been reviewed by the USPTO.[57] The US Court of Appeals for the Ninth Circuit affirmed a district court's authority to cancel the pending applications because the applicant was found to lack actual intent to use the RAW GARDEN trademarks with the goods identified in the pending applications.[58]

The lawful use requirements pose a unique issue for cannabis-related trademarks as marijuana, as mentioned, is listed as a Schedule I drug under the CSA, which means federal trademark applications for cannabis (or marijuana) goods and services will be rejected because the trademark cannot be lawfully used in commerce. This has led to cannabis companies seeking trademark protection for goods and services that are ancillary to cannabis goods and services. The current dominant strategy for establishing trademark rights is for businesses to find federally legal goods and services that occupy trademark classes, which will likely include cannabis after its prohibition. Identifying which trademark classes will include cannabis goods and services is challenging because they are not included in the USPTO Trademark Identification Manual.

Since September 1, 1973, the US has used the Nice Classification System, which harmonized the US trademark classification system for goods and services with the other member countries in the Nice System.[59] Every year, a Committee of Experts from member states of the Nice Agreement 1957 votes on including or removing goods and services from the classification system.

---

[55] RA Mikos, "Unauthorized and Unwise: The Lawful Use Requirement in Trademark Law", (2022) 75 Vanderbilt Law Review 161.

[56] In *re Joy Tea Inc.*, Serial No. 88640009 (September 1, 2021).

[57] *BBK Tobacco & Foods LLP v Cent. Coast Agric.* (9th Cir. Apr. 1, 2024).

[58] ibid.

[59] Trademark Manual of Examining Procedure (TMEP) § 1401.02.

The twenty-ninth session of the Nice Expert Committee was held between April 29 and May 3, 2019, and 34 member state representatives attended.[60] For the first time, some member states proposed six amendments for cannabis goods and services.[61] This resulted in cannabis goods being added to Class 5 and Class 31, for medical purposes and plants, respectively.[62] The US rejected adopting the proposed amendments on the basis that it was against national policy as US federal law prohibits cannabis cultivation and possession, and goods used to cultivate cannabis are viewed as illegal paraphernalia.[63]

The rejection of the new classification for cannabis was consistent with a unique event that occurred in 2010. On April 1, 2010, the classification of medical marijuana was added to the USPTO's Trademark Identification Manual.[64] This inclusion was short-lived, and every application filed for medical marijuana was either outright rejected or received an office action indicating that medical marijuana should never have been included in the identification manual because the goods "did not reflect goods and services that may be in lawful use in commerce."[65] The identification manual was updated shortly after that, removing any reference to medical marijuana and any other marijuana-related identifier from the identification manual.[66]

---

60 L Zimmerman, "Curing the Nice Classification: Expanding Trademark Classes to Include Hemp & Cannabis Goods and Services" (8 August 2020) <https://ssrn.com/abstract=3782739>.

61 ibid.

62 Class 05-050500 Cannabis for medical purposes/marijuana for medical purposes. Class 03 310173 cannabis plants, 310174 cannabis, unprocessed.

63 15 U.S.C. § 1057(a).

64 *See* U.S. Trademark Application Serial No. 76703884 (filed June 6, 2011); *see also* TMEP (5th edn., Sept. 2007).

65 U.S. Trademark Application Serial No. 85049842 (Office Action September 24, 2010).

66 J Scheck, "US: Patent Office Raises High Hopes, Then Snuffs Them Out: Short-Lived Trademark Category for Marijuana is Nipped in the Bud", (2010) Wall St. J. <https://www.wsj.com/articles/SB10001424052748704682604575368783687129488>.

Due to the lawful use requirement, the USPTO will reject goods related to the cultivation,[67] processing,[68] application,[69] or ingesting of cannabis,[70] given that they are federally illegal and viewed as paraphernalia.[71] The USPTO has the right to ask for additional information about the nature of goods and services in applications, so in instances where it believes the goods might be used for illegal purposes, it will ask the applicant to provide additional information about how the goods are intended to be used.

An example of this line of inquiry occurred in the case *In re National Concessions Group, Inc.,* TTAB Ex Parte Appeal No. 87168058 for the trademark "BAKKED".[72] The USPTO here rejected the application for a good that assisted with the application of "essential oils" and argued the goods were intended to be used for the purpose of dabbing cannabis oil extracts.[73] The applicant appealed to the US Trademark Trial and Appeal Board (TTAB), claiming the good could be used with tobacco products. The TTAB found this argument to be unpersuasive as there was no evidence showing a good of this nature has any historical record of being used with tobacco.[74] The TTAB affirmed the refusal of the USPTO to register the application because the good was drug paraphernalia, as defined by the CSA.

The implementation of the 2018 Farm Bill has created much confusion about how the USPTO reviews specimens of goods for both hemp and marijuana because if the good is intended to be used for hemp goods, then the use is lawful, and the trademark registration should be granted. Still, if a good is intended to be used for marijuana, it fails the lawful use requirement and will be rejected. This has led the USPTO to require hemp-related trademark applications to differentiate from marijuana applications by including variations of the following language: "solely derived from hemp with a Delta-9

---

[67] U.S. Trademark Application Serial No. 88528198 (Office Action Aug. 4, 2020).

[68] U.S. Trademark Application Serial No. 86479070 (Office Action Aug. 14, 2015).

[69] U.S. Trademark Application Serial No. 87168058 (Office Action Nov. 7, 2017).

[70] U.S. Trademark Application Serial No. 86002127 (Office Action May 10, 2013).

[71] U.S. Code Title 21 Section 863.

[72] *In Re Nat'l Concessions Grp., Inc.*, No. 87168058, 2023 WL 3244416, at 2 (May 3, 2023).

[73] Dabbing is a term related to consuming cannabis extracts and hash.

[74] *Re Nat'l Concessions Grp., Inc.* (n 72).

tetrahydrocannabinol (THC) concentration of not more than 0.3 percent on a dry-weight basis" in the description of goods and services.[75]

In some countries, cannabis trademark applications are rejected on the basis that the applied marks are "immoral" or "scandalous" in nature. Historically, trademarks in the US could be denied protection because their marks were not protected under the Constitution's First Amendment. There are numerous office actions for trademarks that include cannabis leaves,[76] green crosses,[77] and the names of cannabis cultivars,[78] which had office actions issued because the marks were immoral or scandalous.

Before June 19, 2017, the USPTO rejected trademark applications for marks that "consists of or comprises matter that may disparage, or bring into contempt or disrepute, persons, institutions, beliefs, or national symbols."[79] This is no longer the case, as the Supreme Court found that scandalous or immoral trademarks were protected First Amendment speech, and refusing to register immoral and scandalous trademarks was unconstitutional.[80] Since this ruling, cannabis-related trademarks no longer receive office actions claiming the mark is scandalous or immoral.

Where this is a benefit for cannabis-related trademarks in the US, it will likely pose some issues for US-based cannabis brands trying to move their trademarks into other jurisdictions because what is no longer immoral in the US could still be viewed differently by different countries' trademark offices.

1.4 DISTINCTIVENESS, CULTIVAR NAMES, AND NOVEL CANNABINOIDS

The Lanham Act requires a trademark to be "distinctive" for protection under federal and state laws in the US.[81] The protection given to distinctive

[75] U.S. Trademark Application Registration No. 7239898.

[76] U.S. Trademark Application Serial No. 77654064 (Office Action Nov. 17, 2009).

[77] U.S. Trademark Application Serial No. 77483348 (Office Action Oct. 2, 2008).

[78] U.S. Trademark Application Serial No. 77429217 (Office Action Oct. 13, 2009).

[79] TMEP 1203.01 Other refusals Under 15 U.S.C. 1502(a) No Longer Valid.

[80] *Iancu v Brunetti*, 139 S. Ct. 2294, 204 L. Ed. 2d 714, 2019 U.S. LEXIS 4201, 27 Fla. L. Weekly Fed. S 1057, 2019 WL 2570622 (U.S. June 24, 2019).

[81] *See* Trademark Cases, 100 U.S. 82, 93–94 (1879) (governing trademark cases). *See also* U.S. Const. art. I, § 8, cl. 8. (stating Congress's power). The Intellectual Property Clause (or Patents and Copyrights Clause) gives Congress the power "[t]o promote the Progress of Science and useful Arts, by securing for

trademarks is in the interest of consumer protection, whereas trademarks that are merely descriptive or generic will not be granted registration. Determining if a cannabis-related trademark is distinctive or descriptive is challenging because terms used to describe cannabis evolve constantly; often, these terms come from music or slang from subcultures.[82] Furthermore, the evolution of cannabis terms is sometimes limited to specific geographic locations. These factors make it difficult to evaluate if a cannabis trademark is distinctive.

Many parts of cannabis culture are still developing as a subculture, which means some of the lexicon used in the cannabis industry is not widely known outside of cannabis culture. Words like "Zaza,"[83] "moonrocks,"[84] and "hash holes"[85] might look like distinctly unique words that could be used as trademarks. Yet, for consumers of the cannabis industry, these words describe types of cannabis products, making them descriptive terms.

The development of cannabis trademarks has been stifled by the inability to seek registration. This created a scenario where the cannabis industry did not understand the necessity of creating distinctive trademarks. This is reflected in many of the first cannabis trademarks, including the word "canna," and including green in stylized trademarks, or a cannabis leaf in combination trademarks. This resulted in almost an inability to distinguish the different companies from each other. This problem was further compounded as the cannabis industry repeated these same mistakes when a new state legalized cannabis and started accepting state trademark registrations.

There is a legal relationship between the names of plant cultivars and varietals, names of cannabis "strains",[86] and trademark law. Rule 1202.12 of the Trademark Manual of Examining Procedure (TMEP) explains that plant varietals and cultivars cannot function as trademarks because they lack the

---

limited Times to Authors and Inventors the exclusive Right to their respective Writings and Discoveries." Id.

82 W Bobrow, "DRO, AKA/Hydropic: Luxury Cannabis & Culture for the People in 2020" *Forbes* (22 April 2020).

83 Urban Dictionary defines Zaza as "top-tier weed". <https://www.urbandictionary.com/define.php?term=Zaza>.

84 Urban Dictionary defines Moonrocks as "a nugget of marijuana bud dipped in hash oil and kief". https://www.urbandictionary.com/define.php?term=Moonrocks>.

85 S Ju, "Hash Holes Are Hot in Cannabis: Everything You Need to Know About These Potent Pre-Rolls" *Los Angeles Magazine* (19 October 2023).

86 D Hunt, "Strain? Variety? Cultivar? Which is Which?" (*Plant Law Blog*, 18 November 2018) <https://plantlaw.com/2018/11/18/strain-cultivar/>. The word "strain" is widely used in cannabis culture to identify a specific type of cannabis. The botanically accurate terms for the different types of plants are variety or cultivar.

required distinctiveness, as plant names are considered generic.[87] This restriction on granting trademark protection has been applied to cultivars like the Honeycrisp apple.[88] The name of the Honeycrisp cultivar was identified in a plant patent application,[89] which caused a trademark application filed a year later to receive a refusal to register because "Honeycrisp" was the name of the cultivar and, therefore, was generic and could not function as a trademark.

In the US, novel cultivars are usually identified by being named in utility patents, plant patents,[90] or Plant Variety Protection (PVP) registrations. Fewer than 50 plant and utility patents for cannabis cultivars have been registered with the USPTO, but more than 8,000 strains can be found on Leafly.[91] Since patent registration and defense are expensive, the majority of identified cannabis cultivars are not patent-protected.

In the US, 3,000 seeds must be deposited with each PVP application to the Plant Variety Protection Office (PVPO).[92] Cannabis seeds are included in the CSA definition for marijuana, meaning they are federally illegal.[93] Therefore, the PVPO office will not take possession or deposit cannabis seeds, which makes Breeder's Rights inaccessible for identifying new cannabis cultivars.

Due to cannabis' illegal status, there are no government databases for recording the names of cannabis cultivars. When the USPTO reviews a trademark application to see if it is using a cultivar name for cannabis-related goods or services, the USPTO relies on websites like Leafly.com and Weedmaps.com as resources for determining if the trademark is an identified cannabis cultivar. The issue with this is that both websites allow the cannabis community to submit recommendations for newly identified strains, so they are not reliable or accurate databases.

This has created a situation where the USPTO sometimes issues inconsistent reviews of trademark applications for ancillary goods, claiming they applied for a trademark for a cannabis cultivar name simply because of a listing on a

---

[87] United States Patent and Trademark Office TMEP. 1202.12 Varietal and Cultivar Names (Examination of Applications for Seeds and Plants) (2017).

[88] U.S. Trademark Application Serial No. 74156209 (Office Action Aug. 27, 1991).

[89] J Luby and DS Bedford, "Apple Tree: Honeycrisp". US Patent Plant 7,197, filed Nov. 7, 1988, issued Mar. 20, 1990.

[90] United States Agricultural Marketing Service, "Plant Variety Protection" (*U.S. Department of Agriculture*) <https://www.ams.usda.gov/services/plant-variety-protection> accessed 12 December 2024.

[91] "All Cannabis Strains" (*Leafly.com*) <https://www.leafly.com/strains> accessed 5 December 2024.

[92] 7 C.F.R. 97.6.

[93] 21 U.S.C. §802(16).

website. This occurred with a trademark application for the mark STIIIZY[94] which received an office action that included the following: "The attached evidence from Leafy, All Bud, and Hytiva shows that STIIIZY is a cannabis strain."[95] The supporting evidence in the office action shows there is a strain of cannabis named STIIIZY OG, whereas on the STIIIZY website, the strain is OG KUSH, but it is cultivated by STIIIZY.[96] This issue will most likely not be resolved until after cannabis is legalized because of the limited resources the USPTO has for determining the name of a cannabis cultivar.

Cannabis consumers would benefit from the federal government granting registration for cannabis trademarks. An example of how a lack of trademark protection can cause harm to consumers is when a Colorado company using the "Charlotte's Web" trademark received news coverage for having products that could be used as medicine for some forms of child epilepsy.[97] The company could not register "Charlotte's Web" because the trademark was being used with illegal goods.[98] Because of the news coverage, many other cannabis companies, both state-licensed and illicit operators, started creating products claiming to include "Charlotte's Web," and some of these products contained pesticides and other contaminants.[99] Because cannabis trademarks are not afforded protection under federal law, companies have a hard time restricting other companies from using their trademarks. This is to the detriment of public safety because tested cannabis goods are often confused with illicit, untested goods, which can contain a variety of harmful contaminants.

There have been more than 100 different cannabinoids identified in the *Cannabis sativa L* plant, of which THC and CBD are the most well-known.[100]

---

94 U.S. Trademark Application Serial No. 97802545 (Office Action Dec. 13, 2023).

95 ibid.

96 *"OG Kush Strain: Legendary Classic"* (*Stiiizy*, 7 March 2023) <https://www.stiiizy.com/blogs/learn/og-kush-strain?_pos=36&_sid=177b424b1&_ss=r.>.

97 "Charlotte's Web" (*Leafly.com*) <https://www.leafly.com/strains/charlottes-web> accessed 29 January 2024. Whether "Charlotte's Web" could function as a trademark is debatable, as it has been identified as the name of a hemp cultivar.

98 S Young, "Marijuana Stops Child's Severe Seizures" CNN (7 August 2013) <https://www.cnn.com/2013/08/07/health/charlotte-child-medical-marijuana/index.html>.

99 J Schroyer, "Trademarks: Some, But Not Many, Protections for Cannabis Companies" *MJ Biz Daily* (20 September 2016) <https://mjbizdaily.com/trademarks-some-but-not-many-protections-for-cannabis-companies/>.

100 National Center for Complementary Integrative Health, "Cannabis (Marijuana) and Cannabinoids: What You Need to Know" (*United States Department of Health and Human Services*, October 2019).

These cannabinoids are contained in both hemp and marijuana. With the legalization of hemp, innovation in the hemp industry has allowed for the extraction and distillation of many of these cannabinoids from hemp, including THC. While hemp may only contain 0.3 percent THC, it is possible, with enough biomass, to extract a substantial amount of THC from hemp plants. This creates a legal conundrum because a concentration of THC can be extracted from federally legal hemp, but the THC concentration itself would then be federally illegal.

The Farm Bill created additional confusion about whether cannabinoids like Delta-8-THC are federally legal. While this remains a nationally unanswered question, the US Court of Appeals Ninth Circuit gave some direction in the case *AK Futures LLC v Boyd St. Distro, LLC.*[101] In this case, the plaintiff alleged the defendant infringed on its "CAKE" trademark by selling counterfeit e-cigarette vaping products.[102] The defendant claimed the plaintiff did not have a valid trademark because the plaintiff was using the trademark in connection with selling Delta-8-THC vaporizer products, which the defendant claimed failed the lawful use requirement for trademark protection because Delta-8-THC was federally illegal.[103] The Ninth Circuit held that because the Delta-8-THC was extracted from hemp, it was federally legal, and the plaintiff did have enforceable trademark rights. Based on this court decision, hemp extracts would seem presumptively federally legal, but as of February 20, 2024, the USPTO still has not registered a trademark for Delta-8-THC products, even if the description includes that they are hemp-derived.

The USPTO's requirement to include the THC percentage in the description of goods in hemp trademark applications creates a unique burden for accessing the Madrid Trademark System. The burden is that the legal definition of hemp might be different than 0.3% percent[104] THC could hinder the application from being registered.

A new bill named the Farm, Food, and National Security Act of 2024,[105] or the 2024 Farm Bill, has been proposed and debated in Congress. The bill

---

[101] *AK Futures LLC v Boyd* St. Distro, LLC, 35 F.4th 682 (9th Cir. 2022).

[102] ibid.

[103] ibid.

[104] S DeCarlo and M Weaver, "Keeping the High out of Hemp: Global THC Standards" (*U.S. International Trade Commission*, May 2023) <https://www.usitc.gov/publications/332/executive_briefings/ebot_decarlo_weaver_keeping_the_high_out_of_hemp.pdf> accessed 2 February 2024. The following countries define hemp as having less than 0.3 percent THC: Israel (0.2 percent), United Kingdom (0.2 percent), Ukraine (0.01 percent), South Africa (0.01 percent).

[105] H.R.8467 Farm, Food, and Nation Security Act of 2024 (2023–2024) <https://www.congress.gov/bill/118th-congress/house-bill/8467>.

includes amendments that would redefine hemp by creating two categories of hemp products: "hemp grown for cannabinoid extraction" and "industrial hemp." Congresswoman Rep Mary Miller filed an amendment[106] to the 2024 Farm Bill which would effectively make many of the novel cannabinoids illegal under the CSA. If the 2024 Farm Bill is adopted without Miller's amendment, there will be a significant impact on the hemp industry. However, if Miller's amendment is also adopted, the cannabinoid extraction side of the hemp industry will be devastated, as many of the ingestible products will once again be federally illegal.

Despite the challenges of obtaining trademark registration for cannabis-related trademarks, there is a clear interest in pursuing protection. Since 1996, the number of trademark applications, including the word "cannabis" listed in the application, has increased significantly.[107] The following table illustrates the prolific submission of cannabis-related trademark applications.

1.5 THE BENEFITS AND LIMITATIONS OF STATE TRADEMARKS

An aspect of trademark law that is unique to the US is that each state has its own trademark registry, which is part of the Secretary of State's office. Each state has statutes that apply to trademarks,[108] and therein, there are some differences in the law from state to state. However, these laws generally mirror the Lanham Act. Similar to the Lanham Act, the states also require trademark registrations to be granted only to trademarks used for "lawful" goods and services.[109] The difference is that the scope of protection for state trademark registration is only for the state where it is registered, so state trademarks afford more protection than a common law trademark right but do not provide as much protection as a registered federal trademark. States that have legalized cannabis for medical or adult use have started allowing trademark registration for cannabis goods and services through the Secretary of State's office.

---

106 M Miller, "Amendment to H.R. 8467" (22 May 2024) <https://hemp-supporter.com/wp-content/uploads/2024/05/MaryMillerAmendment-VOTENO.pdf>.

107 R Dickson, *High Hopes: Cannabis Trademarks at the USPTO* (2024). Manuscript submitted for publication in the Ohio State Technology Law Journal, 2025.

108 An example of a few states' trademark statutes: See, e.g., CAL. BUS. & PROF. CODE §§ 14200–14272; N.Y. GEN. BUS. LAW §§ 360 to 360-R; TEX. BUS. & COM. CODE ANN. §§ 16.001–.16.107.

109 California Secretary of State, "Trademarks and Service Marks Frequently Asked Questions #13" <https://www.sos.ca.gov/business-programs/ts/faqs>.

Table 1.1 Cannabis trademark applications at the USPTO, 1996–2023

Application filing year	**Trademark applications that, at the time of searching, have cannabis goods/ services**[a]	**Number of state-legal regimes**	**Relevant historical events**
1996	8	States with Medical Marijuana (MMJ): 1	Medical Marijuana is legalized in California.
1997	10	MMJ: 1	N/A
1998	4	MMJ: 5	Medical Marijuana is legalized in Alaska, Nevada, Oregon, and Washington.
1999	6	MMJ: 6	Medical Marijuana is legalized in Maine.
2000	26	MMJ: 8	Medical Marijuana is legalized in Colorado and Hawaii.
2001	5	MMJ: 8	N/A
2002	4	MMJ: 8	N/A
2003	5	MMJ: 8	N/A
2004	2	MMJ: 10	Medical Marijuana is legalized in Montana and Vermont.
2005	9	MMJ: 10	The US Supreme Court rules in *Gonzales v Raich*[b] that Congress has the power to prohibit intrastate manufacture and possession of marijuana.
2006	5	MMJ: 11	Medical Marijuana is legalized in Rhode Island.
2007	9	MMJ: 12	Medical Marijuana is legalized in New Mexico.
2008	7	MMJ: 13	Medical Marijuana is legalized in Michigan.

Application filing year	Trademark applications that, at the time of searching, have cannabis goods/ services[a]	Number of state-legal regimes	Relevant historical events
2009	47	MMJ: 13	Deputy Attorney General David Ogen releases a memorandum stating that Department of Justice (DOJ) employees should prioritize prosecution of significant traffickers of illegal drugs and not focus on individuals complying with state medical marijuana laws.
2010	161	MMJ: 15	Three medical marijuana goods and services identifications are briefly added to the USPTO Trademark Identification Manual, sparking a temporary surge in cannabis-related trademark applications. Medical Marijuana is legalized in Arizona and New Jersey.
2011	69	MMJ: 16	Medical Marijuana is legalized in Delaware and Washington, D.C.
2012	37	MMJ: 18 States with Adult-Use Marijuana (AUMJ): 2	Medical Marijuana is legalized in Connecticut and Massachusetts. Adult-Use Marijuana is legalized in Colorado and Washington, D.C.

Application filing year	Trademark applications that, at the time of searching, have cannabis goods/ services[a]	Number of state-legal regimes	Relevant historical events
2013	89	MMJ: 21 AUMJ: 2	Deputy Attorney General James Cole issues a comprehensive memorandum that lists specific DOJ priorities regarding marijuana. Many states use this memo as a template in crafting their marijuana laws. Medical Marijuana is legalized in Illinois, Maryland, and New Hampshire.
2014	394	MMJ: 23 AUMJ: 4	The first Rohrbacher-Farr Amendment to the Consolidated Appropriations Act passes Congress, preventing DOJ funds from being used to prevent states from implementing their own medical marijuana laws. Medical Marijuana is legalized in Minnesota and New York. Adult-Use Marijuana is legalised in Alaska and Oregon.
2015	588	MMJ: 25 AUMJ: 4	The Adult-Use Marijuana gifting system is set up in Washington, D.C. Medical Marijuana is legalized in Georgia and Louisiana.
2016	642	MMJ: 30 AUMJ: 8	Medical Marijuana is legalized in Arkansas, Florida, North Dakota, Ohio, and Pennsylvania. Adult-Use Marijuana is legalised in California, Maine, Massachusetts, and Nevada.

Application filing year	**Trademark applications that, at the time of searching, have cannabis goods/ services**[a]	**Number of state-legal regimes**	**Relevant historical events**
2017	1,047	MMJ: 32 AUMJ: 8	Medical Marijuana is legalized in Iowa and West Virginia.
2018	2,764	MMJ: 35 AUMJ: 9	On Dec. 20, 2018, hemp is removed from the definition of marijuana in the CSA in the 2018 Farm Bill. Medical Marijuana is legalized in Missouri, Oklahoma, and Utah. Adult-Use Marijuana is legalised in Michigan.
2019 (as of 11/02/2023)	6,299	MMJ: 35 AUMJ: 10	Adult-Use Marijuana is legalised in Illinois.
2020 (as of 11/02/2023)	4,152	MMJ: 37 AUMJ: 14	Medical Marijuana is legalised in Arizona, Montana, New Jersey, and Vermont. Adult-Use Marijuana is legalised in Arizona.
2021 (as of 11/02/2023)	3,598	MMJ: 38 AUMJ: 18	Medical Marijuana is legalized in Alabama. Adult-Use Marijuana is legalised in Connecticut, New Mexico, New York, and Virginia.
2022 (as of 11/02/2023)	2,352	MMJ: 39 AUMJ: 21	October 2022: President Joe Biden requests the initiation of an administrative process reviewing the scheduling of marijuana and pardons all prior Federal offenses for simple possession of marijuana. Medical Marijuana is legalized in Mississippi. Adult-Use Marijuana is legalized in Maryland, Missouri, and Rhode Island.

Application filing year	Trademark applications that, at the time of searching, have cannabis goods/ services[a]	Number of state-legal regimes	Relevant historical events
2023 (as of 11/02/2023)	1,325	MMJ: 40 AUMJ: 23	January 2023: The FDA releases a statement that a new regulatory pathway is required for handling CBD products. Medical Marijuana is legalized in Kentucky. Adult-Use Marijuana is legalized in Delaware and Minnesota.

Note: [a]TESS Search Strings: (cannabis marijuana marihuana THC tetrahydrocannabinol tetrahyrocannabinol CBD cannabidiol cannabigerol CBG)[gs] and FD > 20160101 < 20161231 (searched year by year on Oct. 8, 2023. Searches for 2022 and 2023 were also run again on Apr. 10, 2023). [b]Gonzales v. Raich, 545 U.S. 1 (2005).
Source: Compiled by Rachael Dickson

State trademarks are currently the only form of trademark registration in the US that allows for the registration of trademarks for cannabis goods and services. These registrations are often the best option for cannabis businesses trying to have at least some form of trademark protection. Still, state trademarks also have some limitations on the scope of protection they can provide.

As previously discussed, the lawful use requirement for federal trademarks does not apply to cannabis. This means that even if a cannabis trademark is registered at the state level, if a legal claim is brought in federal court, the state trademark protection will not be recognized by the federal court because the state registration would fail to fulfill the lawful use requirement.

In the case *Kiva Health Brands LLC v Kiva Brands Inc.*,[110] the plaintiff, a natural food manufacturer, brought a trademark infringement claim against the defendant, a cannabis edibles manufacturer. Both parties claimed ownership rights to the KIVA trademark. As a response, the defendant also filed a counterclaim alleging trademark infringement against the plaintiff based on prior use of the KIVA trademark and, therefore, a superior claim to the trademark.[111] The defendant had also registered the KIVA trademark with

110 *Kiva Health Brands LLC v Kiva Brands Inc.*, 439 F. Supp. 3d 1185 (N.D. Cal. 2020).

111 ibid.

the California Secretary of State for cannabis edibles.[112] The court found the Lanham Act does not recognize the user's priority claim because the use of the trademark was not lawful, so there cannot be any common law rights associated with the cannabis trademark.[113]

This decision of the court made it clear that state trademarks for cannabis cannot be relied upon for claiming priority use in federal court.

One of the shortcomings of state trademarks is that not every state uses the Nice Classification System to classify goods and services. Some states that use the Nice Classification System were confused about what classes would be appropriate for cannabis goods and services. Leading up to California legalizing cannabis for adult use in 2018, which also allowed for the registration of cannabis trademarks with the Secretary of State, there was an active discussion as to whether new classes for identifying cannabis would need to be created.[114] Classification of cannabis goods and services was a novel issue for states because the Federal Trademark Identification Manual did not provide guidance. The manual currently does not include any classification for cannabis goods or services.[115]

Additionally, state trademarks are unenforceable in other states, which means cannabis companies that operate in multiple states must seek trademark registration in every state in which they are operating. This can lead to identical trademarks being registered in different states by different owners, which increases consumer confusion. An example of this would be the trademark BLAZE, which is a registered trademark for cannabis goods in California,[116] Illinois,[117] and Washington,[118] with each of the registrations being owned by a different company. This is problematic for cannabis companies that want to expand into other states and even more so for consumers who might mistakenly believe the same company is operating in multiple states.

---

112 ibid.

113 ibid.

114 S M Hervey, "California Finally Rolling Out Its Own Cannabis Trademark Laws" (*The IP Law Blog*, 24 August 2017) <https://www.weintraub.com/2017/08/california-finally-rolling-cannabis-trademark-laws/>.

115 As of January 2024, the USPTO Trademark ID Manual still excludes cannabis goods or services.

116 California state trademark registration number 02004409.

117 Illinois state trademark registration number 116849.

118 Washington state trademark registration number 58189.

1.6 UNIQUE ISSUES OF TRADE DRESS, CELEBRITY BRANDS, AND GEOGRAPHIC INDICATION

The US cannabis industry has a growing problem of cannabis companies infringing on existing trademarks, especially candy-related trademarks and their trade dress. In 2014, Hershey's Corporation filed lawsuits against the Conscious Care Cooperative, a cannabis dispensary in Seattle, Washington, for trademark infringement.[119] The dispensary was selling cannabis-infused edibles under the names "Reefer's Cups" and "Mr. Dankbar," which Hershey's claimed infringed on its trademarks "Reese's Cups" and "Mr. Goodbar," respectively. The packaging for the infringing products was very similar to the trade dress of Hershey's candies. This lawsuit resulted in a settlement, and the dispensary ceased selling all the infringing goods. Since 2014, instances of infringement of this nature have become increasingly more common in the cannabis industry.[120]

With cannabis consumers now increasingly purchasing branded cannabis products in states that have legalized recreational cannabis, the unfortunate side effect is that the illicit market now creates counterfeit packaging of some state-legal products. Websites operating outside of the US are selling bulk counterfeit packaging for popular cannabis brands. Without the ability to seek a federal trademark registration, cannabis companies cannot register their trademarks with the US Customs and Border Patrol, meaning the packaging can be imported with virtually no recourse because there are limited options for seeking infringement or dilution claims against the producers of the counterfeit mylar packaging.[121] While this is not an entirely new issue, it is starting to happen at an advanced rate with trademarks related to confectionery trademarks.

Confectionery companies generally win any lawsuit they bring for trademark infringement, but this does not necessarily stop the dilution of a trademark. This occurred in a case brought by the candymaker Wrigley, which owns the trademark Skittles,[122] against a California cannabis company named

---

[119] "Candy vs. Cannabis: Hershey's Sues Seattle Dispensary over Reefer's Cups" (*Cannabis Now*, 10 June 2014) <https://cannabisnow.com/candy-vs-cannabis-hersheys-sues-a-seattle-dispensary-over-reefers-cups/>.

[120] S Kalamaras and L Zimmerman, "Weeding Out Imposters: When Cannabis Brands Name Themselves after Well-Known Children's Brands" *The Trademark Lawyer Magazine* (April 2022).

[121] This is because there is usually no easy way to identify the goods' origin source.

[122] U.S. Trademark Application Registration No. 73305850.

Terphogz, LLC.[123] Terphogz bred a famous cannabis strain named Zkittlez and created clothing and merchandise also using the ZKITTLEZ name.[124] Under federal and Illinois state law, Wrigley brought a lawsuit against Terphogz for trademark infringement, false designation of origin, unfair competition, and trademark dilution. Wrigley argued that even if Terphogz's use of ZKITTLEZ did not amount to consumer confusion with Skittles, the use of ZKITTLEZ and the rainbow-themed trade dress diluted the goodwill associated with the Skittles trademark.[125] The case resulted in a settlement in which Terphogz abandoned all use of ZKITTLEZ as a trademark but was allowed to continue using a design of a Z as a trademark.[126] The settlement was in Wrigley's favor, but it did nothing to stop the spread of the use of ZKITTLEZ as a strain name. This case is an excellent example of how confectionery companies can win individual lawsuits against cannabis companies. Yet, at times, this is not enough to stop continued dilution because the trademark is associated with the name of a cannabis strain.

Another widespread trademark infringement issue happened to the Ferrara Candy Company, which has had to file multiple lawsuits for infringements on its NERDS,[127] and TROLLI[128] trademarks. These lawsuits involve cannabis companies selling edibles infused with cannabinoids with unlicensed use of the Ferrara trademarks.[129] Ferrara has diligently enforced its trademark rights by bringing lawsuits against the offenders, but even winning the lawsuits has not deterred other companies from infringing on the NERDS and TROLLI trademarks. A significant part of the continued infringement is that some companies buy pre-printed Mylar packaging from websites like Aliexpress.com, which has resulted in having to file lawsuits against many unrelated parties. Unless Ferrara can address the production of this packaging, continuously filing infringement lawsuits is a Sisyphean act.

There is a new trend of celebrities in the US who are starting their own cannabis brands. Celebrities who are also cannabis activists like Willie Nelson,[130]

---

[123] *WM. Wrigley Jr. Co. v Terphogz, LLC*, No. 21-CV-02357 (N.D. Ill. July 3, 2023).

[124] ibid.

[125] ibid.

[126] ibid.

[127] NERDS, U.S. Trademark Application Registration No. 75417121.

[128] TROLLI, U.S. Trademark Application Registration No. 73387672.

[129] *Ferrara Candy Co. v Akimov LLC*, No. 22-CV-80768-RAR (S.D. Fla. Oct. 27, 2022).

[130] C Casacchia, "Celebrity marijuana brands outperform traditional brands, data suggest", *MJ Biz Daily* (14 July 2023) <https://mjbizdaily.com/celebrity-marijuana-brands-outperform-traditional-brands-data-suggests/>.

Snoop Dog,[131] B-Real,[132] Mike Tyson,[133] and Seth Rogan[134] have all started their own cannabis brands. Sales data indicate that celebrity brands often outperform regular cannabis brands in sales. The brand Cookies, which is arguably one of the most recognized cannabis brands in the world,[135] was started by a rapper named Gilbert Anthony Milam Jr., better known as Burner.[136] Celebrities like Cheech Marin and Tommy Chong are associated internationally with cannabis because of their cannabis-themed movies,[137] so it was easy for them to establish multiple cannabis brands that reference their films.[138] There has also been an increase in cannabis companies getting in trouble for using celebrities' images without permission. Actors like Clint Eastwood[139] and Sacha Baron Cohen[140] have sued CBD companies over false endorsements.

In Chapter 5 of this book, Emma Perot provides a deeper dive into the intersection between marijuana and image rights and shows that celebrity brands of cannabis are starting to be created in countries throughout the world.

In the US, the protection of geographical marks was included in the 1964 Trademark Act as certification and collective marks.[141] The USPTO has the authority to review and grant registration for such marks. When evaluating applications, the USPTO uses a similar set of standards to trademarks to decide if a certification or collective mark related to a geographical area will be granted registration. As of the beginning of 2024, no certification or collective marks that include the words hemp, marijuana, or cannabis in their description have been registered with the USPTO.[142] This means appellations

---

131 ibid.

132 ibid.

133 ibid.

134 ibid.

135 Cookies, "The Cookies Story" <https://cookies.co/about-us/>.

136 ibid.

137 M Lewis, "Every Cheech & Chong Movie in Order, for When You're Feeling the Munchies" *Collider* (6 November 2021) <https://collider.com/cheech-and-chong-movies-in-order-of-release/>.

138 Cheech and Chong Cannabis Co., "Brands" <https://www.cheechandchongscannabis.com/>.

139 J Hoffman, "Clint Eastwood Wins Second Big Lawsuit against CBD Industry" *Vanity Fair* (2 July 2022) <https://www.vanityfair.com/hollywood/2022/07/clint-eastwood-wins-second-big-lawsuit-against-cbd-industry>.

140 BM Adams, "Sacha Baron Cohen Drops $9 Million Lawsuit Over Bogus Weed Ad" *High Times* (19 May 2022) <https://hightimes.com/news/sacha-baron-cohen-drops-9-million-lawsuit-over-bogus-weed-ad/>.

141 15 U.S.C. § 1054.

142 There are also no GIs registered under the WTO Lisbon System that include the words hemp, marijuana, or cannabis in the description of goods.

registered with the California Department of Food and Agriculture (CDFA) could become the first form of GI protection for cannabis in the US.[143]

The Jamaican Government is also exploring expanding GI protection, which has allowed robust protection of geographical names for goods like "Jamaica Jerk" and "Jamaica Rum."[144] It is now also exploring how Jamaican-cultivated cannabis might benefit from GI protection, as analyzed by Yentyl Williams in this volume.[145] The reasoning behind this is that worldwide cannabis consumers know about Jamaica's rich history of cannabis, also known by its Hindi term, ganja, in Jamaica. By granting protection to cannabis GIs, the Jamaican government can give Jamaican ganja farmers a potential competitive advantage for exporting Jamaican cannabis products.[146] This potential competitive advantage in the market is why California created the California Appellations Program (CAP).[147]

The CAP program is a sui generis system that includes legal standards inspired by the US American Viticultural Areas (AVAs) regulations and the Lisbon Treaty for the Protection of Appellations of Origin. The amalgamation of the two standards has created a novel set of laws that only exist in California. Appellation applications will need to provide evidence of how the cannabis produced in a geographic area has a quality or characteristic caused by the area's distinctive geographic features.[148]

The CAP program aims to allow regions of California that are traditionally known for cannabis production to protect and hopefully benefit from

---

143 P-A Chouvy, "Why the Concept of Terroir Matters for Drug Cannabis Production" (2022) 88 Geo J. 89. There are areas around the world that might qualify for protection as cannabis GIs because of the terroir and cultural cannabis history. Still, those countries' governments are not currently seeking protection.

144 E Bonadio and C Poyser, "Protecting Jamaican Geographical Indications: The Cases of 'Jamaica Jerk,' 'Jamaica Rum' and 'Blue Mountain Coffee'" (1 January 2021) European Int. Prop. Rev <http://dx.doi.org/10.2139/ssrn.3803854>.

145 Ministry of Industry, Investment & Commerce, "CLA Seeks Protection for Jamaican Ganja" (*Government of Jamaica*) <https://www.miic.gov.jm/content/cla-seeks-protection-jamaican-ganja> accessed 24 January 2024.

146 E Bonadio, N Corthésy, M Mimler, D Daley McClure, Y Williams, S Deslandes, "Maximizing the Benefits of Origin Products in An Emerging Economy – The Impact of Geographical Indication Protection in Jamaica" (2023) 5 European Intellectual Property Review, 1–16 <https://papers.ssrn.com/sol3/papers.cfm?abstract_id=4368537> accessed 12 April 2023.

147 California Business and Professions Code § 26063 – BPC Division 10. Chap 6. Licensed Cultivation Sites.

148 California Department of Food and Agriculture, "Cannabis Appellations Program Proposed Text of Regulations" (2 February 2024) <https://www.cdfa.ca.gov/oefi/cap/docs/2024020_ProposedText.pdf>.

their cannabis history. There is a region of California known as the "Emerald Triangle," which has been known for cannabis production for over 40 years.[149] Within the Emerald Triangle, there are many sub-regions that cannabis cultivators believe have a unique history of cannabis cultivation, which are distinct enough to qualify as appellations of origin (AO).[150] The cultivators in these areas hope that by receiving AO designation from the CDFA, their cannabis will receive a higher price at the time of sale.[151]

There are a few identifiable legal challenges for the CAP program. The cannabis grown in California cannot be shipped to other states or countries, and certification or collective marks for the appellations cannot be registered with the USPTO due to marijuana's Schedule I status. This means that enforcement and protection of appellation names would be very difficult nationally and internationally in foreign jurisdictions. The US is not a signatory to the Lisbon Agreement for the Protection of Appellations of Origin,[152] so even despite the advances of the CAP program at the state level, there are significant barriers to it receiving international recognition. Lastly, CAP is a state program with no legal power outside of California, making enforcing the appellation regions' names challenging outside the state. The enforcement of appellation names has not occurred because the problem is still in development, but it is safe to assume this could be an issue.

1.7 MARIJUANA RESCHEDULING TO SCHEDULE III

On April 30, 2024, the Department of Justice circulated a proposal to reschedule marijuana from Schedule I to Schedule III.[153] The DEA accepted this proposal, but additional procedural steps must be taken before reclassification.[154] If marijuana is granted reclassification, it will still be a controlled substance.

---

149 E Witt, "How Legalization Changed Humboldt County Marijuana" *The New Yorker* (20 May 2019).

150 J Bryant, "Winemakers Collaborate with Weed Growers on New Cannabis Appellations System" (*Wine Enthusiast*, 8 May 2023) <https://www.wineenthusiast.com/culture/wine/california-cannabis-appellation-guide/>.

151 ibid.

152 Lisbon Agreement for the Protection of Appellations of Origin and their International Registration, art. 2(1), Oct. 31, 1958, as revised July 14, 1967, 923 U.N.T.S. 205.

153 Z Miller, J Goodman, J Mustian, L Whitehurst, "US poised to ease restrictions on marijuana in historic shift, but it'll remain a controlled substance" *The Associated Press* (30 April 2024) <https://apnews.com/article/marijuana-biden-dea-criminal-justice-pot-f833a8dae6ceb31a8658a5d65832a3b8>.

154 ibid.

However, some form of "medical marijuana" would likely be allowed, with oversight from the FDA. At the time of writing this chapter, there are far more unknowns than knowns about the implications that would result from the rescheduling of marijuana.

What rescheduling would mean for marijuana-related trademarks remains to be seen, but a few safe assumptions can be made. What constitutes bona fide intent for intent-to-use trademark applications should be allowed for some marijuana products and services. Applying the lawful use requirement for trademarks will change and might be decided more on standards from the FDA than currently from the DEA.

Suppose there are more pharmaceutical patents registered for drugs that include cannabinoids. In that case, those goods will most likely be registered in Nice Classification Class 05, but Class 34 might also be adopted if smokable medical marijuana is allowed. If there is an increase in pharmaceutical-related cannabis patents that involve specific cannabinoids, then a similar issue could occur preventing CBD being usedas a food additive as CBD is considered a drug.[155] This would restrict any medical cannabis from being classified as foodstuffs or edibles in Class 30.

Based on the implications the 2018 Farm Bill had on allowing for the increased opportunity for trademark protection for hemp goods and services, it is reasonable to assume that rescheduling will also create an opportunity for trademarks related to medical cannabis. It is also reasonable to assume that the regulatory policies related to rescheduling will take significant time to develop and apply.

1.8 CONCLUSION

As the cannabis industry continues to evolve, cannabis trademarks will become more important for the safety of consumers and the growth of cannabis businesses. Until cannabis is removed from the CSA, there will always be barriers for cannabis companies seeking federal trademark protection. Until this occurs, trademark applicants for cannabis-related products must be informed about the unique obstacles to protecting cannabis trademarks in the US. Even with these obstacles, every indication is that the cannabis industry will continue to expand as new states continue to legalize cannabis use, which means new trademarks will continue to be created. If marijuana is rescheduled, then there will be new opportunities, such as a reduction in taxes, access

---

[155] United States Department of Food and Agriculture, "FDA Regulation of Cannabis and Cannabis-Derived Products Including Cannabidiol (CBD)" (2 June 2024) <https://www.fda.gov/news-events/public-health-focus/fda-regulation-cannabis-and-cannabis-derived-products-including-cannabidiol-cbd>.

to banking, and, even if it is limited, some access to registering trademarks for medical cannabis goods.

It is not far-fetched to predict that the rescheduling of marijuana would lead to its eventual descheduling in the US because the regulations relating to cannabis, marijuana, medical marijuana, and hemp – all of which are *Cannabis sativa L* – are becoming overly convoluted and confusing.

2. "A bridge too far?": trade mark protection for cannabis-related products and services in the European Union

Marc Mimler

2.1 INTRODUCTION

On 1st April, many countries celebrate April Fools' Day, a day known for pranks and practical jokes. But in 2024, the German legislator was not fooling anyone when it enacted one of the main electoral pledges of the German coalition government formed by the Social Democratic Party of Germany, the Greens, and the Liberals.[1] The Act on Cannabis expanded the permitted uses of cannabis products within the Federal Republic of Germany.[2] While the law still bans many uses of cannabis, individuals are allowed to possess up to 25 grams of cannabis and grow up to three plants at home for personal use. The law is, however, very restrictive compared to other countries that have legalised and regulated the use of Cannabis products like Canada. One notable difference is that German law does not include provisions for establishing a regulated commercial retail market for cannabis due to concerns about potential violations of EU law.[3]

[1] L Bayer, "Cannabis Users Celebrate Relaxation of Laws on Personal Use in Germany" *The Guardian* (1 April 2024) <https://www.theguardian.com/world/2024/apr/01/germany-legal-cannabis-weed-laws-personal-use> accessed 9 July 2024.

[2] Gesetz zum kontrollierten Umgang mit Cannabis und zur Änderung weiterer Vorschriften (Cannabisgesetz – CanG) vom 27. März 2024.

[3] Transform Drug Policy Foundation, "German Cannabis Legislation Explained" (7 March 2024) <https://transformdrugs.org/blog/german-cannabis-legalisation-explained#:~:text=After%20several%20years%20of%20debate,in%20favour%2050%20to%2016> accessed 9 July 2024.

For companies wishing to use trade marks to advertise their products and services, the German legislation may well just be a "joke"; it clearly is not the hoped-for "dam buster" leading to wider commercial uses of cannabis products and services in the Federal Republic. However, the ongoing debates in other countries about expanding permissible uses of cannabis raise the interesting question of whether trade marks can be obtained for cannabis-related products or services in the EU.[4] Using trade marks to promote illegal substances would obviously be counterproductive in combatting an illegal substance. But should this alleged tendency to "liberalise" continue and commercial uses come into play, the use of trade marks to advertise products or services becomes crucial.

This chapter will address the current situation regarding the possibility of registering so-called EU trade marks for cannabis-related products and services within the EU. These trade marks can be registered for the entire EU territory through the European Union Intellectual Property Office (EUIPO). However, the 27 EU Member States have varying approaches to regulating cannabis, which poses a challenge to granting a unitary right to promote these products: how can a unitary right that will be used to promote products be granted when there is such disunity on whether these products are legal or not? The EU's lack of overall exclusive competence on this matter further complicates the regulatory landscape. The chapter will provide an overview of the EU trade mark focussing on the major obstacles related to trade marks for cannabis-related products or services, such as distinctiveness. A key issue to be discussed is whether trade marks for such products or services would go against public policy or accepted principles of morality, which is a major barrier to registration.

2.2 MAIN BODY

2.2.1 The Trade Mark System in the European Union

The EU's trade mark system comprises two legal elements. First, a Directive was issued to standardise national trade mark laws, reducing differences in national trade mark legislation, especially regarding what can be protected as a trade mark and how trade marks for services are registered.[5] Second, a Regulation was enacted to establish a single trade mark that is valid throughout

[4] Y Basire and S Martin, "Public Policy and Morality in Trademark Examination in the European Union" (2023) The Trademark Reporter 590–629, 613.

[5] First Council Directive 89/104/EEC of 21 December 1988 to approximate the laws of the Member States relating to trade marks, OJ L40, 11.2.1989, p. 1.

the entire EU.[6] This EU trade mark can be acquired by applying to the EUIPO located in Alicante, Spain. Prior to the UK's departure from the EU, these rights extended to the UK, and EU trade marks registered by the EUIPO before 1st January 2021 were automatically replicated as comparable rights in the UK.

In addition to regular EU trade marks that are registered to indicate the source of goods or services from a specific entity, Collective and Certification Marks can also be registered.[7] Collective marks indicate goods or services originating from a specific organisation rather than an individual entity. For example, "Darjeeling" is owned by the Tea Board of India, and "Bavarian Beer" is registered by the Bavarian Association of Brewers. EU Collective Trade Marks can be used by anyone who meets the criteria set out in regulations covering the use of the mark.[8] For instance, they could be used by cannabis licencing authorities, enabling all association members to apply the mark to their goods. Certification marks, on the other hand, indicate that certain goods and services possess specific characteristics rather than designating trade origin. These marks were only added with the recent revision of the EU trade mark system. However, the main focus of this chapter is on the law of trade marks rather than that of certification or collective marks.

2.2.2 Registering Cannabis-related Trade Marks in the European Union

Trade mark registrations for cannabis products can cover more than just the plants or products derived from the cannabis plant. They can also include vaping equipment, shops, cafes, and services related to these products. In the EU, there is no specific legislation regarding the registration of trade marks for cannabis-related goods or services. Instead, the same criteria as for any other trade mark application under the EU Trade Mark Regulation apply. According to EU trade mark law, a trade mark is defined as a sign that is able to distinguish the goods or services of one undertaking from those of other undertakings and which can be represented on the Register of EU trade marks "in a manner which enables the competent authorities and the public to determine the clear and precise subject matter of the protection afforded to its proprietor".[9] The recent amendment to the law eliminated the requirement for a sign to be

---

[6] Regulation (EU) 2017/1001 of the European Parliament and of the Council of 14 June 2017 on the European Union trade mark (hereafter: EU Trade Mark Regulation).

[7] EU Trade Mark Regulation, Articles 74 and 83.

[8] ibid Article 78.

[9] ibid Article 4(a)(b).

graphically represented,[10] making it easier to register so-called exotic marks such as colours and sounds.[11] The Regulation specifies that signs can include words, designs, letters, numerals, colours, the shape of goods or packaging of goods, or sounds.[12]

2.2.2.1 Classes of goods and services for trade mark registration

As mentioned previously, trade marks can be obtained for either goods or services. The EU Trade Mark Regulation mandates the EUIPO to adhere to the Nice Agreement of 1957 concerning the International Classification of Goods and Services.[13] As a result, applicants for an EU trade mark must specify the goods or services for which trade mark registration is sought.[14] There are a total of 45 classes of goods and services (34 classes for goods and 11 classes for services), which are further divided into various sub-categories. For cannabis-related products or services, the class headings, Class 3 (Cosmetics, essential oils), Class 5 (Pharmaceuticals and natural remedies, dietary supplements), Class 29 (Edible oils), Class 30 (Coffee and tea and their substitutes, bakery products, processed plant-based foods), Class 31 (Unprocessed plants), Class 32 (Non-alcoholic beverages), Class 34 (Tobacco products and tobacco substitutes), Class 35 (Retail of cosmetics, retail of food and beverages), and Class 43 (Restaurants and cafes) are likely to be relevant for applicants seeking to register trade marks in the EU.

The EUIPO initially applied a lenient approach by allowing trade mark applicants to claim all sub-classes of a class by simply using the heading of that class. This resulted in trade mark owners obtaining overly broad product

---

10 ibid Recital 10.

11 See the decision of the CJEU in the *Shield Mark BV v Joost Kist* case where the two marks in question were the "crowing of a cock" and the first nine notes of Beethoven's "Für Elise": Case C-283/01 *Shield Mark BV v Joost Kist*, Judgment of the Court (Sixth Chamber) of 27 November 2003, [15]–[19]. Previously, the requirement of having to produce a graphical representation of a sound mark presented difficulties for applicants.

12 EU Trade Mark Regulation, Article 4.

13 Nice Agreement Concerning the International Classification of Goods and Services for the Purposes of the Registration of Marks (as amended on 28 September 1979).

14 Commission implementing Regulation (EU) 2018/626 of 5 March 2018 laying down detailed rules for implementing certain provisions of Regulation (EU) 2017/1001 of the European Parliament and of the Council on the European Union trade mark, and repealing Implementing Regulation (EU) 2017/1431, Article 2(1)(c).

claims,[15] namely by taking the "lazy option"[16] of reproducing just the class heading in their applications. However, after the CJEU issued its IP Translator decision, the EUIPO had to change its approach. The CJEU required that the goods and services for which trade mark protection is sought be clearly and precisely identified by the applicant to enable authorities and businesses to determine the extent of the protection provided by the trade mark.[17] As a result, the EUIPO adopted the Court's ruling,[18] which means that applicants can no longer claim entire sub-classes by using an entire class heading. Instead, they must expressly indicate whether they intend to "cover all the goods or services in the alphabetical list of the class in question".[19] This is relevant for cannabis-related trademarks because applicants should consider which products or services their business is built on before applying for an EU trade mark.

2.2.2.2 Absolute grounds of refusal, Article 7 EU Trade Mark Regulation

The EU's trade mark law prohibits certain trade marks from being registered. These absolute grounds of refusal are assessed by the EUIPO ex officio. One important barrier to trade mark registration is distinctiveness, meaning that trade marks must not be devoid of any distinctive character.[20] Distinctiveness is crucial in trade mark law as it relates to the mark's ability to identify the origin of goods and services.[21] This ground of refusal was applied in a case involving cannabis products, decided by the 4th Board of Appeal of the EUIPO.[22]

---

15 A von Mühlendahl, D Botis, S Maniatis, I Wiseman, *Trade Mark Law in Europe* (3rd edn, OUP 2016) [4.191].

16 J Mellor, D Llewelyn, T Moody-Stuart, D Keeling, I Berkeley, A Chantrielle, *Kerly's Law of Trade Marks and Trade Names* (17th edn, Thomson Reuters 2024) [6-019].

17 *Chartered Institute of Patent Attorneys v Registrar of Trade Marks* [2012] E.T.M.R. 42 [64].

18 Communication No 2/12 of the President of the Office of June 20, 2012, Concerning the Use of Class Headings in Lists of Goods and Services for Community Trade Mark Applications and Registrations.

19 ibid Point VII.

20 Trade Mark Regulation, Article 7(1)(b) EU. This ground often overlaps with Article 7(1)(c) (where the sign is descriptive of the goods and services) and Article 7(1)(d) of the Regulation.

21 In this line, the Court of Justice held that distinctiveness relates to the "capacity of the mark to identify the goods or services for which it has been registered as coming from a particular undertaking" (Case C-342/97 *Lloyd Schuhfabrik Meyer & Co. GmbH v Klijsen Handel BV.*, Judgment of the Court of 22 June 1999, [22]).

22 R2135/2020-4 EUIPO (4th Board of Appeal) 4 May 2021.

The applicant wanted to register their sign (Figure 2.1) for various goods and services in relation to cosmetics, products for medical, medicinal, veterinary, dietetic or sanitary purposes, foodstuff, plants, electronic cigarettes and retail, mail order, catalogue and online services related to these products in Classes 3, 5, 29, 30, 31, 34 and 35.

The EUIPO examiner partially refused the application, stating that the English-speaking consumer would perceive the sign as meaning simply "cannabidiol" and thus "merely informed consumers that the goods for which protection was sought merely contained CBD, that CBD was their principal compound, or that the retailed goods contained CBD as their main compound".[23] The examiner believed that the inclusion of three small leaves in the logo was negligible and did not make the mark distinctive. It would rather reinforce the meaning of CBD. In response, the applicant argued that the leaves may not necessarily depict cannabis leaves, that CBD is just one of 113 cannabinoids, and that the term "just" could also mean "fair". Additionally, the applicant pointed out that most EU consumers may not be native English speakers.[24]

The Board of Appeal found that the entire sign lacked distinctive character. It explained that even though adding the word "just" could be viewed as a form of advertising, it would not make the sign distinctive. The term "just CBD" was considered not unusual or uncommon by the average consumer.[25] The Board also agreed with the examiner's assessment of the figurative element and discarded the appellant's point that the figurative element would render the mark distinctive: "[A] figurative sign remains devoid of distinctive character

Source: R2135/2020-4, JustCBD, EUIPO (4th Board of Appeal) 4 May 2021.

Figure 2.1 *"JustCBD" figurative mark*

23 ibid [3].
24 ibid [5]–[7].
25 ibid [18]–[20].

if its graphical elements do not divert the relevant public's attention from the descriptive message conveyed by the words."[26] It concluded that the figurative elements would not be striking enough as they were smaller compared to the terms "Just" and "CBD", which were considered more striking elements of the mark.

Concepts related to the absolute ground of lacking distinctive character are descriptiveness,[27] and genericism.[28] Descriptiveness is based on a pro-competitive rationale that allows descriptive signs or indications related to the categories of goods or services to be used freely by all, serving the public interest.[29] This means that terms that immediately convey information about the goods or services applied for may not be registrable.[30] Terms such as "weed",[31] "marijuana", or "ganja", often used in relation to cannabis, would thus be considered descriptive. This issue was discussed in a decision by the Board of Appeal at the EUIPO. The applicant sought to register the word mark "Mango Kush".[32] The Board agreed with the examiner in finding that the term would refer to a cannabis variety and supplemented that the term "Kush" would connote "a form of cannabis made from a particular variety or strain of the indica subspecies of the cannabis plant, Cannabis Savita indica, and typically containing a high level of [tetrahydrocannabinol] THC; (also) plants of this variety or strain", according to the Oxford English Dictionary.[33] The addition of "Mango" would mean that the cannabis variety would have a mango taste.[34] The Board concluded that the term would be descriptive for many product groups the applicant wanted to register for in classes 30 and 34, such as "Herbs for smoking", "e-cigarette liquids", "chemical flavourings in liquid form used to refill electronic cigarette cartridges", or "Cartridges sold filled with chemical flavourings in liquid form for electronic cigarettes". However, the Board

---

26 ibid [24].

27 EU Trade Mark Regulation, Article 7(1)(c).

28 ibid Article 7(1)(d).

29 Joined cases C-108/97 and C-109/97 *Windsurfing Chiemsee*, Judgment of the Court of 4 May 1999, [25].

30 EUIPO, Trade Mark Guidelines, Part B Section 4.1.1.

31 In the *Bavaria Weed* decision, which will be discussed below, the examiner and Board of Appeal of the EUIPO found that the term weed would be understood by the relevant consumers as relating to "Marihuana": Case T-178/20 *Bavaria Weed v EUIPO* (BavariaWeed) Judgment of the General Court (Tenth Chamber) of 12 May 2021, [24].

32 Case R 2006/2020-2 *In re Shape Sols. GmbH*, Decision of the 2nd Board of Appeal of the EUIPO of 19 July 2021.

33 ibid [25].

34 ibid.

found that the mark would not be descriptive in relation to smoking equipment without a direct connection to specific ingredients or flavourings, such as "Cigarette paper", "Tobacco storage tins", and "Tobacco pipes".[35]

Article 7(1)(d) of the Regulation prohibits the registration of generic marks as EU trade marks. This means that marks made up exclusively of words or indications that have become part of everyday language or common practice in a specific trade at the relevant time cannot be registered. Such marks lack distinctive character and cannot fulfil "the essential function of the trade mark which is to guarantee the identity of the origin of the marked goods or service to the consumer or end user".[36] It is important to note that this restriction is based on the current usage of the signs in the relevant trade sectors for which the mark is being applied, not on their potential future use.[37] Generic signs are unable to denote the specific source of the goods and services in question, thus failing to fulfil the essential function of trade marks.[38] Classic examples of trade marks that became generic over time include "escalator", which used to be a trade mark for the Otis Elevator company, and "linoleum".

2.2.2.3 Acquired distinctiveness

The bar to registration pursuant to Article 7(1)(b)-(d) of the Regulation discussed above is not absolute but is subject to a proviso. A sign that is inherently unregistrable can still be registered if it has gained distinctive character in relation to the specific goods or services for which registration is sought due to its use.[39] This means that consumers have become accustomed to seeing the sign as indicating a particular trade origin, i.e., where such characteristics have been nurtured.[40] The Court of Justice has ruled that a previously non-distinctive, descriptive, or generic sign can be registered "following the use which has been made of it, it has come to identify the product in respect of which registration is applied for as originating from a particular undertaking and thus to distinguish that product from goods of other undertakings".[41] For

---

[35] ibid [40].

[36] Case C-517/99 *Bravo*, Judgment of the Court of 05 October 2001, [22].

[37] ibid [35].

[38] Case T-322/03, *Telefon & Buch v OHMI – Herold Business Data (WEISSE SEITEN)*, Judgment of the General Court (Third Chamber) of 16 March 2006, [52].

[39] EU Trade Mark Regulation, Article 7(3).

[40] L Bently, B Sherman, D Gangjee, P Johnson, *Intellectual Property Law* (6th edn, OUP 2022) 989.

[41] Joined cases C-108/97 and C-109/97 *Windsurfing Chiemsee*, Judgment of the Court of 4 May 1999, [46].

the trade mark to be registered, it must have gained distinctiveness among a significant proportion of current and potential customers.[42]

The Court has outlined specific types of evidence that can help support a claim that a trade mark has acquired distinctiveness. These include the market share held by the mark, the extent and duration of its use, the investment in promoting the mark, the proportion of consumers who identify goods with the mark, and statements from trade and professional associations.[43] The applicant must request an examination of acquired distinctiveness and demonstrate that the mark had acquired distinctiveness through prior use before the date of the application for registration.[44] Coming back to the "Mango Kush" example discussed above, the applicant might have succeeded in registering the trade mark for the disputed classes where they had shown such acquired distinctiveness as prescribed by the factors laid down by the CJEU in the Windsurfing Chiemsee decision.

2.2.2.4 Morality and public policy, Article 7(1)(f) EU Trade Mark Regulation

The most contentious issue in registering trade marks for cannabis-related products and services is the rule that trade marks "contrary to public policy or to accepted principles of morality" cannot be registered pursuant to Article 7(1)(f) EU Trade Mark Regulation. This rule cannot be overcome by showing that the mark has acquired distinctiveness. Cannabis consumption for recreational use remains illegal in many European Union states.[45] Even medical uses for cannabis are still illegal in some European Union countries.[46] Using trade marks to promote cannabis-related products or services could be seen as counterproductive to a public policy aiming to discourage the use of such products, and their registration seen as a government-agency vetting of such uses. For the EUIPO as an EU Agency, the issue is more complex because criminal

---

42 ibid [52].

43 ibid.

44 *Guidelines for Examination of European Union Trade Marks, European Union Intellectual Property Office (EUIPO) Part B Examination Section 4, Absolute grounds for refusal Section 4 Absolute grounds for refusal – Chapter 14 Acquired distinctiveness through use (Article 7(3) EUTMR) 3.1.* <https://guidelines.euipo.europa.eu/binary/2214311/2000150000>.

45 European Monitoring Centre for Drugs and Drug Addiction, *Cannabis Laws in Europe: Questions and Answers for Policymaking* (Publications Office of the European Union Luxembourg 2023) 19, accessed 16 August 2024.

46 See the illustrative map at The Canimaga, "Where cannabis is legal in Europe" <https://cannigma.com/where-cannabis-is-legal-in-europe/> accessed 9 July 2024.

issues are usually subject to the national law of Member States, as the EU has very limited competence on such matters.[47] The divergent national approaches taken in EU Member States may make a common approach more difficult.

The terms covered within Article 7(1)(f) of the Regulation are challenging to apply because they are abstract and require interpretation by examining bodies and courts.[48] The CJEU recently considered this provision in a decision.[49] Constantin Film Produktion, the production company of the film "Fack Ju Göhte", tried to register the title of the film as a word sign in 2015 at EUIPO. The title is related to the famous German author Johann Wolfgang von Goethe and is a phonetic transcription in German of the term "Fuck you". The examiner rejected the registration, and the 5th Board of Appeal dismissed Constantin Film's appeal. The General Court also upheld the decision to reject the registration.[50]

The CJEU upheld the Advocate General's position, stating that the concept refers to the fundamental moral values and standards adhered to by a society at a given time. These values and norms may change over time and differ from place to place and should be determined based on the social consensus prevailing in that society at the time of the assessment.[51] When making this determination, the social context, including cultural, religious, or philosophical diversities, should be taken into account in order to objectively assess what that society considers morally acceptable at that time.[52] The Court explained how an assessment would take place. It would not be enough for the sign to be in bad taste but rather it must "be perceived as contrary to the fundamental moral values and standards of society as they exist at that time" by the relevant public.[53] The examination would need to be based on "the perception of a reasonable person with average thresholds of sensitivity and tolerance, taking into account the context in which the mark may be encountered and, where

[47] Consolidated Version of the Treaty on the functioning of the European Union [2012] OJ C326/47 (TFEU), Article 83.

[48] Y Basire and S Martin, "Public Policy and Morality in Trademark Examination in the European Union" (2023) The Trademark Reporter 590–629, 597.

[49] Case C-240/18 P *Constantin Film Produktion v EUIPO*, Judgment of the Court (Fifth Chamber) of 27 February 2020.

[50] Case T-69/17 *Constantin Film Produktion v EUIPO*, Judgment of the General Court (Sixth Chamber) of 24 January 2018.

[51] Case C-240/18 P *Constantin Film Produktion v EUIPO*, Judgment of the Court (Fifth Chamber) of 27 February 2020, [39].

[52] ibid.

[53] ibid [41].

relevant, the particular circumstances of the part of the Union concerned".[54] Legislation, administrative practices, and public opinion would be relevant in this context.

Another point barring trade mark registration is public policy. The CJEU did not discuss this ground in the decision as it was not raised. However, Advocate General Bobek provided some guidance within his opinion. He found that the concept would relate to "a normative vision of values and goals, defined by the relevant public authority... Public policy thus expresses the public regulator's wishes as to the norms to be respected in society".[55] The following section will discuss some cases of how this absolute ground was discussed in relation to trade mark applications before the EUIPO for cannabis-related products and services.

2.2.2.4.1 "Cannabis Store Amsterdam"

The examining divisions of the EUIPO have had numerous occasions to assess trade mark applications for cannabis-related products and services.[56] One of the notable cases involving the morality exclusion in relation to cannabis-related products was the Amsterdam Cannabis decision, which was brought before the General Court of the European Union, the EU's second highest court.[57] In this case, the applicant sought to register a specific sign as an EU trade mark and sought registration for Classes 30,[58] Class 32,[59] and 43.[60]

The examiner initially rejected the application due to a lack of distinctive character and descriptiveness. The applicant appealed this decision before the Board of Appeal. Interestingly, the second Board of Appeal additionally raised the ground of refusal based on Article 7(1)(f) EU Trade Mark Regulation,

---

54 ibid [42].

55 Case C-240 *Constantin Film Produktion v EUIPO*, Opinion of AG of Bobek, [76].

56 According to Bourdeau and Martin, the EUIPO rejected a dozen applications that included the word "cannabis" or similar denominations on the absolute ground of public order in 2019 alone: L Bourdeau, S Martin, "General Court Confirms Rejection of Cannabis Trade Mark on the Ground of Public Order pursuant to art.7(1)(f) of European Union Trade Mark Regulation (EUTMR): Cannabis Store Amsterdam (T-683/18) EU:T:2019:855" (2020) EIPR 378–380, 380.

57 Case T-683/18 *Conte v EUIPO* (CANNABIS STORE AMSTERDAM), Judgment of the General Court (Seventh Chamber) of 12 December 2019.

58 "Baked goods, confectionery, chocolate and desserts; Salts, seasonings, flavourings and condiments; Ice, ice creams, frozen yoghurts and sorbets; Savoury pastries."

59 "Soft drinks; Beer and brewery products; Preparations for making beverages.""

60 "Services for providing food and drink."

Source: Case T-683/18, *Conte v EUIPO* (Cannabis Store Amsterdam) Judgment of the General Court (Seventh Chamber) of 12 December 2019.

Figure 2.2 "Cannabis Store Amsterdam" figurative mark

which was not raised by the examiner in its decision. The appeal was dismissed, with the Board finding that the application would be contrary to public policy. It argued that the recreational use of cannabis containing more than 0.2 per cent of THC was illegal in many EU Member States. The applicant then sought to annul this decision, which meant that the General Court of the EU had to decide the issue.

It is important to note that the Court made a significant observation concerning Article 7(1)(f) of the EU Trade Mark Regulation. The Court emphasised that the absolute ground for refusal applies even if the grounds of non-registrability only exist in part of the Union, such as in one Member State, as stipulated in Article 7(2) of the Regulation.[61] The Court made an important finding regarding the relevant public from whose viewpoint the question of immorality would be assessed. The applicant argued that this public would mainly consist of younger people aged between 20 and 30. It was suggested that younger

[61] Case T-683/18 *Conte v EUIPO* (CANNABIS STORE AMSTERDAM), Judgment of the General Court (Seventh Chamber) of 12 December 2019, [29].

people would be less offended by trade marks promoting cannabis products. However, the Court disagreed with this argument and pointed out that the relevant public was broader and included "other persons who, without being interested in those goods and services, will encounter that sign incidentally in their day-to-day lives".[62]

In relation to the assessment of public policy, the applicant argued that the requested registration would not involve any illegal narcotic substances. Even if it did, that would not necessarily violate public policy unless the mark encouraged, trivialised, or approved the use or consumption of an illegal narcotic substance. The applicant also argued that the difference between the classes for which the trade mark was sought and the typical consumption of marijuana by smoking would make the decision of the Board of Appeal unfounded. The applicant referred to a decision of the Cancellation Division of the EUIPO concerning the sign "COCAINE" for goods in Classes 3, 25, and 32 (particularly beer), where consumption patterns were relevant in determining whether Article 7(1)(f) of the EU Trade Mark Regulation would apply.

The Court then outlined the Board's considerations in relation to the term cannabis, which could have three possible meanings. The Board agreed with the applicant's view that the term should not be automatically understood as referring to a narcotic unless there were "further indications" to that effect.[63] Thus the Court agreed that the Board was entitled to investigate these further indications in relation to the public's perception of the sign in question. It held that the Board was correct to analyse the

> combined presence, in the sign at issue, of the stylised representation of the cannabis leaf, the media symbol for marijuana, and the word "amsterdam", referring to the fact that the city of Amsterdam has many points of sale for the narcotic derived from cannabis, due to the sale of cannabis being tolerated under certain conditions in the Netherlands, made it very likely that the consumer, in the circumstances of the present case, would interpret the word "cannabis" as referring to the narcotic substance which is illegal in "many countries of the European Union".[64]

The Court further stated that the dominant element of the sign, i.e., the word "cannabis",

> will be perceived by the relevant English-speaking public as meaning "cannabis shop in Amsterdam" and by the relevant non-English-speaking public as "cannabis in Amsterdam", which, in both cases, coupled with the image of the cannabis

---

62 ibid [33].

63 ibid [62].

64 ibid [64].

leaves, the media symbol for marijuana, is a clear and unequivocal reference to the narcotic substance which is sold there.[65]

The Court then examined whether the sign would go against public policy. To do this, the Court referred to the Attorney General's opinion in the "Fack Ju Göhte" decision. The Court observed that in Member States where the use of cannabis is prohibited, it is a sensitive issue due to its implications for public health. The prohibition of cannabis is seen as safeguarding "an interest which those Member States consider to be fundamental in accordance with their own systems of values".[66] As a result, the regulation of cannabis use becomes a public policy issue under Article 7(1) in conjunction with Article 7(2) of the EU Trade Mark Regulation.[67]

The Court held that it was immaterial whether the Boards omitted to assess whether the sign in question would encourage, trivialise, or convey approval of the use of an illegal narcotic substance. Based on its own assessment of the relevant public and their perception of the sign as containing illegal narcotic substances, the Court found that this would suffice to trigger the absolute ground of Article 7(1)(f) of the Regulation.[68] The fact that signs such as the Cocaine example mentioned by the applicant were registered at the EUIPO would be irrelevant since the decision of the examining division would not bind the Boards of the EUIPO or the EU courts.[69] Thus, the case brought by the applicant was unsuccessful.

2.2.2.4.2 "Bavaria Weed"

A subsequent application of the "Cannabis Store Amsterdam" decision can be seen in the Bavaria Weed decision by the 10th chamber of the General Court.[70] The Bavaria Weed GmbH sought to register a figurative mark (see Figure 2.3)

---

65 ibid [65].
66 ibid [74].
67 ibid.
68 ibid [77].
69 ibid [79].
70 Case T-178/20 *Bavaria Weed v EUIPO* (BavariaWeed), Judgment of the General Court (Tenth Chamber) of 12 May 2021.

Source: Case T-178/20, *Bavaria Weed v EUIPO* (BavariaWeed) Judgment of the General Court (Tenth Chamber) of 12 May 2021.

Figure 2.3 "BavariaWeed" figurative mark

in relation to services in Classes 35,[71] 39,[72] 42,[73] and 44.[74] The examiner at the EUIPO rejected the application based on Article 7(1)(f) of the EU Trade Mark

[71] "Distribution of medical cannabis; Distribution of medical cannabis to pharmacies and doctors, in particular via an online shop; Procurement services relating to medical cannabis; Public relations with the aim of marketing medical cannabis; merchandising."

[72] "Medical Cannabis Storage; Packaging and shipping of medical cannabis."

[73] "Conducting technical tests on pharmaceuticals; Development of pharmaceutical preparations and medications; medical laboratory services; development of pharmaceutical products; Medical and pharmaceutical research services; Services for evaluating the effectiveness of pharmaceuticals; Evaluation of pharmaceutical products; Information on medical and scientific research results on medicines and clinical trials; Quality testing for pharmaceutical products; biomedical research; pharmaceutical research and development; Pharmaceutical development of drugs; Research and development of vaccines and medicines."

[74] "Preparation of prescriptions in pharmacies; pharmaceutical services; Advisory and information services relating to pharmaceutical products; Production of medical cannabis, namely cultivation, refinement and processing of cannabis for medical purposes; preparation and administration of medication; Information on pharmaceutical products; information relating to medicines; Information for patients in the field of medication dosage; Advice and information services relating to pharmaceutical products via the Internet; Preparation of medication according to prescription in pharmacies; Refinement of medical cannabis; dispensing of pharmaceuticals; Preparation and dispensing of medication; Advice in the field of healthcare; Pharmacy consultations; Pharmaceutical advice."

Regulation; the subsequent appeal was rejected by the 5th Appellate Chamber at the EUIPO, against which the applicant sought recourse to the EU General Court. It was submitted that the Board erred in applying Article 7(1)(f) of the Regulation and that it had violated the principles of equitable treatment and good administration.

The Court followed its precedent in Cannabis Store Amsterdam concerning the relevant public and the definitions of public order. The discussion in this case revolved largely around establishing the relevant public for an assessment of Article 7(1)(f) of the Regulation. The Court adopted the approach taken by the EUIPO's Board of Appeal, which considered the relevant public to consist of doctors, pharmacists, patients, and average consumers. Additionally, the assessment included individuals who may encounter the sign in their daily lives but have no interest in the services. It was also noted that English-speaking people were considered relevant in this context. These considerations were not disputed by the claimant.[75]

Arguably, to avoid the application of the absolute ground of refusal, the claimant argued that the term "Weed" in relation to cannabis should be perceived as referring only to its therapeutic uses rather than recreational uses to avoid refusal of the trade mark, as done in other Member States.[76] The Court however found that the juxtaposition of "Weed" with the hemp leaf would not be perceived as a designation for its therapeutic uses by the relevant public but would rather describe the psychoactive substance.[77] The Court relied on the CJEU's approach in the "Fack Ju Göhte" decision that the mark should not be assessed abstractly, but rather how the relevant public would perceive it, taking into account its "concrete and contemporary social context".[78] The Court referred to the Oxford English Dictionary, which states that in slang it would stand for "[t]he cannabis plant, Cannabis sativa; esp. (as a mass noun) this prepared or used especially as a recreational drug".[79] This would mean that the use of the term "weed" would connote the recreational use "to achieve a feeling of intoxication, elation or delirium"[80] and is precisely "not used to designate medicinal products or treatments based on cannabis".[81] The EUIPO

[75] Case T-178/20 *Bavaria Weed v EUIPO* (BavariaWeed), Judgment of the General Court (Tenth Chamber) of 12 May 2021, [21]–[23].

[76] ibid [25].

[77] ibid [21].

[78] ibid [26].

[79] ibid [28].

[80] ibid [29].

[81] ibid [30].

noted that the terms, "pot", "grass", "herb", "boom", "dope", or the German term "Gras" are used as synonyms.[82]

Furthermore, the applicant could not rely on the fact that the services sought to be provided under the sign in question being, presumably, as the Court observed, legal, would not change their perception by the relevant circles. However, such an approach would undermine the application of the absolute ground of refusal.[83] Furthermore, some of the services for which the trade mark has been applied would not relate to therapeutic uses, but rather to merchandising. Moreover, the relevant groups would not be able to distinguish between legal therapeutic uses and illegal ones typically associated with the word "hemp".[84]

The claimant also submitted that public order would not be violated since there would be a shift towards legalising Cannabis concerning therapeutic uses.[85] However, this argument was insufficient to override the absolute ground for refusal. Although Article 7(1) of the EU Trade Mark Regulation does not define public order or regulate the use of narcotics, Article 7(2) of the Regulation makes the absolute ground within Article 7(1) applicable, even if it applies only in part of the Union, leading to discrepancies in assessing public order among Member States. The Court acknowledged that not every violation of the law would constitute a violation of public order. The fact that marijuana is considered an illegal substance, and its consumption is often penalised in many Member States, would lead to the use of the sign in question being regarded, at the very least, as promoting the consumption of an illegal substance. Additionally, combatting the use of marijuana is based on public health concerns, which could be regarded as fundamental in the Member States in question, thus placing its regulation as a matter of public order pursuant to Article 7(1)(f) EU Trade Mark Regulation. Finally, these considerations are reinforced by EU law related to combatting illicit drug trafficking,[86] and the Union's goal to reduce "drugs-related health damage, including information and prevention",[87] according to the Court.

---

[82] ibid [29].

[83] ibid [31].

[84] ibid [33].

[85] The claimant here submitted the European Parliament's resolution on the use of cannabis for medicinal purposes: European Parliament Resolution of 13 February 2019 on use of cannabis for medicinal purposes (2018/2775(RSP)) OJ C449, 23.12.2020, 115–118.

[86] Consolidated Version of the Treaty on the Functioning of the European Union [2012] OJ C326/47 (TFEU), Article 83(1).

[87] TFEU, Article 168(1), 3.

The Court added that these points could not be challenged with the applicant's submission that a tendency to legalise the use and consumption of cannabis products would exist.[88] The Court found that there is no universally accepted or prevalent tendency towards legalising products containing more than 0.2 per cent THC, whether for therapeutic or recreational use.[89] The European Parliament's resolution highlights the ongoing controversy.[90] Finally, the Court stated that the EU legislator does not possess the legislative competence to create laws regarding the therapeutic use of cannabis and dismissed the case.[91]

2.2.2.4.3 "Well Weed"

Similar considerations were applied in the "Well Weed" decision by the EUIPO's 5th Board of Appeal. The applicant sought to register the figurative mark (see Figure 2.4) concerning Class 22 – hemp, and Class 34 – Tobacco and tobacco products, including substitutes.

Again, the examiner rejected the application under Article 7(1)(f) EU Trade Mark Regulation. The word "Weed" within the expression "Well Weed" would provide a positive message to reasonable English-speaking consumers in the EU about an activity that is deemed illegal within many EU Member States.[92] The applicant's request to annul the examiner's decision was rejected by the Board of Appeal as unfounded; the Board held that the term "weed" would include, inter alia, a reference to marijuana by referring to the online Merriam-Webster dictionary.[93] The addition of the term "Well" would create a positive connotation of the characteristics of the goods in question.[94] The Board acknowledged the applicant's submission whereby the CJEU's decision

---

88 Case T-178/20 *Bavaria Weed v EUIPO* (BavariaWeed), Judgment of the General Court (Tenth Chamber) of 12 May 2021, [46].

89 ibid [45].

90 "...whereas EU Member States differ widely in their approach to cannabis legislation, including their legislation on cannabis for medical purposes, such as on the maximum allowed levels of THC and CBD concentrations, which can lead to difficulties for countries applying a more prudent approach": European Parliament Resolution of 13 February 2019 on Use of Cannabis for Medicinal Purposes (2018/2775(RSP)) OJ C449, 23.12.2020, 115–118, F.

91 Case T-178/20 *Bavaria Weed v EUIPO* (BavariaWeed), Judgment of the General Court (Tenth Chamber) of 12 May 2021, [49].

92 Case R 213/2021-5 *WELL WEED*, Decision of the Fifth Board of Appeal of 04 March 2021, [3].

93 ibid [22].

94 ibid [23].

Source: Case R 213/2021-5, WELL WEED, EUIPO (5th Board of Appeal), 4 March 2021.

Figure 2.4 "Well Weed" figurative mark

in CBD would need to be taken into account.[95] There, the Court held that hemp, within statutory limits, may be freely marketed and thus could not be considered contrary to accepted principles of morality.

The Board acknowledged that there are discussions about the use of cannabis containing tetrahydrocannabinol (THC) for therapeutic or recreational purposes, aiming to classify them as non-narcotic. However, the examiner was

[95] Case C-663/2018 *Commercialisation du cannabidiol – CBD*, Judgment of the Court (Fourth Chamber) of 19 November 2020.

not wrong in rejecting the application, as the use of such cannabis remains illegal in many EU Member States.[96] The Board pointed out that in Member States where English is widely spoken, such as Finland, Ireland, and Sweden, products derived from cannabis with a THC content exceeding 0.2 per cent are considered illegal drugs. In addition, the content of THC would not be relevant anyway since the intended use of the products under the trade mark by the applicant would be irrelevant. This is based on the Cannabis Store Amsterdam decision, which states that consideration "must be based solely on the intrinsic characteristics of the sign forming the subject of the trade mark application and on the perception of the relevant public".[97] Thus, the relevant public would link with illegal substances "regardless of whether or not illegal compounds are present in the goods designated by the trade mark".[98] The use of the colour green in the figurative mark would increase the association with the cannabis plant, while the two wavy lines would not distract from that connotation but could be seen as initials of the word elements.[99] The Board then reiterated the findings discussed above in Bavaria Weed in relation to public health being a matter of public interest and the EU dimension.[100] Thus, the applicant's appeal was rejected.

2.3 CONCLUSION

This chapter has outlined the issues that applicants wishing to register EU Trade Marks in relation to cannabis-related products and services face. There are quite substantial hurdles to overcome, as shown. The criteria of distinctiveness and descriptiveness may disallow descriptive or suggestive terms from being registered as EU trade marks, as seen in the "Bavarian Weed", "Well Weed", or "Mango Kush" decisions discussed above. This would also mean that the use of slang words would not be advisable,[101] since relevant consumer groups would easily make a mental connection with cannabis. Here, applicants would likely need to demonstrate that the terms they seek to register as

---

96 Case R 213/2021-5 *WELL WEED*, Decision of the Fifth Board of Appeal of 04 March 2021, [27]–[29].

97 ibid [36].

98 ibid.

99 ibid.

100 ibid [40].

101 The following examples have been listed by Martin and Basire: "Mango Kush", "Durban Poison", "Green Gelato", "Exodus Cheese", "Lickweed", "Amnesia Haze", and "Northern Lights": Y Basire and S Martin, "Public Policy and Morality in Trademark Examination in the European Union" (2023) The Trademark Reporter 590–629, 614.

EU Trade Marks have acquired distinctiveness, which sets separate hurdles in demonstrating that the relevant consumers perceive the sign as designating that the products or services originate from a particular source. For the time being, trade mark referring to cannabis will struggle to get registered as an EU Trade Mark, as observed by Bordeau and Martin, who provide a list of rejections of applications at the EUIPO using the word "cannabis" or similar words.[102]

The other significant hurdle is, of course, Article 7(1)(f) of the EU Trade Mark Regulation. The fact that the consumption of cannabis is still regarded as illegal in many EU Member States will make it difficult for such trade marks to be registered, as discussed due to Article 7(2) of the Regulation. This situation is likely to remain as it is unless a significant change in policies towards wider legalisation of cannabis within EU Member States occurs. A different situation may arise where the mark in question is sought for products in Class 3 (cosmetics) or 44 (medical services), suggesting non-recreational uses. But as seen in the "Bavaria Weed" decision, utmost care should be given not to convey any message with the sign that may be regarded as promoting or inciting the use of illegal drugs. There, the applicant sought to register the sign for services related to cannabis for therapeutic purposes. But the seemingly clever "tongue-in-cheek" approach in choosing the term "weed" backfired. In summary, the bar of public policy is still quite significant for seeking registration for cannabis-related products or services in the EU. This, of course, may change over time and the new German legislation may lead to "the dawn of a new era for cannabis policy in Europe".[103] But much remains to be seen, and Germany's move to legalise some uses of cannabis for recreational purposes may not yet be the expected watershed moment. Or, in short: "Eine Schwalbe macht noch keinen Sommer."[104]

---

102 L Bourdeau, S Martin, "General Court Confirms Rejection of Cannabis Trade Mark on the Ground of Public Order pursuant to art.7(1)(f) of European Union Trade Mark Regulation (EUTMR): Cannabis Store Amsterdam (T-683/18) EU:T:2019:855" (2020) EIPR 378–380, 280.

103 J Manthey, J Rehm, U Verthein, "Germany's Cannabis Act: A Catalyst for European Drug Policy Reform?" (2024) The Lancet Regional Health – Europe 6 <https://doi.org/10.1016/j.lanepe.2024.100929> accessed 15 August 2024.

104 German proverb, which can be translated as "[i]t takes more than a swallow to make a summer".

3. Geographical indications and cannabis

Yentyl Williams

3.1 INTRODUCTION

3.1.1 Jamaican Cannabis, Ganja, and Hemp

Building on research conducted in 2021, and the 2015 amendment to the Dangerous Drugs Act which seeks to regulate cannabis,[1] this chapter focusses on the Geographical Indications (GIs) being considered for Jamaica cannabis, Jamaica ganja, and Jamaica hemp.[2] These three terms are used in the Act, while the word "marijuana" is absent, notably for its derogatory connotation.

According to the Jamaica GI Act, the GI:

> identifies a good as originating in the territory of a country, or a region or locality in that territory, where a given quality, reputation or other characteristic of the good is essentially attributable to its geographical origin.[3]

This definition is in line with that provided by Article 22 of the TRIPS Agreement. While cannabis can benefit from several intellectual property

1 Dangerous Drugs Act (Amendment) 2015.

2 See E Bonadio, N Corthésy, M Mimler, D Daley McClure, Y Williams, S Deslandes, "Maximising the Benefits of Origin Products in an Emerging Economy – The Impact of Geographical Indication Protection in Jamaica" (2023) 5 EIPR. <https://ssrn.com/abstract=4368537> accessed 13 May 2024.

3 Section 2, emphasis added in the Protection of Geographical Indications Act 5 of 2004 (Jamaica).

(IP) rights – new plant varieties,[4] patents, trademarks,[5] copyrights, confidentiality, and trade secrets agreements, amongst others – this article focusses specifically on GI protection, with a specific focus on Jamaica. The interest herein is linked to the conceptual differentiation of GIs as IP rights that cannot be co-opted as private rights, as, for example trademarks,[6] because they are becoming increasingly recognised as a community tool. From this optic, a GI for cannabis can be framed in the context of identifying a good which is the contemporary evolution of former colonial cash crops of extractive plantation economies in a post-colonial setting.[7] Today, GIs can function as valuable IP tools for former plantation economy producer groups to ensure that the economic returns from these signs that underscore the quality-reputation-characteristic link of the given territory return to that location.

In general, a GI must be registered in its home territory before it can seek protection in third-country jurisdictions. According to the Jamaican GI law, a GI is protected whether registered or unregistered.[8] In this case, a GI can be registered at the Jamaican Intellectual Property Office (JIPO), while unregistered GIs may be protected under the common law principle of "passing off". When seeking regional protection through registration at the European Union (EU) level, the jurisdiction that offers these IP rights the most protective regime in the world, the GI is protected as either a Protected Denomination of Origin (PDO) or a Protected Geographical Indication (PGI).[9] The PDO protection underscores an exclusive link between the product and its geographical area, whereas a PGI corresponds to an essential link between the main

[4] The EU's Community Plant Variety Office (CVO) in Angers charges a €2,020 change in fees for testing the cannabis plant per growing period. <https://cpvo.europa.eu/en/news-and-events/news/note-applicants-adjustment-examination-fees-pharmaceutical-cannabis-sativa-varieties-pcs> accessed 15 November 2022.

[5] Since Jamaica's accession to the Madrid Protocol on 27 March 2022, it is expected that several innovative international registrations relating to the cannabis industry will enter the JIPO and subsequently, the Madrid single-filing trademark registry. Protocol Relating to the Madrid Agreement Concerning the International Registration of Marks, adopted at Madrid, June 27, 1989, WIPO Doc. MM/DC/27 Rev. (1989).

[6] S Bowen, "Development from Within? The Potential for Geographical Indications in the Global South" (2010) 13 JWIP 2, 232.

[7] G Beckford, *Persistent Poverty: Underdevelopment in Plantation Economies of the Third World* (OUP 1972).

[8] The Protection of Geographical Indications Act 5 of 2004 (Jamaica).

[9] Regulation (EU) No 1151/2012 of the European Parliament and of the Council of 21 November 2012 on Quality Schemes for Agricultural Products and Foodstuffs [2012] OJ L343.

factors of production of a GI product. As the archetypal GI, Champagne is a PDO, wherein the production and contributing factors to the end product are exclusively done in-region. By contrast, Holland Gouda PGI uses cow's milk from the entire region of the Netherlands, and in some cases, cumin, which comes from outside the territory, can be added.[10] However, for Noord-Hollandse Gouda PDO, the cow's milk comes exclusively from that region of the north of the Netherlands, as do all factors of production and inputs. Additionally, in the European tradition, GI country names are an exception.[11] In the context of Small Island Developing States (SIDS) in the Caribbean, it is more common to have a GI that refers to the entire territory of a given island. The only Caribbean Community (Caricom) country's GI registered in the EU is the Demerara Rum PGI from Guyana. It is registered as a PGI in the EU since some of its production is sold in bulk, while its premium rum production is localised from sugar cane production through to ageing and bottling in-region. To date, Caribbean GI laws do not distinguish between the stricter PDO and the less strict PGI standards. Rather, the laws are drawn up to ensure an essential linkage – akin to the PGI standard – between the product and its territory, which informs the product's quality, characteristics, and reputation.

The chapter is structured as follows. Section 3.2 considers the Jamaican law regulating the industry and the institutions that manage its functioning. Section 3.3 then looks at the practical steps of obtaining a GI in Jamaica through consideration of the technical document needed to register a GI – the specification – and the regulatory body, which is a prerequisite for managing the GI. Section 3.4 considers the outstanding challenges of managing a GI, as well as the opportunities for regulating cannabis, specifically in Jamaica's post-colonial context. Finally, Section 3.5 concludes that obtaining a GI offers opportunities for Jamaican cannabis stakeholders in today's post-colonial context.

---

10 "Gouda Holland PGI Noord Hollandse Gouda PDO" (Europa) <https://agriculture.ec.europa.eu/farming/geographical-indications-and-quality-schemes/geographical-indications-food-and-drink/gouda-holland-pgi-noord-hollandse-gouda-pdo_en> accessed 2 May 2024.

11 For a discussion on this, see N Corthesy, *International Intellectual Property Protection of Country Names; Balancing Nation Brands and Geographic Commons in a Competitive Global Marketplace* (Caribbean Law Publishers 2023).

3.2 THE LAW AND THE INSTITUTIONS

3.2.1 The Law

3.2.1.1 The Dangerous Drugs Act 2021

Originally introduced in 1948, the Dangerous Drugs Act sought to regulate the illicit use of narcotic drugs and grouped together cannabis with cocaine and morphine. The 2015 amendment marked an important shift as it sought to regulate Jamaica's legal cannabis industry in relation to possession and smoking, use by the Rastafari, and use for medical, therapeutic, and scientific purposes.

The term cannabis is a catch-all term for all plants with cannabinoids, although the Jamaican legislation refers to the word "ganja". Under the 2015 amendments to the Dangerous Drugs Act, it is explained:

> …"ganja" includes all parts of the plant cannabis sativa from which the resin has not been extracted and includes any resin obtained from that plant, but does not include –
> (i) medicinal preparations made from that plant;
> (ii) hemp;…[12]

The amendment explains that hemp is an integral part of the cannabis sativa plant with a THC concentration of less than 1 per cent.[13] The Cannabis Licensing Authority (CLA), which was also established under this Act, defined a threshold of 10 per cent of another cannabinoid (Cannabidiol) CBD, which is also recognised as valuable for the evolving industry. A medicinal hemp plant is therefore expected to contain 1 per cent or less THC and 10 per cent or more CBD.

Possession is not an offence on the following grounds: (i) for religious purposes whereby cannabis is recognised as a sacrament in the Rastafari faith; (ii) for medical or therapeutic purposes once prescribed by a registered medical practitioner or health practitioner approved by the Minister of Health; and (iii) for scientific research conducted by the relevant accredited organisation or approved by the Scientific Research Council or Minister.[14]

Alongside the Act, the Dangerous Drugs Order 2016 authorises the University of the West Indies (UWI), Mona campus located in Jamaica, to cultivate cannabis for scientific purposes.[15] The Dangerous Drugs Cannabis Licensing

---

[12] Section 2(a) Dangerous Drugs Act.

[13] ibid.

[14] Section 7(C)(1) DDA.

[15] Dangerous Drug Act Regulations (under Section 7D(3)(a)) The Dangerous Drugs (Cultivation of Ganja for Scientific Research Purposes) (University of the

Regulations set out the licensing regime to be governed by the CLA.[16] It specifies, for example, that "cultivation" refers to the three-step process of harvesting, curing, and drying; and a "herb house" refers to the licensed premises in which cannabis is sold or consumed for medical or therapeutic purposes.[17]

The Act covers several other areas, from penalties including fines for possession beyond the two ounces permitted or smoking in public, to importation for terminal and serious illnesses or scientific research, as well as cultivation by the various groups permitted. The next section considers the role of the institutions and stakeholder groups governed by the Act.

3.2.2 The Institutions

3.2.2.1 The Cannabis Licensing Authority (CLA)

The Cannabis Licensing Authority (CLA) was created with the amendment to Jamaica's Dangerous Drugs Act 2015.[18] The CLA is responsible for the regulation regarding the issuing and regulating of licences and permits, and grants authorisations for ganja for medical, therapeutic, or scientific purposes.[19] The CLA sits within Jamaica's Ministry of Industry, Investment and Commerce. The ministers for agriculture, health, industry and commerce, justice, national security, science and technology, finance, and foreign affairs are responsible for appointing one member each to the CLA.[20] The Minister of Justice is also responsible for appointing a representative from the Attorney General's Department, an academic representative, and four members of civil society organisations (CSO) or non-governmental organisations (NGO).[21] The Chairperson of the National Council on Drug Abuse also sits on the CLA.[22] One of these 16 members is selected as chairperson.[23]

Currently, there are five types of licenses: a cultivator's licence (three tiers depending on acreage of cultivation); a retail licence (with or without on-site consumption and for therapeutic services); a processing licence (two tiers based on the size of the processing area); a transportation licence; and a research and

West Indies) Order, 2015.

[16] The Dangerous Drugs Act Regulations (under Section 9A(2)), The Dangerous Drugs (Cannabis Licensing)(Interim) Regulations 2016.

[17] Section 2(2) The Dangerous Drugs Cannabis Licensing Regulations (2016).

[18] The Dangerous Drugs Act, 1948; The Dangerous Drugs (Amendment) Act, 2015; The Dangerous Drugs (Amendment) Act, 2021.

[19] Section 9A(2).

[20] Section 9A(3)1(a–h).

[21] ibid (j).

[22] ibid (i).

[23] Section 9A(3)2.

development licence.[24] As of December 2023, the CLA has issued 133 licences.[25] Mid-2022, it was recorded that 185 export authorisations had been made and shipped to North America, Europe, Africa, and the Middle East.[26]

3.2.2.2 The Ganja Growers and Producers Association Jamaica (GGPAJ)

The Ganja Growers and Producers Association Jamaica (GGPAJ, formerly the Ganja Future Growers and Producers Association) was launched in 2014. There was resounding interest in the potential of the expected 2015 amendment to the DDA to turn Jamaica into a leader in medical cannabis research, exports, and development of new products, specifically by drawing on Jamaica's heritage and legacy with the cannabis plant.[27] Yet, as more recent literature demonstrates, the perceived Jamaican leadership in medical cannabis has not manifested a decade later. A 2022 article explained the advocacy efforts of Richard Crawford, President of GGPAJ, for greater inclusion of traditional smallholder, Rastafari, and Indigenous growers, as well as the perspective that the once innovative set of amendments to the DDA has become, de facto, a restrictive and prohibitive policy. The article outlines that despite de jure amendments, growers perceive that there has not been sufficient progress in at least three areas: compliance regulations; lack of a Cannabis Industry Stakeholders Council; and the failure of the Alternative Development Programme.[28] As a result, the GGPAJ issues several recommendations: a two-year Special Cultivation Amnesty; a more inclusive licencing system; a national register for all applicants; and revised cultivator provisions concerning fees and acreage, as well as the introduction of a new type of retailer, namely "local retail" to boost local sales. The need to reduce fees and include Indigenous farmers was reiterated in 2023 following the news that the Jamaican government

---

24 "License Types" (CLA) <https://www.cla.org.jm/licence-types/> accessed 12 April 2024.

25 "License Statistics" (CLA) <https://www.cla.org.jm/licensing-statistics/> accessed 12 April 2024.

26 L Linton, "Strategies Being Put In Place to Grow Medicinal Cannabis Industry" *JIS* (16 June 2022) <https://jis.gov.jm/strategies-being-put-in-place-to-grow-medicinal-cannabis-industry/> accessed 12 April 2024.

27 "Ganja Growers Association Officially Launched" *Jamaica Observer* (8 April 2014) <https://www.jamaicaobserver.com/2014/04/08/ganja-growers-association-officially-launched/>.

28 A Morris, "Ganja Lobby Turns Heat on Gov't in Defence of Small Farmers" *The Gleaner* (25 February 2022) <https://jamaica-gleaner.com/article/lead-stories/20220225/ganja-lobby-turns-heat-govt-defence-small-farmers#google_vignette> accessed 12 April 2024.

had permitted the importation of cannabis from Canada, and the concern over competition in the local market.[29]

3.2.2.3 The Jamaican Licensed Cannabis Association

While there was momentum for an association that would regroup licenced cannabis growers, this has not come to fruition or proved sustainable. This is in part due to the evolution of the industry based on cannabis owners acting individually to secure their own market share. Returning to the logic of IP law, and particularly trademarks, these are, after all, private rights holders and without an incentive to work together in a new market, competition is likely to win over collaboration. There are many licenced cannabis brands in Jamaica; for example, Jacana, Kaya, Epican, and Itopia are some of the top in the market.

3.2.2.4 The Cannabis Development/Industry Task Force

In 2021, the Task Force was established to enhance the growth and development of the local cannabis industry, inter alia, to include smallholder farmers. It is spearheaded by the Minister of Industry, Investment and Commerce (MIIC). Minister Dunn, Minister of State, added, "The Ministry recognizes that in order for the industry to truly grow, we must urgently create the necessary policy and regulatory framework in conjunction with all our relevant stakeholders to provide clear guidelines for the success of the industry."[30] The result is expected to be a blueprint for the industry, referred to as a comprehensive national policy.[31] Since 2022, there has been no public communication from the Task Force.

---

[29] H Burke, "Ganja growers renew call for gov't to improve regulations for local industry" *radio Jamaica News Online* (20 March 2023) <https://radiojamaicanewsonline.com/local/ganja-growers-renew-call-for-govt-to-improve-regulations-for-local-industry> accessed 12 April 2024.

[30] "Dunn Developing Blueprint for Jamaica's Cannabis Sector" (*MIIC*, 18 June 2021) <https://www.miic.gov.jm/content/dunn-developing-blueprint-jamaica%E2%80%99s-cannabis-sector> accessed 12 April 2024.

[31] "Govt Fine Tuning Ganja Export" (*Our Today*) <https://our.today/govt-fine-tuning-ganja-export-leveraging-plan-as-dispensaries-ramp-up-cannabis-innovation/> accessed 2 May 2024.

3.2.2.5 Westmoreland Hemp and Ganja Farmers Association (WHGFA)

Westmoreland Hemp and Ganja Farmers Association (WHGFA) is advocating for a Jamaican ganja-free zone,[32] inspired by the Amsterdam model.[33] The designated area would include the West End of Negril, Orange Hill, Broughton, and Mango Hall. Interestingly, this designation could also be used for a GI for Westmoreland Hemp, Ganja, and cannabis. At the inaugural farmers' symposium held in Negril in 2022, Delroy Johnson, the chairman of WHGFA, stated that the growers need the law to change, not monetary incentives.[34] In 2023, the calls for the free zone were amplified, with the chairman stating that the group will petition the government on the issue.[35] In that address, he further substantiated that government expenditure was not needed as consumers purchase cannabis. Drawing on the example of the successes of the free zones in some US states, Johnson also highlighted that Jamaica has the capacity to benefit and absorb cannabis tourists who are being turned away from certain destinations, such as Colorado, due to the town attempting to regulate the inflow of visitors once the law had changed to permit cannabis use. This is a strong argument that would also support the need to ensure an inclusive GI and use of IP to ensure economic returns flow to producer communities.

3.2.2.6 Other actors – unlicensed growers

It is not uncommon to attend a cannabis fair and meet unlicensed growers showcasing their products alongside licenced growers.[36] While there is a legal difference between the growers, and most likely their brands and use of IP, the two continue to co-exist in Jamaica. For example, some are advertising tours of their "award-winning" weed farms on TripAdvisor, despite not being licensed. This raises questions as to how unlicensed growers can be effectively brought within the licensing scheme as a first step to attaining the long-term

---

[32] A Ferguson, "Ganja Farmers to Seek Gov't Support for a Cannabis Free Zone" *Jamaica Gleaner* (24 May 2022) <https://jamaica-gleaner.com/article/news/20220524/ganja-farmers-seek-govt-support-cannabis-free-zone> accessed 12 April 2024.

[33] For an analysis of the intersection between cannabis and IP laws within the Dutch scenario, see Chapter 11, by Lotte Anemaet.

[34] "Westmorelans Hemp and Ganja Farmers Moot Free Zone" *Jamaica Gleaner* (22 May 2022) <https://jamaica-gleaner.com/article/news/20220522/westmoreland-hemp-and-ganja-farmers-moot-free-zone-cannabis#google_vignette> accessed 2 May 2022.

[35] "Govt Urged to Make Westmoreland Ganja Free Zone" *Jamaica Gleaner* (25 April 2023) <https://jamaica-gleaner.com/article/news/20230425/govt-urged-make-western-westmoreland-ganja-free-zone> accessed 2 May 2022.

[36] For example, the Cannabis Expo (CanEx) is held annually in Montego Bay.

gain, which is benefitting from the economic gains that GI protection would afford. The collaborative effort needed to attain a GI would foreground that unlicensed producers should move towards licencing to be recognised as legitimate actors in the GI system. The next section discusses how GI protection can be obtained in more detail by also looking at developments in the broader Caribbean region.

3.3 STEP-BY-STEP OF OBTAINING A GI

GIs can take decades to achieve. A rum GI can take around three decades, irrespective of jurisdiction, as was the case for Ron Dominicano GI and French rum GIs in general.[37] Generally speaking, in the process of formulating a GI, in any jurisdiction, two elements are key. First, the GI specification is the technical file that explains the essential or exclusive linkage of the quality, reputation and characteristics of the GI good with its geographical territory. Second, the GI regulatory body comprises the stakeholders in the given area that manage the GI to ensure that its production processes remain in conformity with the GI specification. This section provides a comparative analysis with GIs for rums, specifically Demerara rum PGI and Ron Dominicano GI.

3.3.1 The Specification – Case Study of Demerara Rum PGI

The technical file of a GI outlines the main specifications of the GI, namely the GI name to be registered, the category it belongs to, and a description of the product. For example, "DEMERARA RUM" is the GI to be protected in the category of the spirit drink "rum", referring to "[a] spirit drink with discernible sugar cane organoleptic characteristics, which is produced exclusively by fermentation and distillation of molasses or sugar-cane based substrate".[38] The description also provides details on the chemical requirements of the GI, such as alcohol content, the organoleptic qualities such as its appearance, colour, aroma, and flavours, and specific characteristics that distinguish it from other GIs in the same category. On this latter point, the traditional production

[37] Y Williams, B Khan, E Bonadio, "Geographical Indication Laws in the Caribbean: Towards Post-Colonial Justice for former Plantation Economy Crops? The Case of Rum (May 9, 2024)" (2025) 1 EIPR.

[38] "DEMERARA RUM" (File number: PGI-GY-02423 – 28.6.2018). Publication of an Application Pursuant to Article 17(6) of Regulation (EC) No 110/2008 of the European Parliament and of the Council on the Definition, Description, Presentation, Labelling and the Protection of Geographical Indications of Spirit Drinks and Repealing Council Regulation (EEC) No 1576/89 [2021] OJ C120/7.

processes and mineral waters of the Demerara region are highlighted. The technical file then delineates the geographic area and the method for producing the rum. Thereafter, the link with the geographic area is set out and covers issues including environmental conditions, climatic conditions, water quality, human and process factors, historical origins, and reputation. The address of the applicant is included, before the final details on specific labelling rules, including a reference to the registered trademark "Demerara rum" and its corresponding image (which we will discuss further).

A technical file for Jamaica cannabis, ganja, or hemp would similarly highlight these specifications. As outlined, the three terms "Jamaica cannabis", "Jamaica ganja", or "Jamaica hemp" would be identified as the GI name, while the category could be "medical, therapeutic, scientific" herb product, referring to Cannabis sativa as similarly set out in the DDA 2015. The description would provide a scientific and technical overview, again similar to the DDA 2015, alongside chemical, organoleptic, and distinguishing factors. The distinguishing factors can draw on the traditional cultivation processes where appropriate and the natural endowments of Jamaica's ecology in production. In the case of the proposed GI, the designated area would be the entire territory of Jamaica, that is, 10,992 km^2 land mass, 18 degrees north and 77 degrees west of the equator, including the land formations of mountains, valleys, and limestone plateaus, as well as coastal plains. The link with the geographic region would underscore the tropical Windward and semi-arid leeward climates and differentials in rainfall that co-exist in Jamaica; the volcanic origins have endowed the island with rich limestone deposits which filter water; as well as the human factors, historical origins, and reputation that link cannabis to Jamaica. The CLA could be the applicant on behalf of the cannabis stakeholders, who should collectively agree upon a trademark to be registered, containing the image of the GI to be protected for all users.

Another option is a series of more localised GIs as opposed to a country name GI. A precedent for this is set with the Montserrat Hills cocoa GI in Trinidad and Tobago, wherein the Montserrat Hills cocoa cooperative successfully applied for the GI rather than opting for a country-wide GI for Trinidad and Tobago cocoa more generally. Indeed, this is also the case with Demerara rum GI, as opposed to a broader Guyana rum. Machel Emanuel, lead scientist at UWI's cannabis lab, has outlined the realities of "Growing Ganja in Jamaica" and its ecologically diverse biogeography. Emanuel also discusses the know-how and traditional techniques, albeit underscoring the heterogeneity in production.

> The artisanal production of ganja in Jamaica represents the ingenuity of the cultivators who reside in these various microclimates throughout the island catering to a plethora of different demographics of consumers located in tourist areas on the

> north coast, rural townships, urban ghettos, and middle- to upper-class communities. The cultivation methods, post-harvest practices, types of genetics, pricing structure, farm sizes, and distribution method present varying disparities in quality dynamics intended for the various local markets.[39]

Based on his extensive research, Emanuel identifies several growing areas that can, equally, all consider their own GI: Sunny Hill, St. Thomas; Nine Mile, St. Ann; Slipe, St. Elizabeth; Orange Hill, Westmoreland Happy Gate, St. Andrew. This sheds light on the fact that the consideration of a Jamaica ganja, cannabis, or hemp GI can co-exist with either trademarked products from the above-mentioned regions, or those producer communities can seek GIs amongst themselves. Given the heterogeneity of production techniques, a push for Jamaica ganja, cannabis, or hemp GIs would de facto need to be inclusive of all producer communities. It would, therefore, necessitate drawing on the essential linkage, rather than an exclusive linkage, of the quality, reputation, and characteristics of Jamaica ganja, cannabis, or hemp across Jamaica in general. The next section discusses how these stakeholders would be grouped together in the regulatory body, drawing on the case study of the Ron Dominicano GI process.

3.3.2 The Regulatory Council/Body – Case Study Ron Dominicano GI

This section draws on the Dominican Rum Regulatory Body and stakeholders in the Trade Mark Opposition (TMO) proceedings to illustrate how a regulatory body can be established. It will demonstrate that the regulatory body should be inclusive; yet, it does not need to include all growers according to the precedent set in this case. This is in contrast to the literature on GIs that critiques the inclusivity of regulatory bodies. The literature on the Tequila GI and the concerns over the government of Mexico's lack of transparency and inclusivity in its stakeholder engagement to define Tequila norms is a case in point.[40]

The application for the Ron Dominicano GI was filed in 2014 by the Dominican Association of Rum Producers (Asociacion Dominicana de Productores de Ron, Inc., ADOPRON). They produced 90 per cent of the local rum, contributed to 95 per cent of rum exports, and generated 97 per cent of internal sales taxes. The application was challenged, inter alia, arguing that

---

39 M Emanuel, "Growing Ganja in Jamaica" *High Times* (16 March 2024) <https://hightimes.com/culture/growing-ganja-in-jamaica/> accessed 10 May 2024.

40 S Bowen, "Development from Within? The Potential for Geographical Indications in the Global South" (2010) 13 JWIP 2, 232.

the regulatory council would be biased in favour of the sole applicant.[41] The defendants included six rum producers with prior rights as trademark owners of Dominican rum in the Dominican Republic and the EU. The TMO Board considered several issues, which are instructive and discussed elsewhere.[42] For the purpose of this chapter, the overview presented herein concerns the TMO Board's pronouncement on the composition of the Regulatory Council. The Board stated that one entity can apply for a GI, as ADOPRON had, and drew on the precedent of other Regulatory Councils such as Café Barahona, Café Valdesia in the Dominican Republic, as well as Ron de Guatemala and Ron de Venezuela.[43] However, it clarified that when a GI is applied for an entire national territory, the Regulatory Council should be inclusive of more producers.[44] Therefore, in this case, the Regulatory Council was adjusted to be more inclusive. It includes representation from various actors within the supply chain: distilleries, sugar producers, sugar processors, the Association of Industries of the Dominican Republic (AIRD), the Ministry of Industry, Commerce and MSMEs of the DR (MICM), the Export and Investment Center of the Dominican Republic (Pro-Dominican) and lastly, the Dominican Institute of Quality (INDOCAL – without voting rights). The Regulatory Council keeps records of all aspects of production, from sugar produced and distilled, to the registration of packaging requirements and distinctive signs.

A Regulatory Council for Jamaica Cannabis, hemp, and ganja should also aim to be inclusive since it uses the country name Jamaica in the GI. It would include cultivator groups, accredited bodies, UWI, herb houses, and governmental institutions (similarly to the CLA structure discussed above).[45] In the

---

[41] ADOPRON consists of Casa Brugal, Ron Barceló SRL, Vinícola del Norte, Isidro Bordas, and Yazoo Investment. B Messina, IP Lugo, "Geographical Indications Dominican Republic View" *IPCA* (November 2017) <https://ipca.website/wp-content/uploads/2019/09/GIDominicanRepublicBufeteMessinaLugoIP.pdf> accessed 7 November 2022. See also, C Acosta, "Marca Pais de Ron Dominicano en Riesgo" *Listindario* (Santo Domingo, 14 June 2017) <https://listindiario.com/economia/2017/06/14/470069/marca-pais-del-ron-dominicano-en-riesgo> accessed 7 November 2022.

[42] For example, it determined that blended rum cannot benefit from a GI; however, blending can be permitted with effective labelling that nonetheless states that the product is "made in [the] Dominican Republic". See E Bonadio, Y Williams, B Khan, "Towards a Pan-Caribbean Geographical Indication? A Case Study on Rum GIs in the English, French and Spanish-speaking Caribbean" in A Zappalaglio and E Bonadio (eds), *The Future of Geographical Indications – European and Global Perspectives* (Edward Elgar Publishing 2024).

[43] Notably, all Spanish-speaking jurisdictions.

[44] Resolution No. 000279, 12 July 2016, TMO.

[45] See also Chapter 8, authored by Natalie Corthésy.

first instance, it would need to convene to draw up the GI specification to be deposited at the JIPO. Thereafter, once the GI is granted, it would record cultivation processes – three steps – to sales and exports, as well as branding requirements related to packaging and signs. Where different producer communities, such as those highlighted by Emanuel, apply for a GI, the Regulatory Council would only need to include those stakeholders in that given geographic area. Cannabis producers, therefore, have options. In the case wherein the option is a country-wide protection, the implications of such an indication should be well understood. Caribbean IP scholar Natalie Corthésy proposes that country names can provide information to consumers about the origin of a product, a valuable co-branding strategy, and a national competitive identity of a State.[46] Corthésy also puts forth that protecting country names is both an economic and moral endeavour, as a sine qua non for a successful branding scheme.[47] One of the claims of this chapter is that GI laws, as a conceptually different type of IP to trademarks, afford an entire producer community GI protection, and as such, the opportunity to strategise to use the GI as a powerful community tool for the socio-economic and sustainable development of the cannabis industry.

3.4 ROADBLOCKS ON THE HIGHWAY TO GI PROTECTION?

This section provides an overview of some challenges that the stakeholders considering a GI for Jamaica ganja, cannabis, or hemp would need to consider, alongside the technicalities of registering and regulating the GI.

3.4.1 An Inclusive GI Suitable for a Post-Colonial Former Plantation Economy

This chapter has underscored the specific nature of the Caribbean SIDS as former plantation economy sites that were subject to the brutality of colonialism and the slave trade. Moving beyond the colonial cash-crop system in today's post-colonial context requires a strategic approach, especially for cannabis, its traditional growers, and uses that have long suffered stigmatisation, criminalisation, and incarceration. This chapter postulates GIs can offer a strategy of protection for producer communities; however, producer communities must

[46] N Corthésy, "Trade Marks Country Names and Misappropriation of National Identity" (2017) 4 JIPLP 2.

[47] N Corthésy, "Brand New IP: 'Country Name Designation' – from France with Love" in D Gervais (ed.) *The Future of Intellectual Property* (Edward Elgar 2021) 336.

be ready to rise above certain challenges that impact GI communities more generally.

While there are many examples of GI processes for European or even Western products, and others in the so-called Global South – Tequila from Mexico, Darjeeling from India, and Ron Dominicano GI – there is little evidence of how GIs are implemented in the English-speaking Caribbean despite the laws existing de jure since the early 2000s. For example, the only publicly available GI in the region exists for Demerara rum GI because it was registered in the EU system in 2021, wherein all GI specifications are made publicly available via the EU Ambrosia database. Similarly, in Jamaica, despite the GI Act of 2006, the first GI specifications registered for Jamaica jerk (2015) and Jamaica rum (2016) are not publicly available online. This section proposes that capacity-building initiatives need to support national Intellectual Property Offices (IPOs) in the region to boost their capacity to enhance GI protections.

The lack of GI registrations in the Caribbean should be contextualised in the broader framework of the lack of IP rights in the broader developing country or Global South context, and the risks that are inherent.[48] For example, in the literature, it is documented that 85 per cent of IP applications in developing countries were filed by non-residents.[49] Additionally, "IP-grabs" impact producer communities such as those involved in neem, soapberry, corn, and cotton.[50] Vandana Shiva, in her work on biological piracy, has estimated that the US would need to repay over US$300 million in agriculture royalties and US$5 billion for pharmaceuticals as a result of "IP-grabs".[51] From

[48] For an overview of the risks with a reparatory justice framing, see Y Williams, B Khan, E Bonadio, "Geographical Indication Laws in the Caribbean: Towards Post-Colonial Justice for former Plantation Economy Crops? The Case of Rum (May 9, 2024)" (2025) 1 EIPR.

[49] African, Latin American and Caribbean, and Oceanian offices, WIPO, 2014 report, 24; A Peukert, "The Colonial Legacy of the International Copyright System" in M Mamadou Diawara and U Röschenthaler (eds), *Staging the Immaterial. Rights, Style and Performance in Sub-Saharan Africa* (Sean Kingston Forthcoming). On the risk of IP entrepreneurship from the West and the conversion of public goods into private IP: K Aoki, "Neocolonialism, Anticommons Property and Biopiracy in the (Not-so-brave) New World Order of International Intellectual Property Protection" (1998) 6 Indiana Journal of Global Legal Studies 6, 46.

[50] K Aoki, "Neocolonialism, Anticommons Property and Biopiracy in the (Not-so-brave) New World Order of International Intellectual Property Protection' (1998) 6 Indiana Journal of Global Legal Studies 6, 50–54.

[51] There is increasing literature on protecting the commons. While this is positive, the commons debate still face the same risks of "protecting" a tyranny of the majority. V Shiva, *Biopiracy: The Plunder of Nature and Knowledge* (North Atlantic Books 2016), 56 in Aoki (n 50) 50.

this optic, the legalisation of the medical cannabis industry comes with risks that could disenfranchise local populations, the traditional custodians of the Cannabis sativa.[52] Thus, the development of GIs in the Caribbean also necessitates considering how all stakeholders can be part of a eudemonic – goodwill – turn to ensure the GI functions as a community tool that returns the economic profits to all producers in an equitable manner.[53] A eudemonic turn can be gleaned from the mission statement of the CLA: "To have a medical, therapeutic and scientific cannabis industry that creates equal opportunities, enables people's health and wellness with safe and diverse products, fosters investor confidence and strengthens the Jamaican economy through an effective regulatory framework."[54] A case in point would be the CLA's specific provisions for smallholder farmers with less than one acre of land to pay the lowest fees, defer fees, or apply for a waiver,[55] wherein provisions are aimed at reducing compliance costs for cooperatives to reduce this barrier to entry. Two such initiatives include the Transitional Permit for Small Farmers and the Alternative Development Plan. The Alternative Development Plan aims specifically to transition traditional cannabis growers from an illicit growing regime to a legal medicinal system.[56] This approach is part of the UN Action Plan on International Cooperation on the Eradication of Illicit Drug Crops and on Alternative Development, which recognises that specifically designed measures can contribute to national economic growth and sustainable development.[57]

A eudemonic turn would also need to be demonstrated by international partners via capacity building, development aid, and trade assistance. For example, through strategic support to IPOs to in turn, build the capacity of producer groups, regulatory bodies, and, where necessary, the protection of GIs in third country jurisdictions. For instance, while the EU's CARIPI programme

---

52 See N Corthésy, E Bonadio, Y Williams (eds), *Intellectual Property and Cannabis* (Edward Elgar Publishing 2025).

53 More generally, see S Ali, "The Eudamonic Attorney – The Virtuous Pursuitof the Greater Good" in Shazeeda Ali and Stephen Vasciannie (eds), *Perspectives on Caribbean Law: A Compendium of Legal Essays* (UWI Press 2024).

54 CLA < https://www.cla.org.jm/> accessed 12 April 2024.

55 "FAQs" (*CLA*) <https://www.cla.org.jm/faqs/> accessed 12 April.

56 "Ganja Growers Encouraged to Participate in Alternative Development Programme" (*MoA*, 27 February 2020) <https://www.moa.gov.jm/content/ganja-growers-encouraged-participate-alternative-development-programme> accessed 12 April 2024.

57 UN, A/RES/S-20/4 8 September 1998 <https://www.unodc.org/documents/alternative-development/UNGASSActionPlanAD.pdf> accessed 12 April 2024.

aims, inter alia, to create stronger IP offices and more effective enforcement mechanisms,[58] it is uncertain given the existing laws in the EU whether support would extend to feature a cannabis or ganja GI. However, a hemp GI may be better received. Support to national IPOs is vital since national registrations are a prerequisite for international protection thereafter in export markets. However, although national registration is a prerequisite for international protection, not all jurisdictions have sui generis GI laws.

In some countries, GIs are regulated via trademark systems. That is, even if Jamaica's cannabis, ganja, and hemp GIs are protected in Jamaica, the regulatory body, in coordination with the government, should seek to ensure that there are no users of these terms in third-party jurisdictions. For example, a general search of the term cannabis brings up 209 trademarks for cannabis across different classes in the UK, 228 trademarks at the EU's IP Office (EUIPO) by 33 owners, 3,615 for cannabis via the USPTO, 3,644 for cannabis in the Canadian registry, and 2,138 registered globally for cannabis in TMView.[59] There are registrations for Ganja,[60] of which there are 77 trademarks across different

[58] "CARIFORUM Intellectual Property Rights and Innovation" (*International Cooperation*) <https://internationalipcooperation.eu/en/caripi> accessed 03 August 2022.

[59] See UK Trade Mark Registry <https://trademarks.ipo.gov.uk/ipo-tmtext/page/Results>, accessed 2 April 2025; the EU IPO <https://euipo.europa.eu/eSearch/#basic/1+1+1+1/100+100+100+100/cannabis>, accessed 2 April 2025. The USPTO <https://tmsearch.uspto.gov/search/search-results>, accessed 2 April 2025; the Canada Trade Marks Database <https://ised-isde.canada.ca/cipo/trademark-search/srch?payload=%257B%2522domIntlFilter%2522%253A%25223%2522%252C%2522searchfield1%2522%253A%2522all%2522%252C%2522textfield1%2522%253A%2522cannabis%2522%252C%2522category%2522%253A%255B%25221%2522%255D%252C%2522statuses%2522%253A%255B%25223%2522%255D%252C%2522display%2522%253A%2522list%2522%252C%2522maxReturn%2522%253A%2522500%2522%252C%2522nicetextfield1%2522%253Anull%252C%2522cipotextfield1%2522%253Anull%257D>, accessed 2 April 2025; and the Trade Mark View International Database <https://www.tmdn.org/tmview/#/tmview/results?page=1&pageSize=30&criteria=C&basicSearch=cannabis&sortColumn=tradeMarkStatus&desc=true&fTMStatus=RegisteredAll> accessed 2 April 2025.

[60] See UK Trade Mark Registry <https://trademarks.ipo.gov.uk/ipo-tmtext/page/Results> accessed 2 April 2025; EUIPO <https://euipo.europa.eu/eSearch/#basic/1+1+1+1/100+100+100+100/ganja> accessed 2 April 2025; USPTO <https://tmsearch.uspto.gov/search/search-result> accessed 2 April 2025; Canadian registry <https://ised-isde.canada.ca/cipo/trademark-search/srch?payload=%257B%2522domIntlFilter%2522%253A%25223%2522%252C%2522searchfield1%2522%253A%2522all%2522%252C%2522textfield1%2522%253A%2522ganja

classes in the UK, 18 trademarks at the EU's IP Office (EUIPO), 227 via the USPTO, 9 in the Canadian registry, and 415 registered globally in TMView. For hemp, there are 392 trademarks across different classes in the UK, 774 trademarks at the EU's IP Office (EUIPO), 3,915 via the USPTO, 2,008 in the Canadian registry, and 5,340 registered globally in TMView.[61] These terms would need to be assessed to ascertain if there may be any that could impact Jamaica's ganja, cannabis, or hemp registrations in foreign jurisdictions. The current scenario of the lack of various IP rights for cannabis in Jamaica ought to be juxtaposed against the appetite for IP abroad and induce the industry with a sense of urgency to seek such protections. In other words, as cannabis stakeholders want to secure their market at home and, for some eventually abroad, a national registration would be a prerequisite.

When defining the technical file to be deposited at IPOs, the applicants should be pragmatic. Currently, there is evidence of a deadlock concerning the Barbados rum GI and the EU registration of Jamaica rum GI because the producer groups have hit a roadblock concerning the exclusive or essential linkages of their products to the geographical areas of GI production.[62] Ironically,

%2522%252C%2522category%2522%253A%255B%25221%2522%255D%252C%2522statuses%2522%253A%255B%25223%2522%255D%252C%2522display%2522%253A%2522list%2522%252C%2522maxReturn%2522%253A%2522500%2522%252C%2522nicetextfield1%2522%253Anull%252C%2522cipotextfield1%2522%253Anull%257D> accessed 2 April 2025; TM View <https://www.tmdn.org/tmview/#/tmview/results?page=1&pageSize=30&criteria=C&basicSearch=ganja&fTMStatus=RegisteredAll> accessed 2 April 2025.

[61] See UK IPO <https://trademarks.ipo.gov.uk/ipo-tmtext/page/Results> accessed 2 April 2025; EUIPO <https://euipo.europa.eu/eSearch/#basic/1+1+1+1/100+100+100+100/hemp> accessed 2 April 2025; USPTO <https://tmsearch.uspto.gov/search/search-results> accessed 2 April 2025; Canada Trademark registry <https://ised-isde.canada.ca/cipo/trademark-search/srch?payload=%257B%2522domIntlFilter%2522%253A%25223%2522%252C%2522searchfield1%2522%253A%2522all%2522%252C%2522textfield1%2522%253A%2522hemp%2522%252C%2522category%2522%253A%255B%25221%2522%255D%252C%2522statuses%2522%253A%255B%25223%2522%255D%252C%2522display%2522%253A%2522list%2522%252C%2522maxReturn%2522%253A%2522500%2522%252C%2522nicetextfield1%2522%253Anull%252C%2522cipotextfield1%2522%253Anull%257D> accessed 2 April 2025; TM View <https://www.tmdn.org/tmview/#/tmview/results?page=1&pageSize=30&criteria=C&basicSearch=hemp&fTMStatus=RegisteredAll> accessed 2 April 2025.

[62] See, E Bonadio, Y Williams, B Khan, "Towards a Pan-Caribbean Geographical Indication? A Case Study of Rum", in A Zappalaggio and E Bonadio (eds) *The Future of Geographical Indications: European and Global Perspectives* (Edward Elgar Publishing 2025).

this need not be a stumbling block since Caribbean GI laws are written into national laws underscoring an essential, and not exclusive, link between a GI product and its territory. In essence, Caribbean producers are infighting over an EU standard that does not even exist de jure in the region. In the EU, the precedent has been established that only in exceptional cases should the PDO be a country name.[63] Further, the PDO requires the quality and characteristics to be linked exclusively to the geographical area of origin, and all the production should equally take place therein. In contrast, the PGI is less strict since, as mentioned, the quality, characteristics, and reputation only need to be essentially linked to the geographic territory, and not all steps of production need take place therein.[64] In sum, a PGI, in contrast to a PDO, allows for some of the production process to happen outside the given territory. This sheds light on the reality that given the existing heterogeneous biogeography in Jamaica, a Jamaica cannabis, ganja, or hemp GI would only underscore an essential linkage with the geographic area of the GI. Whereas, if there was a more localised GI, such as Westmoreland or Portland cannabis, ganja, hemp GI,[65] the linkage can be drawn up to show the exclusive linkage between the quality, characteristics, and reputation with the given geographic area.

3.5 CONCLUSION

In conclusion, this chapter set out how cannabis industry stakeholders could benefit from GI protection for Jamaican cannabis, ganja, and hemp. It also considered localised GIs for producer communities, including Sunny Hill, St. Thomas; Nine Mile, St. Ann; Slipe, St. Elizabeth; Orange Hill, Westmoreland Happy Gate, St. Andrew. It provided an overview of the practical steps of obtaining a GI through consideration of the technical file needed to register a GI based on Jamaica's biogeography. In considering the regulatory body to be established that would be responsible for managing the GI, inclusivity was underscored as a means to harness the opportunities for regulating cannabis for all producers, specifically in Jamaica's post-colonial context. Despite

63 Art 5.1(a) Regulation (EU) No 1151/2012 of the European Parliament and of the Council of 21 November 2012 on Quality Schemes for Agricultural Products and Foodstuffs [2012] OJ L343.

64 ibid Article 5.2(a).

65 See Chapter 15, authored by Toby Moorsom.

outstanding challenges of managing a GI and associated risks, the chapter concluded by emphasising that obtaining a GI offers opportunities for Jamaican cannabis stakeholders in today's post-colonial context. As such, the private sector and the government can work together to use GIs, as a community IP tool, to return economic profits to producer communities long denied such an opportunity.

PART II

Moral rights, image rights, packaging, and plant varieties

4. Copyright, the moral right of integrity, and marijuana

Justin Koo

4.1 INTRODUCTION

Copyright law's interaction with marijuana is limited to depictions of marijuana in artistic works and references to marijuana in literary, musical, and dramatic works.[1] However, there is an open question whether copyright works can be used in relation to marijuana without the permission of the author given the absence of any case law on the issue. Due to the continued controversial nature of marijuana consumption (notwithstanding increasing legal tolerance), the association of a work with marijuana may lead to negative consequences for the author such as being dropped by sponsors, "cancelled" by fans, and being deemed morally reprehensible as a marijuana sympathiser. Therefore, this chapter assesses whether the use or association of a copyright work with marijuana will be deemed legally "derogatory" and "prejudicial to the honour or reputation of the author" giving rise to potential infringement of the moral right of integrity.[2]

[1] For discussion on intellectual property rights and cannabis, see: S Keller, "How Small Cannabis Businesses Can Survive the Hurdles of IP Protection" (2020) 8 Tex A&M L Rev 199; E Pyclik, "Obstacles to Obtaining and Enforcing Intellectual Property Rights in the Marijuana Industry" (2018) 9 Am U Intell Prop Brief 26; C Dyal, "Cannabis IP: How Federal Inconsistencies Have Stifled a Budding Industry" (2021) 16 J Bus & Tech L 163; J Mixon, "Commercializing Cannabis: Confronting the Challenges and Uncertainty of Trademark and Trade Secret Protection for Cannabis-Related Businesses" (2020) 16 Wash JL Tech & Arts 1; J De Beer, A Gaffen, "Intellectual Property Rights in the Recreational Cannabis Market: Craft or Commodity" (2017) 50 UBC L Rev 621; and J Wyse, G Luria, "Trends in Intellectual Property Rights Protection for Medical Cannabis and Related Products" (2021) 3(1) Journal of Cannabis Research 1.

[2] The moral rights of performers are not discussed in this chapter.

4.2 THE MORAL RIGHT OF INTEGRITY

Moral rights vary by jurisdiction[3] and there are significant differences in the scope and operation of moral rights between common law copyright countries and civil law droit d'auteur countries.[4] This divergence of approaches towards moral rights has been an international issue[5] as signified by the contention surrounding Article 6*bis* of the Berne Convention, which reflects a major compromise arrived at between the droit d'auteur countries and the copyright countries.[6] Notwithstanding this conflict, the moral right of integrity under the Code de la Propriété Intellectuelle (French Intellectual Property (IP) Code) can be described as the standard par excellence because it offers a subjective author-centric right[7] that protects both the form and spirit of the work,[8] and moreover is "perpetual, inalienable and imprescriptible".[9] Therefore, authors

---

[3] For an in-depth discussion on moral rights see: E Adeney, *The Moral Rights of Authors and Performers: An International and Comparative Analysis* (OUP 2006).

[4] H Hansmann, M Santilli, "Authors' and Artists' Moral Rights: A Comparative Legal and Economic Analysis" (1997) 26 J Legal Stud 95, 96; R Monte, "The Concept of 'Copyright' Versus the 'Droit D'auteur'" (1959) 32 S Cal L Rev 177, 177–178; and S Newman, "The Development of Copyright and Moral Rights in the European Legal Systems" (2011) 33(11) EIPR 677, 677.

[5] Dietz described moral rights as the "single most contentious issue surrounding Berne adherence": A Dietz, "The Artist's Right of Integrity under Copyright Law – A Comparative Approach" (1994) 25(2) IIC 177, 179.

[6] The compromise included the non-requirement of express moral rights provisions, the ability to use existing causes of action under the common law and equity, and the inclusion of the requirement of "prejudicial to the honour or reputation of the author" given that authorial hypersensitivity should not be permitted. See G Dworkin, "The Moral Right of the Author: Moral Rights and the Common Law Countries" (1995) 19 Colum VLA JL & Arts 229, 232; R Durie, "Moral Rights and the English Business Community" (1991) 2(2) Ent LR 40, 40; E Adeney, "The Moral Right of Integrity: The Past and Future of "Honour" (2005) 2 IPQ 126; and S Ricketson, J Ginsburg, *International Copyright and Neighbouring Rights: The Berne Convention and Beyond, Volume 1* (2nd edn, OUP 2006) 10.29.

[7] See: Adeney (n 3) para 8.65 and I Stamatoudi, "Moral Rights of Authors in England: The Missing Emphasis on the Role of Creators" (1997) 4 IPQ 478, 481.

[8] Adeney (n 3) paras 8.01 and 8.71. Also see: *Chaliapine c Union des Républiques Socialistes Soviétiques et Sté Brenner* (1932) DP 1934, 2, 139; *Sté Gaumont and Luc Besson c Sté Publicis Conseil and Sté Française du Radiotéléphone* (2004) no 04/09673 and *Pontoreau ADAGP c Association Front National* (2002) 192 RIDA 448.

[9] For more on moral rights in France, see: Adeney (n 3) ch 8.

in France and other droit d'auteur countries can object to a wide range of acts that affect both the intrinsic (the work itself/its form or corpus) and extrinsic aspects of the work (context in which the work is placed).[10]

This contrasts with common law copyright countries that offer a more limited moral right of integrity. The language used in the UK statute, which has inspired the approach adopted by many copyright countries, requires that a work be "subjected to derogatory treatment",[11] which has been defined as an objective[12] distortion or mutilation of the work that is "prejudicial to the honour or reputation"[13] of the author.[14] Thus, a literal interpretation suggests that only the intrinsic elements of the work will be protected because infringement requires alteration to the actual body of the work.[15] Unlike the standard par excellence developed in France, the UK approach has been described as a poor

[10] For an account of right of integrity infringements, see: Adeney (n 3) paras 8.73–8.82. For a range of acts that could potentially affect the extrinsic elements of the work, see: J McCutcheon, "Contextual Infringement of the Moral Right of Integrity: A Taxonomy across Jurisdictions" (2023) 3 IPQ 136, 144–164.

[11] Section 80(1), Copyright, Designs and Patents Act 1988. For more on moral rights in the UK see: Adeney (n 3) chs 13–14.

[12] *Tidy v Trustees of the Natural History Museum* (1998) IPR 501 and *Confetti Records v Warner Music UK Ltd* [2003] EWHC 1274 (Ch), paras 153–157. Also see: L Bently, B Sherman, D Gangjee, P Johnson, *Intellectual Property Law* (6th edn, OUP 2022) 318–319; Stamatoudi (n 7) 481; G Davies, N Caddick, G Harbottle, *Copinger and Skone James on Copyright*, Volume One (17th edn, Sweet & Maxwell 2016) 11–50; Ricketson, Ginsburg (n 6) 10.23; and J Griffiths, "Moral Rights from a Copyright Perspective" in F Brison, S Dusollier, MC Janssens, and H Vanhees (eds), *Moral Rights in the 21st Century* (Bruylant Larcier 2015).

[13] For discussion on the terms "honour" and "reputation", see Adeney (n 6).

[14] See: Bently et al. (n 12) 316–317; Davies et al. (n 12) 11–48; *Pasterfield v Denham and another* [1999] FSR 168, 182; *Confetti Records* (n 12) para 150, and *Harrison v Harrison* [2010] FSR (25) 604, 620–624; and Ricketson, Ginsburg (n 6) 10.21. However, contrast with *Tidy v Trustees* (n 12) 504, *Morrison Leahy Music and another v Lightbond Limited and others* [1993] EMLR 144, 150, and *Emma Delves-Broughton v House of Harlot Limited* [2012] EWPCC 29, para 24, where the courts did not require the proving of both "distortion or mutilation" and "prejudicial to the honour or reputation of the author".

[15] Bently et al. (n 12) 315, Stamatoudi (n 7) 490, Dworkin (n 6) 249–250, and W Cornish, "Moral Rights under the 1988 Act" (1989) EIPR 449, 450. Also see: *Morrison Leahy Music* (n 14) 150–151.

example to follow.[16] Despite this, Jamaica and the US[17] have adopted provisions that reflect the UK approach to the moral right of integrity. However, one copyright country that requires special attention is Canada because it is an outlier with regard to the moral right of integrity.[18] Its approach to the right of integrity reflects elements of both the copyright and droit d'auteur approaches[19] because it protects extrinsic treatments of the work and relies on a hybrid two-part subjective and objective test to establish infringement.[20]

Given the divergence in approaches to the moral right of integrity, the value attributed to moral rights in general also varies by jurisdiction.[21] In theory, the moral right of integrity is a strong tool for authors to maintain control over the use of their works, especially where both intrinsic and extrinsic treatments of the work are protected.[22] In such scenarios, authors can use the right of integrity as a veto power to restrict the use of their works where they disagree with the intrinsic or extrinsic use of their work (as permitted by law). As such, it has been argued that the moral right of integrity can take precedence over commercial and public interests, restricting the potential uses of

---

16 *Harrison* (n 14) 619 (per Fysh QC) 304; J Ginsburg, "Moral Rights in a Common Law System" (1990) 1(4) Ent LR 121, 128–129; McCutcheon (n 10) 139, and E Bonadio, "Copyright Protection of Street Art and Graffiti under UK Law" (2017) 2 IPQ 187, 201.

17 Section 106A(a)(3) of the US Copyright Act 1976 provides a similar right of integrity to that of copyright countries, albeit only in regard to works of visual art and accompanied by significant limitations subject to section 106A(c).

18 Section 28.2 Copyright Act 1985. For more discussion on moral rights in Canada, see: Adeney (n 3) chs 11–12.

19 Adeney (n 3) 291. Also note, Canada was the first common law copyright country to adopt moral rights: G Davies, K Garnett, *Moral Rights* (Sweet and Maxwell 2010) 677. Note, the Canadian approach to moral rights is different from that of other common law copyright countries because its development was not influenced by the Berne Convention: Adeney (n 3) 292–295.

20 See: *Snow v Eaton Centre Ltd* (1982) 70 CPR (2d) 105, para 5; *Lawrence Ritchie v Sawmill Creek Golf & Country Club Limited et al.* (2003) 27 CPR (4th) 220, para 50; *Judy Maltz, Barbara Bird and Richie Sherman v Jennifer Witterick and Penguin Canada Books Inc* (2016) FC 254, para 49; and *Wiseau Studio LLC et al v Richard Harper et al* (2020) ONSC 2504, para 203.

21 For discussion on the value of the moral right of integrity, see: B Ong, "Why Moral Rights Matter: Recognizing the Intrinsic Value of Integrity Rights" (2003) 26 Colum JL & Arts 297, 301–312, and L De Souza, C Waelde, "Moral Rights and the Internet: Squaring the Circle" (2002) 2 IPQ 265, 266–267.

22 Dworkin argued that even if moral rights are ultimately waived, they serve as an important reminder in the bargaining process between authors and exploiters – Dworkin (n 6) 258.

works,[23] which creates an impracticality and hindrance for the creative content industries.[24] As a result, it has become an industry norm to waive moral rights in commercial contracts where permitted to mitigate the power of authors.[25] Thus, the value of moral rights in copyright countries has been diminished significantly.[26]

4.3 THE MORALITY OF MARIJUANA

Marijuana has existed and been consumed for thousands of years,[27] yet it remains a divisive and controversial product. The plant remains illegal in most countries. Only a small number of countries have legalised the growth and consumption of marijuana for personal use and even fewer allow its commercial sale. What has become increasingly popular is the decriminalisation of marijuana, the introduction of fines in lieu of prosecution for marijuana offences, and the legalisation of marijuana for medicinal use.[28] Notwithstanding these incremental shifts towards permitting the legal use of this product, albeit with varying constraints, the concept of marijuana remains taboo and immoral to many people due to its continued illegality around the world. Consequently, there is an interesting copyright question regarding whether the use or association of an author's work with marijuana will constitute an infringement of the moral right of integrity, especially because of the taboo and/or illegal status of marijuana.

To aid with this analysis, the table below lists the legal approaches to marijuana in the countries discussed in this chapter.

23 Bently et al. (n 12) 305; De Souza, Waelde (n 21) 269–270; B Ong (n 21) 304; Newman (n 4) 684; Dworkin (n 6) 263.

24 See DP Tackaberry, "Look What They Done to My Son, Ma: The Songwriter's Moral Right of Integrity in Canada and the United States" (1989) 11(10) EIPR 356, 371. Moreover, the major copyright content industries opposed the introduction of moral rights in the USA: K Temple, *Authors, Attribution, and Integrity: Examining Moral Rights in the United States* (United States Copyright Office 2019) 19–20.

25 Dworkin (n 6) 257.

26 Bently et al. (n 12) 321; Stamatoudi (n 7) 56.

27 D Newton, *Marijuana: A Reference Handbook* (2nd edn, ABC-CLIO 2017) chapter 1.

28 T Magrabi, "A Guide to Medical Marijuana Legalization Around the World" (*Leafwell*) <https://leafwell.com/blog/countries-where-weed-is-legal> accessed 14 February 2024.

Table 4.1 Legal approaches to marijuana in Canada, France, Jamaica, and the UK

Country	Legality
Canada (copyright)	The consumption and sale of marijuana is legal.[a]
France (droit d'auteur)	Marijuana is illegal with limited concessions for medicinal purposes.[b]
Jamaica (copyright)	Marijuana is decriminalised, allowing for the personal possession of small quantities. Medicinal marijuana is legal.[c]
UK (copyright)	Marijuana is illegal. Medicinal marijuana is legal when prescribed by a specialist consultant.[d]
US (copyright)	Marijuana is illegal at the federal level, but it is legal in 24 states, 2 territories, and the District of Columbia. Marijuana is decriminalised in 7 states. Medicinal marijuana is legal in 38 states, 3 territories, and the District of Columbia.[e]

Note: [a]See Cannabis Act 2018 (Canada) and accompanying regulations. [b]See Article R 5132-86 Public Health Code (France). [c]See Dangerous Drugs Amendment Act 2015 (Jamaica). [d]See Misuse of Drugs Act 1971 (UK) and Misuse of Drugs (Amendments) (Cannabis and License Fees) (England, Wales and Scotland) Regulations 2018. [e]See National Conference of State Legislatures, "State Medical Cannabis Laws" (22 June 2023) <https://www.ncsl.org/health/state-medical-cannabis-laws> accessed 17 February 2024.

4.3.1 Case Studies

This section adopts a practical approach by assessing the likelihood of establishing infringement of the moral right of integrity across five case studies concerning marijuana in five jurisdictions: France, the UK, Canada, Jamaica and the US. This will expose the difficulties with using the moral right of integrity in contexts involving controversial subject matter like marijuana, which, despite increasing legal tolerance, remains taboo. In this way, the contemporary understandings of what is "derogatory" and "prejudicial to the honour or reputation of the author" will be assessed, which is valuable because there is no existing case law concerning the use or association of copyright works with marijuana. A central issue to be discussed is whether the taboo nature or continued general illegality of marijuana will impact the determination of whether associating a work with marijuana will be considered prejudicial to the author from an objective perspective.

For the purpose of the case studies, focus is only placed on the moral right of integrity, so that infringement of the economic rights is not discussed; it is assumed that the author has honour and/or reputation; and no alternative causes of action are considered.

4.3.1.1 Marijuana parodies

Considering the case study of lyrics of a song that are parodied to be about the consumption of marijuana, this scenario involves the intrinsic treatment of the work as the lyrics are changed for parodic effect. In general, a parody is almost inevitably a distortion or modification of the author's work,[29] and subsequently, an infringement of the author's honour or reputation from a subjective perspective.[30] However, the parody is unlikely to infringe the moral right of integrity because a valid parody makes it clear to its audience that the parodic work is not the work of the original author. Therefore, there can be no prejudice to the honour or reputation of the author from an objective perspective because a reasonable person will not think less highly of the author given that they know that the author is not directly connected with the parody.[31] There is also another approach to obviate any potential right of integrity infringements concerning parodies, where there is an applicable parody exception. Where a parody is permissible under prescribed exceptions or limitations, no integrity infringement should arise because the use of the copyright work is allowed (at least in terms of the economic rights). A contrary decision in this circumstance will undermine the ability of third parties to make parodies because it is very unlikely that an author will authorise the making of a parody.[32]

Given that this scenario involves a literary work, there will be no infringement of the right of integrity in the US as the protection of moral rights is limited to works of visual art as prescribed by the US Copyright Act 1976.[33]

---

29 S Jacques, *The Parody Exception in Copyright Law* (OUP 2019) 168.

30 G Yonover, "The Precarious Balance: Moral Rights, Parody, and Fair Use" (1996) 14 Cardozo Arts & Entertainment 79, 103–104; J de Werra, "The Moral Right of Integrity" in E Derclaye (ed.), *Research Handbook on the Future of EU Copyright* (Edward Elgar 2009) 283; and J Marshall, "Balancing the Right to Integrity with Caricature, Parody and Pastiche" (2018) 13(12) JIPLP 955, 961–962.

31 Davies et al. (n 12) 11–51.

32 Marshall (n 30) 963–965.

33 Given the limited form of statutory moral rights available, reliance has been placed on other causes of action including infringement of economic rights, unfair competition, privacy, defamation, breach of contract, and even potentially the Lanham Act. This is because there was no form of common law moral rights protection to fall back upon. See: *Vargas v Esquire* (1947) 164 F 2d 522, 525; *Shostakovich et al. v Twentieth Century-Fox Film Corporation* (1948) 80 NYS 2d 575, 579; *Crimi v Rutgers Presbyterian Church* (1949) 89 NYS 2d 813; *Terry Gilliam et al. v American Broadcasting Companies Inc.* (1976) 538 F 2d 14, 24–27; *John Carter et al. v Helmsley-Spear Inc.* (1995) 71 F 3d 77, 82; *Dastar Corporation v Twentieth Century Fox Film Corporation et al.* (2003) 123 S Ct 2041, 2050 per Justice Scalia; C Swack, "Safeguarding Artistic Creation and the Cultural Heritage: A Comparison of *Droit Moral* Between France and the United

In the context of the UK, Jamaica,[34] and Canada, it is very unlikely that a marijuana-themed parody will amount to infringement of the moral right of integrity because there will be no objective evidence of prejudice to the author's honour or reputation as the audience will be aware that the parody is not the author's work.[35] Similarly, in France, parodies have not been held to be an infringement of the moral right of integrity where the rules of the parody genre are followed.[36] Consequently, the marijuana parody song will be very unlikely to infringe the moral right of integrity unless the parody departs from the accepted artform and unreasonably prejudices the author.

Therefore, despite the controversial nature of marijuana, a marijuana-themed parody is unlikely to amount to infringement of the right of integrity in any of the jurisdictions discussed, provided that the parody is humorous and will not be confused for the author's work. However, in the absence of the rules of the parody genre being followed, there is nothing precluding a finding of infringement.

4.3.1.2 Marijuana anthems

Considering the case study of the verbatim adoption of the lyrics of a song as the anthem for a pro-marijuana organisation, this scenario involves an extrinsic treatment of the work because the lyrics remain unchanged in its use as

States" (1998) 22 Colum-VLA JL & Arts 361, 383–387; Dworkin (n 6) 232–224; M Roeder, "The Doctrine of Moral Right: A Study in the Law of Artists, Authors and Creators" (1940) 53 Harv L Rev 554; R DaSilva, "Droit Moral and the Amoral Copyright: A Comparison of Artists' Rights in France and the United States" (1980) 28 Bull Copyright Soc'y USA 1, 6, 39–51; and Hansmann, Santilli (n 4) 97. However, note that Dworkin argued that despite the strong opinions present in common law copyright countries that moral rights are protected adequately by other pre-existing causes of action, this is not the case: Dworkin (n 6) 263. That being said, Article 6*bis* does not require express moral rights provisions: Ricketson, Ginsburg (n 6) 10.09. Moreover, US jurisprudence has demonstrated a continued reluctance to expand the scope of express moral rights protection: *John Carter et al.* 82–83; Tackaberry (n 24) 358; Swack 382; B Ong (n 21) 304; A Adler, "Against Moral Rights" (2009) 97 Calif L Rev 263, 266; and Hansmann, Santilli (n 4) 96–97.

[34] Section 15 of the Jamaican Copyright Act 1993 is a near-verbatim copy of section 80 of the CDPA 1988.

[35] Jacques (n 29) 193.

[36] See Jacques (n 29) 189–190, 194. The parodist must differentiate their work from that of the original author so that there is no confusion about authorship, and the parody must be humorous. See Case C-201/13 *Johan Deckmyn and Vrijheidsfonds VZW v Helena Vandersteen and others* [2014] ECLI:EU:C:2014:2132, para 33.

an anthem.[37] Consequently, there is no potential for infringement in the US because the right of integrity does not apply to literary works. Additionally, there is no option of right of integrity infringement in the UK because the extrinsic treatment of the work is not protected. A similar result is likely to follow in Jamaica unless the courts adopt a more expansive reading and neglect to follow the UK approach.[38] In the context of France, infringement of the right of integrity in this regard is highly likely because the case is comparable to *Pontoreau ADAGP c Association Front National*, where a painting used in a political campaign flier was held to be infringement of the right of integrity.

Similarly, in Canada, the conclusion will likely be the same as in France, provided that the author is able to provide supporting evidence that other third parties will also feel that their honour or reputation will be prejudiced. In this specific example, there is a high chance that others may feel similarly aggrieved given the controversial nature of marijuana consumption and, moreover, the politicised nature of its use as the anthem for a pro-marijuana group.[39] However, it should be noted for both the French and Canadian contexts that if the song's lyrics are expressly in support of marijuana usage/consumption, no infringement of the right of integrity is likely to arise.[40] Notwithstanding that situation, songs that involve double entendres (meanings) may prove more difficult to address because the song could have a duality of meaning, which then places the onus on the author to evidence why they disagree with the use of the work.

Given the range of potential outcomes in this scenario due to the divergence in scope of the moral right of integrity across jurisdictions, authors face a significant task in limiting the use of their works in political contexts.

---

37 Such a use will also invoke the right of reproduction and/or public performance. However, even if authorisation is granted concerning the economic rights, the author retains the ability to enforce the moral right of integrity unless that right is waived by contract. This is complicated by the fact that authorisation may be provided by a collective management organisation.

38 The inclusion of the latter phrase "*or is otherwise prejudicial to the honour or reputation of the author*" under section 15(4)(a) of the Jamaican Copyright Act leaves it open to a Jamaican court to protect the extrinsic treatment of the work if it adopts a liberal reading of the provision with the aim of being consistent with Article 6*bis* of the Berne Convention.

39 Where the author is made to appear bigoted, there is a strong likelihood of infringement of the moral right of integrity: Davies et al. (n 12) 11–50.

40 *Ferrat SNAC et autre c Sté GMT Productions* (1998) 177 RIDA 284.

4.3.1.3 Marijuana remixes

Considering the case study of a dance remix of an instrumental song that is "mashed up" with other songs for the purpose of making a music mix advertised for persons to listen to while they consume marijuana, this scenario involves both intrinsic and extrinsic treatments of the work. This is because there is a dance remix version of the song and it is used in a marijuana-themed and/or advertised playlist. Given that this involves a musical work, there will be no option for liability in the US. Addressing the intrinsic element of the work in the first place, determining whether there is a derogatory treatment of the work will depend on the nature of the original song. This is because a mere change in tempo or key is unlikely to amount to moral rights infringement in any jurisdiction, including France. However, if the dance remix constitutes a significant genre change, then it can be considered a derogatory treatment.[41] Assuming that there is a derogatory treatment because the change in genre is drastic and perceived as offensive,[42] there will be liability in France due to the subjective standard adopted by the court.[43] Alternatively, in the common law countries of the UK, Canada, and Jamaica, there is less likely to be infringement because it has been difficult to provide objective evidence that the act of remixing will prejudice the honour or reputation of the author.[44] However, it is conceivable that if an iconic song is remixed in an abhorrent way, there may be a potential case of infringement of the moral right of integrity.

In terms of the use of the work in a marijuana mash-up mix/playlist, this affects the extrinsic elements of the work.[45] Thus, there will be no liability in the UK or Jamaica.[46] Alternatively, in France, there will be liability as the cutting and pasting of a work in a different context has been treated as infringing the right of integrity.[47] Furthermore, the use of a song in a film with a

---

[41] Newman (n 4) 684 and *Confetti Records* (n 12), paras. 153–158.

[42] "Offensive" in the context of the moral right of integrity will include situations where the author is made to look "inept, untruthful, bigoted", or where there is an unfavourable association of the author with another person: Davies et al. (n 12) 11–50.

[43] Note, if the remix involves the disassociation of the song's words and music, there will be infringement: *Editions Zagora c SDRM* (2002) 194 RIDA 325.

[44] See *Confetti Records* (n 12), para 157.

[45] Such a use will also invoke the right of reproduction. However, even if authorisation is granted concerning the economic rights, the author retains the ability to enforce the moral right of integrity unless that right is waived by contract, especially where authorisation is granted through a collective management organisation.

[46] *Morrison Leahy Music* (n 14) 151.

[47] See Adeney (n 3) 8.79; *Sté Média RATP et autre c Scher et autre* (1996) 169 RIDA 372; *Sté Arkadia c Leloir* (1999) 180 RIDA 367; and *B X Y c SARL PML*

political message that was disagreeable to the composer was also held to be infringing.[48] As such, the act of "mashing up" remixed music into a marijuana-themed mix will likely be treated as an infringement of the moral right of integrity,[49] unless the author had consented to such use in the specific project.[50] However, in Canada, a finding of infringement is only likely to ensue if the author can demonstrate that other authors or reasonable persons will feel equally aggrieved by the remix and mashup of the song in a marijuana-themed playlist. Following the case of *Maltz v Witterick*, it was demonstrated how difficult it is to support the sensitivities of the claimant author.[51] Therefore, infringement will depend on how third-party authors view the remix. In the absence of compelling objective evidence, there will likely be no infringement.

This scenario raised the interesting conflict of preserving the moral right of integrity against music industry norms. It is commonplace for songs to be remixed and mashed up, whether in a live performance, on a recording, or for audio-visual synchronisations. Therefore, such an act may not necessarily be seen as objectively prejudicial. However, the marijuana theme of the mashup may push the finding in the direction of being objectively prejudicial because of the controversial nature of marijuana consumption.[52] Notwithstanding, it should be noted that where authorisation is granted to remix, mashup, or synchronise a song, there may be implied consent to distort or modify the song and use it in different contexts. As such, in practice, the economic rights may override any moral rights interests where authorisation is granted by the author.[53]

(2021) No RG 20/04760 (Cour d'Appel de Paris) [unreported].

48 *Société Le Chant du Monde v Société Fox Europe and Société Fox Americaine Twentieth Century* (1953) 13 January 1953 Court of Appeal, Paris [unreported].

49 Infringement of the integrity right will not arise if the author has contractually allowed the use of their music for the context complained of: *J M c Narcos Productions LLC et autres* (2023) No RG 20/06038 (Tribunal Judiciaire de Paris) [unreported], para 28.

50 *K N c V Z YY, H G, ZZ I and S AS Chris Music* (2020) No RG 17/13001 (Cour d'Appel de Paris) [unreported].

51 *Lawrence Ritchie* (n 20) para 50 and *Judy Maltz* (n 20) paras 49–51.

52 See Ricketson, Ginsburg (n 6) 10.30, for the potential negative impacts of associating a work with a disagreeable context.

53 The situation may be different where authorisation is granted by a third-party right holder on behalf of the author, as is the case with collective management organisations.

4.3.1.4 Marijuana adornments

Considering the case study of a public statue with a sash made of real marijuana leaves to celebrate 4/20,[54] this scenario is akin to the fact pattern of *Snow v Eaton Centre*. This is because the placement of the marijuana sash is comparable to the red ribbons hung on the necks of the geese in *Snow*. Given that the sash is made from marijuana leaves, it is not disputed that this constitutes a modification or distortion of the work. However, liability in this scenario will depend on how courts address the issue of prejudice to the honour or reputation of the author. In France, this scenario will almost certainly amount to infringement of the right of integrity because of the subjective standard for determining infringement. Given that the physical work is modified or distorted, once the author deems this to be offensive, there will be infringement.

By contrast, in the common law countries of the UK, US, and Jamaica that do not rely on the subjective standard of proving prejudice, the establishment of infringement will depend on whether the reasonable person will consider their honour or reputation prejudiced as a result of the placement of the sash. Given the controversial nature of marijuana and the fact that the statue was modified and/or distorted by placing the marijuana sash, it is reasonable to conceive that there will be infringement of the right of integrity in the UK and Jamaica. This is because the action in this scenario goes beyond minor alterations in colour or sizing, which were held to be treatments,[55] and is closer to the "gross differences between a black and white film and a colourised version of the same film",[56] which Overend J suggested would amount to a treatment that is prejudicial. Similarly, in Canada, it is a virtual certainty that the same conclusion will be arrived at because the scenario is factually similar to *Snow* (yet more prejudicial) and, moreover, any distortion to a sculpture will be considered prejudicial to the author's honour or reputation.[57]

However, the situation in the US is unclear because there is limited case law addressing the issue of modifications or distortions for the purpose of infringement of the moral right of integrity.[58] Additionally, section 106A(a) begins with tying the rights of attribution and integrity with fair use. Therefore, it

---

54 G Johnson, "How pot holiday 4/20 came to be" *PBS News Hour* (20 April 2023) <https://www.pbs.org/newshour/nation/part-party-part-call-to-action-a-look-at-pot-holiday-4-20> accessed 14 February 2024.

55 See: *Tidy v Trustees* (n 12) 501; *Pasterfield* (n 14) 182; and *Lawrence Ritchie* (n 20) para 49.

56 *Pasterfield* (n 14) 182.

57 See section 28.2(2) Copyright Act 1985 (Canada).

58 US moral rights cases include: *Chapman Kelley v Chicago Park District* (2011) 635 F 3d 290; *Lilley v Stout* (2005) 384 F Supp 2d 83; *Pollara v Seymour* (2003) 344 F 3d 265; *Maria Castillo v G&M Realty LP* (2020) 950 F 3d 155; and

is unknown whether the robust fair use framework can/will act to limit the infringement of moral rights.[59] In the scenario at hand, it is conceivable that if the defendant is able to argue that placing the marijuana sash on the statue creates a transformative work, a court can potentially hold that there is no infringement on the basis of fair use.[60] But, this remains a contested issue with the lack of case law.[61] Provided that fair use does not step in, there is likely to be infringement of the moral right of integrity in the US where the marijuana sash is placed on the statue.

This scenario was designed to assess whether the decision in *Snow v Eaton Centre* would likely be followed in other common law copyright jurisdictions concerning comparable facts. While the scenario is more severe due to the marijuana context, it is very likely that a court will find infringement provided that the author can provide objective evidence of prejudice to their honour or reputation.

4.3.1.5 Marijuana conventions

Considering the final case study of a photograph as the backdrop for a marijuana convention, this scenario relates to the use of a copyrighted work in a context that may be disagreeable to the author and is similar to the facts of *Pontoreau ADAGP c Association Front National*. As such, the extrinsic elements of the work are affected because it is the placement of the photograph that is objectionable, given that the photograph itself was not edited. Immediately, this rules out the potential for liability in the UK and the US where the extrinsic treatment of the work is not protected under the moral right of integrity.[62] A similar result is likely to arise in Jamaica unless the court

---

Massachusetts Museum of Contemporary Art Foundation v Büchel (2010) 593 F 3d 38.

59 R Buker, "On Art Attacks: At the Confluence of Shock, Appropriation, and the Law" (2015) 14 J Marshall Rev Intell Prop L 393, 403; and Adler (n 33) 281.

60 C Smith, "Creative Destruction: Copyright's Fair Use Doctrine and the Moral Right of Integrity" (2020) 47 Pepperdine Law Review 601, 624–637.

61 See J Ginsburg, "Copyright in the 101st Congress: Commentary on the Visual Artists Rights Act and the Architectural Works Copyright Protection Act of 1990" (1989) 14 Colum-VLA JL & Arts 477; P Karlen, "What's Wrong with VARA: A Critique of Federal Moral Rights" (1993) 15 Hastings Comm & Ent LJ 905, 912–913; and D Ciolino, "Rethinking the Compatibility of Moral Rights and Fair Use" (1997) 54 Wash & Lee L Rev 33, 37.

62 Given the limitations set out in section 106A(a)(3) of the US Copyright Act, the extrinsic treatment of the work is unlikely to be protected: *Massachusetts Museum of Contemporary Art Foundation* (n 58) 62. However, Fromer and Sprigman argued that the protection of the spirit of the work is an open question to which the statute does not speak – J Fromer, C Sprigman, *Copyright Law: Cases*

adopts a broader approach to the interpretation of the right of integrity, which will require that UK jurisprudence be ignored.

In the context of France, this scenario will almost certainly be considered an infringement of the right of integrity where the author is offended by the use of the photograph at a marijuana convention because of the precedent set in *Pontoreau*. In *Pontoreau*, the use of an artistic work in a right-wing political campaign was held to infringe the right of integrity. The scenario here is similar in that a marijuana convention is equally objectionable to a right-wing political campaign due to the polarising nature of the context, which is exacerbated by the fact that marijuana is illegal in France and, moreover, the subjective standard used to determine infringement of the right of integrity.

However, in the context of Canada, the situation is more nuanced for two reasons. Firstly, marijuana is legalised, which perhaps reduces the polarising nature of the context in which the photograph is used. Secondly, the hybrid subjective-objective standard used for proving whether the author's honour or reputation is prejudiced means that other authors or reasonable persons will have to agree with the author that the use of the photograph at a marijuana convention is offensive. Notwithstanding these nuances, it is reasonable to suggest that there is a likelihood of infringement being found in this scenario because marijuana remains a taboo subject despite it being legalised in Canada. Consequently, if the author of the photograph is able to find objective support that this specific use of the photograph is offensive, then it is very likely that infringement of the integrity right will be established. Support for this conclusion can be found in the fact that placing red ribbons on the necks of geese in *Snow v Eaton Centre* was held to be infringement of the integrity right. Therefore, association with a controversial matter like marijuana will likely be considered prejudicial.

This scenario demonstrates the broad scope of protection available to authors in jurisdictions where extrinsic treatments of the work are protected. So long as a work is used in a context disagreeable to the author, there will likely be infringement where that context involves some element of controversy or unsavoury aspect because there is a strong likelihood that the reasonable person will be offended.

and Materials, Version 5 (2023) 339 <https://www.copyrightbook.org/download/Copyright%20Law%20-%20Cases%20and%20Materials%20v5.0.pdf>.

4.4 CONCLUSION

This chapter explored the moral right of integrity as applied to examples of marijuana scenarios across the jurisdictions of France, the UK, Canada, Jamaica and the US. To date, there have been no cases concerning the use of copyright works in conjunction with marijuana and therefore the case studies served to test the scope of the integrity right in novel situations, including use of copyright works for a marijuana parody, an anthem for a pro-marijuana group, a marijuana-themed music remix, a marijuana-styled adornment, and as the backdrop of a marijuana convention.

It is concluded that due to the continued controversial nature of marijuana, notwithstanding its increasing legal tolerance, associating a copyright work with marijuana will likely lead to an infringement of the moral right of integrity in countries (Canada, Jamaica, the UK, and the US) where the author is able to adduce objective evidence of the negative impact it has or may have on their honour or reputation. For the droit d'auteur countries (France), the association of a work with marijuana will almost certainly lead to a finding of infringement of the moral right of integrity, except where some other exception or limitation applies, as in the case of parodies. It is this author's opinion that case law on this topic will eventually arise. However, it is accepted that the potential mischief discussed in this chapter can be avoided by contract in the copyright countries where moral rights are waivable and even in droit d'auteur countries where the author has expressly agreed to certain uses.[63]

[63] See: *K N c V Z YY, H G, ZZ I* (n 50) and *J M c Narcos Productions LLC* (n 49) paras 28 and 32.

5. Marijuana and image rights

Emma Perot

5.1 INTRODUCTION

In the past decade, countries around the world have moved to decriminalise marijuana. Some have gone further, legalising consumption for medical use and, more rarely, recreational use. Legislative changes have resulted in a booming marijuana industry,[1] and like any industry that aims to target consumers, the attraction of celebrity magnetism has resulted in brand partnerships. Many celebrities have also launched their own marijuana lines. While these types of uses of persona are agreed to, there exists the possibility that sellers may want to take advantage of celebrity persona. Advertising, as well as the production of accessories and even clothing, might utilise celebrity persona. As such, it is important to understand when permission must be sought to use persona. The ability of celebrities to object to exploitation depends on the laws of the relevant jurisdiction.

In the US, the right of publicity provides protection against unauthorised commercialisation of persona. In Canada, the tort of appropriation of personality provides similar protection. Jamaica adopted the tort of appropriation of personality in the 1994 case of *Dino Michelle*.[2] The UK has remained firmly rooted in the common law tort of passing off, and false endorsement may prove problematic considering the misrepresentation element as marijuana remains illegal. Celebrities' ability to regulate their association with marijuana-related products varies between jurisdictions, as does the legality of marijuana. The legality is most likely to impact the celebrity's ability to claim against unauthorised use in the absence of the right of publicity or tort of appropriation of

[1] I Dorbian, "Global Legal Weed Market Could Soar to $55 Billion in Four Years" *Forbes* (10 February 2023) <https://www.forbes.com/sites/irisdorbian/2023/10/02/global-legal-weed-market-could-soar-to-55-billion-in-five-years/?sh=1fce1cec6630> accessed 16 December 2023.

[2] E Ventose, N Corthésy, "Misappropriation of Personality in the Commonwealth Caribbean" (2009) 12(4) JIPLP 904–912.

personality. However, unauthorised use is likely to be rare since modern consumption of celebrity requires authentic advertising for a successful product and/or advertisement.[3]

This chapter will discuss the success of celebrity-aligned marijuana lines to establish the appeal of capitalising on celebrity persona. The relevant laws of the US, Canada, Jamaica, and the UK will be analysed to establish that the celebrity should not generally be used without permission. The legal status of marijuana and the advertising of marijuana will be examined against the regulation of persona. It will be argued that celebrities can easily pursue unauthorised commercial uses of persona in jurisdictions where there is a strict liability right, and that brands should be aware that celebrities may object to an unauthorised association for financial reasons, as well as conflict with personal values in some instances. In the UK, passing off may prove problematic because the misrepresentation element might be harder to make out since people would not assume a celebrity would enter into a license for an illegal product. But considering the nature of illegality, the unauthorised producer cannot freely advertise the sale of marijuana. Overall, this chapter will help brands understand the value of celebrity and the need to seek permission for use of celebrity in connection with this controversial product.

5.2 MARIJUANA AND CELEBRITY ALIGNMENT

Celebrities have been involved in the promotion of marijuana through their artforms before it was legalised in any of the jurisdictions examined in this chapter. Bob Marley, a pioneer of reggae, celebrated the use of marijuana as part of his Rastafarian faith in songs such as, "Kaya", "Easy Skanking", and "Get Up, Stand Up". Peter Tosh did the same in his famous song, "Legalize It". While marijuana is still not legalised in Jamaica (but the possession of small amounts has been decriminalised and it is permitted for sacramental/religious uses since 2015),[4] or the UK, celebrities like Snoop Dogg, Willie Nelson, and Cheech & Chong, who have openly identified as consumers of marijuana, have capitalised in the US states that have legalised marijuana, as well as in Canada.[5] Celebrity marijuana-owned or supported brands in the US

---

3 E Perot, *Commercialising Celebrity Persona: Intellectual Property Law and Practice* (Hart Publishing 2023) 108–114.

4 See section 7C(2) Dangerous Drugs Act of Jamaica 1948, as amended in 2014.

5 J Weed, "Marley Natural: Yes, Bob Marley Is One of Many Celebrities with a Marijuana Brand" *Forbes* (21 June 2015) <https://www.forbes.com/sites/julieweed/2015/06/21/marley-naturals-yes-bob-marley-is-one-of-many-celebrities-with-a-marijuana-brand/?sh=2682686035dd> accessed 13 December 2023.

on average sold cheaper products and earned higher revenue than their competitors for the first quarter of 2023.[6] Cann Social Tonics, a cannabis-infused carbonated beverage, amassed US$751,760 in monthly sales in the first quarter of 2023. Cann received investments from Gwyneth Paltrow, Rebel Wilson, and Ruby Rose, among others.[7] Co-Founder Luke Anderson stated, "To have taste-making celebrities who don't have a 'stoner' identity attached to their personal brands wanting to help us spread this message to a mass consumer base is a game-changer for Cann, and a sign for how this industry will evolve in the coming years."[8] The alignment with celebrities who are not known for marijuana consumption is notable as it indicates that other marijuana-derived products might make similar associations as they are trying to appeal to consumers who would not usually partake in smoking. This can have consequences in jurisdictions where passing off is the main cause of action since misrepresentation might be a harder barrier to overcome if the person is not known to partake in marijuana. That being said, the legal status of marijuana will also be a determining factor in seeking redress for unauthorised use and will be discussed in the next section.

Other celebrity marijuana brands that have seen success focus on products for smoking and consumption. Seth Rogen's "Houseplant" earned $377,193 in monthly sales for the first quarter of 2023.[9] This figure is nearly half of Cann's earnings, which could indicate a larger market appeal for products that would be purchased by non-smokers. One of the first celebrity cannabis brands is "Tommy Chong's". According to Chong's testimonial on his website, "Look, I'm no doctor and I've never played one on T.V. but I absolutely believe that using CBD and legal cannabis every day helped me recover from cancer not once, but twice … I do everything I can to stay healthy and active: I eat right.

---

6 C Casacchia, "Celebrity Marijuana Brands Outperform Traditional Brands, Data Suggests" *MJBizDaily* (12 July 2023) <https://mjbizdaily.com/celebrity-marijuana-brands-outperform-traditional-brands-data-suggests/> accessed 15 December 2023.

7 "Cann, the First Cannabis-infused Social Tonic, Announces Investment Led by Celebrity Power Players, Including Gwyneth Paltrow, Rebel Wilson, Ruby Rose, Darren Criss, Baron Davis and More" *PR Newswire* (29 October 2020) <https://www.prnewswire.com/news-releases/cann-the-first-cannabis-infused-social-tonic-announces-investment-led-by-celebrity-power-players-including-gwyneth-paltrow-rebel-wilson-ruby-rose-darren-criss-baron-davis-and-more-301162829.html> accessed 15 December 2023.

8 *PR Newswire* (n 7).

9 Casacchia (n 6).

I lift weights 4 times a week and I smoke my body weight in legal cannabis."[10] Chong's CBD products include "Cruise Chews", "Nice Dreams Sleep Tincture Pack", and muscle balm. His cannabis products include infused strips, vape cartridges, pre-rolled joints, and "full spectrum elixir" for chronic pain and stress.[11]

Companies that are not owned by celebrities seek partnerships with them. The largest US company by market capitalisation, Curaleaf, partnered with Sean Paul to feature a package of their "Select" brand edibles in a music video for "Light My Fire".[12] Music videos can be viewed across state lines and are not subject to the various cannabis advertising regulations.[13] Other videos that have included product placement are Wiz Khalifa's "Still Blazin", Kid Cudi's "Cannabis", and Afroman's "Because I Got High".[14] According to the Vice President of Brand Marketing for Curaleaf, Sydney Chernish, "we are definitely looking for more opportunities to integrate into culture whether that's with celebrities or other ways of reaching new consumers."[15] In terms of the type of deal that is desired, Duane Brown of the marketing agency "Take Some Risk" said, "Celebs can work if it feels real. [It will only work if] the person uses that product, or a product in the space, and it is not just a pay-to-play type deal."[16] This need for authenticity is confirmed by empirical research which established that modern consumption of celebrity requires brands to work with the celebrity to get the best possible outcome.[17] This means that reputable brands are unlikely to use celebrities without permission regardless of the legal requirements of the jurisdiction.[18]

Celebrities' alignment goes beyond marijuana consumables and includes clothing. According to Mongolife, a brand that specialises in marijuana-themed

---

10 T Chong, "Mission – Why I Fight" (*Tommy Chong's*) <https://tommychong.com/mission/> accessed 15 December 2023.

11 See range of products via Chong (n 10).

12 S Paul, "Sean Paul – Light My Fire ft. Gwen Stefani, Shenseea" (*YouTube*, 13 July 2022) <https://www.youtube.com/watch?v=Qg_jLLPlv5o> accessed 28 December 2023.

13 K Monllos, "Why Cannabis Company Curaleaf Wants to 'Integrate Into Culture' to Build Its Brands" *Digiday* (8 August 2022) <https://digiday.com/marketing/why-cannabis-company-curaleaf-wants-to-integrate-into-culture-to-build-its-brands/> accessed 28 December 2023.

14 S Jones, "Cannabis and Product Placement Content Partnerships" (*Hollywood Branded*, 2018) <https://blog.hollywoodbranded.com/cannabis-and-product-placement-content-partnerships> accessed 15 December 2023.

15 Monllos (n 13).

16 ibid.

17 Perot (n 3).

18 ibid 115–117.

clothing, "Thanks to weed being legalised in more places, we definitely see a trend in the cannabis industry and the rise of cannabis apparel brands."[19] Several celebrities have been spotted wearing clothing depicting marijuana.[20] Wiz Khalifa has partnered with Diamond Clothing Co. and Weedmaps to launch a cannabis-themed clothing line.[21] From clothing to consumption, there has been an expansion of marijuana-related products as more US states move towards legalisation. Brands that are successful in the US have also been successful in Canada, where marijuana was legalised in 2018. However, the most profitable brands are owned by the Canadian government.[22] Even these brands are seeking celebrity alignment.

High Tide, one of the largest Canadian cannabis retail companies, has licences to produce several celebrity brands including Snoop Dogg's "Pounds" and Cheech & Chong's "Up in Smoke".[23] Snoop Dogg has also granted a licence to Canopy Growth Corporation's "Tweed" brand for the name "Leafs by Snoop" in 2016. As a result,

> Tweed's parent company Canopy Growth Corporation saw its market value climb nearly 17 percent – a record breaker that set the Canadian Cannabis industry in motion. This can definitely be attributed to the company's collaboration with the cannabis culture icon and singer of "Young & Wild & Free" who reaches more than 35 million people all over the world.[24]

---

19 A Lundgren, "10 Best Weed Clothing Brands In Fashion Right Now" (*Mongolife*, 23 November 2022) <https://mongolife.com/blogs/news/10-best-weed-clothing-brands> accessed 28 December 2023.

20 H Southwick, "High Fashion: All the Stars Who've Worn Weed-themed Bikinis, Jewels and More" *Page Six* (20 April 2021) <https://pagesix.com/2021/04/20/high-fashion-all-the-stars-whove-worn-weed-themed-styles/> accessed 28 December 2023.

21 "8 Fashion and Cannabis Collabs to Know About" (*LIM College*, 4 October 2021) <https://www.limcollege.edu/blog/8-fashion-and-cannabis-collabs-know-about> accessed 5 January 2024.

22 M Lamers, "The Most Profitable Businesses in Canada are Owned by Government" (*MJ Biz Daily*, 20 September 2022) <https://mjbizdaily.com/most-profitable-cannabis-businesses-in-canada-are-owned-by-government/> accessed 20 December 2023.

23 "High Tide Announces 9th Celebrity License Secured by Famous Brandz and Renewal of Key Existing License" (*High Tide Inc*, 29 July 2019) <https://hightideinc.com/high-tide-announces-9th-celebrity-license-secured-by-famous-brandz-and-renewal-of-key-existing-license/> accessed 28 December 2023.

24 H Saab, "Cannabis Celebrity Influencer Marketing" (*Hollywood Branded*, 20 April 2018) <https://blog.hollywoodbranded.com/cannabis-celebrity-influencer-marketing-infographic> accessed 28 December 2023.

In addition, Grenco's partnership with Snoop Dogg yielded one of the highest selling portable vaporiser pens in 2016.[25] While this product is no longer available, Grenco currently sells the "Tyson 2.0 x G Pen Dash Vaporizer". The webpage for the product features Mike Tyson using the vape, and the write-up states, "Created in collaboration with legendary boxer, entrepreneur, and advocate Mike Tyson and his new brand Tyson 2.0, G Pen is pleased to announce the Tyson 2.0 x G Pen Dash Vaporizer."[26]

There are no similar success stories of celebrity marijuana promotion in the UK, where only medical use of marijuana has been decriminalised and is heavily regulated.[27] In Jamaica, decriminalisation has been more wide-reaching than in the UK, but there have only been two notable celebrity alignments of brands thus far. Reggae artist Jesse Royal was appointed as the brand ambassador for Jacana, a pioneer in Jamaica of "medical-grade, organic cannabis products" in 2021.[28] Royal will continue to advocate for the legalisation of marijuana as part of the partnership.[29] The Marley Natural Dispensary, a licenced medicinal marijuana retailer, opened in February 2023.[30] This development took place several years after the Marley family licenced "Marley Natural" in the US in 2015.[31]

Given the changes in the legal status of marijuana, it needs to be considered how brands that do not want to be associated with marijuana use can protect their reputations. The answer lies in morality clauses. The perception

---

[25] N Clement, "Snoop Dogg's Business Empire Harvests Green From Marijuana Legalization Trend" *Variety* (13 September 2016) <https://variety.com/2016/biz/spotlight/snoop-dogg-marijuana-martha-stewart-1201858272/> accessed 15 December 2023.

[26] "Tyson 2.0 X G Pen Dash" <https://www.gpen.com/products/tyson-2-0-x-g-pen-dash-vaporizer> accessed 28 December 2023.

[27] D Nutt, S Bazire, L Phillips, AK Schlag, "So Near Yet So Far: Why Won't the UK Prescribe Medical Cannabis?" (2020) 10:e038687 BMJ Open.

[28] "Jesse Royal Welcomed Into JACANA Herb Family", *The Gleaner* (16 February 2021) <https://jamaica-gleaner.com/article/entertainment/20210216/jesse-royal-welcomed-jacana-herb-family> accessed 11 January 2024.

[29] "Jesse Royal Joins Ganja Company Jacana as Brand Strategist" (*Jacana Jamaica*, 16 March 2021) <https://jacana.life/jesse-royal-joins-ganja-company-jacana-as-brand-strategist/#:~:text=International%20reggae%20star%20Jesse%20Royal,a%20tribute%20to%20Rastafarianism's%20endurance> accessed 11 January 2024.

[30] K Rozario, "Jamaica's First Bob Marley-Branded Cannabis Store Comes To Market" *Forbes* (15 February 2023) <https://www.forbes.com/sites/kevinrozario/2023/02/15/first-bob-marley-branded-cannabis-store-comes-to-market/?sh=12c9850e5f81> accessed 23 December 2023.

[31] Weed (n 5).

of marijuana consumption has shifted with time, as has the law regarding legality.[32] Morality clauses can be more prohibitive than the law, so celebrities should be mindful of behavioural restrictions under a contract for endorsement or sponsorship. It is equally important for brands to choose suitable celebrity partners, as inserting a morality clause that is likely to be breached is a futile exercise. Morality clauses are included to allow the partnership to be terminated if the individual acts in a way that could jeopardise the reputation of the brand.

It is important that morality clauses are clear on what behaviour is prohibited. Chris Webber was terminated by Fila after he was stopped for marijuana possession at a Puerto Rico airport while on a promotional trip for Fila.[33] Webber successfully sued for wrongful termination as his morality clause stated that conviction rather than arrest was a ground for termination.[34] In contrast, Benjamin Curtis, known from Dell computer advertisements where the catchphrase was "Dude, you're getting a Dell!", was dismissed after he was arrested in 2003 on a marijuana charge,[35] because Dell had a strict "no drugs" policy.[36] If a company does not want to align with marijuana use, this should be made explicit, particularly where marijuana is now legal, and even celebrities who are not known to smoke are endorsing marijuana-derived products.

---

[32] A Graves, *Pop Culture's Influence on Recreational Marijuana Use & Legislation: A Case Study on Snoop Dogg* (2019) Ohio State Public Law Working Paper No 507, Drug Enforcement Policy Centre, Drug Enforcement and Policy Centre, No 14; J Weiss, "25 years later, Dr. Dre's 'The Chronic' Remains Rap's World-building Masterpiece" *The Washington Post* (15 December 2017) <https://www.washingtonpost.com/entertainment/music/25-years-later-dr-dres-the-chronic-remains-raps-world-building-masterpiece/2017/12/14/8632acda-e00f-11e7-89e8-edec16379010_story.html?noredirect=on> accessed 6 January 2024.

[33] "Fila Drops Webber for Pot Bust" *CBS News* (28 August 1998) <https://www.cbsnews.com/news/fila-drops-webber-for-pot-bust/> accessed 6 January 2024.

[34] N Seth, "Watch Your Steps: Role of Morality Clauses in Talent and Endorsement Agreements" (2022) 5 Int'l J L Mgmt & Human 933, 938–939.

[35] F Pinguelo, T Cedrone, "Morals? Who Cares About Morals? An Examination of Morals Clauses in Talent Contracts and What Talent Needs to Know" (2009) 19 Seton Hall J of Sports and Ent L 347, 372.

[36] I Tech, "'Dude You're Getting a Dell' Guy" (22 February 2016) <https://www.youtube.com/watch?v=5mLGJsxhCHk> accessed 7 December 2023.

5.3 PROTECTING AGAINST UNAUTHORISED USES OF PERSONA

The previous section has demonstrated that celebrity alignment is a prominent feature of marijuana marketing. Whether the celebrity launches their own brands, grants a licence for the use of their persona, agrees to a product placement, or endorses a product, the attraction of celebrity in promotion is clear.[37] The examples given entailed authorised uses that are most likely to have the desired result of attracting consumers, as such uses yield the best quality promotion of the product.[38] It is important for brands to understand that such authorisation is, in fact, legally required in the US, Canada, and Jamaica. In the UK, there is no strict liability right, but marijuana cannot be legally sold for recreational use.

Each jurisdiction will be discussed in the order in which formal protection of persona was recognised. The implications of how the principles would apply in situations where a persona is used in the commercialisation of marijuana without their consent will be considered. The US is at the forefront as the right of publicity was recognised in 1953. In 1973, Canada referred to UK cases on passing off and instead chose to align with Australian passing-off cases that recognised false endorsement before the UK. But ultimately, reference to US cases led to the recognition of the tort of appropriation of personality. In 1994, Jamaica referred to and applied UK cases on passing off, and even though false endorsement was not yet recognised in the UK, it was extended in Jamaica to cover this type of harm. In addition, more recent Canadian cases that recognised the tort of appropriation of personality were considered persuasive precedent for the introduction of this right in Jamaica.[39] Like Canada, Jamaica also referred to US cases, making it apparent that the right of publicity is the basis for the tort of appropriation of personality.[40] In 2002, the UK finally extended passing off to protect against false endorsement but did not follow the approach of their Commonwealth counterparts in drawing on the US jurisprudence and taking a developmental approach.[41] Rather, passing off

---

37 Graves (n 32).

38 Perot (n 3) 99–101, 108–115.

39 *The Robert Marley Foundation v Dino Michelle Limited* (1994) CL R115/1992.

40 G Kodilinye, N Corthésy, "Personality Rights" in *Commonwealth Caribbean Tort Law* (6th edn, Routledge Taylor Francis 2022).

41 Although it should be noted that *Irvine* examined the Australian case of *Henderson*.

was given a broader interpretation to recognise that a misrepresentation could occur when a person's goodwill was used without authorisation.[42]

5.4 THE UNITED STATES

The legal status of marijuana differs across states. The 2022 Marijuana Opportunity Reinvestment and Expungement Bill seeks to decriminalise marijuana on a federal level by amending the Controlled Substances Act to reschedule marijuana.[43] The Bill was passed in the House of Representatives in April 2022 but remains in the Senate as of January 2024.[44] Thirty-seven states have medical marijuana laws, and 19 states permit recreational use.[45] Each state has its own approach to advertising marijuana. The regulations range from a prohibition of advertising altogether, to restricting advertising to consumers over 18, making false claims, and placement of advertisements, to no restrictions.[46]

Just as the status of marijuana is state-dependent, so too is the scope of the right of publicity. Thirty-three states recognise the right of publicity either by statute, common law, or a combination.[47] In contrast, there is a federal trade mark registration system. However, a federal trade mark for a marijuana-related product cannot be granted since there is no legality at the federal level. Instead, celebrities can only use state trade mark law protection for their brands, which would mean multiple applications.[48] Therefore, the right of publicity is important in protecting against unauthorised uses and is a convenient

---

42 Consider the Jamaican perspective examined in G Kodilinye, N Corthésy, "Passing Off" in *Commonwealth Caribbean Tort Law* (6th edn, Routledge Taylor Francis 2022).

43 H.R.3617 Marijuana Opportunity Reinvestment and Expungement Act.

44 "All Actions: H.R.3617 – 117th Congress" (2021–2022) <https://www.congress.gov/bill/117th-congress/house-bill/3617/all-actions?overview=closed#tabs> accessed 17 December 2023.

45 E Laurence, "Your Guide to Cannabis Legalization by State" *Forbes* (10 October 2023) <https://www.forbes.com/health/cbd/cannabis-legalization-by-state/> accessed 16 December 2023.

46 D Hill, "Study: U.S Cannabis Advertising Policies Suffer from a Lack of Consistency" (18 January 2023) <https://www.buffalo.edu/news/releases/2023/01/014.html#:~:text=Among%20the%2031%20states%20that,have%20restrictions%20on%20building%20signage> accessed 23 December 2023.

47 T McCarthy, R Schechter, *The Rights of Publicity and Privacy*, May 2023 Update (Thomson Reuters 2023), § 6:2 "Introduction to the Law of the States – Right of Publicity".

48 N Ghomeshi, "Celebrities Dabbing with Marijuana Trademarks" (2017) 33 Ent & Sports Law 113, 115–117.

mechanism since there is no registration requirement for living people. Some states, such as New York and California, require registration to pursue statutory post-mortem uses of persona.[49]

There are two prongs that need to be considered in accordance with the US approach to the right of publicity. Firstly, the existence of this proprietary right means that individuals can licence their persona for commercialisation. This is not to say that such licencing is not possible in other jurisdictions as celebrity licencing (for legal industries) is also a big business in the UK where there is no equivalent proprietary right.[50] Rather, the implication in the US is that an exclusive licensee can pursue a third party for infringement to preserve the value of their deal rather than having to rely on the individual to do so. Although research suggests that breaching third-party deals is not common,[51] it is unclear what practices might surface in this emerging industry. Therefore, having the ability to enforce this right can be valuable, particularly as the market, while young, already has many producers that are all trying to stand out. Considering celebrity-owned or supported brands are currently dominating, the value of fame appears to translate into lucrative sales.

The second prong is that celebrities have a strict liability right in most states that they can pursue for unauthorised use of persona. Even states that do not yet recognise the right of publicity are subject to the federal false endorsement action under the Lanham Act, which gives a high level of protection.[52] The confusion element under this action is less onerous than the misrepresentation element under passing off in the UK, but it must still be proved that consumers thought there was a connection or association with the celebrity and the product or service. The potential issue that celebrities might have here is that marijuana is not legal in all states, so unauthorised use might be more difficult to pursue in a state where the sale is illegal. However, it is likely that a state that does not currently recognise the right of publicity might do so if a case is brought on such an issue. In some states, there have not been any cases and hence no recognition because of a lack of opportunity for considering whether the right should be recognised. Many states already recognise the common law tort of unauthorised appropriation of personality, so this action can also supplement the protection afforded to celebrities.

The desire to object to associations with products that the individual does not approve of was considered in the US before the right of publicity existed. In 1941, in the case of *O'Brien v Pabst Sales Co.*, an American football player

---

49 See, respectively: New York Civil Code s. 50-f; California Civil Code s. 3344.1.

50 Perot (n 3) 129–141.

51 ibid 117–118.

52 ibid 38–42.

claimed that his right to privacy had been infringed by the inclusion of his image in a calendar that contained the schedule of all major college football games. The calendar featured a photograph of O'Brien juxtaposed beside a glass with the words "Pabst Breweries, Blue Ribbon Export Beer", and to the right of it, a bottle of beer marked "Pabst Blue Ribbon Beer".[53] At that time, Texas did not recognise the right to publicity. O'Brien's claim failed because he was not considered a private person and "the publicity he got was only that which he had been constantly seeking and receiving".[54] The dissenting judgment by Circuit Judge Holmes noted that the beer company in the case had offered O'Brien $400 for endorsing its beer, but O'Brien had refused.[55] Circuit Judge Holmes also recognised that

> [i]f one is popular and permits publicity to be given to one's talent and accomplishment in any art of sport, commercial advertisers may seize upon such popularity to increase their sales of any lawful article without compensation of any kind for such commercial use of one's name and fame. This is contrary to usage and custom among advertisers in the markets of trade. They are undoubtedly in the habit of buying the right to use one's name or picture to create demand and good will for their merchandise.[56]

It is important to recognise that O'Brien's objection was not for financial reasons. In fact, his testimony did not speak to pecuniary loss. Rather, O'Brien was embarrassed by the association with beer as alcohol consumption did not align with his values. O'Brien was a member of the Allied Youth of America, and the main aim of that organisation was to discourage young people from consuming alcohol.[57] It is easy to transpose O'Brien's concerns to an unwanted association with marijuana, as some people may not want to be associated with the substance, regardless of its legality. For example, Melissa Gilbert, as a "celebrity champion" for Partnership to End Addiction, would likely be very upset if her persona was used for the promotion of marijuana.[58]

O'Brien's pleadings focussing on the unwanted association were seemingly detrimental to his case as the court, in affirming the view of the District Judge, held that "nothing in it could be legitimately or reasonably construed as falsely

---

53 *O'Brien v Pabst Sales Co.*, 124 F2d 167, 168 (5th Cir. 1941).

54 ibid [170].

55 ibid.

56 ibid [171].

57 ibid [168]–[169].

58 J Feliz, "Melissa Gilbert is New Celebrity Champion for The Partnership at Drugfree.org" (*Partnership to End Addiction*, October 2010) <https://drugfree.org/newsroom/news-item/melissa-gilbert-is-new-celebrity-champion-for-the-partnership-at-drugfree-org/> accessed 11 January 2024.

stating that he used, endorsed, or recommended the use of Pabst's beer".[59] In the absence of a right of publicity at the time, O'Brien was unable to seek redress for the use of his persona to promote a substance that he was publicly working to stop youth from consuming. Circuit Judge Holmes' concerns in the dissenting judgment were later addressed as the right was recognised in Texas in 1975 in another case involving a football player, *Kimbrough v Coca-Cola/USA*.[60] This development stemmed from the right of privacy in *Billings v Atkinson*.[61] This path of development is not unusual as many states that now recognise the right of publicity did so due to the inadequacies of privacy. This includes the foundational case of *Haelan v Topps Chewing Gum* in 1953 that started the revolution of the common law recognition of the right of publicity.

> We think that, in addition to and independent of that right of privacy (which in New York derives from statute), a man has a right in the publicity value of his photograph, i.e., the right to grant the exclusive privilege of publishing his picture, and that such a grant may validly be made "in gross," i.e., without an accompanying transfer of a business or of anything else. Whether it be labelled a "property" right is immaterial; for here, as often elsewhere, the tag "property" simply symbolizes the fact that courts enforce a claim which has pecuniary worth. This right might be called a "right of publicity".[62]

The Haelan case was brought by the exclusive licensee of the images of baseball players, which illustrates the first prong of the right of publicity discussed above. In terms of the second prong, the threshold for liability for infringement of the right of publicity is low, as a persona must be used in a commercial setting. However, the persona must be identifiable, as recognised in a case brought by former Major League Baseball player Donald Newcombe.[63] A recovering alcoholic, Newcombe objected to the use of his likeness in an advertisement for Killian's Irish Red Beer. The advertisement featured a drawing that was based on a photograph of Newcombe. A pitcher was depicted in the windup position, but the uniform did not identify a team. The court held that there was

---

59 *O'Brien v Pabst Sales Co.* (n 53) [170].

60 *Kimbrough v Coca-Cola/USA* 521 SW2d 719, 720 (Tex Civ App 1975).

61 *Billings v Atkinson*, 489 SW2d 959 (Tex 1973). See K Jaasma, "Star Power in the Lone Star State: The Right of Publicity in Texas" (2009) 18 Tex Intell Prop L J 123, 132–134 for a full discussion of the development of the right of publicity in Texas.

62 *Haelan v Topps Chewing Gum*, 202 F2d 866, 868 (2nd Cir 1953).

63 For a discussion of *O'Brien*, *Haelan*, and *Newcombe*, see J Thomas McCarthy and Paul M Anderson, "Protection of the Athlete's Identity: The Right of Publicity, Endorsements and Domain Names" (2001) 11 Mar Sports L Rev 195, 195–201.

a triable issue of fact "as to whether Newcombe is readily identifiable as the pitcher in the advertisement".[64]

Newcombe's objection to the association with alcohol can again be extrapolated into an objection to association with marijuana. The right of publicity, while generally focussed on financial harm, can be used to pursue unwanted associations in a commercial setting. Since the strict liability right does not require any false endorsement, individuals who object to the use of persona based on personal values are not disadvantaged. Indeed, this is vital because it would seem contrary to allow claims based solely on financial loss to succeed while reputational harm and feelings of embarrassment could go unaddressed. This is not to say that these are separate heads of damages that are often considered under the modern right of publicity. Rather, "modern cases tend to blur the emotional distress/commercial harm distinction between the rights of privacy and publicity and recognize emotional distress injury when a celebrity denominates its claim as one for infringement of the right of publicity".[65]

McKenna, in arguing for the introduction of an "autonomy-based identity appropriation claim", recognised that harm could accrue from unwanted associations with products that are contrary to the values of the individual.[66] Tom Waits was awarded $200,000 for "injury to his peace, happiness and feelings" when a sound-alike was used in an advertisement, as he had publicly disapproved of artists doing commercials.[67] The court in Waits cited the precedent of Motschenbacher, which recognised that "it is quite possible that the appropriation of the identity of a celebrity may induce humiliation, embarrassment, and mental distress".[68] It should be noted that this citation is from footnote 11 of Motschenbacher as mental harm was not substantively discussed in the judgment.

The Waits court also referred to *Grant v Esquire*.[69] Grant's photograph had been published in a 1946 article about clothing tastes. The case centred around a subsequent use of his head from the photograph, which was superimposed onto a model's body. The accompanying caption drew reference to the 1946 article and talked about styles of the 1970s. The caption stated the brand and price of the cardigan. Summary judgment was denied because the jury would have to decide whether the use of the photograph was for "the purposes of

64 *Newcombe v Adolf Coors Co* 157 F3d 686, 692 (9th Cir 1998).

65 McCarthy, Schechter (n 47) § 11:28.

66 M McKenna, "The Right of Publicity and Autonomous Self-definition" (2005) 67 University of Pittsburgh Law Review 225, 231, 281–285.

67 *Waits v Frito-Lay Inc* 978 F2d 1093, 1097, 1103 (1992).

68 *Motschenbacher v RJ Reynolds Tobacco Company* 498 F2d 821 (1974) fn 11.

69 *Grant v Esquire* 367 FSupp 876, 880 (1973).

trade" under New York law as the use was not considered to be "advertising". The Grant court recognised that damages were available for "lacerations to his feelings".[70] However, the reasoning in Grant as conveyed in Waits was not wholly accurate. Waits, in referring to Grant, stated, "the court found that the mere use of a celebrity's identity could cause embarrassment for which mental distress damages would be available".[71] In fact, the Grant court stated that the New York right of privacy which provides publicity protection, "permits a private individual to recover damages for injured feelings and general embarrassment if for purposes of trade he is unjustifiably subjected to the harsh and to him unwelcome glare of publicity".[72] The Grant judgment did not mention the words "mental" or "distress". The emphasis in Grant therefore remained on financial harm although it was noted that Cary Grant, like Tom Waits, did not want his persona commercialised.

Apart from Waits, Grant, and Motschenbacher, which all concerned celebrity plaintiffs, McCarthy and Schechter list several cases where damages have been awarded for indignity and mental distress, but these cases were between the 1950s and 1980s.[73] During this period, the right of publicity was still developing, and in many cases, the plaintiffs were private individuals rather than celebrities.[74] Even where the plaintiffs were celebrities, the use of their persona was for provocative magazines, hence the award of damages for mental distress.[75] Therefore, the most useful precedent for a celebrity whose persona is used to commercialise marijuana and who wishes to claim for mental distress remains Waits. This may seem like an unsatisfactory position, but it must be recalled that the situation in O'Brien has changed as the right of publicity can be used to address unauthorised use. While a court may choose to focus on the financial harm caused, potential plaintiffs still have a strong cause of action, and any personal objection could lead to the award of additional damages. Such objection would not undermine the action as occurred in O'Brien since there is no need for false endorsement. Dissenting Circuit Judge Holmes in O'Brien, in arguing for a right of publicity, mentioned the use of persona for the sale of lawful articles, but the right would not be so limited. While the legality might be relevant to passing off, as will be discussed when looking at

---

70 *Grant v Esquire* 367 FSupp 876, 881 (1973).

71 *Waits v Frito-Lay Inc* (n 67).

72 *Grant v Esquire* (n 69).

73 McCarthy, Schechter (n 47) § 11:30.

74 See: *Manger v Kree Institute of Electrolysis*, 233 F2d 5 (1956); *Leavy v Cooney*, 214 CalApp2d 496 (1963); *Olan Mills Inc. of Texas v Dodd*, 234 Ark 495 (1962); *Spahn v Julian Messner*, 21 N.Y.2d 124 (1967).

75 *Douglass v Hustler Magazine Inc.*, 769 F2d 11228 (1985); *Clark v Celeb Publishing Inc.*, 530 FSupp 979 (1981).

the UK, which turns on false endorsement, in the US, once unauthorised use has been made in a commercial setting, there would be a finding of infringement. US claimants would have little difficulty pursuing unauthorised use, even in a state where marijuana is not a lawful good.

5.5 CANADA

Marijuana was legalised in Canada in 2018. The Federal Cannabis Act 2018 regulates the advertising of cannabis, cannabis accessories, and related services. Advertising is heavily restricted, and promotion by means of a testimonial or endorsement, or depiction of a person or character, whether real or fictional is prohibited.[76] A violation of this Act attracts criminal penalties of a fine or imprisonment.[77] Despite these regulations, "many Canadian licenced producers have found loopholes to compliantly launch cannabis brands backed one way or another by celebrities".[78] These loopholes create ownership partnerships whereby the celebrity owns part of the company, as well as curation partnerships, which entail the celebrity helping the brand with product development. According to AdCann, a cannabis marketing resource that has published cannabis brand and retail marketing guides, "Since the celebrities involved in these companies are heavily restricted in what they are able to communicate about their brands and products, it is questionable whether these partnerships produce a reasonable return on investment for either side."[79] Nonetheless, the appeal of partnering with celebrities is apparent as there have been many partnerships with celebrities such as Drake, Wiz Khalifa, and Snoop Dogg.[80] However, the partnerships can only make limited use of the celebrity's name due to the advertising restrictions.

In the event that unauthorised advertising takes place, it is likely to be a breach of the Cannabis Act 2018. In addition, the featured individual may be able to pursue a claim under the tort of appropriation of personality.[81] The tort of appropriation of personality was recognised in the 1973 case *Krouse*

---

[76] Cannabis Act 2018 s. 17(1)(c)–(d).

[77] ibid s. 44.

[78] "Celebrity Cannabis Brands and Endorsements in Canada" (*AdCann*) <https://adcann.ca/blog/celebrity-cannabis-brands-endorsements-canada> accessed 23 December 2023.

[79] Fn (78).

[80] Fn (79).

[81] The provinces of British Columbia, Manitoba, Newfoundland, and Saskatchewan also have privacy statutes that can protect against unauthorised commercial uses of persona. See A Conroy, "Protecting Your Personality Rights in Canada: A Matter of Property or Privacy?" (2012) 1 UWO J Leg Stud 3.

v Chrysler Canada Ltd.[82] Unlike the US, which has had a host of cases of the right of publicity, only a few cases have been brought to trial in Canada.[83] An examination of Krouse explains how Canada expanded the law of passing off in line with Australia before the UK opted to do so, and illustrates the recognition of the tort of appropriation of personality, which is similar to the US right of publicity. The expansion of passing off is significant as it could be used by celebrities whose persona is used for commercialisation if the public would believe that the celebrity supports marijuana consumption or derivative products. However, it would be problematic if the celebrity is against such use, as misrepresentation might be difficult to prove. Therefore, the celebrity would have to rely on the tort of appropriation of personality. While the tort has little useful precedent on commercialisation of persona that is objectionable for personal reasons, and the case law has often looked at false endorsement, the current state of the law should allow it to be applied in the same way the right of publicity applies in the US. That is, a strict liability right to pursue unauthorised commercial use of persona.

The case of Krouse concerned the use of a photograph of a famous football player, Bobby Krouse, in a Chrysler advertisement. In conducting the analysis at first instance, Justice Haines stated, "In my opinion two separate but closely related lines of cases are controlling. One strand turns on the right of an individual to his elements of identity, the other is passing off".[84] Justice Haines first explored numerous early UK cases[85] before turning to the famous case of *McCulloch v May*, where the common field of activity defeated the claim of an actor who portrayed a character, "Uncle Mac". The actor thus tried to enjoin the sale of "Uncle Mac" cereal.[86] He then turned to the Australian case of *Henderson v Radio Corp Pty.*[87] Justice Haines described Henderson as "a most interesting and persuasive case … the facts of which closely parallel the present case".[88] That case involved professional ballroom dancers who were featured on the cover of a ballroom record. The Australian court held in favour of the plaintiffs and disposed of the need for the common field of activity in this 1969 case.

---

[82] *Krouse v Chrysler Canada Ltd* [1973] 1 OR (2d) 255.

[83] See McCarthy and Schechter's Treaties (n 47).

[84] *Krouse v Chrysler Canada Ltd* [1972] 2 OR 133 at [41].

[85] *Routh v Webster* [1847] 50 ER 698; *Clark v Freeman* (1848) 50 ER 759; *Maxwell v Hogg* (1867) LR 2 Ch App 307; *Williams v Hodge* (1887) 4 TLR 175; *British Medical Association v Marsh* (1931) 48 RPC 565.

[86] *McCulloch v May* [1947] 2 All ER 845.

[87] *Henderson v Radio Corp Pty* [1969] RPC 218.

[88] *Krouse* (n 84) [55].

Justice Haines departed from the UK approach to a common field of activity in Krouse before the UK relaxed the misrepresentation requirement in *LegoSystems v Lemelstrich*.[89] Alternatively, one could suggest that Haines recognised the spirit of the doctrine of passing off in justifying a finding of confusion. However, he turned to the US right of publicity case of *Haelan Laboratories v Topps*, and cited the paragraphs that established the right.[90] He then noted that, "Once it is established that Krouse is in the business of being used in advertisements, it becomes apparent that either line of cases will support an award."[91]

The Krouse case was appealed. The appeal court acknowledged in paragraph 38 that, " … the common law does contemplate a concept in the law of torts which may be broadly classified as an appropriation of one's personality". In coming to this holding, the appeal court examined the English case of *Tolley v Fry*, where an amateur golfer successfully claimed defamation for the unauthorised use of his photograph in an advertisement for chocolate.[92] Justice of Appeal Estey distinguished the situation in Tolley and Krouse:

> … a prominent amateur golfer, recovered damages for the unauthorised use of his photograph in an advertisement by the defendant of its products which it was held would lead the public to believe that the plaintiff had been paid for this use of his image (when in fact he had not), with the result that his amateur standing, which was of considerable value to him, would be in jeopardy. The respondent Krouse is, of course, in a diametrically opposite position, namely, he is asserting the right to compensation for the use of his image by another for commercial purposes. While this case is of no assistance in the disposition of the issue herein arising, it does illustrate the extent to which customs of the community and commercial practices change so radically over a relatively short period of time, sometimes requiring modification on the application of recognized legal doctrines to meet these new circumstances.[93]

The appeal court then proceeded to highlight the US right of publicity cases as "a more imaginative basis for this type of action" before stating that "neither the courts of England [n]or of this country have as yet recognised such a right".[94] The Krouse appeal court reflected on the trial court's application of UK and Australian passing-off cases, namely *McCulloch v May* and *Henderson v Radio Corporation* respectively, before concluding that passing

89 *LegoSystems A/S v Lego M Lemelstrich* [1983] FSR 155.

90 Cited in *Krouse* (n 84) [59].

91 *Krouse* (n 84) [60].

92 *Krouse v Chrysler Canada Ltd* (1973) 13 CPR (2d) 28 at [26] citing *Tolley v JS Fry and Sons Limited* [1931] AC 333.

93 *Krouse* (n 82) [26].

94 ibid [28].

off was not applicable as the public would not think the product or the advertisement had been designed by the respondent, and there was no similar product of the respondent that was in competition with the appellant.[95] No false endorsement was found, but the court left open the possibility for passing off to be applied in this way as it was stated that

> [h]ad the respondent been depicted standing by or sitting in an automobile such an inference might arise, but I do not believe that a reasonable inference of endorsement or approval by the respondent of the applicants' products can be drawn from the presence of the respondent in the photograph included on one side of the Spotter.[96]

Despite the inapplicability of passing off, the court found that *Tolley v Fry* and the US right of publicity cases justified protecting the commercial value of persona.[97] There was little analysis suggesting that the court agreed with such protection and no reasoning as to why Canada would recognise it. In fact, the court seemed opposed to such an action and found little value in it, stating, "The danger of extending the law of torts to cover every such exposure in public not expressly authorized is obvious."[98] After holding that such a claim could exist, the judge denied Krouse's claim on reasoning more akin to passing off by referring to the absence of any endorsement. Tying the tort of appropriation of personality to false endorsement from the inception thus created a cause of action which added little since passing off, which is arguably a bit more onerous in terms of the goodwill and misrepresentation requirements, could address false endorsement.

A few years later in *Athans v Canadian Adventure Camps*, a water-skier successfully claimed against the unauthorised use of a drawing of him in a brochure advertising a summer camp.[99] Justice Henry held that

> [t]he commercial use of his representational image by the defendants without his consent constituted an invasion and pro tanto an impairment of his exclusive right to market his personality and this, in my opinion, constitutes an aspect of the tort of appropriation of personality.[100]

This holding was followed by a discussion that the camp had attempted to get Mr Athan's endorsement. While it was not as focussed on this endorsement

---

95 ibid [29]–[31].
96 ibid [34].
97 Krouse (n 82) [37]–[38].
98 ibid [42].
99 *Athans v Canadian Adventure Camps Ltd* [1977] 17 OR (2d) 425.
100 ibid [28].

element as Krouse, the later case of *Gould Estate v Stoddart Publishing Co.* echoed Krouse as "the tort of appropriation of personality is restricted to endorsement-type situations".[101]

The risk of restricting the tort of appropriation of personality to endorsement-type situations is that people who have publicly renounced marijuana consumption would have difficulty bringing a claim. However, subsequent cases have moved away from the emphasis on endorsement, resulting in the tort of appropriation of personality being similar to the right of publicity. In *Joseph v Daniels*, the use of a photograph of a bodybuilder's torso was examined, and the court confirmed that the tort of appropriation of personality existed.[102] There was no mention of false endorsement. More recently, in *Hay v Platinum Equities*, a professional chartered accountant was found to have had his right violated despite not being a celebrity, and no mention was made of endorsement: "despite the lack of 'celebrity' of the plaintiffs, the tort of appropriation of personality has been made out. A professional's name and reputation is entitled to be protected from unauthorised commercial exploitation every bit as much as a celebrity's name and likeness."[103] However, it should be noted that the act of including the accountant's name on review engagement reports in support of financing is an endorsement in the traditional sense of the word when dealing with financial institutions.

In terms of using persona in the commercialisation of marijuana, the tort of appropriation of personality in its current form will provide a clear avenue for redress when it is likely that the public would believe that the celebrity has agreed to the association. There is less helpful precedent to support that unwanted associations would fall squarely within the tort of appropriation of personality since no case has articulated this. Rather, cases have moved away from false endorsement without explicitly distinguishing the scope of the tort from passing off. Yet, this developmental move indicates that even associations that the public would not believe to be approved could be redressed under the tort of appropriation of personality. However, the stronger avenue for redress is the Cannabis Act as it would be a violation for a company to include a celebrity's persona in promotion. The criminal penalties of this Act should be a deterrent against unauthorised use as, in addition to the penalties, the renewal of a licence can be refused if the Act was breached within the ten years preceding the application for renewal.[104]

---

101 *Gould Estate v Stoddart Publishing Co* [1996] 30 OR (3d) 520.

102 *Joseph v Daniels* [1986] 11 CPR (3d) 544.

103 *Hay v Platinum Equities* [1202] ABQA 24 [73].

104 Cannabis Act 2018 62(7)(c).

5.6 JAMAICA

Contrary to popular belief, marijuana is not legal in Jamaica. It was partially decriminalised in 2015 under the Dangerous Drugs (Amendment) Act 2015. This Act allows for medical uses, research purposes, and religious purposes as a sacrament in adherence to the Rastafarian faith. There does not appear to be any legislation relating specifically to the advertising of marijuana. Rather, there is a general prohibition of advertising drugs under section 3(1) of the Jamaica Dangerous Drugs Regulations 1948. "Advertise" is not defined in the Regulations, so it is unclear as to what falls within this prohibition. Clarifying advertising is important because advertising the brand can be achieved without explicitly mentioning the sale of a drug. In any event, if an individual's persona is used without permission, the person can avail themselves of passing off and the tort of appropriation of personality.

The case of *Dino Michelle* is the first case in the Caribbean that dealt with the issue of personality rights, and interestingly, the plaintiff in this case is relevant to the topic at hand as it was the estate of the late Bob Marley. There was nearly no analysis of passing off before concluding that this action had occurred. In addition, the court decided to recognise a post-mortem right of publicity to further protect Marley's legacy:

> I hold, therefore, that Bob Marley, a celebrity of renown at home and abroad, had a right to the exclusive use of his name and likeness or image. The right entitled him to exploit it commercially. He could, for instance, for a fee, license persons to use his name and likeness etc. for commercial gain. That right survived his death. The plaintiff is the assignee of that right in Jamaica. And as the statement of claim pleads, the plaintiff is invested with the proprietary right in the exclusive marketing for gain in Jamaica of the license to use his image, photograph, name, all indicia of his personality. In my judgment, the commercial use of Bob Marley's name and likeness or image by the defendant without the plaintiff's consent constitutes an invasion or impairment of the plaintiff's exclusive right as aforesaid resulting in damage to the plaintiff. Such conduct on the defendant's part constitutes the tort of appropriation of personality, separate and distinct from the tort of passing off.[105]

There has been little litigation concerning persona in Jamaica, but in 2010, in the case of *Georgia Messam v Clive Morris and Milton Williams*,[106] Justice Sykes confirmed that the tort of appropriation of personality existed and applied to non-celebrities as well. Unlike the development of the tort in Canada, it was clear from the outset that false endorsement is not a requirement for the tort, as there was no question of endorsement in either case. This lack of endorsement

---

105 *The Robert Marley Foundation* (n 39).

106 *Georgia Messam v Clive Morris and Milton Williams* [2010] 3 JJC 1901.

undermines the finding of passing off in the *Dino Michelle* case. However, it should be a warning to brands that any inclusion of celebrity persona could potentially be considered passing off, and if not, the broad tort of appropriation of personality will be used for redress in Jamaica.

The position of claimants in Jamaica is stronger than those in Canada because the existing law is not based on false endorsement. It is unclear how damages for mental distress might be treated because, similar to Canada, there have not been any cases that examined this. However, the objection to an association with marijuana would not be detrimental to a claim, unlike in the UK, where passing off is more confined and remains consumer-focussed. Given the cultural phenomenon of reggae music and the promotion of marijuana, it would be a strange choice for a Jamaican entity to associate with an individual who does not support marijuana. Rather, it is more likely that brands will want to draw on famous reggae artists. It should be clear, though, that using the image of Bob Marley would definitely attract litigation by the estate, and the court would not hesitate to deploy either avenue of protection. This precedent can easily be applied to the use of any other persona.

5.7 THE UNITED KINGDOM

Recreational marijuana use is illegal in the UK, while medical use is legal in limited circumstances.[107] Cannabidiol (CBD) as an isolated substance in its pure form is not a controlled substance under the Misuse of Drugs Act 1971 and Misuse of Drugs (Fees) Regulations 2010. This is because pure CBD does not contain controlled cannabinoids such as THC and THC-V. However, according to the Home Office "Drug Licencing Factsheet", a CBD product that contains controlled cannabinoids would be considered as controlled.

> It is our understanding that it is very difficult to isolate pure CBD, and in our experience many products in fact do not fully disclose their contents or provide a full spectrum analysis at an appropriate level of sensitivity to accurately and consistently determine their true content or control status.[108]

---

[107] "Cannabis Law in the UK" (*360 Business Law*, 1 June 2022) <https://www.360businesslaw.com/blog/cannabis-law-uk/> accessed 23 December 2023.

[108] "Drug Licensing Factsheet – Cannabis, CBD and Other Cannabinoids" (*Home Office*) <https://assets.publishing.service.gov.uk/media/5d56c5fae5274a075f04a102/factsheet-cannabis-cbd-and-cannabinoids-2019.pdf> accessed 22 December 2023, 3.

Additional regulatory oversight by the Medicines and Healthcare products Regulatory Agency is applicable for products that claim any medicinal benefit.[109]

The UK does not have a statutory right of publicity. Instead, celebrities must rely on passing off. Passing off was first applied to false endorsement in *Irvine v Talksport*, where race car driver Eddie Irvine's photograph was edited to appear that he was listening to Talksport radio.[110] This case established that the elements of passing off – goodwill, misrepresentation, and damage – must be made out for a successful claim. The more recent case of *Fenty v Arcadia* confirmed that passing off could also apply to the use of persona on merchandise.[111] In this case, a photograph of Rihanna was used on a T-shirt that was sold by TopShop. TopShop had secured the necessary copyright licence but had not obtained permission from Rihanna to use her image. The Appeal Court confirmed the High Court's holding of infringement.[112]

The main hurdle in bringing a claim of passing off for commercialisation of persona in connection with marijuana would be that the misrepresentation element might be difficult to prove due to the illegal status of the product. Consumers may not think that an individual consented to the use for an illegal product because such a contract would be illegal and thus void. There are two salient points from *Fenty v Arcadia* that indicate the problems that could arise when trying to claim for passing off in relation to the sale of marijuana. Firstly, the status of Topshop was assessed in determining misrepresentation. Topshop was a national retailer that often entered into licences for their products, even if they were not required to do so in the absence of a right of publicity. Justice Birss stated:

> I reject the claimants' suggestion that Topshop's customers think that any garment bearing an image of a famous person and on sale in Topshop will be authorised by that person. Nevertheless Topshop is not a market stall. It is a leading high street fashion retailer and purchasers would not be surprised to find goods on sale in Topshop which have been endorsed or approved by celebrities.[113]

Since marijuana cannot be legally sold for recreational use, the status of the seller as a potential defendant would be far removed from that of Topshop as a reputable entity that often contracts with celebrities. However, since the product itself is illegal, it is questionable whether circumstances that could

---

109 Fn (78).

110 *Irvine v Talksport* [2003] EWCA Civ 423.

111 *Fenty v Arcadia* [2013] EWHC 2310 (Ch).

112 *Fenty v Arcadia* [2015] EWCA Civ 3.

113 *Fenty v Arcadia* (n 111) [55].

be objected to by a celebrity would even arise, since dealers cannot openly advertise their goods. To purchase marijuana outside of exceptional medical circumstances requires knowledge that is somewhat guarded.[114]

Secondly, the nature of the photograph used was a point of discussion in the Fenty case.

> One of the debates was about whether the image on the T-shirt was flattering or not … I do not believe the question of whether this particular photograph of a young woman is flattering or not has much to do with the key issues I have to decide. Indeed if anything the less flattering the image the less likely it is that it would be thought to be authorised.[115]

While the image of the celebrity itself might be flattering in advertising the product, as rare as such advertising might be, it would be difficult to argue misrepresentation since consumers would not think that a celebrity had endorsed an illegal product. That being said, perhaps if the individual is known for marijuana consumption, there might be a greater likelihood of the court finding misrepresentation.

Due to the mainly illegal nature of marijuana in the UK, celebrities are unlikely to be faced with instances of unauthorised use for the purpose of advertising or selling marijuana products. One issue they might face is the inclusion of their face on a T-shirt or other items of clothing or accessories depicting support for marijuana. This would be difficult to pursue unless the T-shirt is sold by a reputable clothing brand akin to Topshop, and even then, the illegality of marijuana would probably still weigh against a finding of misrepresentation. Another issue could be the use of a deceased celebrity's persona. It is unclear as to whether passing off could protect deceased celebrities. A legal CBD shop opened in Soho in Covent Garden in 2019 under the name "Mr Nice". This is one of the aliases of the deceased drug trader, Howard Marks. According to the UK *Guardian*, "Mr Nice has the blessing of Mark's daughter Amber Marks."[116] The use of this alias is done by an international cannabis company, Equinox International. Such companies are likely to seek permission to use persona even where they are not required to do so,[117] so the

---

114 "How to Buy Weed in the UK" (*Hemp Elf*) <https://hempelf.com/blogs/news/how-to-buy-weed-in-the-uk> accessed 23 December 2023.

115 *Fenty v Arcadia* (n 111) [66].

116 Z Wood, "High Finance: Mr Nice 'Cannabis Lifestyle' Shop Opens in London" *Guardian* (16 May 2019) <https://www.theguardian.com/society/2019/may/16/high-finance-mr-nice-cannabis-lifestyle-shop-opens-in-london> accessed 23 December 2023.

117 Perot (n 3) 190–194.

absence of a right of publicity is unlikely to be detrimental where legal products are being sold by reputable entities.

5.8 CONCLUSION

The legal marijuana industry has expanded in recent years as several US states and Canada legalised recreational use. However, marijuana remains illegal in the UK with limited medical use exceptions. Jamaica has taken a broader decriminalisation approach, inter alia, recognising religious uses. In the unlikely event that persona is used without permission in the UK, passing off may be difficult to prove because of the illegality of the product.

That being said, the kinds of entities that sell illegal marijuana in the UK are likely to be difficult to pursue,[118] and would probably not be deterred by a civil law claim brought by a celebrity given that they are risking criminal law penalties. In contrast, in Jamaica, passing off would probably be easily made out as there was little analysis on the misrepresentation element in the foundational *Dino Michelle* case. In addition, there is the tort of appropriation of personality, which has broad application. In the US, the right of publicity is easily deployed against unauthorised use, which is important considering the disjointed approach to advertising. There is limited jurisprudence on damages for emotional distress, which may be sought if a person who does not want to be associated with marijuana brings a claim. But, the right of publicity is robust enough in its current form to pursue unauthorised use of persona, even if the focus is on the financial rather than reputational harm. Canada's advertising restrictions on marijuana are much stricter than the US as Canada prohibits endorsements and testimonials. As a result, unauthorised use of persona could result in a criminal penalty, even where a civil claim of passing off would be difficult in the absence of false endorsement. The tort of appropriation of personality has moved away from false endorsement in more recent iterations, bringing it closer to the US-style right of publicity and the Jamaican approach to appropriation, providing claimants with a viable cause of action. In conclusion, brands should seek permission to use persona in advertising marijuana due to both the legal requirement to do so in jurisdictions where sale is permitted, and because the best outcome can only be arrived at by collaborating with celebrities as discussed in the first section of this chapter.

---

[118] Perot (n 3) 144–146.

6. Packaging of cannabis: a regulatory overview

Enrico Bonadio and Akshita Rohatgi

6.1 INTRODUCTION

Design and stylistic elements are a standard way to attract consumers' attention to a particular product.[1] An established body of research proves that appealing designs and logos are a significant factor in encouraging customers to buy products.[2] Yet, in the case of addictive substances like cannabis, this appeal is especially hard to control. As decriminalisation and legalisation of the recreational and medical use of cannabis gradually grow across jurisdictions, regulators are trying to minimise the appeal of addictive substances. One way to achieve this end is to introduce regulations related to packaging. Research in the US and Canada shows that such measures have made cannabis less appealing and reduced the positive association of the product in consumers' minds.[3] As this chapter demonstrates, regulators of countries legalising cannabis are increasingly adopting such measures as a mechanism to limit its appeal by making packaging visually neutral, unattractive, and at the same time, informing people about the risks of consuming such products.

The measures analysed in this chapter are not very different from the rules related to packaging adopted by various countries to reduce tobacco consumption. For example, Australia was the first country in the world to adopt the so-called plain packaging of tobacco, with a law that entered into force in December 2012.[4] The UK, France, Ireland, Norway, and others rapidly

---

1 S Goodman, VL Rynard, M Iraniparast, D Hammond, "Influence of Package Colour, Branding and Health Warnings on Appeal and Perceived Harm of Cannabis Products among Respondents in Canada and the US" (2021) 153 Preventive Medicine 106788. <doi:10.1016/j.ypmed.2021.106788>.

2 ibid.

3 ibid.

4 Tobacco Plain Packaging Act 2011 <https://www.legislation.gov.au/Details/C2011A00148>.

followed this health policy option. This measure entails removing from the packaging all logos and other colourful elements that attract consumers' attention, with the obligation to display visible health warnings and images aimed at informing consumers about the devastating effects of tobacco consumption. The effect of this measure is that it significantly restricts the ability of tobacco manufacturers to use their registered trademarks and other trade dress elements on the pack. As a result, plain packaging rules have been challenged in different fora,[5] including at the World Trade Organization (WTO).[6] Yet, in all these disputes, the arguments brought by the challengers, focussing on an alleged violation of trademark rights and unlawful expropriation of a form of property (among other grounds), were all rejected. As cannabis is also a product that produces negative effects on human health, it is likely that any legal challenges to the measures analysed in this chapter would also be unsuccessful.

Against this background, the chapter is structured as follows. Section 6.2 highlights the cannabis packaging measures adopted by various US states, Canada, the Netherlands, and Uruguay. Section 6.3 then focusses more specifically on labelling and warning requirements in some US states, Canada, and Uruguay. Section 6.4 concludes that while these measures restrict the ability of cannabis producers to use brands on their packaging, governments have the right to introduce such requirements to protect citizens' health against addictive substances like cannabis.

---

[5] See, for example *Philip Morris Asia Limited v The Commonwealth of Australia*, UNCITRAL, PCA Case No. 2012–12 Australia; *JT International SA v Commonwealth of Australia*; *British American Tobacco Australasia Limited and others v Commonwealth of Australia* [2012] HCA 43 (*JTI/BATA v Commonwealth*).

[6] This is the challenge brought at the WTO against the Australian law on tobacco packaging, for an alleged violation of several provisions of the TRIPS Agreement and Paris Convention (including provisions protecting trademarks). See the WTO Panel Report, Australia – *Certain Measures Concerning Trademarks, Geographical Indications and Other Plain Packaging Requirements Applicable to Tobacco Products and Packaging*, WT/DS435/R; WT/DS441/R; WT/DS458/R; and WT/DS467/R (28 June 2018); Appellate Body Report, Australia – *Certain Measures Concerning Trademarks, Geographical Indications and Other Plain Packaging Requirements Applicable to Tobacco Products and Packaging*, WT/DS435/AB/R and WT/DS441/AB/R (9 June 2020). On these disputes see E Bonadio, "Bans and Restrictions on the Use of Trade Marks and Consumers' Health" (2014) 4 Intellectual Property Quarterly 323–342; E Bonadio, "How Big Tobacco is Losing the Fight to Stop Plain Packaging of Cigarettes" *The Conversation* (19 May 2016); E Bonadio, A Marsoof, "Logo? No Logo? The WTO Dispute on Plain Packaging of Tobacco, and Beyond" in C Geiger (ed.) *Research Handbook on Intellectual Property and Investment Law* (Edward Elgar 2020).

6.2 PACKAGING

A variety of packaging measures have been adopted by regulators in those jurisdictions which allow and regulate the production, distribution, and consumption of cannabis. Most of these rules aim at making the product less attractive by prohibiting the use of logos, colours, and other eye-catching elements, which are often protected by trademark law and other intellectual property (IP) laws. This section considers some provisions adopted in selected US states, Canada, the Netherlands, and Uruguay.

6.2.1 The United States

The US has taken several varying approaches to the regulation of the cannabis industry, instead of a uniform one across the country. The country does not have federal legislation on cannabis packaging. Some states have legalised the use of cannabis, while others still criminalise its possession. In 2014, Missouri joined a host of US states in legalising cannabis and became one of the first states to introduce extensive regulations for its packaging.[7] As of November 2023, Ohio became the twenty-fourth US state to legalise marijuana for adult recreational use.[8]

Massachusetts was the first state on the East Coast to legalise cannabis, but it prohibits using "bright colours", meaning colours that are "neon" in appearance, to appeal to minors.[9] The regulations do not explain what is meant by colours that are "neon" in appearance despite being critiqued for their vagueness at the drafting stage.[10] A clearer approach seems to be that of the state of

---

[7] R Rivas, "Missouri to be Testing Ground on Plain Packaging for Cannabis Products" *Missouri Independent* (22 June 2023) <https://missouriindependent.com/2023/06/22/missouri-to-be-testing-ground-on-plain-packaging-for-cannabis-products/> accessed 23 January 2024.

[8] JC Smyth, "Ohio Votes to Legalise Marijuana for Adult Recreational Use, Becoming 24th State to Do So" *AP News* (8 November 2023) accessed 29 January 2024.

[9] 935 CMR 500.105: Adult Use of Marijuana (USA) [hereinafter "Massachusetts Regulations"]; "Regulations" (Cannabis Control Commission Massachusetts) <https://masscannabiscontrol.com/public-documents/regulations/> accessed 22 January 2024; A Rodriguez CS, "Cannabis Plain Packaging Rules: Examples and Opportunities" (Regulatory Oversight, 12 September 2023) <https://www.regulatoryoversight.com/2023/08/cannabis-plain-packaging-rules-examples-and-opportunities/> accessed 23 January 2024.

[10] Draft Packaging Relevant Sections of Adult Use Statutes CAB, "Commonwealth of Massachusetts" (*Mass.gov*) <www.mass.gov/doc/draft

New York, which explicitly provides that colours that are bright and "neon" in appearance refer to any colour that consists of over 60 per cent saturation when listed only in terms of hue, saturation, and lightness.[11] New York state regulations contain design mandates to ensure child-resistant packaging via a prohibition on marketing to minors, along with colour, font, and image restrictions.[12] This state also has also a relatively unique requirement that the label must incorporate at least 25 per cent post-recycled consumer content, monitored by an annual report mechanism on implementation.[13]

The variances between different US states extend to how they conceptualise the required packaging. For instance, Connecticut's regulations mandate cannabis packaging to be entirely in one colour and without any embossing, debossing, hidden features, or graphics apart from the requisite labels.[14] In the case of edible cannabis, the regulations require packaging to be completely and uniformly white.[15] However, cannabis-based beverages may be in a single uniform colour other than white.[16] Similarly, regulations in New Jersey ask for packaging to be in a single colour. However, it contains different supporting requirements of opaque and light-resistant packaging.[17] New Jersey also allows logos or symbols up to 1 inch in length and height to be in a different colour.[18]

-packaging-relevant-sections-of-adult-use-statutes-cab> accessed 22 January 2024.

[11] Packaging, labelling, marketing, and advertising regulations (New York) (United States); "Packaging and Labelling & Marketing and Advertising Guidance for Adult-Use Licensees" (Office of Cannabis Management, updated 10 March 2012) <https://cannabis.ny.gov/system/files/documents/2023/03/packaginglabeling-and-marketingadvertising-guidance.pdf> accessed 22 January 2024, 3.

[12] ibid.

[13] ibid.

[14] Conn. Agencies Regs. § 21a-421j-32 (Packaging) Connecticut (USA); "CANNABIS REGULATION FACT SHEET" Home (*Network for Public Health Law*, 25 October 2022) <www.networkforphl.org/wp-content/uploads/2022/11/Packaging-Regulation.pdf> accessed 22 January 2024.

[15] N.J.S.A. 24:6I-35 (packaging) New Jersey (USA); "CANNABIS REGULATION FACT SHEET" Home (*Network for Public Health Law*, 25 October 2022) <www.networkforphl.org/wp-content/uploads/2022/11/Packaging-Regulation.pdf> accessed 22 January 2024.

[16] "Cannabis Plain Packaging Rules: Examples and Opportunities" (*Regulatory Oversight*, 12 September 2023) <https://www.regulatoryoversight.com/2023/08/cannabis-plain-packaging-rules-examples-and-opportunities/> accessed 23 January 2024.

[17] ibid.

[18] ibid.

Due to the vagueness of some regulations and definitions, especially in the design of packaging, many states adopt a policy of pre-approval. In the case of Massachusetts, the Cannabis Control Commission must pre-approve the packaging before sales and before implementing changes in approved packaging or labels for both recreational use and medical marijuana.[19] The applications for approval require pictures of the entire packaging and all labels.[20] Similarly, Oregon mandates pre-approval of cannabis packaging and labels before sale.[21] Oregon contains detailed regulations for the packaging of cannabis apart from requiring it to be plain and unattractive to minors. It contains no explicit requirements concerning the colour of the packaging or label; the state regulates the design elements of the label by requiring the font to be easy to read and in contrast with the label.[22] While the information could be in any font or size, it must be typed and legible with the font being at least 1/16 of an inch and in English.[23] Oregon then requires packages to be "child-proof", explained as packaging that is difficult for a child to open but easy for an adult.

Missouri legalised cannabis via a constitutional amendment in 2023.[24] Following the amendment, the state released packaging regulations for cannabis. The initial drafts of such regulations allowed only one colour on the label.[25] This was later changed to allow "limited colours" after pushback from some legislators, along with a concession to allow QR codes on the label to send consumers to the brand website for more information.[26] The packaging was required to be in a primary colour and could contain up to two logos or symbols in different colours. The 2023 amendment legalising cannabis also contained a provision that packaging for cannabis should not be made

---

19 395 CMR 500.104 (4)-(6), 500.105 Massachusetts (USA). 395 CMR 501.505 Massachusetts (USA).

20 ibid (7)(b)(1)–(2).

21 *Packaging and Labelling Guide for Medical and Recreational Marijuana – Version 5.0* (*oregon.gov*, July 2023) <www.oregon.gov/olcc/marijuana/Documents/Packaging_Labeling/PackagingandLabelingGuide.pdf> accessed 23 January 2024.

22 ibid.

23 ibid.

24 Missouri Const. amend. XIV § 2; "XIV Section 2" (Missouri Revisor of Statutes – Revised Statutes of Missouri, RSMo, Missouri Law, MO Law, Joint Committee on Legislative Research) <https://revisor.mo.gov/main/OneSection.aspx?section=XIV%20%20%202&constit=y> accessed 22 January 2024.

25 "Missouri will soon require 'plain packaging' for legal weed products so they don't appeal to kids" *KCUR – Kansas City News and NPR* <www.kcur.org/health/2023-06-25/legal-weed-missouri-recreational-marijuana-edibles-cannabis-packaging> accessed 22 January 2024.

26 ibid.

appealing to children.[27] Missouri regulations also prohibit any designs that use the shape or any part of the shape of a human, animal, or fruit, whether it is a realistic, artistic, caricaturist or cartoon version, as a measure to "child-proof" the package;[28] they also bar selling marijuana candy that may be confused with regular candies.[29] Yet, such regulations were criticised by the Missouri Cannabis Trade Association, which highlighted that companies invested millions in attractive, attention-grabbing packaging and advertising, and that these measures hurt business profitability. [30]

California has perhaps the most demanding requirements for child-resistant packaging.[31] A straightforward way to get packaging certified as "child-resistant" is to be approved as meeting the prescribed requirements under the Poison Prevention Packaging Act 1970.[32] Single-serving bottles of cannabis are child-resistant if they contain a pry-off, metal crown, and cork-style cap.[33] A single serving of cannabis intended for inhalation or that can be applied topically must be packaged in at least 4 millimetre-thick plastic without easy openings. Such servings may be child-resistant only until opened but must contain a warning that the package is not child-resistant after opening.[34]

California, Connecticut, and Maine add a condition of tamper-evident packaging for cannabis products. Such packaging is intended to make it evident if the packaging has been opened or tampered with before purchase. In the case of California, the packaging must be resealable if the product is for multiple uses to ensure that it remains child-resistant throughout its life cycle.[35] In addition to tamper-evident packaging, California also disallows packaging with bright colours or cartoons to keep them child-resistant.

---

27 ibid.

28 *Regulatory Oversight* (n 16).

29 *KCUR* (n 25).

30 ibid.

31 *Network for Public Health Law* (n 14).

32 Poison Prevention Packaging Act 1970, 16 CFR 1700 California (USA).

33 4 CCR § 17412 (Child Resistant Standards) California (USA).

34 ibid.

35 "Packaging Requirements – Cannabis and Cannabis Products" Home (*California Department of Public Health*) <www.cdph.ca.gov/programs/ceh/dfdcs/mcsb/cdph%20document%20library/packagingchecklist.pdf> accessed 23 January 2024.

6.2.2 Canada

In 2018, Canada enacted the Cannabis Act to legalise recreational cannabis while simultaneously introducing packaging rules.[36] According to the Cannabis Act and Cannabis Regulations, cannabis packaging should have a single uniform colour.[37] This colour must contrast with the yellow of a mandated health warning on the label and the red of the standard cannabis symbol, and it must be the same for one surface but may be different for interior and exterior surfaces. The wrapper colour cannot be fluorescent or metallic for containers. The container coverings are required to be transparent and colourless. However, metallic colours are allowed if the surface is made of metal and is not on the label or image. Any depiction of people, characters, or animals, whether real or fictional, is barred. No inserts or leaflets are allowed.[38] The package cannot contain any testimonials, endorsements, or brand elements conveying glamour, excitement, vitality, daring, or recreation.[39] The packaging should have a smooth texture and not contain any stylistic elements like raised features, embossing, engravings, or decorative ridges in wrappers. Any features necessary for the assistance of visually impaired people are exempted from this requirement.

6.2.3 The Netherlands

For many years, the Netherlands tolerated the production, sale, and consumption of cannabis.[40] After years of tolerance, it introduced the Regulated Cannabis Experiment starting in 2021 for four years, where several designated municipalities would be permitted to sell cannabis in accordance with pre-

---

[36] Cannabis Act (SC 2018, c 16) (Canada) [hereinafter "Cannabis Act of Canada"].

[37] Cannabis Act of Canada, Schedule 3 (Canada); "Packaging and Labelling Guide for Cannabis Products" (*Canada.ca*) <www.canada.ca/en/health-canada/services/cannabis-regulations-licensed-producers/packaging-labelling-guide-cannabis-products/guide.html> accessed 23 January 2024.

[38] Cannabis Act (n 36) 26(e) and 27(e).

[39] ibid.

[40] See Chapter 11 in this volume, authored by Lotte Anemaet. On the Dutch scenario, see also JA Knottnerus, T Blom, SV Eerden, JHH Mans, DV Mheen, JNDD Neeling, DCL Schelfhout, JC Seidell, AHV Wijk, CGKV Wingerde, WVD Brink, "Cannabis Policy in The Netherlands: Rationale and Design of an Experiment with a Controlled Legal ('Closed') Cannabis Supply Chain" [2022] 129 Health Policy 104699 <http://dx.doi.org/10.1016/j.healthpol.2022.12.007> accessed 23 January 2024.

scribed regulations. In order to limit the appeal of visual cannabis products under the experiment, Dutch law allows only "unattractive" cannabis packaging with transparent wrappers or wrappers in one unique colour.[41] Once a colour has been decided, sellers cannot change the packaging while the Regulated Cannabis Experiment is ongoing.[42] Labelling requirements are less comprehensive. Experimental regulations provide that the label must take up at least 30 per cent of the packaging. Additionally, the wording must be in black and in Helvetica font, including only the brand name, cigarette type, and health warning.[43]

6.2.4 Uruguay

Uruguay introduced a law legalising cannabis in 2013 with the aim to control its black market for drugs, becoming the first country to formally legalise this product for recreational use. After a delay of four years, in 2017, legalisation was finally implemented.[44] It adopted a light-touch approach to packaging regulations, allowing packages in blue and white without any branding.[45]

6.3 LABELLING AND WARNINGS

Accurate labels and warnings are essential in ensuring consumer trust in any product. This is even more pertinent when it comes to controversial products like cannabis. A major reason for the distrust of cannabis products is a fear of overuse and addiction. Communicating accurate information about the proper method and dosage to consume can help alleviate this distrust and encourage consumers to make informed decisions. Research shows that those who purchase cannabis from legal sources have a higher likelihood of noticing warnings than those who purchase it from illegal sources.[46] Compulsory warnings are expected to increase exposure to and communication of the health risks of

---

41 ibid.

42 ibid.

43 Knottnerus et al. (n 40).

44 "Ley 19.172" (in Spanish). *Parliament of Uruguay* <http://archivo.presidencia.gub.uy/sci/leyes/2013/12/cons_min_803.pdf> accessed 21 September 2014.

45 Moodie, Crawford, "Plain Tobacco Packaging: Progress, Challenges, Learning and Opportunities" (2022) 31(2) Tobacco Control 263–271 <doi:10.1136/tobaccocontrol-2021-056559>.

46 S Goodman, D Hammond, "Noticing of Cannabis Health Warning Labels in Canada and the US" [2021] 41(7–8) Health Promotion and Chronic Disease Prevention in Canada: Research, Policy and Practice 201–210. <https://doi.org/10.24095/hpcdp.41.7/8.01>.

cannabis.[47] The next section summarises the rules on cannabis-related labelling and warnings adopted by various jurisdictions, namely the US, Canada, and Uruguay.

6.3.1 The United States

Similar to regulations on the design of packaging, the US takes different approaches to regulate the labelling of cannabis products in different states.[48] Basic requirements for most states include a depiction of the cannabinoid profile and standard warnings. In the case of Alaska, labelling mandates include the total estimated amount of THC (tetrahydrocannabinol, the main psychoactive constituent of the plant).[49] It also requires several warnings, including that marijuana is intoxicating and may be addictive. Other warnings state that marijuana impairs coordination, concentration, and judgement, contains health risks, and should not be used by those under 21 or women who are pregnant or breastfeeding.[50] Alaska includes some less common requirements like disclosure of the soil amendments, fertilisers, and other crop production aids like pesticides, herbicides, and fungicides used.[51] Regulations also mandate a mention of the names of licenced marijuana testing facilities and the results of such tests.[52]

California's compliance requirements for packaging are among the most extensive. All label information must be in English, unobstructed, and conspicuous.[53] California law mandates that cannabis packaging can neither

---

47 ibid.

48 Ariz. Admin. Code § 9-17-317.01 Section R9-17-317.01 Analysis of Medical Marijuana or a Marijuana Product, Ariz, effective 10/1/2023; Title 9, Chapter 17. Department of Health Services Medical Marijuana Program, Arizona (USA); "Cannabis Labelling Requirements by State – A Quick Reference Listing" (*Weber Packaging*) <www.weberpackaging.com/pdfs/Cannabis%20Laws%20by%20State.pdf> accessed 23 January 2024.

49 3 AAC 306.345. Marijuana Regulations, Department of Commerce, Community, and Economic Development Alaska (USA) <www.commerce.alaska.gov/web/Portals/9/pub/MCB/StatutesAndRegulations/3AAC306.pdf> accessed 23 January 2024; "Marijuana Regulations, Board of Alcoholic Beverage Control" (*Department of Commerce, Community, and Economic Development*) <www.commerce.alaska.gov/web/amco/MarijuanaRegulations.aspx> accessed 23 January 2024.

50 ibid.

51 ibid.

52 ibid.

53 Department of Cannabis Control, Medicinal and Adult-Use Commercial Cannabis Regulations, California Code of Regulations; Cal. Code Regs., tit. 4, Div.

make health claims nor use the word "organic" on its packages.[54] Moreover, no county should be mentioned on packages unless the plant was grown and sourced in its entirety from that particular county.[55] The package's informational panel must be in a size not lower than six points and proportional to the size of the primary panel and container.[56] The panel should list the name of the licenced manufacturer of the product and their number or website.[57] In case the product exceeds the level allowed for recreational use, the package must contain the statement "For Medical Use Only" in uppercase.[58] The date of packaging for retail sale must be mentioned, along with the Unique Identification code, batch, and lot number.[59]

Also, under Californian law, all product ingredients, including those containing allergens, should be listed on the pack in descending order of weight and volume.[60] In case the product contains sub-ingredients, the list can include its common name and a parenthetical listing of sub-ingredients in a similar order as the others or list them as individual ingredients.[61] If the cannabis product contains ingredients, colours, or incidental additives with a major food allergen, it shall list such allergens preceded by the word "contains", also conforming with food allergen labelling requirements in other statutes.[62] Artificial colourings used in the product must also be mentioned on the label.[63] The requirement does not apply in the case of flavouring, to which other federal requirements apply.[64] For edible products, the amount of sodium, sugar, carbohydrates, and total fat per serving in grammes or milligrammes must be expressed on the label.[65] If applicable, statements saying, "KEEP REFRIGERATED" or "REFRIGERATE AFTER OPENING" must also be mentioned.[66] Most importantly, under Californian law, the packaging needs a

---

19, § 17402 [hereinafter "California Regulations"]; "Requirements for Cannabis Goods" (*Department of Cannabis Control*) <https://cannabis.ca.gov/licensees/requirements-cannabis-goods/#:~:text=Download%20the%20universal%20symbol,by%20%C2%BD%20inch%20in%20size> accessed 23 January 2024.

54 California Regulations (n 53) § 17408.

55 ibid.

56 ibid.

57 ibid § 17406.

58 ibid.

59 ibid.

60 ibid.

61 ibid.

62 ibid.

63 ibid.

64 ibid.

65 ibid.

66 ibid.

section on instructions for use, including the method of consumption or application and information about any preparation needed before use.[67] The label may contain more information unless such information violates regulations. Listing of ingredients may be communicated through supplemental labelling like package inserts, fold-outs, booklet labels, or hanging tags.[68]

Californian law also requires the cannabinoid content to be detailed on the primary information panel on the outermost packaging and not to obscure any other label information.[69] In the case of manufactured products, content may either be included in the label before release to the distributor or added to the label at the distribution premises after issuance of a regulatory compliance testing certificate under regulations.[70] THC and CBD (Cannabidiol, the active principle of the plant that is not addictive) content in each package or serving must be expressed in milligrammes per package and per serving.[71] Especially in the case of edible products or cannabis concentrate, when manufacturers establish serving designations, the THC and CBD concentrate should also be expressed in servings.[72] Topical cannabis or those without serving designations may express cannabinoids as THC and CBD concentrate per package,[73] and non-manufactured cannabis goods can express the total THC content as percentages.[74] Packages or infused pre-rolls of cannabis products may be labelled with the cannabinoid content in milligrammes or express the cannabinoid content of the dried flower as a percentage and the added cannabinoid content in milligrammes.[75] Cannabis-based products are tested by designated labs, which issue a Certificate of Analysis to indicate whether the product has passed or failed their safety requirements.[76] Cannabis goods labelled at distribution premises after issuance of a Certificate of Analysis should reflect the amount in the certificate, rounding it off to the nearest whole number, but the amount cannot be greater than the allowable THC limits.[77]

---

[67] ibid.

[68] ibid.

[69] ibid.

[70] ibid.

[71] ibid.

[72] ibid.

[73] ibid §17407. Topical Cannabis refers to cannabis products that can be applied directly to the skin. See L Mnekin, L Ripoll, "Topical Use of Cannabis sativa L. Biochemicals. Cosmetics" [2021] 8(3) 85. <https://doi.org/10.3390/cosmetics8030085>.

[74] ibid §15717.

[75] ibid.

[76] ibid.

[77] ibid.

Californian law also provides that the package must have a "universal" cannabis symbol.[78] The prescribed government-mandated warning should be indicated in uppercase, informing buyers that the package contains cannabis, which is a Schedule I controlled substance. The warning should include a statement that the product should be kept out of reach of children and animals. Adults may partake only if they are 21 years or over or if they are qualified patients. The product's effects may be delayed up to two hours, may cause an adverse effect on pregnant or breastfeeding people, and impair the ability to drive and operate machines. The warning statement also asks buyers to use "extreme caution" in dealing with the product.[79]

When it comes to marijuana provided by dispensaries, Arizona has introduced several provisions unique to medical marijuana. Arizonian regulations provide for labelling cannabis products with the dispensary's registration identification number and the registry identification number for the qualifying patient.[80] If the substance is not cultivated by the dispensary, the label must mention whether it was obtained from a qualifying patient, designated caregiver, or another dispensary.[81] In case a dispensary provides medical marijuana to a cannabis establishment or another dispensary, it must ensure that it is accompanied by laboratory testing results.[82] The amount, strain, and batch number, along with the date of manufacture, harvest, or sale of the medical marijuana, must be provided on the label.[83] Moreover, the form and weight of the product must be mentioned,[84] and if cannabis is part of an edible food product, the dispensary shall also include the total weight of the edible food product.[85] A list of all chemical additives, including non-organic pesticides or herbicides and other fertilisers used in the production packages, must be given.[86] The labelling must also contain the total THC, CBD, and other cannabinoids, the effects of which the dispensary makes a claim about.[87] Arizonian regulations also require the warning to include a statement about how the carcinogenicity in marijuana smoke may lead to an increased risk for cancer, tachycardia, hypertension, heart attack, and lung infection.[88]

---

78 ibid § 17406.

79 ibid.

80 9 AAC 17 Supp 23-3 R9-17-317 Arizona (USA).

81 ibid.

82 ibid.

83 ibid.

84 ibid.

85 ibid.

86 ibid.

87 ibid.

88 ibid.

Massachusetts has different regulations for the medical and recreational use of marijuana.[89] In terms of packaging of products, there is not much difference, except that the manufacturers and licensees responsible for appropriate packaging are different: the Marijuana Product Manufacturer in the case of recreational use marijuana and the Medical Marijuana Treatment Centre (MTCs) in the case of medical marijuana.[90] Massachusetts further divides marijuana into five categories for labelling regulation: marijuana not sold as a marijuana product, labelling of edibles, labelling of marijuana concentrates and extracts, labelling of marijuana-infused tinctures, topical or other non-edible marijuana-infused products, and repackaged marijuana.[91] Massachusetts mandates pre-approval for marijuana packaging and labelling to ensure that the submitted labelling complies with all the requisite regulations.[92] While requirements differ slightly in each category, the basic ones remain the same. The manufacturer or MTC shall firmly affix a legible label not less than 1/16 of an inch for each retail sale packet prior to any sale or transfer. The label shall contain information about the name, registration number, phone number, and email of the MTC or Marijuana Product Manufacturer, along with the retail licensee's business phone, email, and website information (if any).[93] The date of packaging and the name of the licensee performing the packaging must be mentioned.[94] Other basic information like the net weight or volume and batch number, sequential serial number, and barcode, if used, should be included in the labelling.[95] Under Massachusetts law, the package must also contain a cannabinoid profile, including THC and other cannabinoid levels, along with a seal and statement certifying testing for contaminants without adverse findings.[96] Additional requirements like delta-nine-tetrahydrocannabinol, thinning agents, and terpenes should be expressed when applicable.[97] Warnings under Massachusetts regulations also include a statement that the product is not US Food and Drug Administration (FDA)-approved and that the information on side effects is limited.[98]

---

[89] 935 CMR 500.105 Massachusetts (USA); 935 CMR 501.105 Massachusetts (USA).
[90] ibid.
[91] ibid.
[92] 935 CMR 500.105(7) Massachusetts (USA); 935 CMR 501.105(7) Massachusetts (USA).
[93] ibid.
[94] ibid.
[95] ibid.
[96] ibid.
[97] ibid.
[98] ibid.

While THC and CBD labelling is common across most jurisdictions, the law of the state of New York expressly mandates the terpene profile to be mentioned on the labelling. It also requires the product to be labelled with the lot's unique identifier, lot number, or barcode to determine the product's complete history of cultivation, manufacturing, processing, testing, distribution, or recall.[99] The New York state's warning provision is slightly different from other states in stating that cannabis effects may be delayed by four or more hours.[100] There is also an express prohibition against making any false or misleading claims or claims of health or therapeutic benefits.[101] New York regulations bar the use of the term "organic" in many phrases, as there is no organic standard for cannabis federally.[102] Apart from this, the terms "craft", "gluten-free", "kosher", and "vegan" cannot be used unless the applicable regulations are met.[103]

As an international commercial hub, the state of New York also expressly bars labelling that may cause reasonable consumer confusion of trademarks, marks, or labels that violate any federal trademark regulation.[104] In the case of recreational-use cannabis, falsely portraying the cannabis products as being authorised as medical cannabis or cannabinoid hemp and hemp extracts is prohibited.[105] The label may not depict any cannabis products or paraphernalia.[106] Promotion of overconsumption or price reductions and any discounts or coupons are also barred,[107] but this requirement does not prohibit any dispensary from lowering or otherwise altering the price.[108] Other special branding material should not find a place on the label unless it is authorised.[109] Additionally, the Office of Cannabis Management – the body tasked with the regulation of recreational and medical-use cannabis – may set out additional prohibitions for the labelling.[110]

Finally, the state of Connecticut requires additional warnings about physical and mental health problems, including rotating warnings about the use of cannabis creating mental health issues like anxiety, depression, stunted brain

99 ibid.
100 ibid.
101 ibid.
102 ibid.
103 ibid.
104 ibid.
105 ibid.
106 ibid.
107 ibid.
108 ibid.
109 ibid.
110 ibid.

development, and impaired memory over time.[111] The cannabinoid profile listing also differs from most of the other states. Chemotypes should be displayed in terms of the ratio of THC to CBD: “High THC, low CBD” means when the ratio is greater than five to one and total THC is at least 15 per cent.[112] Similarly, “moderate THC, moderate CBD” means the ratio is at least five to one and total THC is less than 15 per cent. “Low THC, high CBD” means the ratio is less than one to five, and total THC is not greater than 5 per cent.[113] A recommended use-by or expiration date must be mentioned on the package for all types.[114]

6.3.2 Canada

Canada was a frontrunner in coming up with comprehensive cannabis labelling requirements. Canadian law usually requires the label to be in English and French.[115] And the label should be clear, prominent, and legible.[116] The principal display panel on the principal display surface of the container must contain the standardised cannabis symbol, health warning messages, and the THC and CBD content. It should also include the brand name with a size not more than the health warning message, an additional brand element like a slogan or logo not larger than the cannabis symbol or health message, and the international radiation symbol, if applicable.[117] The manner of representation and requirements for cannabinoid content information depends on the category of cannabis in which the product is classified.[118] These classifications are dried or fresh cannabis, cannabis extract, cannabis topical, and edible cannabis.[119] In the case of cannabis extract and dried or fresh cannabis, labelling requirements also consider whether the unit is intended for inhalation or not.[120] The cannabinoid profiles should accurately reflect the values found in testing.

Other information about the product may be displayed either on the principal display panel or another exterior display surface. This information must be represented in black colour with a white background, in standard Sans Serif

111 Public Act No. 23-79 Connecticut (USA).
112 ibid.
113 ibid.
114 ibid.
115 Cannabis Regulations SOR/2018-144 (Canada).
116 ibid.
117 ibid 130–132.
118 ibid.
119 ibid.
120 ibid.

font, with at least a six-point type size.[121] Most requirements cut across different categories of cannabis. The most basic requirements are the class and lot number, along with the licence holder's name, phone, and email.[122] The packing date and recommended storage conditions, like humidity requirements, must be mentioned on the package.[123] Expiry dates mentioning the end date of stability, or the lack of determination thereof, are required for all forms of cannabis except edible ones.[124] Instead, the durable life date, or "best before" date, is applicable in the case of edible cannabis.[125] The list of bilingual symbols of months can be used to display the packaging and expiry date.[126] The net weight in grammes or volume in millilitres, calculated with reference to tolerance limits, must be mentioned.[127] The equivalence of cannabis in the package with dried cannabis must be given if the cannabis is not dried or a cannabis plant.[128]

The label should set out the number of discrete units of the product in the package, if applicable.[129] The common name of the product, like capsule or chocolate, should be given on the label.[130] The labelling should also provide for intended uses of the product, like inhalation or use on skin.[131] In the case of allergens or edible cannabis, sources of food allergens, gluten, or added sulphites must be mentioned clearly.[132] Similarly, a statement on the risk of cross-contamination resulting in food allergen or gluten should be mentioned, if applicable.[133] In the case of edible, extract, or topical cannabis, a complete list of ingredients and constituents must be accurately given on the label.[134] Edible cannabis products also require nutritional facts as set out in the directory of nutritional facts for edible cannabis.[135]

Canadian regulations also mandate a warning to keep cannabis out of the reach of children.[136] They also contain a general prohibition on associating

121 ibid.
122 Canada Cannabis Act (n 36) 123.
123 ibid.
124 ibid.
125 ibid 132.
126 ibid.
127 ibid 124, 125, 132.
128 ibid.
129 ibid.
130 ibid.
131 ibid.
132 ibid.
133 ibid.
134 ibid.
135 ibid.
136 ibid 123.

cannabis with tobacco products, vaping products, or any alcoholic beverage.[137] There should be no assertion or impression of health or cosmetic benefits unless cannabis is a health product. Additional prohibitions apply in the case of edible cannabis and cannabis extracts with respect to representations of nutrients and flavour.[138] False, misleading, or deceptive information, especially about the safety, effects, and health risks of the product, is prohibited.[139] Additionally, all containers need to display the required information. However, if a container is too small to fit information not mandated to be displayed on the principal display panel, an additional panel that is not easily removed under normal conditions and is resealable may be used to display such additional information.[140] Still, the label should include a statement about where the additional information is located and may also provide a black-and-white image instructing users how to open the panel.[141]

Licence holders must provide appropriate additional information, if needed, about the proper use of their product.[142] This may include directions for use, information about the form and formulation of the product, and other warnings or precautions.[143] Such additional information is allowed subject to compliance with the Cannabis Act and accompanying regulations. Other applicable Canadian regulations specific to the product also need to be complied with.[144]

6.3.3 Uruguay

Licenced companies cultivating non-medical cannabis for sale in pharmacies are responsible for the packaging of cannabis products.[145] The cannabis in pharmacies must display only necessary information like potency and consumption.[146] Recommendations for use, along with warnings, must be given on the front and back end of the product. Uruguay mandates two copies of

137 Canada Cannabis Regulations (n 115) 132 and 104.12(2).

138 ibid.

139 Canada Cannabis Act (n 36) 26(e) and 27(e).

140 ibid 132.

141 ibid.

142 Canada Cannabis Regulations (n 115) 130.

143 ibid.

144 "Packaging and Labelling Guide for Cannabis Products" (Canada) (n 37).

145 M Pardal, B Kilmer, S d'Auria, T Strabel, S Galimberti, S Hoorens, T Decorte, B Senator, *Alternatives to Profit-maximising Commercial Models of Cannabis Supply for Non-medical Use* (RAND Corporation 2023) <https://www.rand.org/pubs/research_reports/RRA2190-1.html>.

146 ibid.

original packaging labels in Spanish and English.[147] The regulation is overseen by the Institute for Regulation and Control of Cannabis.[148] However, in the case of Cannabis Social Clubs and home-grown cannabis, there are no packaging and labelling requirements.[149]

6.4 CONCLUSION

The measures analysed in this chapter aim predominantly at discouraging people from consuming cannabis, which is considered harmful to human health. The fact that they have been adopted in jurisdictions where cannabis has been legalised or is tolerated does not constitute a paradox; quite the contrary. As happens with tobacco, a product can remain legal while governments and parliaments have the right (and duty) to protect their citizens' health by obliging manufacturers to remove brands and eye-catching elements from the packaging and to introduce and make highly visible health warnings. The mantra is, therefore: we do not want to prohibit, but we want to discourage unhealthy behaviours by nudging consumers in the right direction.

There is no doubt that these measures have a negative impact on cannabis producers and distributors. They indeed restrict their ability to use packaging, trademarks, and other subject matter protected by various IP rights, including copyright, design, and passing off, as well as unfair competition rules. Yet, it is unlikely that any challenge against these measures under international and national IP regimes would be successful. Indeed, as mentioned in the introduction to this chapter, similar challenges against plain packaging of tobacco have failed.[150] It should also be noted that the measures in question are often based on scientific evidence which shows that exposure to brands and other attractive features of packaging may convince people who have never consumed those products to start doing so, or to make it harder for those who regularly use such products to quit. Such evidence has been taken into due consideration by the WTO adjudicators when ruling in favour of the Australian regime on plain packaging of tobacco.[151]

---

147 "Uruguay – Labelling/Marking Requirements" (*International Trade Administration*) <www.trade.gov/country-commercial-guides/uruguay-labeling-marking-requirements> accessed 25 January 2024.

148 M Cerdá, B Kilmer, "Uruguay's Middle-ground Approach to Cannabis Legalisation" (2017) 42 International Journal of Drug Policy 118–120, <http://dx.doi.org/10.1016/j.drugpo.2017.02.007> accessed 25 January 2024.

149 ibid.

150 WTO Panel Report, Australia (n 6).

151 ibid.

7. Protecting cannabis cultivars in the United States: utility patents, plant patents, and plant variety protection certificates

Larry Sandell

7.1 INTRODUCTION[1]

Even before the federal illegality of marijuana[2] is accounted for, the U.S. intellectual property (IP) protections for plants are an anomaly. There are three different but overlapping forms of protection: (i) utility patents, (ii) plant patents, and (iii) plant variety protection ("PVP") certificates. Each offers about 20 years of protection against infringement by others and each is enforceable in U.S. District Courts, but they diverge with respect to breadth of protection, statutory requirements – including those relating to biological deposits, and difficulty in securing exclusive rights. Contrasted with the availability of U.S. federal trademark protection in the cannabis industry, there is no "lawful use" requirement for utility patents or plant patents, all of which are examined and issued by the U.S. Patent and Trademark Office ("USPTO"). Still, the continued federal illegality of marijuana has the potential to complicate patent

[1] The author would like to thank the U.S. Plant Variety Protection Office; clients Steve Robinson of Robinsons of Maine, Lyndsey Shaw and Frank Haughton of Brighterside Canopy and Brighterside Operations, and Dr. Chanda Macias, PhD of National Holistic; his Mei & Mark colleagues Steven Liang Sun, Brian Su, and Robert Hall; and the editors of this ground-breaking book for their assistance and input in preparing this chapter. He would also like to thank his wife Nicole, and sons Shane, Justin, and Ryan for their love and support.

[2] Marijuana or *marihuana* is defined as any part of a *Cannabis sativa L* plant (except fibrous stalks) that is not *hemp* (21 U.S.C. § 802(16)). *Hemp* is defined as cannabis with <0.3 percent THC by dry weight (7 U.S.C. § 1639o(1)). *Cannabis* or *Cannabis sativa* L encompasses both marijuana and hemp.

enforcement efforts. PVP certificates, on the other hand, are issued by the U.S. Department of Agriculture ("USDA") and are strictly limited to legal crops. In effect, they are currently available for hemp, but not for marijuana.

Utility patent protection for plant and other living inventions may be relatively unusual among international jurisdictions but has readily fit within the U.S. patent system for decades, perhaps dating back to the late 1800s or even earlier.[3] In short, U.S. utility patent law has long considered biological material created by man patentable as a "composition of matter" or "an article of manufacture."[4] Thus, as long as other rigorous requirements for utility patents are met – often with the aid of biological depositions – plants are patentable as utility inventions in the U.S.

While many countries now permit the protection of plant varieties via protection certificates pursuant to the 1991 International Union for the Protection of Varieties of New Plants ("UPOV") Convention, or a similar framework, the U.S. patent system first provided IP protection to plant breeders, and the USPTO remains the only authority to provide such rights in the form of a plant patent. Plant patents provide their owners with "the right to exclude others from asexually reproducing the [patented] plant," and from importing, using, offering for sale, or selling such asexually reproduced plant or any of its parts.[5] While unavailable for plants that are tuber propagated or discovered in an uncultivated state, plant patents are otherwise obtainable by anyone who "invents or discovers and asexually reproduces any distinct and new variety of plant, including cultivated spores, mutants, hybrids, and newly found seedlings."[6]

The Plant Variety Protection Act ("PVPA") (1970) provides patent-like protections for breeders of Cannabis sativa L and other crops, including for seeds and asexually reproduced clones. Under the PVPA, the Plant Variety Protection Office ("PVPO") – which is part of the Agricultural Marketing

---

[3] *Application of Bergy*, 596 F2d 952, 985 (CCPA 1979) (noting that, in 1873, Louis Pasteur was issued US Patent 141,072 for "yeast," which was claimed "as an article of manufacture.")

[4] ibid; *Diamond v Chakrabarty,* 447 US 303, 309–310 (1980) ("human-made, genetically engineered bacterium" with a property "which is possessed by no naturally occurring bacteria" "plainly qualifies as patentable subject matter" because the patent claims are "not to a hitherto unknown natural phenomenon, but to a nonnaturally occurring manufacture or composition of matter – a product of human ingenuity having a distinctive name, character and use."); *see also* Manual of Patent Examining Procedure ("MPEP") § 2105(II)(A), USPTO <https://www.uspto.gov/web/offices/pac/mpep/> accessed 11 March 2024).

[5] 35 USC § 163.

[6] 35 USC § 161.

Service of the USDA[7] – examines PVP applications and issues PVP certificates to the owners of plant varieties that are distinct, uniform, stable, and appropriately named. A PVP certificate entitles the owner, subject to several exceptions, to exclusive rights to the plant variety for 20 years and the right to sue infringers in federal district court. While the PVPO accepts applications and has issued PVP certificates for more than a dozen hemp varieties since the passage of the 2018 Farm Bill, cannabis varietals with greater than 0.3 percent delta-9 tetrahydrocannabinol ("THC") concentration levels – i.e., marijuana varietals – are not currently eligible for protection.

This chapter briefly addresses issues raised by the application of each of these different, but overlapping, forms of plant IP to cannabis and expands on how the cannabis industry to date has used these types of IP.

7.2 THE THREE PLANT IP PROTECTIONS AVAILABLE FOR CANNABIS SATIVA L

7.2.1 Utility Patents

To obtain a utility patent for a new cannabis plant invention, an applicant must meet the same statutory requirements that apply to any utility patent invention – regardless of whether the cannabis invention violates the Controlled Substances Act.[8] A patentable invention must be directed to statutory subject matter, novel and non-obvious in view of the prior art, and sufficiently disclosed.

Patentable Subject Matter: While "the distinction between living and inanimate things [is] not relevant for subject matter eligibility, ... living subject matter with markedly [different] characteristics from any found in nature" may be patented.[9] To assess if a cannabis plant invention is eligible subject matter, it is compared to its closest naturally occurring counterpart with respect to relevant characteristics, such as "biological or pharmacological functions," "functional and structural characteristics such as the shape, size color, and behavior," and genotype.[10] The hurdle is cleared if "there is a change in at least one characteristic as compared to the counterpart, and the change came about or was produced by the inventor's efforts or influences."[11]

---

[7] 7 CFR § 9.2.

[8] 21 USC Ch 13.

[9] MPEP § 2105(II)(A).

[10] MPEP § 2106.04(c)(II).

[11] MPEP § 2106.04(c)(II)(C).

Novelty[12] and Nonobviousness:[13] Utility patent claims must be novel (new) and nonobvious (akin to "inventive step") over the prior art.[14] Prior art includes patents,[15] publications,[16] public uses,[17] sales and offers for sale,[18] and any other public disclosure[19] before the patent application's effective filing date.[20] The U.S. provides a one-year grace period for public disclosures by the inventor.[21] The fact that a prior sale or public use of cannabis might have been illegal does not disqualify it from being prior art, but it is likely to mean that the USPTO is unaware of it.[22] Claim limitations reciting specific ranges, amounts, and proportions – which can be common in utility patent claims on Cannabis sativa L plants with respect to cannabinoid and terpene content – may be presumed obvious where claimed measurements overlap with those of the prior art, and even when they "do not overlap … but are merely close."[23] Such obviousness, however, may be rebutted where a claimed range is shown to be critical, that the prior art teaches away from it, that the prior art did not recognize the importance of the range, or that the prior art range is unreasonably expansive.[24]

Disclosure: Aside from the requirement that it conclude with its claims,[25] a cannabis utility patent's disclosure must meet three requirements: written description, enablement, and best mode.[26] "The essence of [the written description] requirement is that the patentee, 'as part of the bargain with the

---

12 35 USC § 102(a).

13 35 USC § 103.

14 The claims must also be sufficiently definite. 35 USC § 112(b); MPEP 2173 ("The primary purpose of this requirement of definiteness of claim language is to ensure that the scope of the claims is clear so the public is informed of the boundaries of what constitutes infringement of the patent.").

15 MPEP § 2152.02(a).

16 *See* MPEP § 2152.02(b), 2128 and 2128.01.

17 *See* MPEP § 2152.02(c).

18 *See* MPEP § 2152.02(d).

19 *See* MPEP § 2152.02(e).

20 35 USC § 102(a)(1); *see also* MPEP §§ 2152 and 2152.01.

21 35 USC § 102(b)(1)(A); MPEP §§ 2153.01 and 2153.01(a).

22 RR Esfahani, H Bromberg. "Marijuana and Patents: The Complicated Relationship between Patent Rights and the Federal Criminalization of Marijuana" 2022 50(3) AIPLA Quarterly Journal 365, 380–381.

23 MPEP § 2144.05(I).

24 MPEP § 2144.05(III).

25 35 USC § 112(b).

26 35 USC § 112(a); MPEP § 2161; e.g., *Monroe Truck Equip., Inc. v Universal Truck Equip., Inc.*, 120 F Supp 3d 884, 899 (WD Wis 2015), *clarified on denial of reconsideration*, No. 4-CV-49-JDP, 2015 WL 4715279 (WD Wis, Aug 7, 2015).

public, must describe his or her invention so that the public will know what it is and that he or she has truly made the claimed invention.'"[27]

The enablement requirement is met if the disclosure enables a person skilled in the art to produce and use the claimed plant invention "without undue experimentation."[28] Enablement, however, imposes challenges for cannabis plant and genetic code-based inventions because words and pictures alone are unlikely to permit one to make and use such claimed inventions.[29] Accordingly, the "deposit of biological organisms for public availability satisfies the enablement requirement for materials that are not amenable to written description or that constitute unique biological materials which cannot be duplicated."[30] Thus, the enablement requirement may condition cannabis plant patent issuance on the provision of biological deposits, and under the condition that those deposits will be made available to the public, viable, and capable of self-replication (at least indirectly) upon patent issuance and through the life of the patent.[31] For genetic code-based inventions, an applicant may (i)

---

[27] *Universal Truck Equip., Inc.* (n 26), (quoting *AbbVie Deutschland GmbH & Co., KG v Janssen Biotech, Inc.*, 759 F3d 1285, 1298 (Fed Cir 2014)).

[28] *MagSil Corp. v Hitachi Global Storage Technologies, Inc.*, 687 F3d 1377, 1380–1381 (Fed Cir 2012); *Alcon Rsch. Ltd. v Barr Labs, Inc.*, 745 F3d 1180, 1188 (Fed Cir 2014); MPEP §§ 2164, 2164.01; *See also* MPEP § 2164.07 I (indicating that if a claim fails to meet the utility requirement of 35 USC § 101 due to being "nonuseful or inoperative, then it necessarily fails to meet the how-to-use aspect of the enablement requirement"). The best mode requires that the patent "set forth the best mode contemplated by the inventor … of carrying out the invention," but is a hollow requirement because the applicant need not disclose any embodiment as its "best mode" and because the USPTO assumes this requirement is met absent evidence to the contrary (35 USC § 112(b); MPEP §§ 2165(III), 2165.03).

[29] MPEP § 2164.06(a)(II).

[30] *Ajinomoto Co. v Archer-Daniels-Midland Co.*, 228 F3d 1338, 1345–1346 (Fed Cir 2000).

[31] ibid (citing *In re Lundak*, 773 F2d 1216, 1220–1221, 227 USPQ 90, 93–94 (Fed Cir 1985)); *Enzo Biochem, Inc. v Gen-Probe Inc.*, 323 F3d 956, 965 (Fed Cir 2002) (noting that reference to a biological deposit can also meet the written description requirement); 37 CFR §§ 1.806–1.808; MPEP §§ 2410, 2410.01, 2409, 2403.01; *Summary of the Budapest Treaty on the International Recognition of the Deposit of Microorganisms for the Purposes of Patent Procedure*, WIPO (1977) <https://www.wipo.int/treaties/en/registration/budapest/summary_budapest.html>; *Budapest Treaty on the International Recognition of the Deposit of Microorganisms for the Purposes of Patent Procedure*, WIPO (1977) <https://www.wipo.int/treaties/en/registration/budapest/>; *WIPO-Administered Treaties: Contracting Parties > Budapest Treaty*, WIPO <https://www.wipo.int/wipolex/en/treaties/ShowResults?search_what=C&treaty_id=7> accessed 11 March 2024.

deposit biological material that is indirectly capable of replication, for example "viruses, phages, plasmids, symbionts, and replication defective cells,"[32] and/or (ii) provide a sequence listing to the USPTO.[33]

The 47 U.S. utility patents issued to date that are directed to cannabis or hemp plants (including genetic manipulations of such plants) have taken an average of two years and eight months from application filing to patent issuance.[34]

Utility patent owners may sue for infringement through civil actions in U.S. District Courts. Additionally, if infringing goods are imported into the U.S., patent holders may submit complaints to the U.S. International Trade Commission ("ITC"), a non-judicial federal agency, to launch an unfair import investigation regarding allegedly infringing goods and, correspondingly, obtain an order for U.S. Customs to bar their entry into the U.S.[35] Thus far, no suits have been filed for infringement of cannabis plant utility patents.

7.2.2 Plant Patents

Before applying for a plant patent, an applicant "must have asexually reproduced the [new cannabis] plant and observed the clones so produced for a sufficient amount of time to have concluded that the clones are identical to the parent plant in all characteristics."[36] Beyond this, the requirements to obtain

---

[32] MPEP § 2403.01.

[33] 37 CFR § 1.821–1.835; MPEP § 2412–2415.03; *See also* MPEP 2418, 2420 and 2422–2426 (addressing corresponding WIPO Standards).

[34] "Patent Public Search 3.0.9" (*USPTO*) <https://ppubs.uspto.gov/pubwebapp/> accessed 8 March 2024. To derive a set of qualifying patents, the author searched the USPTO database for issued patents with the following query: "(Cannabinoid$.clm. OR Cannabinoid$.ti. OR Cannabinoid$.AB. OR Cannabis$.clm. OR hemp$.clm. OR Cannabis$.ti. OR hemp$.ti. OR Cannabis$.AB. OR hemp$.AB.) AND (A01H5$.cpc. OR A01H6$.cpc. OR A01H5$.IPC. OR A01H6$.IPC. OR C12N$.IPC. OR C12P$.IPC. OR C07H$.IPC. OR C07K$.IPC. OR "PLT/236.1" OR "PLT/258") NOT PP*.did. AND (seed$.clm. OR plant$.clm.) AND (deposit$ OR "sequence listing" OR "SEQ ID")." Patents that were not directed to Cannabis sativa L plants or the genetic modification of cannabis plants were removed from consideration. Additionally, patents directed to the genetic modification of a broad swath of plant species were not included, even where "hemp" or "cannabis" was recited in the claims among the other plant types.

[35] 19 USC § 1337(a)(1)(B); *See also About Section 337* (*USITC*) <https://www.usitc.gov/intellectual_property/about_section_337.htm> accessed 11 March 2024.

[36] "General Information About 35 U.S.C. 161 Plant Patents" (USPTO) <https://www.uspto.gov/patents/basics/apply/plant-patent> accessed 11 March

plant patent protection for a cannabis plant largely parallel the requirements for utility patent protection, with several key differences discussed below.[37]

Patentable subject matter and claim: A plant patent may only claim an "asexually reproduce[d,] distinct and new variety of plant, including cultivated sports, mutants, hybrids, and newly found seedlings, other than a tuber propagated plant or a plant found in an uncultivated state."[38] It must include "a single claim" ... "in formal terms to the plant shown and described."[39] According to the USPTO, the following language would be exemplary: "A new and distinct variety of [Cannabis sativa L] plant, substantially as illustrated and described herein."[40]

Novelty and Nonobviousness: A plant patent's scope is narrowly limited to the "single plant, the plant shown and described in the specification" and its asexually reproduced progeny – that is, exact genetic copies.[41] Accordingly, provided that a cannabis plant was not asexually reproduced from a prior art plant, the novelty requirement is readily met.[42] Given plant patents' basis in asexual reproduction, the nonobviousness requirement is not meaningfully applicable and the USPTO appears to consider it as inherently met.[43]

Written Description: The requirement that a utility patent's disclosure "enable any person skilled in the art ... to make and use"[44] its invention is tempered for plant patents, where such disclosure need only be "as complete as reasonably possible."[45] Still, requirements for a plant patent's disclosure are detailed

---

2024; 37 CFR § 1.163(a).

37 35 USC §§ 161 ¶2, 162; 37 CFR § 1.161; MPEP § 1608.

38 35 USC § 161 ¶1.

39 37 CFR § 1.163 (c)(10); 35 USC § 162 ¶2.

40 MPEP § 1605.

41 *Imazio Nursery, Inc. v Dania Greenhouses*, 69 F3d 1560, 1568–1570 (Fed Cir 1995); *See also* MPEP § 2421.03.

42 ibid 1568–1570; e.g., *Miller v Eagle Mfg. Co.*, 151 US 186, 203 (1894) ("that which infringes if later, anticipates if earlier").

43 While at least one court in the 1970s attempted to grapple with the question of what obviousness might mean in the context of plant patents, no clear answers have emerged. *Yoder Bros. v California-Fla. Plant Corp.*, 537 F2d 1347, 1378–1379 (5th Cir 1976); W Lesser, "From Penury to Prodigal: Protection Creep for U.S. Plant Varieties" (2009) 14 Va JL & Tech 235; J Mueller, D Brean, "Overcoming the "Impossible Issue" of Nonobviousness in Design Patents" (2011) 99 Ky LJ 419, 523; S Locke, "Intellectual Property for the Botanist and the Plant Breeder: An Overview of Protection Afforded by Plant Patents and Plant Variety Protection Certificates" (2007) 6 Chi-Kent J Intell Prop 198, 202. *See* 35 USC § 161 ¶2.

44 35 USC § 112(a).

45 35 USC § 162 ¶1.

and specific.[46] It must include "a complete detailed description of the plant and the characteristics thereof that distinguish the same over related known varieties, and its antecedents, ... the origin or parentage," the physical location "and in what manner the variety of plant has been asexually reproduced," and a "positive statement that the clones or propagules of the claimed plant are identical to the original plant in all distinguishing characteristics so as to establish that the claimed plant is stable."[47] Such "reasonably complete botanical description" must provide "genus and species, habit of growth, cultivar name,[48] precocity (if applicable), botanical characteristics of plant structures (i.e. buds, bark, foliage, flowers, fruit, etc.), fertility (fecundity), [and] other characteristics which distinguish the plant such as resistance(s) to disease, drought, cold, dampness, etc., fragrance, coloration, regularity and time of bearing, quantity or quality of extracts, rooting ability, timing or duration of flowering season, etc."[49] – all "expressed in botanical terms in the general form followed in standard botanical textbooks or publications dealing with the varieties of the kind of plant involved."[50] Drawings or photographs that "disclose all the distinctive characteristics of the plant capable of visual representation" are also required.[51]

There are also important differences in how the USPTO examines utility and plant patents.[52] First, a cannabis plant inventor pursuing a plant patent is given considerably more leeway in revising the written disclosure of a pending application. While a utility patent applicant who adds new disclosure after filing is likely to receive a "new matter" rejection, a plant patent applicant may add "additional description of the plant, or even a wholesale substitution of the original description so long as not totally inconsistent and unrelated to the

[46] 37 CFR § 1.163; MPEP § 1605; *See also General Information About 35 U.S.C. 161 Plant Patents* (USPTO) <https://www.uspto.gov/patents/basics/apply/plant-patent> accessed 11 March 2024.

[47] ibid.

[48] Applicants should be cautious about how they name their plant within the application and avoid using an actual or potential brand name because, as discussed above, the official varietal name is deemed generic per se and precludes trademark rights to it.

[49] USPTO (n 36) (punctuation added and capitalization modified).

[50] MPEP § 1605; *See also* USPTO (n 36).

[51] 37 CFR § 1.165(a); MPEP § 1606; USPTO <https://www.uspto.gov/web/offices/pac/mpep/s1606.html> accessed 11 March 2024.

[52] MPEP § 1608.

original description and photograph of the plant."[53] Without this flexibility, many initially inadequate plant patent applications could never issue.

Second, plant patent examiners have discretion to request that an applicant "furnish specimens of the plant, or its flower or fruit, in a quantity and at a time in its stage of growth as may be designated, for study and inspection."[54] However, the author has been unable to find any cannabis plant patent specimen requests. In view of the current federal illegality of marijuana, this appears to have enabled cannabis plant patents' issuance without subjecting applicants or their patent attorneys to criminal liability.

With respect to cannabis and hemp plant patents issued to date, and with the exception of the first cannabis plant patent filed in 2010 and issued in 2016 (discussed below), applications have taken between 8 and 34 months from application filing to issuance, with most taking between 12 and 24 months.[55]

Plant patent infringement includes asexually reproducing the plant without authorization, as well as unauthorized use, offering for sale, selling, or importing into the U.S. such a plant or any of its parts.[56] Although plant patents may be enforced in the same manner as utility patents, plant patent litigation is significantly less common than utility patent litigation, and no suits have yet been filed for infringement of cannabis plant patents.

7.2.3 Plant Variety Protection Certificates

Unlike plant and utility patents, PVP certificates are only available for federally legal plants: marijuana plant breeders must await a change in law. To obtain protection, a hemp plant varietal must be new, distinct, uniform, stable, and appropriately named.[57] Beyond these requirements, the owner of the varietal must be a resident of the U.S., another UPOV member state,[58] or a foreign

---

[53] MPEP § 1605 (citing 35 USC § 132 and *Jessel v Newland*, 195 USPQ 678, 684 (Dep Comm'r Pat 1977)).

[54] 37 CFR § 1.166; MPEP §§ 1607, 2403.02.

[55] "Patent Public Search 3.0.9" (*USPTO*) <https://ppubs.uspto.gov/pubwebapp/> accessed 19 February 2024). To derive a set of qualifying plant patents, the author searched the USPTO database for issued plant patents with the following query: "PP*.did. AND (Cannabis*.clm. OR hemp*.clm. OR Cannabis*.ti. OR hemp*.ti.)." Patents that were not directed to Cannabis sativa L plants or the genetic modification of cannabis plants were removed from consideration.

[56] 35 USC § 163.

[57] "PVPO Program Requirements" (*USDA*) <https://www.ams.usda.gov/services/plant-variety-protection/pvpo-requirements> accessed 11 March 2024.

[58] "Members of the International Union for the Protection of New Varieties of Plants" (*UPOV*) < https://www.upov.int/edocs/pubdocs/en/upov_pub_423.pdf>

nation that grants reciprocal plant varietal protection rights.[59] The applicant must also deposit (or maintain) sufficient germplasm specimens.

New: The PVPA's "new" requirement differs from patent law's "novelty" requirement in several notable ways. First, the PVPA, consistent with the 1991 UPOV Convention, provides a four-year grace period for sales outside of the U.S., as opposed to the one-year grace period provided for an inventor's sales outside of the U.S. (and in the U.S.).[60] Second, U.S. patent law considers publications, public uses, and (unexecuted) offers for sale to be prior art; the PVPA considers only effectuated sales and actual provision of the varietal to third parties to preclude protection.[61] Given the significant amount of time required for field trials and that newness of a varietal is determined as of a PVP application's filing date, hemp breeders seeking PVP protection should avoid selling or distributing their varietal too early, especially in the U.S., lest the window to obtain PVP rights close.[62]

Distinct, Uniform, and Stable: To demonstrate DUS, field trials comparing the subject variety ("SV") to the most similar variety ("MSV") must be completed before application filing.[63] The MSV and SV should be of the same species and have similar morphological characteristics, especially for characteristics for which the SV is being selected.[64] Additionally, if the SV is a Genetically Modified Organism or cross-bred product line, the MSV should follow suit.[65] Field trials must comport with published UPOV Test Guidelines that provide crop-specific characteristics for measurement and visual assessment of DUS characteristics, as well as appropriate cultivation parameters; be conducted at the same location for two years or in two separate locations for one year; and reflect normal growing conditions for the relevant crop type.[66] The SV and MSV should be subjected to identical growing conditions to ensure that distinguishing characteristics result from genetic variation and not environmental factors.[67]

DUS is substantially documented in a PVP Application's Exhibit C. This "Objective Description of the Variety form … collects morphological,

---

accessed 2 February 2024.

59 7 CFR § 9.5(a); 7 USC § 2421.

60 cf 7 USC § 2402(a)(1)(B) *with* 35 USC § 102(b)(1).

61 cf 7 USC § 2402(a)(1) *with* 35 USC § 102(a)(1).

62 7 USC § 2402(a)(1).

63 "Guidelines for Demonstrating DUS" (*USDA*) <https://www.ams.usda.gov/services/plant-variety-protection/dus-guidelines> accessed 11 March 2024.

64 ibid.

65 ibid.

66 ibid.

67 ibid.

physiological, and other characteristics, and documents variety distinctness [and] is equivalent to the Table of Characteristics in the UPOV Test Guidelines."[68] Although the PVPO publishes Exhibit C for the most commonly protected crop types on its website, hemp is not among them.[69] The Hemp Exhibit C form is provided upon request; it corresponds to the table of characteristics from the UPOV Test Guidelines for Cannabis sativa L, but also requires express confirmation that the subject variety has less than 0.3 percent THC by dry weight to ensure that it is not marijuana.[70]

Appropriately named: Consistent with Article 20 of the UPOV Convention, PVP certificates are only issued when a varietal is properly named.[71] And, for most crops, a varietal's official name must be used for sales, even after the expiration of PVP rights.[72] A varietal's denomination must be unique and consist of a single, permanent name that remains consistent throughout the world.[73] These and other naming requirements ensure that a varietal's denomination does not cause confusion or mislead.[74]

Hemp breeders seeking PVP protection should be wary of trademark implications. Denominations are forbidden to undermine trademark rights of third parties.[75] Moreover, a "trademark by itself cannot be a variety name and a variety name cannot be trademarked."[76] Thus, while a trademarked term may

---

68 USDA (n 57); *See also* ST-470 <https://www.ams.usda.gov/sites/default/files/media/PVPOST470ApplicationWithExhibitsAndInstructions.pdf> at 5.

69 "PVPO Exhibit C Forms" *USDA* <https://www.ams.usda.gov/services/plant-variety-protection/pvpo-c-forms> accessed 11 March 2024.

70 ibid; email from PVPO Hemp Examiner David Chalkley on behalf of PVPO Commissioner Jeffery S. Haynes to Larry Sandell (20 February 2024); cf Form ST-470-113 (Exhibit C for Hemp) *with* "Cannabis Sativa L Guidelines for the Conduct of Tests for Distinctness, Uniformity and Stability" (*UPOV*, 26 October 2021) <https://www.upov.int/edocs/tgdocs/en/tg276.doc> accessed 15 March 2024.

71 7 USC § 2422(1); S*ee also* "Variety Naming" (*USDA*) <https://www.ams.usda.gov/services/plant-variety-protection/variety-names> accessed 11 March 2024; *Explanatory Notes on Variety Denominations under the UPOV Convention* (*UPOV*, 27 October 2023) https://www.upov.int/edocs/expndocs/en/upov_exn_den.pdf>.

72 7 USC § 2568(4); UPOV Conv Art 20(1)(a), (3), and (7); Variety Naming (n 70); *See also* 7 USC § 201.34(d).

73 UPOV Conv Art 20(2) and (5); "Seed Variety Name Clearance Program" (USDA) <https://www.ams.usda.gov/services/seed-testing/applying-for-variety> accessed 11 March 2024.

74 UPOV Conv Art 20(2); *See also* 7 CFR § 97.121.

75 UPOV Conv Art 20(4).

76 Variety Naming (n 71).

be used within a denomination, such use forfeits trademark rights "even if the name was originally arbitrary" because the formal denomination is "the generic name of the plant or seed by which such variety is known to the U.S. consumer."[77]

Germplasm requirement: The germplasm submission differs based on its type, but in all instances must include "material that is capable of self-replication."[78] For sexually reproduced hemp varietals, 3,000 viable seeds must be deposited at the National Laboratory for Genetic Resources Preservation ("NLGRP") in Colorado within three months of application filing.[79] For the first three years after the 2018 Farm Bill authorized asexually reproduced vegetative varietals (January 6, 2020 through January 6, 2023), no germplasm deposit was required provided that the applicant maintained their owned sample, declared where it was maintained, consented to PVPO inspection, and agreed to provide a sample within three months of a PVPO request.[80] Since then, the PVPO has readily granted indefinite "delay waivers" upon submission of a "Germplasm Deposit Waiver Form" until the "technical difficulties" in receiving and storing such specimens is resolved.[81]

With respect to hemp PVP certificates issued to date, applications have taken between 9 and 15 months from application filing to issuance, with most taking 11 or 12 months.[82] PVP protection for hemp varietals lasts for 20 years

---

77 *Trademark Manual of Examining Procedure*, TMEP § 1202.12 (USPTO, 20 October 2010) <https://www.uspto.gov/sites/default/files/documents/TM-TMEP-7th-edition.pdf> (citing *In re Pennington Seed Co.*, 466 F3d 1053, 80 USPQ2d 1758, 1761–1762 (Fed Cir 2006) and *Dixie Rose Nursery v Coe*, 131 F2d 446, 447, 55 USPQ 315, 316 (DC Cir 1942); Variety Naming (n 71); *See also* 7 USC § 2568(4) (requiring use of the formal name in marketing).

78 7 CFR § 97.7(a).

79 7 CFR § 97.7(b)(1), (d); USDA (n 57); "Deposit Germplasm" (USDA) <https://www.ars.usda.gov/plains-area/fort-collins-co/center-for-agricultural-resources-research/paagrpru/docs/plants/pages/deposit-germplasm/> accessed 11 March 2024; *PVP Voucher Seed Submission Protocol* (*USDA*) <https://www.ars.usda.gov/ARSUserFiles/30123030/Plants/StephanieGreeneFiles/PVP%20SEED%20VOUCHER%20DEPOSIT%20FORM.pdf> accessed 11 March 2024; ST-470 at 4.

80 7 CFR § 97.7(d)(3) and 97.7(d)(2(i)–(ii)).

81 Email from PVPO Hemp Examiner David Chalkley on behalf of PVPO Commissioner Jeffery S. Haynes to Larry Sandell (20 February 2024); USDA (n 56) ("Asexually Reproduced (Vegetative) Samples – Samples are to be maintained by the applicants themselves."); *See also* 7 CFR § 97.7(d).

82 This calculation was performed based on publicly available PVPO status data as of 19 February 2024. "PVPO Application Status" (*USDA*) <https://www

from certificate issuance.[83] Germplasm samples are made available to the public after certificate expiration.[84]

PVP certificates may be enforced in U.S. District Courts or the ITC.[85] However, PVP infringement lawsuits are relatively rare, with an average of less than one per year since the early 1980s.[86] Contrasted with patent infringement, PVP infringement has a similar scope,[87] but excludes private noncommercial use;[88] use and reproduction for plant breeding or bona fide research;[89] and sales of plant matter resulting from authorized cultivation for non-reproductive purposes (e.g., hemp fiber, hemp seed sold as a food product, etc.). Additionally, plants sold under a formal varietal denomination are presumed to infringe.[90] No suits have been filed for infringement of hemp PVP certificates.[91]

7.3 CURRENT USAGE AND STRATEGIES OF IP PROTECTIONS FOR THE CANNABIS PLANT

7.3.1 Utility Patents and Cannabis sativa L

7.3.1.1 Survey of issued cannabis plant utility patents

The USPTO has issued at least 47 utility patents directed to cannabis plants and cannabis plant genetics.[92] Of these, 22 are essentially directed to particular plant cultivars and supported by biological deposits of plant specimens,

---

.ams.usda.gov/sites/default/files/media/PVPOApplicationStatus.xlsx> (updated monthly).

[83] 7 USC § 2483(b).

[84] 7 CFR § 97.7 (h); *See also* "U.S. National Plant Germplasm System" (*USDA*) <https://npgsweb.ars-grin.gov/gringlobal/search.aspx> accessed 11 March 2024; "PVPO Frequently Asked Questions" (*USDA*) <https://www.ams.usda.gov/services/plant-variety-protection/pvpo-frequently-asked-questions> accessed 11 March 2024.

[85] 7 USC § 2561; 19 USC § 1337(a)(1)(A); *See also* "About Section 337" (*USITC*) <https://www.usitc.gov/intellectual_property/about_section_337.htm> accessed 11 March 2024. The author is unaware of any PVP-based Section 337 investigations having been filed.

[86] The author searched Westlaw for all case citations for §7 USC §2541, which defines PVP infringement: 43 opinions spanning 1982–2022 were returned, with many relating to the same litigations.

[87] 7 USC § 2543.

[88] 7 USC § 2541(e).

[89] 7 USC § 2544.

[90] 7 USC § 2563.

[91] ibid.

[92] Patent public search (n 34).

with the remainder directed to generic cannabis plants with specified genetic material inserted, genetic sequences to produce or enhance production of cannabinoids, or methods of breeding or testing cannabis based on the presence of specified genetic sequences.[93]

In May 2008, U.S. 9,035,130, the first issued cannabis plant utility patent, was filed by GW Pharmaceuticals (now Jazz Pharmaceuticals), the purveyor of Epidiolex®, an epilepsy treatment that was the first FDA-approved CBD-based drug.[94] The USPTO issued the patent in May 2015, and independent claims directed to the plant and a method of producing are provided below:

1. An inbred reference Cannabis sativa plant characterized in that it:
   a) comprises stalked glandular trichomes having small dull heads free of white trichomes;
   b) does not express cannabinoids; yet expresses a profile of entourage compounds quantitatively substantially similar to a profile of entourage compounds of a comparator Cannabis sativa plant which expresses cannabinoids from which it has been bred; and
   c) comprises a cannabinoid knock out factor or monogenic mutation that blocks cannabinoid biosynthesis in Cannabis sativa governing a reaction in the pathway towards the phenolic moieties olivetolic and divarinic acid, wherein the source of said cannabinoid knock out factor or monogenic mutation is Cannabis sativa industrial hemp cultivar USO-31 deposited as NCIMB Accession number 42357. …

18. A method of producing an inbred reference Cannabis sativa plant which comprises stalked glandular trichomes having small dull heads free of white trichomes and does not express cannabinoids yet generates a reference extract with a reference chemical profile which resembles that of a comparator plant less the cannabinoids comprising:
   a) selecting a plant which comprises a cannabinoid knock out factor or monogenic mutation that blocks cannabinoid biosynthesis in Cannabis sativa governing a reaction in the pathway towards the phenolic moieties olivetolic and divarinic acid, where the source of said cannabinoid knock out factor or monogenic mutation is Cannabis sativa industrial hemp cultivar USO-31 deposited as NCIMB Accession number 42357;
   b) selecting a therapeutically active comparator plant; and

---

[93] ibid.

[94] *Jazz Pharmaceuticals to Acquire GW Pharmaceuticals plc, Creating an Innovative, High-Growth, Global Biopharma Leader*, Press release (*Jazz Pharmaceuticals*, 3 February 2021) <https://investor.jazzpharma.com/news-releases/news-release-details/jazz-pharmaceuticals-acquire-gw-pharmaceuticals-plc-creating>; *FDA Approves First Drug Comprised of an Active Ingredient Derived from Marijuana to Treat Rare, Severe Forms of Epilepsy*, Press release (*FDA*, 25 June 2018) <https://www.fda.gov/news-events/press-announcements/fda-approves-first-drug-comprised-active-ingredient-derived-marijuana-treat-rare-severe-forms>.

c) crossing the plants from (a) and (b) to obtain F1 progeny and self-crossing the F1 progeny to obtain an F2 progeny which is selected for the characteristics comprising stalked glandular trichomes having small dull heads free of white trichomes and does not express cannabinoids.

The next six issued cannabis plant utility patents were filed with the USPTO between 2014 and 2017.[95] The Biotech Institute LLC owns five of these early cannabis utility patents, and they are all in the same patent family, claiming priority to at least one U.S. provisional patent filed in 2013. The disclosures of this patent family are massive, with nearly 250 columns of specification text, 19 sheets of figures, and references to biological deposits of cannabis cell cultures. The broadest claim from U.S. 9,095,554, the first of the Institute's plant utility patents to be issued, is provided below:

1. A hybrid cannabis plant, or an asexual clone of said hybrid cannabis plant, or a plant part, tissue, or cell thereof, which produces a female inflorescence, said inflorescence comprising:
   a) a BT/BD genotype;
   b) a terpene profile in which myrcene is not the dominant terpene;
   c) a terpene oil content greater than about 1.0% by weight; and
   d) a CBD content greater than 3%;

   wherein the terpene profile is defined as terpinolene, alpha phelladrene, beta ocimene, [carene], limonene, gamma terpinene, alpha pinene, alpha terpinene, beta pinene, fenchol, camphene, alpha terpineol, alpha humulene, beta caryophyllene, linalool, cary oxide, and myrcene, and wherein the terpene oil content is determined by the additive content of the terpenes in the terpene profile; and wherein the terpene contents and CBD content are measured by gas chromatography-flame ionization detection (GC-FID) and calculated based on dry weight of the inflorescence; wherein a representative sample of seed producing said plants has been deposited under NCIMB Nos. 42246, 42247, 42248, 42249, 42250, and 42254.

This claim stands out because multiple biological deposits – "one or more varieties of this invention" – are recited as "representative samples[s]" but the claim is not directed to any specific plant.[96] Accordingly, the claim language suggests that a broad swath of cannabis genomes might fall within its scope and thereby infringe. The Biotech Institute continues to extend this patent family, obtaining utility patents that claim priority back to the 2013 provisional application filings. For example, US 11,528,861, directed to cannabis extracts, was issued on December 20, 2022, and as of the publication of this chapter, a Continuation application remains pending, leaving the door open for more

95 Patent public search (n 34).

96 US Pat No 9,095,554, col 244, ll, 15–28 (filed 17 March 17 2014).

patent applications grounded in the extensive disclosure.[97] Accordingly, there is justifiable fear in the cannabis industry that the Biotech Institute may attempt to legally dominate the space once federal legalization occurs – for example, by extracting substantial patent license fees from a broad swath of the industry and filing infringement lawsuits against those who decline such licenses. Indeed, as early as 2017, cannabis industry participants have expressed worries that, allegedly, the Biotech Institute is "owned by a mysterious billionaire with an unclear agenda" and "all of the company's desired patents would be worth hundreds of millions of dollars and could eventually affect every marijuana strain currently being bred."[98]

The remaining cannabis plant utility patents issued to date and essentially directed to particular plant cultivars appear to be more narrowly drawn to their corresponding biological deposit. Several companies have been particularly active in this space, with Charlotte's Web, Inc. holding six such patents; GennCann, LLC holding three; and New West Genetics holding two.[99]

Of the 23 cannabis utility patents directed to a generic cannabis plant with a specified genetic insert or otherwise directed to cannabis genetics, seven are owned by Trait Biosciences, Inc. and claim priority to a provisional filed in January 2018.[100] As an example, US 10,724,048 entitled "Systems and methods for enhancing trichome formation and density in cannabis" is illustrative of such genetic engineering claims. Its sole independent claim is directed to a method and provides:

> 1. A method of increasing trichome formation in a plant comprising the steps: stably transforming a cannabinoid producing plant to express a heterologous polynucleotide sequence according to SEQ ID NO. 7, wherein expression of the heterologous polynucleotide sequence independently upregulates trichome formation and metabolic flux through the cannabinoid biosynthetic pathway in said cannabinoid producing plant; and
>   wherein said cannabinoid producing plant is Cannabis.

As another example of a cannabis plant utility patent directed to a generic cannabis plant with a specified genetic insert, US 10,400,222, titled "Desaturase

[97] US Pat App No 18/084,042, US Pat App Pub No 2023/0284578, titled "Extracts of CBD and THC." The company also obtained two unrelated utility patents, US 11317577 and US 11432488, directed to specific hemp cultivars in 2022 and may have additional patents pending.

[98] A Lewis, "The Great Pot Monopoly Mystery" (*GQ*, 23 August 2017) <https://www.gq.com/story/the-great-pot-monopoly-mystery>.

[99] Patent public search (n 34).

[100] ibid.

nucleic acids and polypeptides" is assigned to the University of York in the United Kingdom. This patent is a U.S. national phase of a PCT application that, in turn, claims priority to two December 2013 British applications, which makes it the first and (to date) only cannabis plant U.S. utility patent that claims foreign priority.[101] Its sole independent claim provides:

> 1. A modified Cannabis spp. plant generated by mutagenesis with a chemical mutagen or physical mutagen, comprising:
>
> a modified delta-12 desaturase gene comprising a termination codon at position 167 of SEQ ID NO: 3, resulting in a truncated and non-functional delta-12 desaturase polypeptide in the modified Cannabis spp. plant,
>
> wherein the modified delta-12 desaturase gene comprising a termination codon at position 167 of SEQ ID NO: 3 is homozygous, and
>
> wherein the modified plant has an oleic acid content of between 70–85% of the total oil content of the modified plant.

7.3.1.2 Enforcement of cannabis-related utility patents

To date, there have been no attempts to enforce any cannabis plant utility patents or any utility patents. Rather, the limited cannabis-related patent enforcement cases to date have been directed toward legal CBD products,[102] extraction technologies,[103] and vaporizer products.[104] To be sure, the federal illegality of marijuana and the exclusive jurisdiction of federal district courts to hear civil

---

[101] ibid.

[102] *United Cannabis Corporation v Pure Hemp Collective Inc.*, DCO-1-18-cv-01922 (D Co); *Canopy Growth Corporation v GW Pharmaceuticals plc*, WDTX-6-20-cv-01180 (WD Tex).

[103] *Gene Pool Technologies, Inc. v Coastal Harvest*, Case 5:21-cv-01328-JWH-SHK (CD Cal); *Gene Pool Technologies, Inc. v ANM, Inc.*, CDCA-2-21-cv-08756 (CD Cal); *ExtractionTek Sales LLC v Gene Pool Technologies, Inc.*, IPR2022-01011, IPR2022-00832, IPR2022-0625 (PTAB); *Canopy Growth Corporation v GW Pharmaceuticals plc*, WDTX-6-20-cv-01180 (filed 22 December 2020).

[104] *Certain Oil-Vaping Cartridges, Components Thereof, and Products Containing the Same* (Inv. No. 337-TA-1286) (ITC Investigation instituted 4 November 2021); *Shenzhen Smoore Technology Co., Ltd. v A&A Global Imports, Inc. d/b/a Marijuana Packaging*, CDCA-2-22-cv-08014 (CD Cal); *Shenzhen Smoore Technology Co., Ltd. v Next Level Ventures, LLC et al.*, CDCA-2-22-cv-07646 (CD Cal); *Shenzhen Smoore Technology Co., Ltd. v Greentank Technologies Corp.*, CDCA-2-22-cv-07638 (CD Cal); *Shenzhen Smoore Technology Co., Ltd. v The Calico Group Inc.*, CDCA-2-22-cv-07633 (CD Cal); *Certain Vaporizing Devices, Components Thereof, and Products Containing the Same* (Inv No 337-TA-1392) (ITC Investigation instituted 6 March 2024); *PAX Labs, Inc. v ALD Group Limited et al.*, CDCA-2-24-cv-00782 (CD Cal); *PAX Labs, Inc. v Stiiizy IP LLC et al.*, CDCA-2-24-cv-00788 (CD Cal).

actions regarding patents make patent enforcement awkward.[105] While one U.S. District Court has ruled that the illegality of an accused infringer's marijuana-based product does not deprive federal courts of jurisdiction to hear a patent case,[106] many questions remain. For example, it could be asked whether a federal court can award a reasonable royalty based on the accused infringer's illegal sales, or award a patent owner their lost illegal profits. Similarly, in view of the constitutionally based right to avoid self-incrimination,[107] can litigants refuse to give testimony or comply with interrogatory requests on the basis that they would implicate themselves in a marijuana-related federal crime?

7.3.1.3 Plant patents and Cannabis sativa L

On December 20, 2016, the USPTO issued US PP27,475 titled "Cannabis Plant Named 'Ecuadorian Sativa'" issued to the late cannabis author, activist, and expert Steven Kubby.[108] The application was filed on March 13, 2010, and received six office actions,[109] substantially all rejections of the "written description" due to inadequacies in the disclosure, even more amendments to the application, and even an inadvertent abandonment and subsequent revival before being allowed and issued.

To date, 41 plant patents directed to the Cannabis sativa L species, including hemp, have been issued, and their disclosures all appear to hew closely to the template established by Mr. Kubby's "Ecuadorian Sativa" and its extended examination by the USPTO. A review of a subset of the publicly available prosecution histories of these plant patents reveals that almost all rejections concerned the sufficiency of the "written description," and that cannabis plant patents are increasingly issued with fewer, if any, office actions. Other types of rejections are rare. For example, US PP31535, titled "Cannabis plant named 'Lemon Crush OG,'" received a rejection for lack of novelty after the USPTO Examiner discovered internet postings discussing the availability of "Lemon Crush" medical marijuana in 2010.[110] The rejection was easily overcome by an affidavit from the inventor explaining that although the name was the same, it

---

105 28 USC § 1338.

106 *Gene Pool Technologies, Inc. v Coastal Harvest*, Case 5:21-cv-01328-JWH-SHK, Dkt 101 (22 November 2022 Tr, 9–17) (CD Cal 4 January 2023).

107 *See McCarthy v Arndstein*, 266 US 34 (1924).

108 *See also* "Steve Kubby" (*Wikipedia*) <https://en.wikipedia.org/wiki/Steve_Kubby> accessed 11 March 2024.

109 "File History for U.S. Pat. App. No. 12/661,271, Cannabis plant named 'Ecuadorian Sativa'" (*USPTO Patent Center*) <https://patentcenter.uspto.gov/applications/12661271/ifw/docs?application=> accessed 20 March 2024.

110 "File History for U.S. Pat. App. No. 15/932,562, Cannabis plant named 'LEMON CRUSH OG'" Non-Final Office Action (*USPTO Patent Center*, 13

had to be a different cultivar because it predated the claims of "Lemon Crush OG" by seven years.[111]

Ten of the 41 cannabis plant patents are assigned to a single entity, the already mentioned Biotech Institute, and illustrate a technique that may be used to establish a cannabis plant portfolio. The applicant filed a single provisional application on December 18, 2017 (Ser. No. 62/596,591) that purported to disclose 43 distinct cannabis varietals.[112] The Biotech Institute filed eight plant patent applications claiming priority to the provisional within a year, and another as a continuation the year after. In this manner, the applicant was able to conserve resources while determining which varietals might be most valuable – presumably through competitions and sales to the cannabis-consuming public – while preserving the early priority date and, accordingly, the newness of each varietal pursuant to 35 U.S.C. § 102.

7.4 PVP CERTIFICATES AND CANNABIS SATIVA L

7.4.1 Hemp

On April 24, 2019, following the passage of the 2018 Farm Bill, the PVPO began accepting PVP applications for sexually reproduced hemp varieties, that is seeds[113] of Cannabis sativa L "with no more than 0.3% delta-9 tetrahydrocannabinol (THC) concentration level on a dry weight basis, as determined by using post-decarboxylation or other similarly reliable method (i.e., total THC, including THC acid)."[114] On January 6, 2020, the PVPO instituted final rules integrating the 2018 Farm Bill's incorporation of asexually reproduced

May 2019) https://patentcenter.uspto.gov/applications/15932562/ifw/docs?application=> accessed 20 March 2024.

[111] "File History for U.S. Pat. App. No. 15/932,562, Cannabis plant named 'LEMON CRUSH OG'" Affidavit of Steven Haba, 19 August 2019, Amendment and Response, 24 July 2019.

[112] "Continuity for U.S. Pat. App. No. 62/596,561, CANNABIS PLANTS" (*USPTO Patent Center*) <https://patentcenter.uspto.gov/applications/62596561/continuity?application=> accessed 11 March 2024).

[113] "USDA Now Accepting Applications of Seed-Propagated Hemp for Plant Variety Protection" (*USDA*) https://www.ams.usda.gov/content/usda-now-accepting-applications-seed-propagated-hemp-plant-variety-protection> accessed 11 March 2024.

[114] Email from PVPO Commissioner Jeffery S. Haynes to Larry Sandell (6 February 2024).

varietals into the PVPA.[115] That same day, the PVPO began accepting PVP applications for asexually reproduced hemp.[116]

In the interim period before the PVPO began accepting applications for asexually reproduced hemp, six PVP hemp seed applications were filed; four of these issued into PVP certificates, with the first issued on June 24, 2020.[117] Since January 6, 2020, sixteen additional hemp PVP applications were filed and ten have been issued as PVP certificates. Of these, five are asexually reproduced clones and four are seeds. To date, a majority of PVP applications have been filed by two entities: Arcadia Biosciences Inc. in California and New West Genetics in Colorado.

Currently, observed and analyzed Cannabis sativa L characteristics listed in the UPOV's table of characteristics – and correspondingly, the PVPO's Exhibit C form – pertain to embryo features (e.g., cotyledon shape and color, and hypocotyl and crown pigmentation intensity), mature leaf features (e.g., leaf and petiole color intensity, petiole length, central leaflet length and width, number of leaflets), reproductive features (e.g., coloring of male flowers, timing of male flowering; proportions of male, female and female plants; and THC content of inflorescence), mature stem features (e.g., internode length, thickness, pith in cross-section, depth of grooves, main stem coloration); and seed features (e.g., weight, color of testa, and marbling).[118] These identified characteristics appear directed to important and distinguishing features for industrial hemp, namely the plant's fibrous stalk, nutritious seeds, and reproductive characteristics.

---

115 *Regulations and Procedures under the Plant Variety Protection Act*, 85 FR 422 (*Federal Register*, 6 January 2020) <https://www.federalregister.gov/documents/2020/01/06/2019-27636/regulations-and-procedures-under-the-plant-variety-protection-act>; Pub L 115–334, 20 December 2018, 132 Stat. 4906; 7 USC §§ 2401(a)(1), 2402, 2541(a)(3), 2568.

116 Email from PVPO Commissioner Jeffery S. Haynes to Larry Sandell (6 February 2024).

117 "PVPO Application Status" (*USDA*) <https://www.ams.usda.gov/sites/default/files/media/PVPOApplicationStatus.xlsx> (updated monthly); "Plant Variety Protection Office – Scanned and Redacted Issued Certificates" (*USDA*) <https://apps.ams.usda.gov/CMS/> (click "hemp" to access PVP certificates).

118 "Guidelines for the Conduct of Tests for Distinctness, Uniformity and Stability" (*UPOV*, 26 October 2021) <https://www.upov.int/edocs/tgdocs/en/tg276.doc.>

7.4.2 Marijuana

As to high-THC Cannabis sativa L in the U.S., the PVPO will readily accept PVP applications once the anticipated federal legalization of "marihuana" in the U.S. becomes law; no regulatory change by the PVPO would be required.[119] At that time, other varietal characteristics of this unique plant species may gain importance. For example, psychoactive Cannabis sativa L varietals may demonstrate value and be rendered distinctive by their concentrations of various terpenes, Cannabidiol (CBD), Cannabigerol (CBG), and other cannabinoids in the female flowers and other plant components. Such concentrations may be ascertained at specified times in the cultivation cycle and, perhaps, in relation to common cultivation stresses, such as vertical stress and scrog stress.[120]

Indeed, to capture distinctive characteristics likely to correspond to commercial value in marijuana, future versions of the PVP Application Exhibit C form and the corresponding UPOV Guidelines for Cannabis sativa L may recite descriptors of trichomes, colas, buds, bud hairs, scents, and the like. For example, trichomes may be characterized by length, development structure – e.g., mushroom shape with long stems extending therefrom, straight stems with mushroom-shaped tops, long and squiggly stems with mushroom-shaped tops – and timing of transition to trichome development.[121] Colas may be objectively assessed by comparative height, width, density, and proportion of inflorescence versus leaf content. Buds may be characterized by color; trichome density; and structure or growth measures, such as box shape, cone shape, hair density, false finishes (e.g., visual indications of completed bud development followed by ripening or "creaturing"), and fox tail growth

[119] Email from PVPO Hemp Examiner David Chalkley on behalf of PVPO Commissioner Jeffery S. Haynes to Larry Sandell (20 February 2024).

[120] Email from Lyndsey Shaw and Frank Haughton to Larry Sandell (29 February 2024); ("Throughout the flowering cycle, [marijuana] plants are physically manipulated by bending and training their growth using netting and/or other outside materials to support and hold plant matter in place. This bending causes micro-breaks in the stalk, which send signals for rapid enzyme movement, thus generating increased cannabinoids, flavonoids, and terpene spikes. ... Measuring the effects of vertical and scrog stress can be performed through the following methods: gas chromatography coupled with tandem mass spectrometry (MS/MS) with liquid and headspace sampling; ultra-high-performance liquid chromatography (UHPLC) with UV-PDA detection and MS/MS; ICP-MS; Quantitative Polymerase Chain Reaction (qPCR); culture-based microbial analysis techniques; and microscopy.") (13 June 2024).

[121] Email from Lyndsey Shaw and Frank Haughton of Brigherside Farms to Larry Sandell (29 February 2024).

(e.g., light leakage, which may indicate instability or horticultural defects).[122] Additionally, marijuana bud hairs may be distinguished among varietals by length, thickness, and color.[123]

7.5 CONCLUSION

Cannabis breeders and genetic scientists seeking IP protections in the U.S. have three different, overlapping options at their disposal. Utility patents are often the most difficult, expensive, and time-consuming to obtain, but – as the mysterious billionaire behind the Biotech Institute undoubtedly appreciates – their scope can be wide and (sometimes) nebulous, providing powerful competitive advantages and emboldening lucrative, industry-wide patent licensing and enforcement campaigns. Plant patents narrowly protect from cloning prized cultivars and are relatively straightforward to prepare and prosecute in view of the increasing number of issued cannabis plant patents that may serve as templates. PVP certificates grant similar protections where the USDA's (and UPOV's) clear roadmap is followed, but also offer IP rights for seeds of stable strains. While, at the time of publication, only hemp – not marijuana – breeds are eligible for PVP protection, the U.S. Drug Enforcement Agency's May 2024 proposal to federally legalize marijuana for prescription-based medical use[124] suggests that this limitation may soon be removed. While it is unlikely that the floodgates of cannabis plant IP infringement litigation will open until full federal legalization of marijuana comes to pass, breeders who hope to protect and receive full value for their contributions to this future legal U.S. cannabis industry should act now to perfect their IP rights – and do so to the maximum extent that their resources and plant inventions permit.

---

122 ibid.

123 ibid.

124 "Notice of Proposed Rulemaking, Drug Enforcement Administration, Department of Justice, 89 FR 44597" (*Federal Register*, 21 May 2024) <https://www.federalregister.gov/documents/2024/05/21/2024-11137/schedules-of-controlled-substances-rescheduling-of-marijuana>.

PART III

Case studies

8. The development of an IP protection strategy for Jamaican cannabis

Natalie Corthésy

8.1 INTRODUCTION

It might seem strange that Jamaica, the birthplace of Bob Marley, the most globally recognised Jamaican icon and Rastafarian,[1] often portrayed as the place where there is "No Problem", has not legalized ganja, nor has it taken advantage of Jamaica's robust intellectual property regimes to protect ganja, cannabis, or hemp. Early efforts were concentrated on controlling and regulating the manufacture, sale, use, export, and import of cannabis as a dangerous drug pursuant to The Hague Convention 1912, the Geneva Convention (No.1) 1925, and the Geneva Convention (No.2) 1935, in respect of which Jamaica is a signatory.[2] Subsequent advances towards legislative tolerance of the cannabis industry have been made, notably the Dangerous Drugs (Amendment) Act 2015[3] (DDAA), which introduced a limited scope of decriminalisation, and is discussed below; and the successful first-ever legal exportation of pharmaceutical products with cannabis-derived THC, as well as hemp-derived CBD, by Pure Jamaican and Seven 10 Pharmaceuticals to the US, Brazil, and

[1] Note the significant investment made by Bob Marley's heirs in 2023 in the cannabis industry through the launch of Marley Natural dispensary, which not only relies on the name of the reggae superstar, but leverages the Bob Marley Museum as its flagship location at 56 Hope Road, as well as his image. Technically, Marley Natural is a licenced medicinal outlet and cannabis retailer of THC (tetrahydrocannabinol) products, including flower, pre-rolls, smoking accessories, and edibles, while CBD (cannabinoid) products span beverages, topicals, and confections. <https://www.marleynaturalshop.com> accessed 11 April 2024.

[2] Note Jamaica's succession on December 26, 1963 <https://treaties.un.org/pages/ViewDetailsIV.aspx?src=TREATY&mtdsg_no=VI-2&chapter=6&Temp=mtdsg4&clang=_en>.

[3] The Dangerous Drugs Act 1948 was amended in 1954, 1961, 1964, 1974, 1985, and 1987. This latest amendment entered into force on 15 April 2015.

other major international markets.[4] It can be inferred from the positive financial trend in the cannabis market internationally, that the economic climate is ripe for expansion and growth of Jamaica's cannabis industry.[5] This is evidenced by the efforts of the Cannabis Licensing Authority (CLA),[6] the success of international conferences on cannabis such as CANEX and Jacana 420, and the proliferation of (legal and illegal) smoke shops across the island. Arguably, this paradigm shift in the perception of the commerce around cannabis, and consumption of cannabis-derived products, represents a business opportunity that Jamaica's legislative framework is not suited to accommodate. At a time when no country in the world has yet registered a geographical indication for cannabis,[7] given the potential for the registration of GIs for Jamaica ganja, Jamaica cannabis, and Jamaica hemp, serious consideration must be given to adopting the necessary policies to remove existing legislative and administrative hurdles to conducting legal cannabis business in Jamaica, with Jamaican cannabis, within and without Jamaica.

Against this background, the chapter will consider the status quo and gaps in the legal and policy framework that underpin the cannabis industry in Jamaica, and whether increased use of IP protection mechanisms can provide

---

4 https://www.prnewswire.com/news-releases/pure-jamaican-through-its-pharmaceutical-division-seven-10-announces-the-acquisition-of-the-production-and-cultivation-assets-of-timeless-herbal-care-the-first-company-to-achieve-gmp-certification-for-medical-cannabis-productio-301449204.html.

5 Legal cannabis industry analyst Brightfield Group says that the US market is estimated to reach close to $32 billion in annual sales by the end of 2023, and top $50 billion by 2028: I Dorbian, "Despite Some Stumbles, Total Sales in U.S. Cannabis Market Could Soar to $50.7 Billion by 2028, Says Top Researcher" *Forbes* (15 February 2023) <https://www.forbes.com/sites/irisdorbian/2023/02/15/despite-some-stumbles-total-sales-in-us-cannabis-market-could-soar-to-507-billion-by-2028-says-top-researcher/?sh=3d8bee49164d> accessed 15 February 2023.

6 The CLA, since its establishment in 2016, regulates cannabis production from seed to sale for medical and research purposes only, and has issued 133 licences as of 7 December 2023, across five categories – cultivator (tier 1 for less than an acre, tier 2 for 2–5 acres, tier 3 for over 5 acres), processing, retail, research and development, and transportation. This represents well over one hundred million US dollars, with application fees ranging between US$300 for individuals to US$500 for companies, and tier 1 cultivator licensing fees at US$2,000, tier 1 processor at US$3,500 trending up each tier; transport for the first vehicle at US$10,000; retail at US$2,500, and research at US$5,000: "Schedule of Fees" (*Cannabis Licensing Authority Jamaica*) <https://www.cla.org.jm/schedule-of-fees/> accessed 29 August 2023.

7 See Chapter 3 in this volume, authored by Yentyl Williams.

the springboard needed to enable and support cannabis stakeholders in their quest for heightened economic growth and market sustainability.

8.2 THE HERB – NOT YOUR ORDINARY AGRICULTURAL CROP

On 7 August 2001, the National Commission on Ganja, chaired by the late Professor Barry Chevannes, presented its findings to the then Prime Minister, the Most Honourable P.J. Patterson. The key elements of the recommendations made were the decriminalisation of ganja for personal private use by adults and for use as a sacrament for religious purposes. It was noted that despite medical evidence that use of the herb can have harmful effects, there was growing evidence that the herb had therapeutic properties as well. Accordingly, continued criminalisation of its use by Jamaicans in ways and with beliefs that were deeply rooted in the culture of the people was adjudged unwarranted.[8] Importantly, the Commission reported that possession of herb for personal use did not pose the same mischief as trafficking in substances like crack cocaine; thus, decriminalisation should be considered as this measure would in no way breach the United Nations Drugs Conventions which Jamaica ratified.

Two of the seven specific steps recommended by the Commission are of particular importance in the context of intellectual property: firstly, to avoid Jamaica being left behind, a research agency should be established in collaboration with other countries to coordinate research into all aspects, including its epidemiological and psychological effects, pharmacological and economic potential, as was then being pursued by other countries; secondly, that it is critical to expeditiously engage CARICOM partners and international trading partners, in particular the European Union, to entreat the international community to revise their stance on the criminalised status of dealing in, and consumption of, the herb.

Over a decade later, on 17 September 2013, the Honorable House of Representatives was once again urged to consider "What prevents Jamaica from optimizing our academic and economic potential in legal cultivation and research of a plant which has been part of Jamaica's natural history and heritage for the better part of at least two centuries?"[9] Further, the House was entreated to contemplate the injustice occasioned by the criminalisation of cannabis in all forms, which had the effect of threatening social development

---

[8] Chevannes, Barry, National Commission on Ganja "Report of the National Commission on ganja". Jamaica Information Service, 2001; National Library of Jamaica, Pam 362.295 Ja Rep.

[9] Submission made by Raymond Pryce. *Jamaica Hansard* 17 September 2013, vol 39(2), Session 2013–2014, 1559.

through arrests of youths incarcerated for possessing small quantities of herb and the overcrowding of prisons, unduly overwhelming the criminal justice system. This was buttressed by a statement made by Deputy Superintendent of Police, Steve Brown, that statistics compiled by the Criminal Records Office of the Jamaican Constabulary Force for the period January to July 2013 showed that a total of 6,150 Jamaicans were convicted in the Corporate Area Residents Magistrates Court and were sentenced to serve a total of 1,254 years and given fines amounting to $37.5 million; 71 per cent of these were convicted of drug-related offences like smoking and possession of ganja.[10]

8.3 THE LIVITY – INTRODUCING POLICY AND AMENDING LEGISLATION TO ENHANCE JAMAICA'S STRENGTHS, REDRESS WEAKNESSES, INCREASE OPPORTUNITIES, AND DEBUNK THREATS

The social mischief presented by the trade in and consumption of cannabis is complex. On the one hand, as with all smoking, health risks to smokers and persons who are exposed to secondhand smoke are problematic and a matter of public health concern.[11] Further, the rights of Indigenous groups like Rastafarians, who use the herb as a sacrament, stop where the rights of others begin. The conundrum is that this relatively small community, estimated in 2011 by the national census to represent 2 per cent of the counted population, is arguably responsible for the widespread perception worldwide of Jamaica as the land of good ganja, Jamaicans as ganja smokers, or at any rate, ganja-tolerant. This underpins the political mischief, namely, the arguments of the Ganja Law Reform Coalition for decriminalisation of marijuana, on the basis of international human rights to freedom of religion or the right to privacy, and the unjustifiable continued classification of ganja as a dangerous drug simpliciter, must be counterbalanced with the possible negative trade implications with international actors who support criminalisation. As a corollary, the economic mischief is rooted in herb as a dangerous drug rather than as an extraordinary agricultural crop that can yield lucrative pharmaceutical and other

---

[10] Cited in "Ganja arrests worry HEAD OF the Constabulary Communication Network of people who are acquiring criminal records due to them possessing marijuana" *The Daily Gleaner* (9 September 2013).

[11] K Powell-Booth, W De La Haye, S Longman-Mills, "Impact of Cannabis on the Neurocognitive Performance of Jamaican Adolescents" The University of the West Indies Study 2004–2005 <https://www.researchgate.net/publication/368156399_Impact_of_cannabis_on_the_neurocognitive_performance_of_Jamaican_adolescents> accessed 11 April 2024.

byproducts. Indeed, the demonisation of cannabis as a crop has proved to be a fetter on imparting know-how to farmers on how to grow the crop consistent with industry standards for the purpose of pharmaceutical exploitation.[12] In summary, to redress the social, economic, political, and economic mischiefs that the cannabis trade and consumption engender, the proposed policy solution must disaggregate the issue of decriminalisation from legalisation and the bespoke question of developing the medical cannabis industry; in particular, pharmaceuticals, nutraceuticals, and health tourism.

The debate of the House on 24 September and 8 October 2013, served to ratify the position that had been tabled as far back as 9 March 1977, when the then Committee rejected the recommendation that there should be no punishment prescribed for the personal use of ganja up to a quantity of two ounces by persons on private premises.[13] It is therefore unsurprising that this approach to decriminalisation is adopted in the DDAA. However, the decision to codify a quantum of two ounces remains an enigma, especially in light of arguments cautioning that qualitatively all ganja is not equal, not just in quality but in THC content.[14] All the more so because the definition of "ganja" in section 2 of the Act gives no guideline for the concentration of THC required vis-à-vis the two ounces limit imposed for illegality to arise. In contrast, the definition of "hemp" makes specific reference to THC concentration of more than 1.0 per cent.[15] The relevance of this distinction is of particular importance where IP is concerned and will be considered below.

---

[12] Pure Jamaican, "Pure Jamaican, Through Its Pharmaceutical Divison Seven-10, Announces the Acquisition of the Production and Cultivation Assets of Timeless Herbal Care, the First Company to Achieve GMP Certification for Medical Cannabis Production in Jamaica" *PR Newswire* (21 December 2021) <https://www.prnewswire.com/news-releases/pure-jamaican-through-its-pharmaceutical-division-seven-10-announces-the-acquisition-of-the-production-and-cultivation-assets-of-timeless-herbal-care-the-first-company-to-achieve-gmp-certification-for-medical-cannabis-productio-301449204.html> accessed 21 December 2021.

[13] *Jamaica Hansard* 8 October 2013, vol 39(2), Session 2013–2014, 1688.

[14] ibid 1685.

[15] The CLA has authority to regulate ganja and not hemp generally. It does, in practice, regulate "craft hemp" containing less than 1 per cent THC or more than 10 per cent CBD, for medicinal use or research purposes. It does not, however, regulate "industrial hemp" because of the inherent risk of cross-pollination with ganja.

Rychert, Emanual, and Wilkins in their article "Issues in the Establishment of a Therapeutic Cannabis Market under Jamaica's Dangerous Drugs Amendment Act 2015"[16] resolve that:

> [There are] … a number of challenges in implementing therapeutic market provisions under DDAA [Dangerous Drugs Amendment Act of 2015], including a limited buy-in from key government agencies; delays in developing a framework for quality assurance; and lack of access to banking services. Public sector actors stressed the challenges imposed by the UN drug conventions and [the] need to maintain favourable diplomatic relationship[s] with the US federal government, with the consequence of prioritising enforcement to prevent diversion and inversion. Implementation of the Alternative Development Programme in two traditional cannabis-growing communities experienced challenges with land titles and frictions in local communities. High compliance costs and limited skills to meet the envisioned medical standards presented barriers for traditional farmers. Many KIs conceptualised the purchasing of cannabis from the regulated market as "recreational" rather than medical, reflecting the marketing and limited information on medical applications at point of sale. Licensees' reliance on foreign investment puts local industry at risk of predatory shareholder agreements, but also provides needed investment and expertise.

Emanual and Wilkins conclude that the financial system also has to be adapted to facilitate the proceeds of cannabis commerce.

Similarly, Araujo in "Ganja and the Laws of Men: Cannabis Decriminalization and Social (In)Justice in Jamaica"[17] expressed reservations about the DDAA and whether it had successfully made strides towards decriminalisation. Specifically, he argues that the current framework does not promote social justice for actors historically engaged in the cannabis trade and suggests that it should be revised and aligned with policies geared towards reparations. He focusses on the historical entanglements between Rastafarians, law enforcement, and criminal justice once the prohibition had been weaponised against these actors. He discusses the involvement of the US in the attempt to eradicate cannabis in Jamaica, the massive investment in militarisation, and the state violence embodied in the war against cannabis to then unpack the issues with the process of decriminalisation and legalisation. He concludes by suggesting that the Cannabis Licensing Authority and the Jamaican government develop

---

16 M Rychert, MA Emanuel, C Wilkins, "Issues in the Establishment of a Therapeutic Cannabis Market under Jamaica's Dangerous Drugs Amendment Act 2015" (2020) 86 International Journal of Drug Policy 102945 <https://www.sciencedirect.com/science/article/abs/pii/S095539592030284X.> accessed 11 August 2023.

17 F Neis Araujo, "Ganja and the Laws of Men: Cannabis Decriminalization and Social (In)Justice in Jamaica" (17 February 2023) 50(2) Sage Journal on Criminology and Criminal Justice.

deeper engagement with traditional farmers to design and implement policies that will allow them to enjoy the benefits of the current legal cannabis market.

Perhaps the better view is that while decriminalisation and legalisation will immediately impact Jamaica socially and politically once appropriate policies and related legislative steps are implemented, economic resonance will depend on the country's ability to champion the uptake and proprietorship of intellectual property assets and create added value to cannabis goods and services by leveraging brand Jamaica. Such a framework should contemplate an IP audit of cannabis businesses, including registered trademarks, business names, and patents. It must include the creation of a consortium; the registration of GIs for Jamaica ganja, Jamaica cannabis, and Jamaica hemp; registration of plant varieties; and the establishment of a national seed bank. Leveraging brand Jamaica by mandating country of origin labelling for all cannabis raw materials, irrespective of their use in local or export goods and services, is also of paramount importance. Collectively, these actions have the potential to solidify Jamaica's national competitive identity in the international cannabis market.

8.4 THE HIGH – VALUE-ADDED IP ASSETS

The Trade Mark Amendment Act 2021 (TMAA) and the Patent and Designs Act of Jamaica 2020 (PDA) reimagined the significance of the use of country names, Jamaica's country name and insignia of sovereignty in commerce, and the rights of Indigenous or local communities in respect of their traditional knowledge or cultural expression, and personality rights. The proposition that the official name of a state serves to indicate not merely that a product is "made in, made by or made of" Jamaica(n) people, ingredients or provenance, but a country's national competitive identity, is compelling.[18]

The TMAA entrenches protection for the country name "Jamaica" in its own right, not merely as an indicia of sovereignty, but as a sui generis intellectual property asset. It introduces the nomenclature "originate in Jamaica" but no definition is given. There is no requirement to show proof of constituent elements and means of production for cannabis goods and services to be said to originate locally, to be co-branded locally with "Jamaica" as a registered trade mark. This provision would unlikely pose an impediment to the registration of Pure Jamaican as a trademark in Jamaica as the source of the cannabis

[18] N Corthesy, *International Intellectual Property Protection of Country Names: Balancing Nation Brands and Geographic Commons in a Competitive Global Marketplace* (Caribbean Law Publishers 2023).

pharmaceuticals manufactured by the company is Jamaica, made of, made in, and made by Jamaican industry.[19]

The TMAA also makes reference to a list of national emblems and symbols in respect of which the legislation shall apply, and uses restricted. However, no definition of "national symbol" is given, thus statutory interpretation will be necessary to determine the parameters of the genus. This would include the Coat of Arms, the National Flag, and the National Emblem, which are expressly listed. Presumably, the genus would also include the National Bird, the National Flower, the National Tree, the National Fruit, the National Anthem, the National Song, the National Pledge, the National Motto, and the National Prayer.

Further, the conspicuous absence of approved guidelines outlining the criteria and procedure regarding the use of national emblems and symbols could prove to be a bureaucratic niggle for cannabis undertakings seeking to co-brand with Jamaican iconography of this kind. Requests to do so must be directed to the Jamaica Intellectual Property Office (JIPO), which has authority to approve the use of Jamaica's symbols and emblems, and they currently carry out this function free of charge; at any rate, there is no additional charge for use over and above the cost of the trade mark application itself. It is, however, unclear whether failure to procure authorisation is an offence or attracts a penalty as section 5 of TMAA is silent on this. Seemingly, there is no legislative disincentive in the TMAA for the commercial exploitation of unregistered signs that co-brand with the country name Jamaica or insignias of sovereignty. Perhaps recourse could be had in such cases to consumer protection law.

Nevertheless, JIPO has received numerous applications to register signs related to ganja for, inter alia, herbal teas, ganja cafes, a number of festival trademarks, and clothing lines, including "Ganja Babie" applied for by Wallace Melbourne, and Medicanja, owned by Dr Henry Lowe,[20] which applied for "Ganja Café". Notable successful registrations for ganja include: Caribbean Dreams High Grade Ganja Tea owned by Jamaican Teas Limited since August

[19] The company and trademark "Pure Jamaican" is registered in Canada, although the place of business operations is in Jamaica. However, the eligibility criteria established by the CLA regulations for applicants seeking a licence require that an individual (for cultivation) must be "ordinarily resident", i.e., living in Jamaica for three or more years; a company must be registered with the Companies Office of Jamaica with "substantial" ownership and control by persons "ordinarily resident"; and cooperatives must have proof of registration or application for registration in Jamaica.

[20] Dr Henry Lowe is a Jamaican scientist who invented the drug Canasol, which is patented in Jamaica and has received approval from the US Patent Office as a drug that treats glaucoma and myopia, or nearsightedness.

2016; Ganja Cup and Medical Ganja Cup, registered in March 2016 by Trans High Corporation; and 16Ganja owned by Prime Sports Jamaica as a lottery symbol for its games, registered in June 2016.[21]

As a corollary, section 83(7)(a) of the PDA provides that the Registrar shall not register a design which, in his opinion, incorporates a representation or imitation of the Coat of Arms, the national flag, official signs or hallmarks, or other national symbols or emblems, unless the Government of Jamaica has so consented. Subsection (7)(b) further extends the category of prospectively unregistrable designs to include the country name Jamaica, abbreviations or homonyms thereof, the map of Jamaica, or the national colours of Jamaica, save where the Registrar believes the use made is "not likely to mislead the public as to the existence of a connection between the origin, nature or quality of the articles to which the design is to be applied and the country Jamaica". Subsections (7)(c)–(e) similarly make provision for the names of other countries, Convention countries and international organisations, respectively. Further, the rights of unregistered and registered trade mark owners, copyright owners, a person's image rights, and the rights of Indigenous and local communities who are custodians of traditional knowledge and traditional cultural expressions must all be considered by the Registrar, who must verify that their consent has been obtained. The use of Bob Marley's name and image by heirs in association with cannabis goods and services is a notable example.[22] This provision would also impact the wider Rastafarian community where applications to register cannabis-related designs are submitted to JIPO.

8.5 "ONE CANNABIS" REGIME IMAGINED

It is difficult to imagine Jamaican cannabis growers, distributors, and retailers disentangling themselves from the stigma of illegality to maximise their contribution to GDP through legal channels, supported by legitimate financial systems; especially not as individual undertakings with fragmented industry goals. Acquiring IP rights such as trademarks, geographical indications, patents, and plant varieties can furnish public and private sector stakeholders with economic leverage to recoup investments and commit to further research and

[21] "Ganja Babie, Other Trademarks in the Pipeline" *The Gleaner* (7 February 2017) <https://jamaica-gleaner.com/article/business/20170208/ganja-babie-other-trademarks-pipeline> accessed 8 February 2017.

[22] See "Marley Natural" <https://www.marleynaturalshop.com/> accessed 11 April 2024.

development, which would augur well for giving local communities an economic and cultural boost.[23]

Could "Jamaica Ganja" become to Jamaica what Café de Colombia is to Colombia? Can Jacana[24] become a symbol of high-quality "Jamaica Cannabis"-derived goods and services in the way Juan Valdez is synonymous with Café de Colombia? The passage of the DDAA has seemingly increased the gap between cannabis production and supply that are legal and illegal. This shroud of illegality does at least in part explain the lag in local registration of IP rights. The persistent illegality in foreign regimes that are trading partners with Jamaica has not aided the advancement of the industry either. It is noteworthy that Jamaica's most important trading partner, the US, recently tabled a bill for the legalisation of cannabis at the federal level, but no predictions can be made on the outcome or possible impact of this motion just yet.

The cannabis tolerance framework introduced by the DDAA, while it does not stop the registration of IP assets per se, is incongruous with the commercial flexibility required for the cannabis industry to flourish. That is, if Jamaica's commercial prowess in the global cannabis market reposes in its national competitive identity as epitomised by Rasta and Reggae, the regime of illegality on which ganja trade is propped is arguably a bigger commercial boulder than the lacuna of regulations for the pharmaceutical cannabis market.[25] What is more, best efforts have to be made to avoid repeating the mistakes made with the sugar industry. That is, by treating cannabis as unbranded raw material, the value added that could be garnered in the pharmaceutical cannabis market would be lost as well. Regulations must entrench a requirement for country of origin labelling so that Jamaica Cannabis will be to Jamaica what Demerara Gold is to Guyana.[26]

Against the backdrop of these challenges, there is an inescapable inference that a long-felt want for a cannabis consortium exists; one that will advocate for advancing solutions to redress these challenges. To transform commerce in cannabis from a trade in raw materials to an industry of high-quality branded and marketed cannabis-derived products and services, what is required is

---

23 Two notable research initiatives exist: The University of the West Indies Mona Cannabis Group, spearheaded by the Faculty of Medical Sciences but comprising academics from all faculties conducting cannabis-related research; and The University of the West Indies Mona Law Faculty – City University London joint research project on GIs funded by Higher Education Fund UK.

24 See "Jacana Jamaica" <https://jacana.life/> accessed 11 April 2024.

25 Mandatory testing of cannabis is expected to be implemented by the Cannabis Licensing Authority in collaboration with the Ministry of Health. Draft regulations exist but are not yet gazetted, and are thus not in force.

26 See Chapter 3 in this volume, authored by Yentyl Williams.

Figure 8.1 Model for a Jamaica Cannabis Consortium

a lobby for a more pragmatic but tightly regulated framework for cannabis, ganja, and hemp, that has the endorsement of most, if not all, the private and public sector stakeholders. A successful consortium must be erected on the edifice of strong public-private partnership. The model may contemplate diverse stakeholders as demonstrated in Figure 8.1.

The first order of business the consortium would be advised to undertake is the registration of at least three geographical indications (GIs) – Jamaica cannabis, Jamaica ganja, and Jamaica hemp; and not necessarily in that order. Under Jamaica's Geographical Indications Act of 2004 and Regulations of 2009, as amended by the GI Act of 2018 (the GI Act), oversight of the registration process is administered by the Registrar of Industrial Property of JIPO.

The GIs may be registered by producers, groups of producers, or any competent authority such as the recommended consortium.[27]

The consortium's application would have to indicate the chosen nomenclatures for the GIs being registered – Jamaica cannabis, Jamaica ganja, and Jamaica hemp. It would also have to make a determination as to the physical geographic limits of the locality in Jamaica to which the GI would apply, and specify Westmoreland, for example, as the provenance of the goods in respect of which the GI will be used. Alternatively, the consortium could determine that the GI is applicable to the entire country of Jamaica and give an ample and acceptable description justifying this designation in the specification. The application must also iterate the quality, reputation, or other characteristics of the goods for which the GI is used, any conditions under which the GI may be used, and any additional information. The application must be accompanied by a Control Manual and a Code of Practice for the manufacturing of the product in question.

The objective of the *Control Manual* and *Code of Practice* is to identify the relationship between the product and the geographical area in which it originates. A detailed explanation must be given of how the geographical area imbues the product with unique qualities, rendering it an inimitable product compared to like products not produced in the indicated geographical place. Defining characteristics for cannabis include but are not limited to soil, rain fall, altitude, water supply, and traditional knowledge. Specificities for which the product is renowned should also be highlighted, such as its fragrance, visual appearance, flavour profile, and emblematic reputation. Whilst the *Control Manual* can be said to be a qualitative description of the product, the *Code of Practice* must outline the process involved in producing it. The CLA could be instrumental in providing guidance in developing the manuals. In principle, the CarIPI project could also be approached for funding to elaborate the specification, develop the manual, and identify a mentor.[28] Substantial assistance was given to Trinidad and Tobago Fine Cocoa Company when developing a national GI for cocoa,[29] and more poignantly, assistance was given for plant varieties

27 "Producers" refers to producers of agricultural products, persons who exploit natural products, manufacturers of products of industry or handicraft, and persons who deal or trade in the above-mentioned products. A "competent authority" is "any association of persons recognized in the prescribed manner". Sections 2, 9(1) and (2) and 9(5) GI Act.

28 See "About CARIPI" (*carIPI*) <https://internationalipcooperation.eu/en/caripi/about-caripi> and "IP Documents" (*carIPI*) <https://internationalipcooperation.eu/en/caripi/ip-information>.

29 *Case Study: Trinidad and Tobago Fine Cocoa Company* (carIPI) <https://internationalipcooperation.eu/sites/default/files/caripi-docs/2021-11/CarIPI_Nov

of tomato[30] and rice.[31] However, assistance from CarIPI would be dependent on getting government stakeholders to champion the cause, especially given that collaborations in the region have all been in respect of non-controversial products:[32] no doubt a reflection of other trade-related implications associated with the underlying European Union – CARIFORUM Partnership Agreement which underpins the technical assistance offered by CarIPI.[33]

If the proposition is that the GI should apply to all of Jamaica, it must be possible to replicate the prescribed quality and process standards specified in the entire country. This may prove impracticable. Consideration could be given to the pragmatic approach taken by the Jamaica Rum consortium, which cleverly devised a specification of cultivation, processing, product testing, manufacturing, and labelling for rum that allowed for a broad geographic area of provenance beyond the boundary of Appleton.[34]

Successful registration of the GIs is one side of the coin.[35] Equitable interest and ownership in the IP asset created, and administration thereof, is the other.[36] In the ideal scenario where the consortium is comprised of a balanced number of public and private stakeholders, critical decisions about criteria for use of the GI by members, licencing registered users, and enforcement and

-2021_Trinidad-and-Tobago_Fine-Cocoa-Company-Case-Study.pdf> accessed 11 April 2024.

30 See *Case Study: Plant Variety Solanum Licopersicum L.-Kivu* (carIPI) <https://internationalipcooperation.eu/sites/default/files/arise-docs/2022/CARIPI_REGISTRATION-PLANT-VARIETY_SOLANUM.pdf> accessed 11 April 2024.

31 See *Case Study: Plant Variety Oriza* (carIPI) <https://internationalipcooperation.eu/sites/default/files/arise-docs/2022/CARIPI_REGISTRATION-PLANT-VARIETY_ORIZA.pdf> accessed 11 April 2024.

32 CarIPI is an EU-funded project, and part of the EU programme to support CARIFORUM states in the implementation of their Economic Partnership Agreement commitments. Among CarIPI's goals is to offer technical assistance to CARIFORUM states to facilitate compliance and help them realise the expected benefits of the EPA. This includes fostering a regional framework and cooperation on intellectual property.

33 *Economic Partnership Agreement* (Official Journal of the European Union) <https://eur-lex.europa.eu/legal-content/EN/TXT/PDF/?uri=CELEX:22008A1030(01)> accessed 11 April 2024.

34 See Chapter 3 in this volume, authored by Yentyl Williams.

35 The cost to register a GI in Jamaica is estimated to be between JMD$160,000.00 and JMD$250,000.00, inclusive of the Government Fees of JMD$30,000.00. This does not include the cost of preparing and reviewing the *Code of Practice* or *Control Manual*, and legal fees.

36 Note GI Act Section 4(2) and 11, GI Act.

protection of the GI against infringement locally and abroad will be tough to arrive at and adhere to. The recent dispute involving Jamaica Rum is illustrative of the dexterity required.[37] It would also be necessary to ensure that international standards for cannabis production are borne in mind to maximise the opportunities afforded in the export market.

In addition to GI registration in Jamaica and target export markets external to Jamaica, the Consortium must also take cognisance of its trademark registrations and those of its constituent members. International trade mark registration is desirable and possible as a result of the Madrid system to which Jamaica is party.[38] Local cannabis undertakings can take advantage of the facility provided by this system that allows for the international application and registration of a bundle of national trade marks through a single local application. Ironically, given the restrictions in the TMA of Jamaica on the use of the country name Jamaica, the use of Rastafarian iconography, and general grounds of refusal based on morality, it may prove more difficult to register signs that incorporate any of these elements in Jamaica than in other priority countries designated in the Madrid application. It will therefore be important for the consortium and its members to conduct trade mark searches, decide on suitable and available signs for registration, have a clear trade mark registration strategy to determine priority foreign countries where trade mark protection is necessary, and confirm whether those countries are signatories to the Madrid Protocol. It would also be beneficial to develop an IP inventory. This would contemplate executing an IP audit to ascertain and classify the ordinary trademarks, collective marks, and/or certification marks owned by the consortium and its members, and ultimately conducting an IP valuation exercise to determine the value of the IP assets vis-à-vis the consortium's business worth.

Another IP protection demarche that should be considered is the collection and testing of cannabis samples, with a view to depositing seeds with seed banks locally and internationally, and updating the inventory of existing cannabis varieties in Jamaica to determine eligible candidates for New Plant Variety protection (Jamaica is currently negotiating its membership of the 1991 UPOV Convention for the protection of plant varieties).[39] Also, the

---

[37] A Monteith, "National Rums Reinforces Position GI" *Jamaica Observer* (13 October 2023) <https://www.jamaicaobserver.com/2023/10/13/national-rums-reinforces-position-on-gi-20231018-1640-470855/> accessed 13 October 2023.

[38] The Madrid Protocol for the International Registration of Trademarks has 126 member countries. The Madrid Protocol came into force in Jamaica on 27 March 2022.

[39] EXAMINATION OF THE CONFORMITY OF THE NEW PLANT VARIETIES (RIGHTS OF BREEDERS) BILL, 2021, OF JAMAICA WITH THE

Protection of Plant Genetic Resources for Food and Agriculture Act 2013[40] facilitates Jamaica's compliance with its obligations under the International Treaty on Plant Genetic Resources for Food and Agriculture.[41] The underlying policy objective of this regime is to grant breeding rights to Jamaican farmers for a restricted term of up to 25 years while balancing the benefits to be realised by facilitating access to new varieties. It was also espoused that a system of registering new plant varieties would strengthen the capabilities of developing countries and countries with economies in transition like Jamaica, with respect to conservation and sustainable use of plant genetic resources.[42]

The example of the new pineapple variety developed in Costa Rica, which is easily identifiable by its red outer skin, is instructive.[43] Produced in small quantities by Fresh Del Monte Produce Inc., it will be retailed at approximately US$400 per fruit. The IP strategy involved obtaining a US plant patent No. 33,544 in 2021, wherein the specification cites the variety denomination as "Vintage Ruby". It is not permissible to adopt this denomination as a trademark under 1991 UPOV Convention,[44] to guarantee the homogeneity of the nomenclature used to refer to the plant variety in commerce. The US Plant Patent system adopts this approach, as does the EU Trade Mark system[45] as denominations are deemed generic.

Consequently, Fresh Del Monte Produce Inc. has registered the trade mark "Rubyglow" for the new pineapple. This is nothing short of branding genius as

1991 ACT OF THE UPOV CONVENTION, October 4, 2021. See <https://www.upov.int/edocs/mdocs/upov/en/c_55/c_55_15.pdf> accessed 11 April 2024.

40 See <https://laws.moj.gov.jm/library/statute/the-protection-of-plant-generic-resources-for-food-and-agriculture-act> accessed 11 April 2024.

41 The Treaty was approved by the United Nations Food and Agriculture Organisation (FAO) in November 2001, and came into effect in June 2004.

42 See <https://jis.gov.jm/senate-passes-bill-to-protect-plant-genetic-resources/#:~:text=A%20Bill%20providing%20for%20the%20protection%20of%20Jamaica%E2%80%99s,on%20Plant%20Genetic%20Resources%20for%20Food%20and%20Agriculture>; and <https://www.miic.gov.jm/content/new-plant-varieties-be-protected-intellectual-property> accessed 22 January 2013.

43 J Bosse, "What's in a Trademark? By Any Other Name, Would a $400 Pineapple Taste as Sweet?" (*The IPKat*, 11 May 2024) <https://ipkitten.blogspot.com/2024/05/whats-in-trademark-by-any-other-name.html>.

44 Article 20(1)(b) UPOV 1991 stipulates that "... no rights in the designation registered as the denomination of the variety shall hamper the free use of the denomination in connection with the variety, even after the expiration of the breeder's rights".

45 Article 7.1(m) EU Trade Mark Regulation provides that it is grounds for rejection or invalidity if a trade mark consists of, or reproduces in its essential elements, an earlier plant variety denomination.

the breeders stand to continue reaping benefits beyond the expiry of the plant variety protection by leveraging their infinite monopolistic trade mark rights. The crux of the matter for Jamaican cannabis breeders in mirroring this strategy is to ensure that corresponding trade marks of registered plant varieties are so effectively marketed to consumers that the variety is synonymous with the trade mark rather than the variety denomination of the cannabis plant. Post-expiry of plant variety rights, although other breeders will be free to sell the variety and use the variety denomination, they will not be permitted to use or associate their product with the hopefully well-known cannabis trade mark for the variety.[46] However, there is a catch. As with all trade marks, the function is to guarantee the source of the undertaking, not the provenance of the goods themselves. Buyers will have to be aware that they may not necessarily be purchasing the cannabis variety. Brand loyalty is everything.

Further, registering top-level and country-level domain names for Jamaica cannabis, Jamaica ganja, and Jamaica hemp is paramount. Indeed, the registration of trade marks identified in the previously recommended IP audit should correlate to domain name registrations by the undertakings concerned.

Finally, careful thought must be given not just to extrinsic IP but also to intrinsic IP. That is, access to and use of information created by the consortium, or in the event that trade secrets are divulged, confidentiality agreements, non-disclosure, and non-compete agreements among stakeholders internal to the consortium would be necessary. Although these agreements are not, strictly speaking, IP assets, their value relative to the security of the industry is inestimable. Their existence is a sine qua non of successful business operations and financial health, for individual undertakings and the consortium as a whole.

8.6 CONCLUSION – WHO JAH BLESS, NO MAN CURSE

The status quo of the legalisation of cannabis in Jamaica has thus far been characterised by the economic ambitions of farmers, government, and middlemen, and what can be described as the noble aspirations of the Rastafarian community and scientists, to elevate the herb to more than a symbol of illegality and dread. The gaps in the legal and policy framework that underpin the cannabis industry in Jamaica demonstrate a need for a wider approach:

---

46 Note the case involving the apple variety "Cripps Pink", named after British Australian breeder, John Cripps. The registered trade mark for the variety is "Pink Lady". Retailer Asda was entitled to market the apples as "Cripps Pink" but was not permitted to label the fruit with the trade mark "Pink Lady". See E Bedington, "Asda Performs U-turn on Pink Lady" (*Fresh Produce Journal*, 2 July 2005) <https://www.fruitnet.com/fresh-produce-journal/asda-performs-u-turn-on-pink-lady/136759.article> and Bosse (n 43).

removing the stigma and illuminating the disingenuous distinction between commerce in cannabis, ganja, and hemp. Cannabis production for cultural recreational purposes, religious rites, manufacturing pharmaceuticals, and nutraceutical THC/CBD cannabis-derived products, means one thing – commerce in cannabis. To attract investment and grow the industry, it has to be possible to deal in the proceeds of cannabis production legally, not in cash but rather by conducting banking and financial transactions legally.[47] Sound social policy dictates that this crucial step must be accompanied by the introduction of a bespoke regime for restricting sales to youth, which incorporates educational programmes and health programmes to advocate for addiction prevention and to counteract abuse.

This course of action can only be substantiated by reference to empirical projections of the market value of the cannabis industry and its ability to exponentially escalate its contribution to Jamaica's GDP. The fantastic possibility that market price and access to the global export market will increase must be weighed against the likely probability that softening the legislative stance on illegality and opening up the cannabis market could result in oversupply and a fall in price. Much of the success being enjoyed presently is arguably due to the illegal nature of the cannabis business and the absence of an established transparent process for regulating the production, testing, and export of cannabis and THC/CBD cannabis-derived products.

Assuming this shift in policy is adopted, should a shift away from current economic activity centred around smoke shops and tourism, towards an increase in the development and export of pharmaceutical and nutraceutical THC/CBD cannabis-derived products be anticipated? If so, the importance of acquiring value-added IP and co-branding with the country name Jamaica, to reap the benefits of Brand Jamaica's global recognition, cannot be overstated.[48] It is espoused that heightened IP protection mechanisms can provide

---

47 Note the US Senate Banking Committee successfully tabled The SAFER Banking Act, which will allow cannabis businesses to conduct banking transactions with local banks and safeguard those banks that need to protect their corresponding banking relationships with foreign banks. See commentary by the American Bar Association: H Urness, A Kouhoupt, "SAFER Banking Act: Marijuana May Soon Become a Bigger Deal" (*ABA*, 15 February 2024) <https://www.americanbar.org/groups/business_law/resources/business-law-today/2024-february/safer-banking-act/> accessed 1 March 2024.

48 It is anticipated that the nation brand strategy for Jamaica, currently under development for adoption in 2024, will include recommendations on narratives to be used in relation to medical cannabis, cannabis-related health tourism, and guidance on how to avoid negative misconceptions. It will also likely make separate recommendations on ganja narrative development intended to address consumer

the springboard needed to enable and support cannabis stakeholders in their quest to transform Jamaica's cannabis business into a performing and sustainable industry worthy of international acclaim. This is best achieved through collaboration and the establishment of a public-private sector lobby and/or consortium. A strong argument can be made for establishing a consortium to take advantage of economies of scale, minimising the costs associated with devising an IP strategy – the cost of research and cannabis testing, conducting an IP inventory and audit, procuring the services of IP experts to put together applications for the registration of IP assets, obtaining licences where mandated and authorisation to export,[49] and implementing enforcement strategies, administrative costs, and of course legal fees.

concerns about quality control, certification of suppliers and shops, protocols related to export, and encouragement of local entrepreneurs to enter into licences.

[49] Pure Jamaican, the first and only company to export thus far, obtained licenses and/or approval from CLA; JAMPRO; the Ministry of Health; the Ministry of Industry, Commerce, Agriculture and Fisheries; and the Bureau of Standards.

9. The Canadian scenario

Cameron Hutchison

9.1 INTRODUCTION

In 2018, Canada became the first of the most developed economies globally – the G20 countries – to create a national marketplace for legalised cannabis.[1] Even so, the industry is heavily regulated by federal and provincial governments. Like any industry, its viability is, at least in part, connected to intellectual property (IP) law and the innovation it spurs. This chapter explores the relationship between IP law regimes in Canada, on the one hand, and the cannabis industry and cannabis regulation, on the other. The IP regimes addressed in this chapter include registered trademarks, patent law, and plant breeders' rights. The chapter does not address copyright or industrial designs as these are areas more incidentally connected to the cannabis industry.[2] Since Canada is a party to the major IP treaties in the areas discussed, the reader can assume that harmonised procedures and priority dates are available for foreign applications.

The chapter proceeds accordingly. Part 9.2 provides an overview of the federal Cannabis Act,[3] which is the main source of cannabis regulation in Canada. As there are 13 sub-national jurisdictions in Canada, only a general reference will be made to the notable features of some of these laws. Part 9.3

---

[1] Ernst Young, *Executive Summary The State of Canada's Cannabis Industry* (*ey.com*, January 2023).

[2] Copyright has obvious application to expressive elements in trademark logos and designs, and advertising more generally. Industrial designs concern designs that are pleasing to the eye. To date, four designs relating to cannabis devices are registered as industrial designs in Canada: two for a "cannabis cone" (Registration Nos. 182958, 208988), and one each for a "tailored container" and an "extinguisher" (Registration Nos. 207292 and 207530). As I mention under Section 3 "Registered Trademarks", I also do not address unregistered trademarks (aka common law tort of passing off) which is, in many important ways, similar to the law of registered trademarks.

[3] SC 2018 c. 16 [hereinafter "the Act"].

discusses registered trademarks, which are severely impacted by advertising and promotion restrictions for cannabis. Part 9.4 addresses patent law with a particular emphasis on the patenting of higher life forms, including plants. Part 9.5 focusses on the Plant Breeders' Rights Act,[4] and the emergence of cannabis plant varieties applications thereunder.

9.2 OVERVIEW OF THE CANNABIS ACT

In 2018, Canada passed the Cannabis Act, which "legalized" (albeit heavily regulated) the production, distribution, sale, export, import, and possession of cannabis for adults of legal age. Prior to this, Canada had already regulated the area of medical cannabis, a regime now subsumed under the Act. Initially, cannabis consumption in Canada grew, and the value of the sector increased from $6.4 billion in 2018 to $10.8 billion in 2023.[5] However, owing to several factors including overproduction and competition from the illicit market, the industry has since been in decline with businesses closing, workers laid off, and share prices plummeting.[6]

Under the Act, "cannabis" is broadly defined to be "any part of a cannabis plant … any substance or mixture that contains or has on it any part of such a plant … [and] any substance identical to any phytocannabinoid produced by, or found in, such a plant, regardless of how the substance was obtained".[7] This definition appears to capture anything to do with a cannabis plant or its phytocannabinoid properties, even if synthetically engineered. In addition, the Act also regulates cannabis accessories.[8]

The purposes of the Act are also wide-ranging, with heightened regard to protecting public health, restricting access to young persons, and deterring the illicit market. Section 7 provides that the purposes of the Act are to:

- protect the health of young persons by restricting their access to cannabis;
- protect young persons and others from inducements to use cannabis;
- provide for the licit production of cannabis to reduce illicit activities in relation to cannabis;

---

4 SC 1990, c. 20.

5 Statistics Canada, "Five Years Since Legalization, What Have We Learned about Cannabis in Canada?" *The Daily* (16 October 2023).

6 T Deschamps, "Canada's Cannabis Industry Burning Out 5 Years after Legalisation" *Global News* (16 October 2023). For a more detailed account of problems in the industry, see Ernst and Young (n 1).

7 The Act (n 3), s. 2, Schedule 1.

8 A defined term under ibid s. 2.

- deter illicit activities in relation to cannabis through appropriate sanctions and enforcement measures;
- reduce the burden on the criminal justice system in relation to cannabis;
- provide access to a quality-controlled supply of cannabis; and
- enhance public awareness of the health risks associated with cannabis use.

The Act regulates cannabis comprehensively and, as such, is a long and complicated piece of legislation consisting of 12 parts and over 200 provisions, not including the regulations. The basic regulatory framework is to prohibit all activities relating to the production, sale, or distribution of cannabis unless authorised by licence or permit.[9] Of particular relevance to IP law, Part 1 of the Act strictly regulates the promotion and packaging of cannabis products,[10] as well as the production and cultivation of cannabis products.

With respect to patent law, section 12 of the Act restricts the ability to obtain cannabis by means of a method or process:

12 (1) Unless authorized under this Act, it is prohibited
(a) to obtain or offer to obtain cannabis by any method or process, including by manufacturing, by synthesis or by using any means of altering the chemical or physical properties of cannabis; or
(b) to alter or offer to alter the chemical or physical properties of cannabis by the use of an organic solvent.

Patent law does not prohibit the patenting of illegal subject matter, though this regulation makes the practical and commercial viability of such an invention questionable. With respect to plant breeders, authorisation is required to cultivate, propagate, and harvest any cannabis, beyond a personal use exception of four plants for dwelling houses.[11]

The detailed regulations on packaging and promotion of cannabis under the Act have strong implications for trademark law. As for promotion, sections 16 to 24 create several prohibitions. Section 17 provides:

17 (1) Unless authorized under this Act, it is prohibited to promote cannabis or a cannabis accessory or any service related to cannabis, including
(a) by communicating information about its price or distribution;

---

[9] BA MacFarlane, R Frater, C Michaelson, *Cannabis Law* (Thomson Reuters 2018) at 2-2.

[10] On the packaging-related measures for cannabis products, see Chapter 6 in this volume, authored by Enrico Bonadio and Akshita Rohatgi.

[11] See the Act (n 3), at ss. 12(5) and (6).

(b) by doing so in a manner that there are reasonable grounds to believe could be appealing to young persons;
(c) by means of a testimonial or endorsement, however displayed or communicated;
(d) by means of the depiction of a person, character or animal, whether real or fictional; or
(e) by presenting it or any of its brand elements in a manner that associates it or the brand element with, or evokes a positive or negative emotion about or image of, a way of life such as one that includes glamour, recreation, excitement, vitality, risk or daring.

Importantly, "brand element" is defined to include a "brand name, trademark, tradename, distinguishing guise, logo, graphic arrangement, design or slogan that is reasonably associated with, or that evokes, (a) cannabis, a cannabis accessory or a service related to cannabis, or (b) a brand of any cannabis, cannabis accessory or service related to cannabis". Sections 21 and 22 prohibit cannabis brand sponsorship of a "person, entity, event, activity or facility" (including naming rights).

The Act creates limited exceptions by allowing promotion:

- by certain methods and in places inaccessible to young persons;[12]
- at the point of sale of an authorized vendor but only in relation to price and/or availability;[13]
- for things not associated with or appealing to young persons or "associated with a way of life such as one that includes glamour, recreation, excitement, vitality, risk or daring".[14]

Of equal importance to trademark law are sections 25 to 28 dealing with the packaging and labelling of cannabis. Sections 26 and 27 basically mirror the prohibitions set out in section 17 with respect to promotion. Further restrictions on labelling are set out in detailed regulations.[15] These include mandatory requirements for health warnings, prohibitions regarding access to children, a standardised cannabis symbol, general information about the supplier, the type of cannabis and the amount of THC and other active cannabinoids. Most importantly, while brand names and logos are permitted, these must be in a

[12] ibid s. 17(2) and (3).
[13] ibid s. 17(4) and (5).
[14] ibid s 17(6).
[15] Cannabis Regulations SOR/2018-144.

single uniform colour and cannot be larger than the health warning, thus making branding elements non-prominent on packaging.

Canada has a federal system of government, with strong jurisdictional powers conferred upon its ten provinces and (to a lesser extent) three territories.[16] This means that, in addition to the federal Act, there are myriad laws and regulations promulgated under provincial and municipal law. Some of these powers overlap with federal jurisdiction; for example, the provinces may create additional rules for the sale and distribution of cannabis.[17] Many provinces "require all cannabis products to remain sealed until sold and stored behind a locked display case", while some allow for sensory "smell jars" for cannabis strains.[18]

9.3 REGISTERED TRADEMARKS

As in any jurisdiction, trademark law in Canada concerns the protection and promotion of source identification in the marketplace. As the Canadian Supreme Court pithily observed, trademarks function as "a kind of shortcut to get consumers to where they want to go, and in that way perform a key function in a market economy".[19]

Distinctiveness of the mark, as it pertains to a single source, is the essence of trademark law. There are some restrictions on what signs may be registered as trademarks. Some of these are standard bars, including a mark that is confused with an existing mark or that illegitimately uses (part of) a geographical indication (GI).[20] Subject to the mark developing a secondary meaning, a trademark cannot be registered if it is "primarily merely a name or surname" or "clearly descriptive or misdescriptive" of, among others, the character or quality of the goods or services, or their place of origin.[21] Finally, there are a number of prohibited marks listed under the Act, including "any scandalous,

---

16 The Act (n 3) s. 69 imposes minimum legislative requirements that the provinces and territories must follow.

17 J de Beer and A Gaffen, "Intellectual Property Rights in the Recreational Cannabis Market: Craft or Commodity?" (2017) 50 UBC Law Rev 621 at 629.

18 B Cheung, "Marketing an Unmarketable Product: The Need for a Less Stringent Cannabis Legal Framework in order to Develop a Sustainable Licit Market" (2019) *Canadian Bar Association* 5 <https://ssrn.com/abstract=3406119>.

19 *Mattel Inc v 3894207 Canada Inc* 2006 SCC 22 at para 21. While Canadian law also protects the use of unregistered trademarks, this will not be addressed in this section.

20 Trademarks Act RSC 1985, c T-13, s. 12(d)(g)(h) and (h.1). Geographical indications in Canada are limited to wines, spirits, agricultural products, and food.

21 ibid s. 12(1)(a) and (b), (2).

obscene or immoral word or device",[22] and plant variety denominations registered under the Plant Breeders' Right Act.[23]

To date, 11,343 "cannabis" signs appear on the Canadian Intellectual Property Office (CIPO) trademarks database, 7,631 of which remain active, and 2,844 of which are registered. Almost all of these pertain to traditional trademark subject matter, i.e., words, designs, standard characters, and colours. A few three-dimensional and hologram signs appear on the register, but none have progressed to the examination stage. There are 18 position signs on the register, only 5 of which are registered.

Only one application for a cannabis scent appears on the CIPO database. Now abandoned, the scent is described as a "pungent skunky, earthy, woody odor with subtle hints of diesel and fruit aromas".[24] The examiner of the scent required evidence of both the distinctiveness of the scent, as well as clarification with respect to "fruit aromas", i.e., the specific fruits claimed.[25] The registration of taste trademarks is similarly underwhelming. To date, there have been five applications, two of which are abandoned and none of which have entered the examination stage. There are no GIs pertaining to "cannabis". There are, however, five registered certification marks connected with cannabis, all of which pertain to general standards that incidentally include cannabis products, e.g., certified organic standards.

The "Tokyo Smoke" family of registered marks merits consideration given the use of a GI. Tokyo Smoke is both a retailer and maker of cannabis products and accessories, as well as merchandise such as clothing. There are close to 100 stores in Canada, making it a major player.[26] The business pitches itself as "an award-winning, design focused, legal cannabis retailer". Curiously, the retail use of the name is still awaiting examination and has yet to be registered.[27] There are five registered trademarks of Tokyo Smoke in connection with recreational cannabis products – Go, Pause, Rise, Equalize, and Ease – denoting the different effects arising from specific cannabinoid combinations associated with each mark.

The word "Tokyo" in these trademarks raises questions about their eligibility for registration. To be clear, the concern is not that "Tokyo" is a GI, defined in the Act as a sign distinguishing wine, spirit, agricultural product, or food possessing "a quality, reputation or other characteristic … essentially

22 ibid s. 9(1)(j).

23 ibid ss. 10.1, 12(1)(f).

24 Cannabis Order, #2023681.

25 ibid Examiner's First Report, 2023-01-25.

26 "Tokyo Smoke" <https://ca.tokyosmoke.com/> accessed 6 June 2024.

27 It is also noteworthy that the mark was registered in 2016 in connection with clothing and related products unrelated to cannabis.

attributable to its geographical origin".[28] Cannabis from Tokyo has no distinctive quality, reputation or other characteristics. Still, these marks are clearly misdescriptive of the place of origin of these products, which is normally a bar to registration.[29] Registration must, therefore, have been based on these products developing a secondary meaning in the marketplace.

There have also been a handful of infringement actions brought by famous brand names against cannabis companies using names that play off of well-known trademarks. In *Toys "R" Us (Canada) Ltd. v Herbs "R" Us Wellness Society*,[30] the Federal Court of Canada ruled on infringement claims brought by the plaintiff against a Vancouver cannabis dispensary, which did not defend the action. The plaintiff is the registered owner of 16 trademarks, consisting of word and/or design elements. The mark most closely resembling the defendant's use was TMA 777,641 [hereinafter "641 mark"] comprised of the words "Toys R Us" running together with multicoloured lettering, a prominent "R" in the middle (which is inverted) and a star shape in the centre of the R. The defendant's Herbs R Us also used a similar hue of multicoloured lettering with the words running together, a prominent R in the middle (not inverted), and a cannabis leaf in the centre of the R (rather than a star).

The infringement actions were grounded in section 20 (confusion) and section 22 (goodwill depreciation) of the Trademark Act. The test for confusion is premised on "first impression in the mind of a casual consumer somewhat in a hurry at a time when [they] have no more than an imperfect recollection of the registered mark and without giving the matter detailed consideration or scrutiny".[31] The analysis is guided by section 6(5) of the Act, in which the court considers all surrounding circumstances including the inherent and acquired distinctiveness of the marks, the length of time in use, the nature of the goods and services, the nature of the trade, and the degree of resemblance between the marks.

The court found there were "striking or unique" similarities between the two marks, "as well as similarities in font, use of varying coloration, and the appearance, sound and connotation of the R US element".[32] Moreover, the plaintiff's mark had both inherent and acquired distinctiveness, as well as 35 years of use in Canada. The defendant's mark was not well known and appeared only to have been in use since 2018. Despite those favourable elements of the analysis for the plaintiff, the court ultimately ruled that there was no confusion or infringement. As so often happens, substantial differences in

---

[28] Trademarks Act (n 20) s. 2.
[29] See (n 21) and accompanying text.
[30] 2020 FC 682.
[31] ibid para 19.
[32] ibid para 21.

the nature of the goods and services and nature of the trade led to a finding that an ordinary consumer would not be confused. In essence, the business of selling toys, on the one hand, and that of selling cannabis, on the other, are too different for the ordinary consumer to likely think that the defendant's business was affiliated with that of the plaintiff.

The plaintiff was, however, successful in their goodwill infringement action. For this action to succeed, a plaintiff must prove that: the defendant used the mark; there is significant goodwill attaching to the mark (as proven by the number of sales and extent of advertising, for example); and the use is likely to have the effect of depreciating the value of the goodwill.[33] The last element is determined based on whether the use would evoke a "mental association" in an ordinary consumer's mind, which is arguably a much easier threshold than confusion for a plaintiff to establish. It also requires depreciation of the goodwill, meaning either dilution or tarnishment of the mark. The court inferred a mental linkage based on the marked similarities between the marks and the "extensive use, sales, and advertising associated with the "641 Mark".[34] The court also found both dilution due to the reduced distinctiveness caused by the mental association, as well as disparagement, based on the association with a cannabis dispensary, "particularly one that appears to be operating without a license, and one that markets through social media with adult-themed content said to include nudity and swear words … utterly inconsistent with the reputation of Toys R Us".[35]

In sum, the severe advertising and promotion restrictions in place under the Cannabis Act have obvious implications for branding and trademark law. The inability for brands to advertise their products adequately, even in store, means that consumers are less able to distinguish between brands. In turn, there is less incentive for businesses to invest in quality or innovative products. As one commentator observes, when consumers are not made aware of the differences between products or their quality, two things might happen: "(1) consumers will only purchase brands they are familiar with, which discredits new entrants and generally keeps prices high; or (2) profitability becomes the key source of survival and competitors continue to cut costs, and with it, quality in an industry-wide race to the bottom."[36]

[33] ibid para 51.
[34] ibid at para 59.
[35] ibid at para 61.
[36] Cheung (n 18) 16.

9.4 PATENT LAW

The fundamentals of Canadian patent law mirror those of other countries. Patents may be issued for eligible subject matter inventions. Eligible inventions must also meet the requirements of novelty, usefulness, and non-obviousness. Determinations about eligible subject matter, and whether the three requirements have been satisfied, depend on a purposive construction of the claims read as a whole.[37] The patent monopoly includes the exclusive right to make, use, and sell the invention and lasts 20 years from the date of filing.[38]

The story of patenting life forms in Canada is a complicated one. A noteworthy patent infringement action was brought by Monsanto against a Canadian farmer who claimed that patented canola seed blew onto his property and therefore his infringement was not intentional.[39] The claimed invention was for the process of genetically modifying a canola plant cell with Round Up Ready herbicide resistance. In another 5:4 ruling, the court left the Harvard Mouse ruling undisturbed but found that practising the invention – growing the plant that is made up of patentable genetically modified cells – was "use" of the patent and therefore infringement on a purposive reading of the process claim. The fact that the patented invention, namely the pesticide-resistant properties of the genetically modified cell, formed part of a larger unpatented structure – the plant as a life form – was not a bar to infringement.[40] In effect, then, so long as the patent claim does not go beyond the cellular level, higher life forms are protected by patent law at the infringement stage.[41]

Canada's patent office follows the Manual of Patent Office Procedure (MOPOP).[42] While this is a policy document and not legally binding, it is relied upon by patent examiners in their assessment of patent applications. Following Supreme Court case law, lower life forms, referred to as unicellular, are eligible subject matter but the multicellular higher life forms are rejected

---

37 That is to say, the claims are read in light of the specification, which describes the invention. Needless to say, the disclosure must be adequate such that a person skilled in the art can work the invention from it.

38 Patent Act RSC 1985, c P-4, ss 42, 44.

39 *Monsanto Canada Inc. v Schmeiser* 2004 SCC 34.

40 ibid para 58.

41 There is one caveat. For living organisms, a patent infringement claim may be defeated by evidence of innocent infringement, i.e., the plant seed blew onto your property and efforts were made to eradicate it.

42 Available at *Manual of Patent Office Practice (MOPOP)* (Government of Canada) <opic-cipo.gc.ca>.

outright.[43] Furthermore, the MOPOP seems to specifically reject the possibility of crossbreeding as patent eligible.[44]

From the above, it is uncontroversial that many important innovations relevant to the cannabis industry may be eligible for patent protection. As one source noted, innovations in the cannabis industry may include novel packaging, paraphernalia such as pipes, novel cannabis processing methods, novel food products and e-liquids, novel extracts and extraction methods, novel (drug) formulations, new or improved systems, processes or equipment for cultivation and harvest or pest control, novel compositions of cannabinoids,

---

43 ibid at 23.02.02, Higher and Lower Life Forms: "Lower life forms are generally deemed to fall within the scope of section 2 as being either 'manufactures' or 'compositions of matter' since they can be produced *en masse* (bearing similarity to how chemical compounds are prepared) and formed in such large numbers that any measurable quantity will possess uniform properties and characteristics … Note that the fact that a claimed cell could form part of a higher life form does not mean that the claim to the cell should necessarily be construed to be a claim to the higher life form. However, where, upon a purposive construction, a claim to a cell is construed to be a claim to a higher life form, the claim lacks compliance with section 2 of the Patent Act. Where a claim is construed as an isolated cell, there is no need to specify in the claim that the cell is "as found in the laboratory" or is "in isolated form". Lower life forms include: microscopic algae; unicellular fungi (including moulds and yeasts); bacteria; protozoa; viruses; transformed cell lines; hybridomas; and embryonic, pluripotent and multipotent stem cells.

44 ibid at 23.02.03, Processes to Produce Life Forms: "The patentability of a method or process is independent of whether or not the product of the method or process is statutory. Processes to produce higher life forms, organs or tissues are not, therefore, defective on the grounds that they produce non-statutory products. An especially important consideration is the degree of human intervention embodied in the claimed process. A process which occurs essentially according to nature, with no significant human intervention, is not patentable. Thus, for example, a claim construed to be directed to a process for producing a plant solely by traditional cross-breeding techniques is not patentable (even where one of the cross-bred plants is transgenic or otherwise modified). A process that is a result of both human intervention and the laws of nature, however, is patent-eligible subject-matter where at least one step of human intervention is an essential element of the claim. Processes that are considered to include significant human intervention include: processes to produce a lower life form, processes to produce a higher life form (if more than traditional breeding techniques), processes to produce an organ or a tissue through genetic transformation; processes for the *in vitro* culturing or manipulation of cells; processes to separate cells; and processes to generate mutants using a chemical or physical agent."

molecular methods for plant breeding, and novel plant varieties.[45] As outlined below, the current patent register bears many such patents. However, it seems from case law and the MOPOP that novel plant varieties will require an element of human ingenuity that forms a significant part of the plant and not, for example, mere traditional crossbreeding methods to become patentable.

Since 2018, 151 patents have been issued for inventions that contain the word "cannab*" in their title. This is a vast increase from the 17 that were issued prior to legalisation. A review of the titles suggests that most inventions relate to cannabinoid compound uses, methods of extracting or changing the composition of cannabinoids, and preparation of products with cannabinoids, or in one case, a method for detecting cannabis use.[46] None of these inventions pertain to plant varieties at the cellular level. Three pertain to genetically engineered sativa plants, though the actual claims of those inventions relate to pharmaceutical compounds derived therefrom.[47] Unfortunately, there is no record in the patent search database of unsuccessful patent applications; as a result, it is therefore difficult to understand whether plant cellular patents are not being applied for, or whether they are being rejected by the patent office. As for genetic engineering specifically, one source notes that as of 2018, "no reliable genetic engineering of cannabis is currently available".[48]

9.5 PLANT BREEDERS' RIGHTS

The development of new plant varieties for enhanced agricultural properties is a long-standing practice of ancient origin. While traditional methods of crossbreeding continue, modern biotechnology has introduced methods of

---

45 M Pidkowich, TW Sum, "Key Intellectual Property Issues in the Cannabis Industry" in Legal Education Society of Alberta, *Legalization of Marijuana* (2018) 12–13.

46 Canadian patent No. 2893697 is noteworthy. It protects an invention defined as "Single serve beverage pod containing cannabis". Specifically, according to the patent abstract, this invention consists of "Single-serve containers for use in brewing a cannabis-based beverage are described, as are methods for preparing a single-serve container configured for receipt in a single-serve brewing machine. The method includes: adding a processed cannabis product to the single-serve container; adding, to the single-serve container, at least one of an extraction or flavoring agent; and sealing the single-serve container" <https://www.ic.gc.ca/opic-cipo/cpd/eng/patent/2893697/summary.html?query=title%3A%28cannabis%29+AND+%28current-status%3APatents%29&type=advanced_search>.

47 Canadian patent No. 3091776. "Genetically Modified Cannabis Sativa Plants and Modified Cannabinoid Compounds for Treatment of Substance Addiction and Other Disorders."

48 Pidkowich, Sum (n 45) 23.

molecular manipulation for the development of new plant varieties.[49] Whether by traditional or modern means, plant breeders invest significant time and resources into the development of new plant varieties.[50] Since 1990, Canada has offered special protection for the development of new plant varieties. As in other countries, this protection is for new varieties of plant species possessing a new characteristic or improved agricultural property. Canada's Plant Breeders' Rights Act was amended in 2015 to implement the treaty commitments of UPOV 1991.[51] The Act applies to all categories of the plant kingdom except algae, bacteria, and fungi.[52] To obtain exclusive rights, the plant variety must be new, distinct, stable, and uniform.

Despite concerns that cannabis plant varieties present problems of stability generally and uniformity with respect to cannabinoids, which, as mentioned are two essential requirements for protection,[53] this has not prevented the registration of over 60 cannabis plant variety applications. Only five of these have been granted rights, all in connection with the taxon Cannabis sativa hemp. Twelve others in this taxon have been given provisional protection, and one application has been abandoned. In the Cannabis sativa taxon, 25 applications have provisional protection, while 17 others have been withdrawn or abandoned. There is one abandoned application in the Cannabis sativa subsp. indica taxon dating back to 2013. Most applications have occurred in the past three years and almost all since legalisation. The only exceptions are six Cannabis sativa hemp applications, most of which have still not resolved.

Particularly with respect to cannabinoid-bearing plants, there has not been much success so far in the granting of plant variety rights, except on a provisional basis. It is difficult to know whether this is due to the inherent instability and uniformity of these plants, lack of investment, long research and development periods, or long trial testing periods – or some combination of these.

9.6 CONCLUSION

There is no doubt that the legalisation of recreational cannabis use in Canada has incentivised some innovation in this emerging industry. In all areas discussed in the chapter – trademarks, patents, and plant varieties – there have

[49] de Beer, Gaffen (n 17) 633.

[50] ibid.

[51] SC 1990, c 20. UPOV International Convention for the Protection of New Varieties of Plants.

[52] Section 4, Plant Breeders' Rights Regulation SOR 91/594, Schedule 1.

[53] de Beer, Gaffen (n 17) 646–647. As the authors note, these attributes may also have negative implications for patent-eligible plants, particularly in connection with the utility requirement.

been modest but marked increases in the number of applications for protection in the eight years since legalisation. These are still early days and, as research and development in this area matures, we might see dramatic increases in innovative activity. Still, there are reasons to be pessimistic. The severe promotion and labelling restrictions in the industry imposed under the Cannabis Act hinder revenue generation and disincentivise brand and product development. More generally, despite high expectations and initial growth, the industry is currently in decline. In tandem with the feasibility of genetic engineering and plant variety development of cannabis, we might wonder whether IP is able to play much of a role in the immediate future of this industry.

10. Cannabis regulation and IP rights in Uruguay

Maximiliano Marzetti

10.1 INTRODUCTION[1]

The first part of this chapter introduces the comprehensive regulatory framework for cannabis liberalization in Uruguay, which was the first of its kind in the world. Understanding the unique Uruguayan regulatory framework and its evolution is essential, as each market and its corresponding regulations impact the incentives for economic actors and the utilization of intellectual property (IP) rights differently. The second part of this chapter examines how existing IP rights in Uruguay have been employed to support cannabis research, development, and commercialization. The conclusion provides an overview of some general observations on the role of economic incentives and IP rights in relation to cannabis products and services in developing countries.

10.2 URUGUAY, AN EXCEPTIONAL CASE IN LATIN AMERICA

In 2013, Uruguay became the first country to regulate the cannabis market for recreational, medicinal, and industrial purposes. With a population of approximately 3.5 million, residing primarily in the capital, Montevideo, and an area of 176,215 square kilometers (68,037 square miles), Uruguay is one of Latin America's smallest countries. It is an exceptional case of political and economic stability in a region often marked by instability and structural inequality.[2] Moreover, Uruguay is distinguished by its social democratic tradition,

[1] All Spanish-to-English translations contained in this chapter belong to the author.

[2] Albeit with one exception, the civil and military de facto regime which ruled the country from 1973 to 1985, from which the country managed to escape in a

adherence to the rule of law, secularism, and tolerance, earning it the moniker "the Switzerland of Latin America."[3] Over the years, Uruguay has successfully developed and maintained a liberal democratic model and a welfare state unparalleled in the region. Furthermore, Uruguay is the least religious country in the region, characterized by a secular state tradition comparable to the French concept of "*laïcité*."[4] The strict separation of state and church may in part explain Uruguay's distinctive policymaking style – pragmatic and progressive, detached from conservative religious and moral stances.[5]

On December 20, 2013, Uruguay passed the Cannabis Act No. 19.172 (CA), which legalized cannabis for recreational, industrial, and medicinal uses. Uruguay was the first country to do so, and to date, its approach remains somewhat unique. Uruguay's tradition of democratic alternation and policy continuity facilitates the implementation of radical legal reforms; the CA was signed by President Pedro Mujica (Frente Amplio, center-left), and continued by Tabaré Vázquez (also Frente Amplio) in 2015 and then by Luis Alberto Lacalle Pou (Partido Nacional, center-right) in 2020, indicating bipartisan support across different political affiliations and ideologies.

10.3 A BRIEF HISTORY OF CANNABIS IN LATIN AMERICA

Cannabis sativa, a species within the family Cannabaceae, was first classified by Carl Linnaeus in 1753. In 1785, Jean Baptiste Lamarck identified another species, naming it Cannabis indica.[6] To date, at least 13 different cannabis species have been identified.[7] For simplicity, this chapter will use the term "cannabis" to refer to all its species and varieties, including those used in industry (where it is known as hemp) and for recreational consumption (where it is known under a plethora of different names, such as marijuana, Mary Jane, weed, pot, dope, ganja, etc.).

---

consensual manner. See CG Gillespie, *Negotiating Democracy: Politicians and Generals in Uruguay* (Cambridge University Press 1991).

[3] Also, in the past, due to its banking secrecy.

[4] See N da Costa, "Religion and Public Space in the Uruguayan 'laïcité'" (2018) 65(4) Social Compass 503–515.

[5] Uruguay was the first Latin American country to allow divorce on the sole will of the woman (1907), to provide universal poor relief at the expense of the state (1910), and to grant the women's vote (1932).

[6] GE Ángeles López, F Brindis, S Cristians Niizawa, R Ventura Martínez (2014) "Cannabis sativa L., una planta singular" 45(4) Revista Mexicana de Ciencias Farmacéuticas 1–6.

[7] ibid.

Cannabis contains numerous compounds such as cannabinoids, flavonoids, alkaloids, terpenes, stilbenes, and phenolic amides. Cannabinoids are the most studied and abundant, with THC (delta-9-tetrahydrocannabinol) being the primary psychoactive compound, predominantly found in the flowers, leaves, and stems of the female cannabis plant. THC induces relaxation and euphoria, commonly referred to as "a high," and possesses some therapeutic properties alongside potential harmful side effects, including intoxication. The second most prevalent cannabinoid is CBD (cannabidiol), which lacks psychotropic effects. CBD is a key ingredient in many cannabis-derived medicines used to treat anxiety, insomnia, chronic pain, arthritis, and inflammation, and is also added to various food, drinks, and beauty products. The origins of cannabis are traced to Asia, with some scholars suggesting its cultivation began approximately 10,000 years ago. Initially, cannabis was used for producing fibers for paper, clothing, and navigation equipment, such as sails and ropes. Medicinal and recreational uses are ancient, with evidence found in ancient Chinese and Indian texts.[8]

Cannabis reached the Americas in the late fifteenth or early sixteenth centuries, possibly brought by Christopher Columbus. Hemp[9] production was officially promoted by the Spanish King during the colonial period for its valuable fibers used in navigation. In 1532, the Royal Audience authorized cannabis planting for textiles in the Viceroyalty of New Spain (now Mexico and the Southwestern United States). In 1545, King Charles I authorized the planting of cannabis in all colonial territories and ordered the instruction of Indigenous people in spinning and weaving. Jesuits later taught and experimented with the medicinal uses of cannabis.[10]

10.4 THE REGULATION OF CANNABIS IN URUGUAY

10.4.1 The Situation up to 2013

Uruguay's first Criminal Code of 1889 criminalized drug consumption, a stance continued in the 1934 Criminal Code, which imposed penalties for trading or possessing narcotics, including cocaine, opium, and derivatives. Act No. 9.692 of 1937 listed prohibited substances, including hashish, with

[8] See S Pisanti, M Bifulco, "Medical Cannabis: A Plurimillennial History of an Evergreen" (2019) 234(6) Journal of Cellular Physiology 8342–8351.

[9] Hemp refers to Cannabis sativa used for industrial purposes and typically contains 0.3 percent or less THC in most countries.

[10] See P Leal-Galicia, D Betancourt, A González-González, H Romo-Parra, "A Brief History of Marijuana in the Western World" (2018) 67(4) Revista de Neurología 133–140.

consumption punishable by up to two years' imprisonment, doubled for recidivism. However, there was a divorce between *law-in-books* and *law-in-action*; as a consequence, criminal sanctions were rarely applied to individual users, focusing instead on drug trade organizations. The first milestone towards liberalization occurred in 1974 when Decree Law 14.299 decriminalized substance consumption while maintaining penalties for storage, trafficking, and supply, aligning legal norms with the prevailing social norms.

Despite decriminalization, drug abuse remained a government concern. In 1988, Decree No. 463 established the National Board for the Prevention and Repression of Illicit Drug Trafficking and Abuse (Junta Nacional de Prevención y Represión del Tráfico Ilícito y Uso Abusivo de Drogas), under the Office of the President, to propose policies for reducing drug supply and demand, drug-related crime, and citizen insecurity, and to create an assistance network for addicts. In 1999, a new National Drug Board (Junta Nacional de Drogas) and National Drug Secretariat (Secretaría Nacional de Drogas) were created to implement prevention, treatment, rehabilitation, and repression policies. A series of drug-related crimes in 2012 opened a "window of opportunity" for legal reform.[11]

10.4.2 The Current Framework

In July 2012, then-President José "Pepe" Mujica proposed comprehensive cannabis legalization. Subsequently, on December 7, 2013, Cannabis Act No. 19.172, regulating access to recreational, industrial, and medicinal cannabis, was published. The CA came into force on December 20, 2013, positioning Uruguay as the first country to comprehensively legalize cannabis. The CA was complemented by a series of Executive Decrees: No. 120/014 (for recreational use), No. 372/014 (for industrial use), No. 46/015 (for medicinal use and research, repealed on April 2, 2015), and No. 56/023 (for the production and sale of cannabis-derived products through pharmacies).

According to some authors, the Uruguayan model for the legalization of recreational cannabis has attempted to strike a middle ground between two opposing models,[12] i.e., prohibition and free commercialization. Moreover, in the case of Uruguay, the decision to liberalize cannabis followed a top-down

---

11 See R Queirolo, C Rossel, E Álvarez, L Repetto, "Why Uruguay Legalized Marijuana? The Open Window of Public Insecurity" (2019) 114(7) Addiction 1313–1321.

12 See M Cerdá, B Kilmer, "Uruguay's Middle-Ground Approach to Cannabis Legalization" (2017) 42 The International Journal on Drug Policy 118.

approach.[13] The decision was taken by the political elite, disregarding or even contradicting the aspirations of the majority of citizens at the time.[14] Over time, as legalization did not lead to increased public security concerns, public opinion began to change.[15]

Even if the U.S. states of Colorado and Washington legalized cannabis a little earlier, they remain to this day constrained by limiting federal rules.[16] The regulatory approach followed by Uruguay is unique. While the supply of recreational cannabis in Colorado and Washington relies on free markets, there is no mandatory registry for users,[17] or marketing and branding restrictions;[18] Uruguay does so via monitored channels, relies on a state monopoly for production with fixed prices, a registry of users, and "plain packaging." The Uruguayan policy also differs from the more recent approach implemented by Canada, which allows private actors in the recreational cannabis market.

While a revenue-maximizing monopoly sets prices above market equilibrium, Uruguay's state monopoly on cannabis was instituted as a public policy measure, allowing the government to set legal cannabis prices at a competitive level relative to the black market. The slightly higher price of official

---

13 See R Queirolo, "Uruguay: The First Country to Legalize Cannabis" in Queirolo, "Uruguay: The First Country to Legalize Cannabis" in T Decorte, S Lenton, C Wilkins, *Legalizing Cannabis* (Routledge 2020) 116–130.

14 See JM Cruz, MF Boidi, R Queirolo "Saying No to Weed: Public Opinion towards Cannabis Legalization in Uruguay" (2018) 25(1) Drugs: Education, Prevention and Policy 67–76.

15 See JM Cruz, MF Boidi, R Queirolo, "The Status of Support for Cannabis Regulation in Uruguay 4 Years after Reform: Evidence from Public Opinion Surveys" (2018) 37(Suppl.1) Drug and Alcohol Review S429–S434.

16 At the federal level, cannabis remains a prohibited substance, at least for the moment, pursuant to the Controlled Substances Act.

17 For a comparison, see, for example, B Pardo, "Cannabis Policy Reforms in the Americas: A Comparative Analysis of Colorado, Washington, and Uruguay" (2014) 25(4) International Journal of Drug Policy 727–735; M Gandilhon, I Obradovic, N Lalam, D Alimi, D Weinberger (2018) "Colorado vs Uruguay: Deux Modes Opposés de Légalisation du Cannabis" (2018) 16(1) Drogues, Santé et Société 70–85; B Pardo, "Cannabis Policy Reforms in the Americas: A Comparative Analysis of Colorado, Washington, and Uruguay" (2014) 25(4) International Journal of Drug Policy 727–735.

18 Most federal trademark registrations for cannabis-related products at the USPTO are rejected, with some limited exceptions based, for instance, on the *commercial free speech* doctrine. In this regard, see LG Jacobs, "Regulating Marijuana Advertising and Marketing to Promote Public Health: Navigating the Constitutional Minefield" (2018) 21(4) Lewis & Clark Law Review. See also Chapter 1 in this volume, authored by Luke Zimmermann.

cannabis is offset by its consistent quality and guaranteed origin, aiming to undermine the black market without significantly incentivizing new consumer groups, particularly minors.[19] For similar reasons, the government decided not to excise taxes on recreational cannabis.[20]

However, this monopoly system presents challenges, as it results in an insufficient supply to meet existing demand, thereby encouraging unserved consumers to turn to the black market – the very issue the legislation aims to address. This reflects a well-documented regulatory failure in economics, where even well-intentioned central planners lack the information spontaneously produced by markets, making it difficult to set prices that balance supply and demand effectively.[21]

The government advanced three reasons for legalizing cannabis: (a) reducing drug trafficking-related crime by establishing a legal market, (b) promoting public health through controlled market access, education, and prevention campaigns, and (c) decriminalizing cannabis use and consumption. While the Act aimed to regulate both industrial and medicinal cannabis markets, the initial focus was primarily on recreational cannabis.

The CA distinguishes three markets for cannabis, all regulated, but with different levels of intensity: (1) the planting, cultivation, and harvesting of psychoactive cannabis for recreational purposes; (2) the planting, cultivation, harvesting, and industrialization of non-psychoactive cannabis for non-medical purposes; and (3) the planting, cultivation, harvesting, and industrialization of psychoactive and non-psychoactive cannabis for medicinal purposes and scientific research.

The CA initially prioritized the regulation of recreational cannabis. However, the increased public and private interest in the industrial and medicinal cannabis markets demonstrated the need for additional legislative measures. In response, two acts were passed in December 2019: Act No. 19.845, which promotes scientific research on cannabis and establishes a new agency to provide tax exemptions for research equipment and inputs, and Act No. 19.847, which facilitates access to cannabis-derived medicines, promoting their medical and therapeutic use.

The regulation defines psychoactive cannabis as the flowering tops of the female cannabis plant with a THC content equal to 1 percent or more (Section 3B of Law Decree No. 14.294, modified by Act No. 19.172). Non-psychoactive

---

[19] See E Cohen, R McGowan, "Grass is Always Greener When it is Legal: Policies for State Regulated Marijuana" (2012) 9(1) Economists' Voice 1–6.

[20] See M Castaldi, "Uruguay to Sell Marijuana Tax-free to Undercut Drug Traffickers" *Reuters* (18 May 2014).

[21] See F Hayek, "The Use of Knowledge in Society" (1945) XXXV(4) American Economic Review 519–530.

cannabis contains no more than 1 percent THC, with seeds not exceeding 0.5 percent THC (Section 3C). Recreational cannabis must have a THC content between 2 percent and 9 percent. Only Uruguayan citizens or accredited permanent residents aged 18 or older can access recreational cannabis through three mutually exclusive regulated channels.

Pursuant to the CA, the three available channels for accessing recreational cannabis are: (1) *home growing*: authorized individuals can grow up to six female flowering plants per household, with production capped at 480 grams per year. Surplus production must be surrendered. Licenses are valid for three years and renewable; (2) *cannabis clubs*: these are non-profit associations ranging from 5 to 45 adults that can collectively grow up to 99 plants, with annual dispensation capped at 480 grams per member. Clubs must be located more than 150 meters from educational, cultural, or sports centers and addiction treatment institutions;[22] and (3) *retail purchases in authorized pharmacies*. In either case, Uruguayan citizens can buy up to 40 grams per month, limited to 10 grams per week.

Not many Uruguayan pharmacies have agreed to sell cannabis; most have opted out due to reputational concerns and the threat of financial sanctions (see Section 10.5 below). Non-residents are currently prohibited from accessing recreational cannabis through any of the three legal channels. Journalistic reports suggest that the government may be considering the removal of this restriction. The use of recreational cannabis is limited in public spaces where tobacco smoking is also prohibited.

A 2023 report estimates that 250,000 individuals use legal channels, representing 34 percent of all cannabis consumers.[23] The same report suggests that 51 percent of users access cannabis legally, indicating that a majority of recreational users now rely on legal channels. Consequently, nearly a decade after the CA passage, the black market, which offers lower-quality imported cannabis (mainly from Paraguay), has become a minor source. The report lists 61,129 authorized purchasers, 14,592 authorized home growers, and 306 authorized cannabis clubs. Currently, 38 pharmacies are authorized as official sales points, primarily in Montevideo and Maldonado.

The Institute for the Regulation and Control of Cannabis (IRCCA) is the state agency charged with overseeing the implementation of the CA, regulating all aspects of cannabis production and distribution, and maintaining registries for home growers, cannabis clubs, and purchasers.[24] IRCCA also determines

---

[22] See R Queirolo, MF Boidi, JM Cruz, "Cannabis Clubs in Uruguay: The Challenges of Regulation" (2016) 34 International Journal of Drug Policy 41–48.

[23] IRCCA, Informe N°16 de monitoreo del mercado regulado del cannabis al 30 de junio de 2023.

[24] Instituto de Regulación y Control del Cannabis.

the prices for various types of psychoactive cannabis sold at pharmacies. The production of recreational cannabis is delegated by the government to three private companies, which were licensed by the IRCCA through a competitive bidding process.[25] These are the only entities authorized to produce and distribute recreational cannabis in Uruguay.

According to Article 6 of Law 14.294, both the import and export of medicinal cannabis require prior authorization from the Ministry of Public Health (MSP), which issues the necessary certificates for these activities. Producing medicinal cannabis necessitates authorization from both the IRCCA and the MSP. No medicinal cannabis may be advertised or sold without prior registration with the MSP. To date, the MSP has approved 14 medicinal products containing cannabis. The production of non-psychoactive cannabis for industrial purposes (hemp) requires prior authorization by the Ministry of Livestock, Agriculture and Fisheries (MGAP). In all cases, cannabis production must comply with stringent anti-money laundering and anti-terrorist financing regulations.[26]

10.5 ISSUES CONCERNING INTERNATIONAL COMMITMENTS AND FINANCIAL REGULATIONS

When Act No. 19.172 was passed, it apparently contravened Uruguay's earlier international commitments under the United Nations' 1961 Single Convention on Narcotic Drugs (SCND), which Uruguay ratified without reservations on October 31, 1975. The SCND categorizes cannabis in Schedule I, indicating probable addiction and serious abuse risk, and in Schedule IV, as among the most dangerous substances with minimal medical value. The International Narcotics Control Board, which monitors the implementation of UN drug control conventions, has indeed accused Uruguay of violating its obligations. Despite these allegations, Uruguay has not withdrawn from the SCND, asserting that its human rights obligations, particularly the rights to freedom and health for its citizens, take precedence over international commitments related to drug control. The SCND's enforcement capabilities are limited, primarily offering criticism rather than imposing sanctions.

The U.S. Federal Government, a major supporter of drug prohibitionism, could have exerted political pressure on Uruguay. However, this was unlikely,

[25] At the moment, Jabelor S.A., Legiral S.A., and Faises S.A.

[26] The concerned agency in Uruguay is the National Secretariat for the Fight against Money Laundering and the Financing of Terrorism (SENACLAFT). For an analysis of this and other compliance challenges firms face in Uruguay, see J Hurtado, "La Industria del Cannabis en Uruguay, los Desafíos Frente a la Banca y al Compliance" (*LexLatin*, 6 June 2023).

as in 2012, Colorado and Washington legalized cannabis, challenging federal drug policy. When Uruguay legalized cannabis, these states had already done so, making it hypocritical for the U.S. to pressure Uruguay. This timing was likely exploited by the Uruguayan government.

International signals suggest a shift in stance. In 2020, the UN Commission on Narcotic Drugs, following a World Health Organization (WHO) recommendation, reclassified cannabis to acknowledge its medical value, removing it from Schedule IV.[27] However, tensions persist between countries legalizing drugs and those adhering to prohibitionist treaties.[28]

It should also be noted that the U.S. indirectly hindered Uruguay's reforms through the banking system. In 2017, Bank of America and Citibank notified Uruguayan banks to cease services to pharmacies selling recreational cannabis, citing the Patriot Act.[29] Under threat of asset seizure, Uruguayan banks warned pharmacies to stop selling cannabis or face account closures. Some pharmacies chose to stop selling cannabis to maintain banking services, while others adopted a cash-only model. The Patriot Act's extraterritorial effect proved more effective in constraining Uruguay's cannabis policy than international drug treaties.[30] In 2018, Canada legalized cannabis, prompting Uruguayan firms to use Canadian banks to avoid U.S. sanctions. However, Canadian banks must also comply with U.S. regulations, making this solution uncertain.

10.6 INTELLECTUAL PROPERTY ASPECTS OF CANNABIS UNDER URUGUAYAN LAW

Uruguay recognizes and protects a comprehensive range of IP rights, including trademarks, patents, utility models, design rights, geographical indications,

---

[27] See K Riboulet-Zemouli, MA Krawitz, "WHO is First Scientific Review of Medicinal Cannabis: From Global Struggle to Patient Implications" (2022) 23(1) Drugs, Habits, and Social Policy 5–21.

[28] See J Walsh, M Jelsma, "Regulating Drugs: Resolving Conflicts with the UN Drug Control Treaty System" (2019) 1(3) Journal of Illicit Economies and Development 266–271.

[29] The Uniting and Strengthening America by Providing Appropriate Tools Required to Intercept and Obstruct Terrorism (USA PATRIOT) Act of 2001, among other things, precludes involvement with controlled substances, including cannabis, and has extraterritorial reach.

[30] See RA Barry, "'We Never Thought This Would Be Considered Drug Trafficking': International Finance Rules, Policy Space and Uruguay's Regulation of Recreational Cannabis" (2023) 18(1) Global Public Health 2283042.

appellations of origin, trade secrets, copyrights, and related rights, as well as plant breeders' rights.

At the international level, Uruguay is a member of the World Intellectual Property Organization (WIPO) and the World Trade Organization (WTO) and a signatory to most major international IP treaties. Therefore, Uruguay's domestic IP domestic legislation is largely harmonized with international minimum standards of IP rights protection. In addition, Uruguay is a member of the Southern Common Market (MERCOSUR), which has some rules to harmonize IP rights.[31]

Section 33 of the Uruguayan Constitution states that the rights of authors, artists, and inventors shall be legally recognized and protected. The most relevant domestic IP laws, of relevance for the cannabis industry, are the Trademark Act No. 17.011 (TA) of 1998, amended by Act No. 19.670 of 2018; the Patent Act No. 17.164 of September 2 (PA) of 1999, amended by Act No. 19.924 of 2020; and the Seeds Act No. 16.811 of 1997 (PBR Act). While other IP rights, such as utility models, design rights, geographical indications, and copyrights, may provide some benefit to cannabis producers, their overall impact is comparatively limited. Trade secrets, while relevant, are not directly observable and are therefore also excluded from the scope of this discussion.

10.6.1 Trademarks

It is important to emphasize that trademarks cannot be used in the recreational cannabis market. According to the CA, all forms of branding for recreational cannabis are prohibited. This includes "any form of direct or indirect advertising, promotion, sponsorship, or sponsorship of psychoactive cannabis products by any of the various media: written press, radio, television, cinema, magazines, filming in general, posters, billboards, flyers, banners, e-mail, Internet technologies, as well as by any other suitable means" (CA Article 11). The regulatory Decree No. 120/014 adds that the packaging and distribution of psychoactive cannabis shall be carried out by the producer from the site directly to the pharmacies (Article 13).

The guidelines for the labeling and packaging of recreational cannabis have been established through a series of unpublished IRCCA decisions. The label specifies the name of the variety using Greek letters (Alpha, Beta, Gamma, and Delta) and a system of Roman numerals to identify the authorized producers

[31] The 1995 Protocol for the harmonizing of rules for trademarks, indications of source, and appellation of origin; and the 1998 Protocol for the harmonization of rules on industrial designs.

(II, III, and IV). THC and CBD content and net weight are also visible on the label.

No company branding is permitted on the packaging; however, IRCCA assigns, besides the distinct Roman numeral mentioned above, a different color to each producing firm. Moreover, the producing company's name appears on the back of the packaging, allowing consumers to identify the product's origin and, in principle, choose the variety they prefer, provided it is in stock. Notably, the price remains uniform across all varieties. The only distinct logo on the packaging is that of the IRCCA.[32]

The rationale for the minimalistic labeling for recreational cannabis in Uruguay echoes, *mutatis mutandis*, the plain packaging for tobacco products.[33] Uruguay was indeed the first Latin American country to implement plain packaging rules for tobacco products, a decision contested by the tobacco industry, but similar measures adopted by Australia, the UK, and other countries ultimately have been upheld by both national and international bodies.[34] Such a semiotic policy seems to suggest governments do not endorse the neoclassical economic theory that suggests brands are purely informative vehicles allowing rational consumers to make better informed purchase decisions (Search-Cost Theory),[35] but, under certain circumstances, may persuade and even incite some consumers to purchase what they otherwise would not.[36]

---

32 Which is not a registered trademark in Uruguay.

33 Without graphic warnings or pictures. For more on plain packaging, see Chapter 6 by Enrico Bonadio and Akshita Roghati.

34 See also the relevant WTO Appellate Body and Panel reports concerning DS435, Australia – Certain Measures Concerning Trademarks, Geographical Indications and Other Plain Packaging Requirements Applicable to Tobacco Products and Packaging, also relevant to the Uruguayan situation; for a discussion, see, *inter multis*, E Bonadio, A Marsoof, "Logo? No Logo? The WTO Dispute on Plain Packaging of Tobacco, and Beyond" in C Geiger, *Research Handbook on Intellectual Property and Investment Law* (Edward Elgar Publishing 2020) 339–365. As far as a Uruguayan measure similar to plain packaging, and the related legal dispute, see ICSID Case No. ARB/10/7, *Philip Morris Brands Sarl, Philip Morris Products S.A. and Abal Hermanos S.A. v Oriental Republic of Uruguay*, ICSID Case No. ARB/10/7 (formerly *FTR Holding SA, Philip Morris Products S.A. and Abal Hermanos S.A. v Oriental Republic of Uruguay*), concerning the international investment front.

35 This represents the traditional *Law & Economics* perspective on trademarks; for a detailed explanation, see, *inter multis*, WM Landes, RA Posner, "Trademark Law: An Economic Perspective" (1987) 30(2) The Journal of Law and Economics 265–309.

36 For a theoretical discussion, see NS Economides, "The Economics of Trademarks" (1988) 78 The Trademark Reporter; and B Beebe, "Search and

There is no explicit prohibition on the use of trademarks for cannabis products or services in the medicinal or industrial markets. Consequently, such use is permitted, as evidenced by a quick trademark search at the Uruguayan Intellectual Property Office (officially known as the DNPI). Nonetheless, trademark rules and other relevant legal requirements must be observed. In Uruguay, as elsewhere, a sign must be distinctive to qualify for trademark registration. Additionally, the sign must not fall under any absolute or relative grounds for refusal. Absolute grounds include prohibitions against signs that contravene public policy or morality.[37]

Pursuant to Article 7 of the 1883 Paris Convention, to which Uruguay is a member, "[t]he nature of the goods to which a trademark is to be applied shall in no case form an obstacle to the registration of the mark." Therefore, a trademark should not be rejected solely for identifying cannabis products or services. Article 6*quinquies* (B) adds that trademarks may be neither denied registration nor invalidated except in the following cases: (iii) "when they are contrary to morality or public order and, in particular, of such a nature as to deceive the public." However, the same provision adds that "a mark may not be considered contrary to public order for the sole reason that it does not conform to a provision of the legislation on marks, except if such provision itself relates to public order."

Since the passing of the CA, it is not possible to claim that a trademark containing the word cannabis or any of its components, or a graphical representation of them, is contrary to public policy or morality in Uruguay. For example, a trademark such as "Cannabis Store Amsterdam,"[38] denied by the EUIPO as contrary to public policy and morality, could in principle registered in Uruguay if considered distinctive and not misleading. Nevertheless, a trademark for cannabis products or services may still be subject to prohibition if it includes words or symbols that contravene current legal and moral standards accepted in Uruguayan society.

Certainly, to commercialize products or services containing or related to cannabis or its components, it is not necessary to make explicit reference to them. The *principle of trademark specificity* relates the distinctiveness of a sign to the product or service it identifies. The more arbitrary this connection,

---

Persuasion in Trademark Law" (2004) 103 Michigan Law Review 523–539.

[37] "Drawings or expressions contrary to public order, morals or good customs" (TA Article 4 para 13).

[38] See Judgment of the General Court (Seventh Chamber) of December 12, 2019, in *re Santa Conte v European Union Intellectual Property Office, Case T-683/18*; and, for an analysis of the latest judgments concerning morality and trademarks in the EU see B. van der Donk (2022) 17(3) Journal of Intellectual Property Law & Practice 303–307.

the more distinctive the trademark becomes. However, arbitrary or fanciful trademarks, lacking evocative elements, tend to be more challenging and costly to market. Consequently, many firms opt to incorporate generic, descriptive, or evocative terms in their trademarks.

The TA includes, among the absolute grounds for refusal, the registration of generic and descriptive words. However, a search in the trademark registry of the DNPI suggests words such as "cannabis," "CBD," or "THC," or images such as the cannabis plant, are commonly found in registered trademarks for cannabis products or services. The explanation for this practice can be found in TA Article 7, which states that signs falling into the absolute grounds for prohibition of paragraphs 9, 10, 11, and 12,[39] may yet be registered as part of a larger semiotic ensemble, without giving the trademark owner any exclusive rights over each sign, individually considered. For instance, trademarks containing the term "CBD" have been granted for products in class 3,[40] class 5,[41] and "THC" for products in class 25[42] and class 30.[43]

In the DNPI register, one can find registered trademarks for the commercialization of cannabis products in class 3 (non-medicated cosmetics,

---

[39] "Technical, commercial or common denominations used to express qualities or attributes of products or services" (TA Article 4 para 9); "designations usually used to indicate the nature of the products or services or the class, genus or species to which they belong" (TA Article 4 para 10); "words or locutions that have entered into general use, and signs or designs that are not fanciful, that is to say, that do not present characteristics of novelty, specialty and distinctiveness (TA Article 4 para 11); and "words or combinations of words in a foreign language whose translation into the Spanish language is included in the prohibitions of the preceding paragraphs 9, 10 and 11 (TA Article 4 para 12).

[40] KALMA CBD COSMETICS, mixed mark, application no. 537309, granted on June 2, 2023, class 3 (limited to non-medicated cosmetic products and toilet preparations; perfumery products; essential oils), owned by ARAL CORPORATE, S.L. (Spain).

[41] CBD TEDAL COMPLEX, mixed mark, application no. 472875, granted on May 11, 2018, class 5 (complete), owned by Marcelo Fabián González Machín (Uruguay).

[42] THC URUGUAY, mixed mark, application no. 459784, granted on November 12, 2015, class 25 (complete), owned by José Ignacio Quintana Moreno (Uruguay). Note that, albeit granted, this is considered a "weak" trademark since the distinctive sign is composed of a generic term (CBD) and a country name (Uruguay, over which the applicant waived any exclusive use).

[43] YERBA MATE CON CBD "LA POSTERGADA" SIN THC, mixed mark, application no. 479999, granted on January 2, 2019, class 30 (limited to "yerba" mate [*ilex paraguariensis*], a very popular herbal drink in Uruguay), owned by González Machín and Marcelo Fabián (Uruguay).

perfumes, oils, etc.); class 5 (pharmaceuticals, medical, and veterinary preparations); class 9 (batteries for electronic cigarettes); class 32 (non-alcoholic cannabis-infused beverages or cannabis extracts); class 33 (cannabis-based wines); class 34 (herbs for smoking); class 40 (manufacturing of pharmaceutical preparations containing cannabidiol); class 41 (medical education in the field of medical cannabis); class 44 (medical advice in the field of medical cannabis), etc. Also, it is worth noting that the current Nice Classification only explicitly refers to cannabis in class 5 (050500: cannabis for medical purposes/ marijuana for medical purposes) and class 31 (310173: cannabis plants; 310174: cannabis, unprocessed), and to cannabidiol in class 5 (050506: cannabidiol for medical use). Some countries do not allow trademark registration for products not explicitly mentioned in the Nice Agreement Classification, but that is not the case in Uruguay, which allows a more flexible interpretation.

Moreover, Chapter VIII of the TA regulates certification or guarantee trademarks. Some scholars suggest the potential strategic advantage of using ethical labels to promote agricultural products coming from developing countries, such as *Fair Trade*,[44] what could also benefit cannabis producers.[45] Also, in recent decades, the Uruguayan government has been promoting its national brand "Uruguay Natural," registered both as a word and mixed mark by the Presidency before the DNPI in 2002, covering all 45 classes of the *Nice Agreement*, and renewed regularly. According to the "Uruguay Natural" use handbook, any Uruguayan company that shares the values of the brand can use it, and it is particularly appealing to firms with export potential. While no evidence has been found thus far, it is plausible that ethical labels or the nation's brand may be utilized in the future to promote cannabis exports, potentially fostering co-branding strategies.[46]

10.6.2 Patents

TRIPS Agreement Article 27.1 enunciates the *principle of technological neutrality*, according to which patents should be granted for any product or process, in all fields of technology, provided that they are new, involve an inventive step, and are capable of industrial application. This resulted in the patentability of pharmaceutical products in developing countries, where such protection was previously unavailable, with detrimental consequences according to

---

[44] S Kay, M Jelsma, D Bewley-Taylor, "Fair Trade Cannabis: A Road Map for Meeting the Socio-economic Needs and Interests of Small and Traditional Growers" (2020) 2(1) Journal of Fair Trade 27–34.

[45] This author is not aware that such labels are currently in use.

[46] On co-branding, see Chapter 8 by Natalie Corthésy.

some authors.[47] However, the TRIPS Agreement provides some *flexibilities*. For instance, Article 27.3(b) states that plants and animals, except microorganisms, and essentially biological processes for the production of plants or animals, except non-biological or microbiological processes, *may* be deemed non-patentable. For the legal protection of plants, Uruguay adopted a *sui generis* model of Plant Variety Protection Rights or Plant Breeder Rights (PBR).

Yet, in congruence with the aforementioned *principle of technological neutrality*, biotechnological patents that do not fall within the scope of the options provided in TRIPS Agreement Article 27.3(b) should in principle be patentable. Due primarily to developmental concerns, some scholars from the Global South oppose this interpretation.[48] Thus, it should come as no surprise to find a small number of patents granted related to plants in developing countries. The author identified only 13 patent applications filed at the DNPI over the past 20 years containing terms such as "cannabis," "THC," or "CBD" in their descriptions.[49] All of these applications were submitted by foreign applicants; of these, nine have been abandoned, one was rejected, and three remain pending substantive examination.

Uruguay, like many countries in the Global South, is not characterized by a high volume of patent activity. In 2022, it ranked 95th out of 170 countries in terms of total patent applications (including both resident and non-resident filings), according to the WIPO statistics database.[50] By way of comparison, a study on IP rights trends for the protection of medical cannabis and related products found that patent filings are concentrated in a few developed countries: the U.S. (26.25 percent), Europe (12.26 percent), Canada (10.25 percent), and Australia (7.20 per cent).[51]

---

[47] See C Vaitsos, "Patents Revisited: Their Function in Developing Countries" (1972) 9(1) The Journal of Development Studies 71–97. More moderate authors suggest that the link between economic growth and (stronger) patent protection is less accentuated in developing countries than in developed ones. In this regard see, PC Neves, O Afonso, D Silva, E Sochirca, "The Link between Intellectual Property Rights, Innovation, and Growth: A Meta-analysis" (2021) 97 Economic Modelling 196–209.

[48] In this sense, see C Correa, *Patent Protection for Plants: Legal Options for Developing Countries* (Research Paper 55 2014) The South Centre; and CM Correa, JI Correa, B de Jonge "The Status of Patenting Plants in the Global South" (2020) 23(1–2) The Journal of World Intellectual Property 121–146.

[49] <https://pamp.miem.gub.uy/pamp/pages/patentSelect.xhtml>.

[50] WIPO IP Statistics Data Center (December 2023).

[51] J Wyse, G Luria, "Trends in Intellectual Property Rights Protection for Medical Cannabis and Related Products" (2021) 3(1) Journal of Cannabis Research 1–22.

Moreover, in Uruguay, the majority of patent applications are submitted by non-residents. For example, in 2017, Uruguay received 23 patent applications from residents and 500 from non-residents, according to the World Bank database.[52] In 2024, Uruguay acceded to the Patent Cooperation Treaty (PCT), a development expected to primarily benefit non-residents.[53]

10.6.3 Plant Breeder's Rights

The early forms of PBR were first recognized in Czechoslovakia and France in the early 1920s, with subsequent adoption in Austria, the Netherlands, and Germany.[54] An international framework for plant variety protection was provided by the UPOV Convention, signed in 1961 and amended in 1972, 1978, and 1991. Uruguay became a party to the UPOV Convention in 1994, adhering to the Act of 1978.

As mentioned in the previous section, TRIPS Agreement Article 27.3(b) reflects the differing perspectives between developed and developing countries regarding plant patents and highlights the challenges faced during the Uruguay Round negotiations in reaching a consensus. Uruguay, like most developing countries, has chosen to protect plant varieties through the issuance of PBRs rather than plant patents. In this area, member states retain significant discretion; PBRs are considered more amenable to developing goals.[55] In contrast, the U.S. system of plant patents is a distinctive feature of American law.[56]

Uruguay's national framework for PBR was established with the Seed Act No. 16.811 in 1997 (PBR Act), later amended by Act No. 18.467 in 2009, complemented by Regulatory Decrees No. 104/997 of 1997, and 438/004 of 2004. The PBR Act emphasizes the national interest in breeding, producing, and commercializing seeds and phytogenetic creations. To obtain PBR protection, a plant variety must meet specific criteria, including novelty, distinctiveness, uniformity, and stability (DUS).

---

[52] World Bank Open (searched terms "Patent applications," "residents," "non-residents," "Uruguay").

[53] JI Correa, CM Correa, "Impact of the Patent Cooperation Treaty in Latin America" (2020) 69(8) GRUR International 803–822.

[54] See M Blakeney, "Agricultural Innovation: Patenting and Plant Variety Rights Protection" in G Steier, KK Patel, *International Food Law and Policy* (Springer International Publishing 2016) <https://doi.org/10.1007/978-3-319-07542-6_6>.

[55] See LR Helfer, *Intellectual Property Rights in Plant Varieties: International Legal Regimes and Policy Options for National Governments* (FAO 2004).

[56] ibid.

The PBR Act also established the National Seed Institute (INASE) to promote seed quality and grant PBRs. To those ends, INASE oversees two registries: the Cultivar Property Registry (RPC) and the National Cultivar Registry (RNC). Registration in the RPC grants breeders exclusive rights over a plant variety for 20 to 25 years, including rights to introduce, produce, market, and engage in transactions involving the variety. However, inclusion in the RNC is required to commercialize the variety within Uruguay. Consequently, some plant varieties are registered in both registries (providing both protection and marketability), while others are registered in either the RPC (protected but not marketable) or the RNC (marketable but not protected).

Finally, it is worth noting that Section 72 of the PBR Act outlines three exceptions to the exclusive rights granted to the PBR holder, permitting certain uses without the holder's authorization. These exceptions are (a) the use or sale of the product derived from the plant variety as a raw material; (b) the reservation and sowing of seeds for personal use, excluding commercialization, referred to as the *farmer's exception* or *farmer's privilege*, which is classified as *ordre public* and cannot be waived or contracted out; and (c) the use of the plant variety by other breeders for experimental purposes or as genetic material for developing new plants, provided it is not used repeatedly and systematically for commercial production. These exceptions arguably prioritize the economic interests of farmers and individuals seeking to experiment with existing plant varieties, potentially at the expense of the rights and interests of PBR holders. Due to pressure from agricultural producers, Uruguay is unlikely to adhere in the short term to UPOV's 1991 Act, which offers a more restrictive interpretation for the farmer's exception.

At the moment of submitting this chapter, there were 105 cannabis plant varieties registered in the RNC, of which 20 were of the psychoactive type (*cannabis sativa* sp., containing more than 1 percent THC), and 85 were non-psychoactive (*cannabis sativa,* containing less than 1 percent THC).[57] Inscription in the RNC does not grant any exclusive PBR but the right to market the variety in Uruguay. Nineteen cannabis plant varieties have been registered in the RPC, of which 14 have also been registered in the RNC for commercialization. IRCCA owns four PBRs for these plant varieties, specifically for psychoactive cannabis. These varieties are inscribed in the RPC but not in the RNC, since they cannot be freely marketed. The four plant varieties owned by IRCCA are produced by three local firms, under IRCCA's authorization and subject to a plant variety license agreement.

Similar to what happens in the case of patents, the INASE database suggests most PBRs are registered by foreign firms. For instance, Silk Hemp Uruguay

---

[57] INASE RPC (last accessed 10 July 2024).

S.R.L., a subsidiary of Silk Hemp S.L. (Spain), has three PBRs on non-psychoactive cannabis plant varieties (under the denominations BELATE, SASARI, and URBE, Nos. 2019090, 2019091, and 2019100 respectively) also registered for commercialization in the RNC. Phytoplant Research S.L., another Spanish company, obtained three PBRs on non-psychoactive cannabis plant varieties (under the denominations MAGDA, GOUYA, and OCTAVIA, Nos. 2022204, 2022206, and 2019100 respectively) in Uruguay, also registered in the RNC.

The greater number of plant varieties registered in the RNC compared to those in the RPC can be attributed to several factors. Not all plant varieties fulfilll the criteria for obtaining PBRs, such as distinctiveness, uniformity, and stability; there may also be a lack of interest in securing exclusive rights. Additionally, some PBRs may have expired, or certain hybrid plants are maintained exclusively by the breeder who controls access to the parent breeding lines, preventing others from reproducing them. Moreover, infringing PBR rights is relatively easy and difficult to detect, making it impossible to maintain strict control and traceability of resales of cultivars containing PBR. Established in 1994, URUPOV is a non-profit association composed of the primary companies and institutions involved in the research, development, production, and commercialization of new plant varieties in Uruguay.[58] Alongside INASE, URUPOV contributes to enforcing PBR and the related contracts between plant breeders and producers.

To foster investments in agribusiness, in 2015 Uruguay enacted Act No. 19.317 for the promotion of biotechnology, which was declared of *national interest*. Among other things, the Act provides tax cuts and the creation of a stimulus fund. Concerning cannabis investments, the industrial and medicinal markets seem to be the most attractive to local and international investors. According to Uruguay XXI, the national export promotion agency, Uruguay has been exporting cannabis for six years with sales totaling more than US$27 million. Uruguay primarily exports cannabis flowers and seeds for medicinal and industrial markets. In recent years, Brazil has been the principal market for cannabis flowers, with other significant markets including New Zealand, Australia, the Czech Republic, and Spain. Regarding cannabis seeds, Argentina constitutes the main export destination, followed by Paraguay, Costa Rica, Switzerland, the Czech Republic, the US, and Spain.[59]

---

58 <https://www.urupov.org.uy/>.

59 *UruguayXXI* <https://www.uruguayxxi.gub.uy/es/noticias/articulo/la-exportacion-de-cannabis-uruguayo-diversifico-productos-y-amplio-mercados/>

10.7 CONCLUSION

Uruguay was the first country to legalize access to recreational, medicinal, and industrial cannabis. However, IP rights have played a limited role in the development of these sectors. Two possible explanations can be proposed. First, as a small economy in Latin America, Uruguayan firms often lack the sophistication and resources necessary to fully leverage IP protection. Second, the Uruguayan government maintains a legal monopoly with fixed prices and a strict no-brand policy for the sale of recreational cannabis, which diminishes private firms' incentives to invest in IP rights.

Given the costs associated with obtaining IP rights and the absence of markets to transact or capitalize on the competitive advantages they provide, their limited use is unsurprising. The case of Uruguay underscores the often-overlooked premise that IP rights are effective when there is a functioning market for intangible assets, not to mention other necessary conditions such as effective enforcement mechanisms. However, it is worth acknowledging the use of IP rights by public authorities. The IRCCA holds four PBRs on cannabis varieties for recreational sale in pharmacies. However, the production of these varieties has been delegated to private firms.

There is greater scope for private enterprise in the medicinal and industrial cannabis markets. Nevertheless, investment in IP rights is not widespread either in these sectors. This may be due to the relatively recent implementation of essential reforms required for the development of these industries. If this explanation is accurate, it is anticipated that there will be an increase in IPRs, especially in trademarks and PBRs, in the forthcoming years, though not to the same extent as expected in developed countries.

11. The Dutch scenario

Lotte Anemaet

11.1 DRUGS POLICY IN THE NETHERLANDS

The Netherlands applies a policy of tolerance to "soft drugs": possession is a criminal act,[1] but under certain circumstances, it is not subject to criminal prosecution. Users are allowed to possess small amounts of soft drugs, equivalent to a maximum of 5 grams of weed or hash, or a maximum of five hemp plants.[2]

Meanwhile, coffeeshops are allowed to sell weed and hash under strict conditions, meaning no hard drugs and no more than 5 grams soft drugs per person per day. If they fail to meet these strict conditions, coffeeshop holders can be subject to criminal prosecution, and the coffeeshop can be temporarily or permanently closed.[3]

Under Dutch law, the Opium Act[4] regulates the distinction between soft and hard drugs: List I contains all substances that give rise to unacceptable risks (heroin, cocaine, and hash oil) and List II all solid substances of the cannabis plant (hashish, marihuana), together with the substances that appear on Lists III and IV of the Convention on Psychotropic Substances.[5] The rationale

---

[1] Art. 3 Opium Act: "It is not permitted to: A. enter or leave the territory of the Netherlands with; B. grow, prepare, process, sell, deliver, provide, or transport; C. own; D. manufacture a product as referred to in List II appended to this Act, or designated pursuant to Article 3a(5)."

[2] Art. 4 Aanwijzing Opiumwet (2015A003).

[3] <https://www.rijksoverheid.nl/onderwerpen/drugs/gedoogbeleid-softdrugs-en-coffeeshops#:~:text=Minderjarigen%20mogen%20niet%20in%20een,voor%20de%20omgeving%20worden%20veroorzaakt.>.

[4] Wet van 12 mei 1928, tot vaststelling van bepalingen betreffende het opium en andere verdoovende middelen. See: <https://wetten.overheid.nl/BWBR0001941/2023-09-12>.

[5] T Blom, *Opiumwetgeving en Drugsbeleid. Studiepockets Strafrecht 37* (Wolters Kluwer 2015) 48, 187. <https://www.rijksoverheid.nl/onderwerpen/drugs/wet-maakt-verschil-harddrugs-en-softdrugs>.

behind this distinction between soft drugs and hard drugs is preventing cannabis users from gaining access to drugs with bigger health risks, such as hard drugs.[6] Access to a coffeeshop is subject to a residence criterion, meaning that only inhabitants of a Dutch district are allowed to purchase cannabis. However, this residence criterion has been enforced only in some districts with coffeeshops at the border.[7] Despite the sale and possession of soft drugs being accepted, growing soft drugs for recreational use remains prohibited.[8]

The production and supply of cannabis for medicinal and scientific purposes is permitted and falls under the responsibility of the Office for Medicinal Cannabis (Bureau voor Medicinale Cannabis; BMC) of the Ministry of Health, Welfare and Sport.[9] A company that has obtained authorisation to produce and sell cannabis for medicinal and scientific purposes must comply with strict quality standards.[10] Medicinal cannabis is checked and tested in independent laboratories before it can be supplied to Dutch pharmacies.[11] Thereafter, it is possible and legal to obtain medicinal cannabis from the pharmacy with a doctor's prescription.[12]

Cannabidiol (CBD) products can be purchased on the Internet or from the drugstore. These CBD products have a low THC content (tetrahydrocannabinol; maximum of 0.05 percent), but they do fall under the Opium Act, which means that selling these products is formally forbidden. However, since the

---

[6] ibid; <https://www.om.nl/onderwerpen/beleidsregels/aanwijzingen/algemeen/aanwijzing-opiumwet-2015a003>.

[7] <https://www.eumonitor.eu/9353000/1/j9vvik7m1c3gyxp/vm4ioflnw9z2>

[8] It is not permitted to grow medicinal cannabis yourself. In highly exceptional circumstances, this may be allowed: Dutch Supreme Court, 16 September 2008, ECLI:NL:HR:2008:BC7923.

[9] <https://www.cannabisbureau.nl/>.

[10] BMC has commissioned Bedrocan to grow medicinal cannabis. They have a long-term contract and grow only what is ordered by BMC. BMC is the official producer. The Bedrocan company has two production locations in the Netherlands, one research facility, and one laboratory of their own in Amsterdam. The company started out as a family business in Groningen, and worked on specialised indoor farming, for example witloof; See <https://bedrocan.com/nl/wie-zijn-er-verantwoordelijk-voor-de-levering-van-medicinale-cannabis-in-nederland/>.

[11] The Ofichem Labs company tests whether heavy metals, pesticides, moulds, and other contaminants are present in the cannabis, and whether the cannabis has the right amount of ingredients. The Steris company irradiates the cannabis with gamma radiation on the orders of BMC (ibid).

[12] "Medicinaal middelengebruik" (*Nationale Drug Monitor*) Trimbos-instituut, Utrecht & WODC, The Hague <https://www.nationaledrugmonitor.nl/wetgeving-en-beleid-medicinale-cannabis/>; <https://www.cannabisbureau.nl/productie>.

CBD substance does not itself have a psychoactive effect (as is the case with THC), the sale of CBD products is allowed.[13] This means that CBD products are increasingly being used.[14] The Court of Justice of the European Union (CJEU) ruled that CBD is not a narcotic drug under the international treaty when it is extracted from the Cannabis sativa plant in its entirety and not solely from its fibre and seeds.[15] CBD products are considered food supplements, as novel foods. To launch CBD products onto the market, an approval procedure with the European Commission is necessary.[16] In the Netherlands, growing industrial hemp for fibres and seeds is permitted. The THC content of hemp should not exceed 0.2 per cent.[17] Yet, it is not permitted to grow hemp for fibre for the production of substances, such as CBD oil, or to process these in food supplements.[18]

The Dutch Opium Act was established in 1919 and amended in 1928 and 1976. The first International Opium Conference took place in The Hague on 1 December 1911 and resulted in the establishment of the Opium Convention on 23 January 1912. Several countries,[19] were signatories to the Convention, including the Netherlands. Initially, the Dutch wanted to delay the organisation of the conference because of the important interests they had in trading opium and cocaine, and the uncertainty regarding the impact of the conference on that lucrative trade.[20] Under pressure from the US, where problems associated with drug use emerged earlier and were more pressing, the Netherlands agreed to organise the conference.[21] In the literature, it is suggested that this was probably due to fear of a too rigid convention text if the US were to organise it.[22]

---

[13] Nationale Drug Monitor (n 12).

[14] Because of its popularity, a large range of CBD products can be purchased at Dutch pharmacies (for example: Lucovitaal CBD oil from Kruidvat).

[15] Case C-663/18 *B S and C A* [2020] ECLI:EU:C:2020:938, para 76.

[16] Nationale Drug Monitor (n 12).

[17] <https://hempcollective.nl/waarom-hennep/wetgeving/>.

[18] "Vezelhennepteelt in het Teeltplan" (*groen kennisnet*, 4 October 2023) <https://wiki.groenkennisnet.nl/space/HNPN/109772801/2.+Vezelhennep+in+het+teeltplan> accessed 31 March 2024.

[19] Twelve countries signed the Opium Convention in 1912: China, France, Germany, Great Britain, Iran, Italy, Japan, Netherlands, Portugal, Russia, Thailand, and the United States. See: UNTC, <u></u><<https://treaties.un.org/doc/Treaties/1922/01/19220123%2006-31%20AM/Ch_VI_2p.pdf>.

[20] In 1910, the Nederlandsche Cocaïnefabriek (NCF), which was established in 1900, was considered to be the largest cocaine factory in the world. See: M de Kort, *Tussen patiënt en delinquent. Geschiedenis van het Nederlandse drugsbeleid* (Hilversum, 1995) 44, 60–61.

[21] de Kort (n 20) 65–66.

[22] Blom (n 5) 2–3. The US realised that China was an important sales market for American products, but that market had already been divided between the

Until World War II, the economic interests of the Netherlands in drugs remained determinative.[23] After the war, the Dutch East Indies, now Indonesia, gained its independence, resulting in the Netherlands losing revenues from opium and cocaine. The US also became more powerful worldwide, and their strict policy towards drugs predominated.[24] In response, Dutch legislators amended the Opium Act in 1953, and the possession and production of cannabis were criminalised. In this way, the Opium Act was brought into accordance with the provisions of the Convention signed in Geneva on 26 June 1936 for the Suppression of Illicit Traffic in Narcotic Drugs, amended by the Protocol amending the Conventions, Treaties, and Protocols on Narcotic Drugs signed in New York on 11 December 1946.[25]

In the 1960s, cannabis became popular among young people, and a subculture emerged around drug use. Drugs symbolised the fight against the established order.[26] Around 1970, the Netherlands introduced its drug tolerance policy, under the wary eye of other countries. This was due to growing criticism of the long sentences with deprivation of freedom imposed on young users of cannabis products.[27] Doubts were also increasingly raised about all drugs being subject to the same regime. It was increasingly considered less useful to pursue criminal action against users of hemp products.[28]

Initially, no distinction was made between soft and hard drugs, such that an open trade in hard drugs began to grow, resulting in an amendment of the Opium Act in 1976.[29] Two lists were introduced: List I contained all substances that give rise to unacceptable risks, and List II all solid substances of the cannabis plant, together with the substances that appear on Lists III and IV of the Convention on Psychotropic Substances. The concept of risk came to the fore, i.e., the risk of potentially harmful effects. The two lists represented an attempt to separate the trade in hemp products from drugs with unacceptable risks as much as possible and to ensure that hemp users were less likely to come into contact with traders in drugs with an unacceptable risk.[30]

West and Japan. In their fight against opium, the US hoped to create favourable relationships with China in order to establish trade agreements.

23 Before World War II, the Netherlands deducted income from the trade in opium and cocaine that was imported from the Dutch East Indies (former Dutch colony); Blom (n 5) 19; de Kort (n 20) 65.

24 Blom (n 5) 19; de Kort (n 20) 78.

25 <https://nl.wikipedia.org/wiki/Drugsbeleid_in_Nederland#cite_note-21>; Blom (n 5) 19–20, 35.

26 Blom (n 5) 35, 41.

27 ibid 41.

28 ibid.

29 Drugsbeleid in Nederland (n 25). See also: Blom (n 5) 43, 48, 187.

30 Blom (n 5) 41–43, 187.

In 1996, the tolerance policy with regard to coffeeshops was strengthened by applying the AHOJG conditions (Geen Affichering; Geen Harddrugs; Geen Overlast; Geen verkoop aan Jeugd; Geen voorraad of verkoop van Grote hoeveelheden) more strictly.[31] For example, it was no longer permitted to advertise soft drugs.[32] Furthermore, coffeeshops could no longer offer alcoholic beverages, and districts were allowed to apply additional conditions, such as a maximum of permissible trading stock.[33] To regulate the front and the back door of coffeeshops, an experiment was recently conducted by the Dutch government to investigate whether it is possible to create a chain of legal sale, production, purchase, and supply.[34] The growers who have come forward to join the experiment can legally produce and sell cannabis, and their cannabis is examined against quality standards.[35] The laboratory that examines

---

[31] Coffee shops are not allowed to advertise (A), possess or sell hard drugs (H), cause a nuisance (O), be accessible to and sell to juveniles (J). They may only sell a limited quantity per transaction and have only a limited trading stock (G). They must not be accessible to or sell to persons who are not residents of the Netherlands (I). See: <https://www.om.nl/onderwerpen/beleidsregels/aanwijzingen/algemeen/aanwijzing-opiumwet-2015a003>.

[32] A number of coffeeshops were acquitted for presenting cards on the counter on which the word "coffeeshop" was depicted, together with a name, logo, or URL. The Court of Appeal of Amsterdam ruled that the concept of "making available" should not be stretched so far as to include this information without a reference to drugs (Court of Appeal of Amsterdam, 15 September 2010, ECLI:NL:GHAMS:2010:BN7280). One coffeeshop was, however, convicted for possessing cards depicting a weed plant and advertising "Cannabis cup winter 2010" (Court of Appeal of Amsterdam, 15 September 2010, ECLI:NL:GHAMS:2010:BN7285). The placement of menus and the prices of soft drugs that could be purchased in the coffeeshop was also interpreted as a publication in the sense of Art. 3b(1) Opium Act (Supreme Court, 25 May 2004, ECLI:NL:HR:2004:AO6423). One coffeeshop holder who had prepared a supply of joints preprinted with the name of their specific coffeeshop, the text "support your local dealer", and a picture of a dog with a cigarette/joint in its mouth was also convicted of advertising (AG D.J.C. Aben, 28 October 2014, ECLI:NL:PHR:2014:2292).

[33] Blom (n 5) 73.

[34] This was agreed in the coalition agreement of 2017. See: <https://www.rijksoverheid.nl/onderwerpen/experiment-gesloten-coffeeshopketen-wietexperiment/tijdlijn-experiment-gesloten-coffeeshopketen>.

[35] Art. 28(1) Besluit van 15 juni 2020, houdende regels over het experiment met een gesloten coffeeshopketen (Besluit experiment gesloten coffeeshopketen); Art. 12 Regeling van de Minister voor Medische Zorg en de Minister van Justitie en Veiligheid van 12 mei 2020, kenmerk 1681487-204740-VGP, houdende regels in verband met het experiment met een gesloten coffeeshopketen (Regeling

the cannabis must have an exemption under the Opium Act.[36] This experiment aims to investigate the effects of the closed coffeeshop chain on public health, crime, safety, and nuisance. After being regulated and examined for quality, the cannabis is delivered by up to ten growers to ten participating municipalities.[37] Growers are also allowed to produce and deliver pre-rolled joints and edibles. Concentrates of cannabis obtained by extraction of hemp or hashish in a mixture with oil are prohibited.[38]

The experiment involves a number of phases. In the preparation phase, which began on 1 July 2020, growers were selected and enabled to start a cultivation farm. In the start-up phase that began on 15 December 2023 and for up to six months thereafter, growers are allowed to deliver to coffeeshops in the Dutch cities of Breda and Tilburg. During the transitional phase, a period of up to six weeks, all coffeeshops in the participating municipalities can participate. In the experimental phase, which lasts for four years, with up to 18 months extension, coffeeshops are only allowed to sell regulated cannabis. The final phase lasts six months. During the transition phase, coffeeshops are only allowed to have one stock per week and must store their stock safely. Coffeeshops at the border (Dutch cities of Breda, Heerlen, and Maastricht) are not allowed to sell cannabis to non-Dutch residents.[39]

Growers are also responsible for packaging the cannabis. Each package should be sealed with an irreplaceable seal. The appearance of the packaging and the label are subject to standard requirements. For example, the packaging should be smooth and free of imprints, the inside should be one colour like the outside, and the texture should also be smooth.[40] For example, the label should

---

experiment gesloten coffeeshopketen). See also: "Voorwaarden Coffeeshops in Wietexperiment" (*Rijksoverheid*) <https://www.rijksoverheid.nl/onderwerpen/experiment-gesloten-coffeeshopketen-wietexperiment/voorwaarden-coffeeshops-in-wietexperiment>.

[36] Art. 6 Opium Act; Art. 28(2) Besluit experiment gesloten coffeeshopketen.

[37] Art. 2 and Art. 13 Besluit experiment gesloten coffeeshopketen: The municipalities that participate in the experiment are Arnhem, Almere, Breda, Groningen, Heerlen, Maastricht, Nijmegen, Tilburg, Voorne aan Zee, and Zaanstad. All coffeeshops in the participating municipalities take part (80 in total). A procedure has been initiated to amend the law such that Amsterdam East can also take part in the experiment.

[38] *Spelregels experiment gesloten coffeeshopketen*, 10. <https://www.rijksoverheid.nl/onderwerpen/experiment-gesloten-coffeeshopketen-wietexperiment/documenten/brochures/2019/04/11/spelregels-experiment-gesloten-coffeeshopketen>.

[39] Art. 4(4) Besluit experiment gesloten coffeeshopketen. See also: <https://www.rijksoverheid.nl/onderwerpen/experiment-gesloten-coffeeshopketen-wietexperiment/documenten/brochures/2024/02/28/factsheet-experiment-gesloten-coffeeshopketen>.

[40] Art. 7 Regeling experiment gesloten coffeeshopketen.

be white in colour, contain a unique identification number as well as the name of the variety, the date of the harvest and the packaging, and display health warnings, the universal THC symbol in red, the weight and content of THC and CBD, the weight of the finished product, the composition of the finished product, the ingredients,[41] the trade name, and the contact details for the consumer of the designated grower from whom the product originates.[42] The label must cover at least 30 per cent of the whole outside of the packaging.[43] The text and the label must also have a standardised appearance.[44] The packaging must also include health warnings and an information leaflet.[45] The Netherlands Food and Consumer Products Safety Authority (Nederlandse Voedsel en Warenautoriteit (NVWA)) checks the quality of the cultivated hemp and the packaging requirements.[46]

11.2 TRADEMARKS

The pragmatic approach that has been adopted in the Netherlands with regard to drugs is reflected in the Benelux trademark register. Several cannabis trademarks have been registered. Think of Benelux trademark registrations such as "Cannabis Sativa"[47] and "Cannabis Energy Drink" for drinks,[48] "Cannabistro"

---

[41] Art. 29(e) Besluit experiment gesloten coffeeshopketen. According to the Dutch Commodities Act (Warenwet), the product packaging should indicate the product ingredients. Regulations on product labelling are incorporated in the Commodities Act Decree (Warenwetbesluit informatie; WIL) and based on the EU Regulation nr. 1169/2011. Article 9 of EU Regulation nr. 1169/2011 contains a list of references that should be included on the product packaging. See also: <https://www.nvwa.nl/onderwerpen/etikettering-van-levensmiddelen/documenten/consument/eten-drinken-roken/etikettering/publicaties/handboek-etikettering-van-levensmiddelen>.

[42] Art. 29(2) Besluit experiment gesloten coffeeshopketen; Art. 8 Regeling experiment gesloten coffeeshopketen.

[43] ibid.

[44] Art. 8 Regeling experiment gesloten coffeeshopketen.

[45] Art. 29(g) Besluit experiment gesloten coffeeshopketen. See also: <https://open.overheid.nl/documenten/35dc2729-2c0e-4ce8-bc4f-af587cfef675/file>.

[46] Spelregels experiment gesloten coffeeshopketen (n 38). From 1 October 2021, the Netherlands Food and Consumer Products Safety Authority will also check whether all cigarettes and shag are sold in neutral packaging (dark green and brown). The packaging has an unattractive colour, the health warnings are easier to read, and the product packaging is no longer an advertising product. <https://www.rijksoverheid.nl/actueel/nieuws/2020/09/29/alle-sigaretten-en-shag-vanaf-1-oktober-in-donkergroen-bruine-verpakking>.

[47] Registration number 1441644.

[48] Registration number 880575.

for tobacco,[49] "Bon Fire" for cannabis plants and pharmaceutical products,[50] or "Cannabis Career" for courses and in-company training programmes.[51]

In the Netherlands, trademark law is regulated by the Benelux Convention on Intellectual Property (BCIP) under Title 2. This convention applies in all three Benelux countries, with the exception of overseas territories in the Caribbean as per Article 1.16 BCIP.[52] Benelux trademarks are always acquired, refused, or nullified for the entire Benelux territory, with the exception of the overseas territories.[53] Rights are acquired by registering a trademark in the Benelux or, in the case of an international trademark, at the World Intellectual Property Organization (WIPO) with a reference to the Benelux territory, in line with the right of priority, as prescribed by the Paris Convention or the TRIPS Agreement as laid out in Article 2.2 BCIP.[54] Applications for Benelux trademarks can be submitted to the national services in Brussels and Luxembourg, or to the Benelux Office for Intellectual Property (BOIP) in The Hague.

Article 2.1 of the BCIP prescribes that a trademark may consist of any signs that (a) make it possible to distinguish the goods or services of one undertaking from those of other undertakings and (b) can be represented on the register in a clear and precise manner. The distinctive character of the trademark must be assessed in the light of the goods and services for which the trademark is

---

[49] Registration number 840343.

[50] Application number 1495634.

[51] Registration number 1031667.

[52] The Kingdom of the Netherlands has existed since 1813. From 1986 until 2010, the Kingdom consisted of three countries: the Netherlands, Netherlands Antilles, and Aruba. In 1986, Aruba was already an independent country within the Kingdom. On 10 October 2010, Netherlands Antilles withdrew from the Kingdom. From then on, Curaçao and Saint Martin became independent countries within the Kingdom. Bonaire, St. Eustatius, and Saba, also referred to as the BES islands, were given the status of "special municipalities" of the Netherlands. The BCIP only has effect within the European territories of the Kingdom (Art. 1.16 BCIP). Aruba has had its own trademark regulation since 1989. The special municipalities of the Netherlands are subject to the BES Trademark Act. In Curaçao, the old Antillean legislation still applies (Merkenlandsverordening 1995). Saint Martin has its own Merkenlandsverordening. See: "Kingdom of the Netherlands" (*Wikipedia*) <https://en.wikipedia.org/wiki/Kingdom_of_the_Netherlands>; PGFA Geerts and AME Verschuur (eds), *Kort Begrip van het Intellectuele Eigendomsrecht* (Wolters Kluwer 2022) 268.

[53] Trademark rights, in principle, offer protection for ten years, although this can be renewed indefinitely (Art. 2.9 BCIP).

[54] See the Paris Convention for the Protection of Industrial Property of 20 March 1883 (amended on 28 September 1979) and the Agreement on Trade-Related Aspects of Intellectual Property Rights (as amended on 23 January 2017).

requested and the perception of a consumer who is reasonably well informed and reasonably observant and circumspect.[55] For cannabis products, as for tobacco, the relevant public consists of the general public with a higher level of attention. The relevant consumer will pay more attention when purchasing cannabis products because of the specific legal framework that applies to these products and the fact that they can only be purchased from special traders.[56] Whether a trademark has distinctive character is assessed by considering all relevant facts and circumstances of the case.[57]

11.3 DESCRIPTIVE SIGNS

Despite the broad definition of a trademark, not every sign can be a trademark. In practice, the BOIP refuses quite a few trademark applications,[58] most commonly on grounds relating to descriptive trademarks under Article 2.2bis(1)(c) BCIP,[59] i.e., trademarks that consist exclusively of signs or indications that can serve to designate the characteristics of the goods or services in question. Additionally, general interest requires that descriptive signs remain freely available to third parties.[60]

Cannabis trademarks that are used for particular classes, such as cannabis for recreational use (class 34) or the raw plants themselves (class 31), could fall under this ground for refusal. Such trademarks are not likely to be perceived by the consumer as a source identifier, but rather as an indication of the kind of good. The same applies to the English variant "weed", because the English language is used frequently in the Benelux countries.[61] However, a little twist could be sufficient: the figurative mark "CannaBizz" is, for instance, a valid trademark and registered in the Benelux for cannabis.[62]

---

55 Joined Cases C-456/01 P and C-457/01 *P Henkel/OHIM* [2004] ECR I-5089, para 47.

56 BOIP, opposition decision 2014692, MOHAWK/MOHAWK, para 58.

57 Joined Cases C-108/97 and C-109/97 *Windsurfing Chiemsee* [1999] ECR I-2779, para 49; Case C-104/01 *Libertel* [2003] ECR I-3793, para 76.

58 Within two months of the publication of the application, the trademark owner can file an opposition on relative grounds (Art. 2.14 BCIP; Art. 2.2ter BCIP).

59 PGFA Geerts, *Bescherming van de Intellectuele Eigendom* (Wolters Kluwer 2021) 97. See also: BOIP, *Guidelines for Examining Absolute Grounds* (2020) 24. The Benelux Office for Intellectual Property (BOIP) established these guidelines: <https://www.boip.int/en/ip-professionals/regulations-policy/refusals/guidelines>; <https://www.boip.int/en/ip-professionals/news/new-guidelines-on-refusals-published>.

60 Case C-363/99 *Postkantoor* [2004] ECR I-1619, para 55; Joined Cases C-108/97 and C-109/97 *Windsurfing Chiemsee* [1999] ECR I-2779, para 30.

61 Case C 2018/7/6 *Bimbo v BOIP* [2019] IEF 18777, para 45.

62 Registration number 1434344. See also the Benelux trademark "Sweed" which is depicted with a green weed leaflet against a black background and that

In addition, under Article 2.2bis(1)(b) BCIP, a descriptive sign can also be refused due to a lack of distinctive character. This ground for refusal is, for example, also applicable to descriptive signs that are applied for in a specific layout. The addition of a graphic element does not necessarily cancel the lack of distinctive character because the consumer may perceive the sign as a descriptive indication with a nice font, and therefore not as a trademark.[63] For example, a trademark that consists only of the word "Cannabis" and is registered for cannabis plants will be refused, even though the word is italicised or capitalised and pictured with a cannabis leaf.

It is, however, possible to register descriptive and non-distinctive signs once they have acquired distinctiveness through use in trade. Trademark owners could opt for higher investments in marketing campaigns to educate consumers to recognise a sign as a source identifier. If trademark owners succeed in this, descriptive and non-distinctive signs could be registered due to the secondary meaning acquired by the sign in line with Article 2.2bis(3) BCIP.[64] The trademark must acquire distinctiveness throughout the entire Benelux territory, or a substantial part thereof, or in the case of a trademark in one of the Benelux languages, at least in the area where the language in question is spoken.[65]

11.4 PUBLIC POLICY AND ACCEPTED PRINCIPLES OF MORALITY

Another relevant refusal and invalidity ground concerns signs that conflict with public policy or accepted principles of morality under Article 2.2bis(1)(f) BCIP. In contrast to descriptive signs, this refusal ground cannot be overruled through acquired distinctiveness through use in trade; even if the consumer perceives the sign as a source identifier, the sign will be definitively refused.

---

has been registered validly for cosmetics based on CBD Cannabis and super aliments (registration number 1390159).

[63] Guidelines for Examining Absolute Grounds (n 59) 20.

[64] See, for example, District Court of The Hague, 25 October 2006, ECLI:NL:RBSGR:2006:BB2076 (Substral/Substra(flores)), paras 4.9, 4.10. The trademark had become highly distinctive because of its long-term use (it has been on the market since 1947) and significant market share.

[65] Case C-108/05 *Europolis* [2006] ECR I-7605, paras 24–28. For example, if someone wants to register the sign "Green Cannabis" for cannabis plants, this trademark application will probably be rejected due to a lack of distinctive character. However, if the company succeeds in educating consumers to perceive the sign as a source identifier for a special cannabis plant, this sign could potentially be registered. However, a company will not succeed in this easily because they are not allowed to advertise soft drugs.

This ground for refusal is intended to ensure that offensive trademarks are excluded from the trademark register.[66]

There is considerable overlap between the concepts of "public order" and "morality".[67] Nevertheless, public order is assessed on objective grounds, while morality relates to subjective grounds, such as the values and beliefs of a specific society.[68] The term "public" refers in this case to a reasonable person with an average sensitivity and tolerance threshold.[69] Unlike other refusal grounds, this assessment not only concerns consumers for whom the trademarked product is intended but also takes into account any person who might come into contact with the trademark.[70] The assessment concerns the sign itself in relation to the goods or services, not whether the goods or services are marketed illegally.[71]

In contrast to descriptive signs, this refusal ground is rarely applied.[72] In the Benelux, trademarks referring to drugs will not be refused on grounds of conflict with public order and morality.[73] The principle here is that the Benelux public is not easily shocked.[74] By contrast, elsewhere in the EU, as highlighted by Marc Mimler in Chapter 2 of this volume, trademarks referring

---

66 For example, the trademark "Flikker" (English: faggot) was considered contrary to public order and morality and was therefore refused (application number 1458029).

67 A-G M. Bobek, 2 July 2019, Case C240/18 P, *Fack Ju Göthe*, para 81.

68 ibid para 77.

69 06/07/2006, R 495, SCREW YOU; 27/02/2020, Case C240/18 P, *Fack Ju Göthe*, EU:C:2020:118.

70 05/10/2011, Case T-526/09, *PAKI*, ECLI:EU:T:2011:564.

71 13/09/2005, Case T-140/02, *Intertops*, EU:T:2005:312.

72 Guidelines for Examining Absolute Grounds (n 59) 37.

73 See also: L Coenen, A Weemaes, "The 'Public Policy or Accepted Principles of Morality'-exclusion in EU Trade Mark Law and Practice" (2/2021) 47 BMM Bulletin 106; B Kist, W Heemskerk, "Lul de Behanger en Andere Dubieuze Merken", (1/2008) 34 BMM Bulletin.

74 Trademarks such as "Neleman Just Fucking Good Wine" (registration number 1442360), "Jesus" (registration number 699762), and "Shiva" (registration number 1486598) have been registered. This is different for signs consisting of references to World War II. For example, a picture of a Nazi swastika was refused (Guidelines for Examining Absolute Grounds (n 59) 37; application number 947182). However, the same gnome without the Nazi swastika but with the same Hitler salute was accepted (registration number 691996). The trademark "Joden" for shower heads was refused because it was found to conflict with public order and accepted principles of morality. Criticism towards the head of state, "Trix is Nix" (application number 862689), as well as racist expressions such as "Nederlanders eerst" (application number 862690), were refused.

to drugs can definitely be refused on the ground of conflict with public order or accepted principles of morality, and this has perhaps more frequently been the case of late.[75] For example, in the Cannabis Store Amsterdam case,[76] the EU General Court ruled that the fact that the cannabis sign could be perceived by the relevant public as an indication that the foodstuff and drinks contained narcotics that were prohibited in many member states for reasons of public health was sufficient to refuse the trademark.[77] Therefore, it might be safer to register a cannabis trademark in the Benelux provided that the trademark is not too descriptive.[78]

11.5 CONFLICTS WITH PLANT VARIETIES' DENOMINATIONS

Under Article 2.2bis(1)(l) BCIP, trademarks that consist of, or reproduce in their essential elements, an earlier plant variety denomination shall be refused. The name of the variety bred by the breeder is automatically the generic designation of the variety and must be freely available to anyone. Even if the variety was bred by the trademark owner themselves, the trademark will be refused.

New variety denominations are registered with the competent authorities and listed in the EU's Community Plant Variety Office database (CPVO). As soon as the plant variety denomination is recorded, the trademark will be refused for the relevant plant variety, even if the registration has already expired. Furthermore, trademarks are refused for plants that are closely related to the relevant variety. This refusal ground is only applicable to a trademark or an essential part thereof that is identical to the name of the protected plant variety and does not apply to its variants.[79] For example, the plant variety

---

75 In 2014, the trademark "Cocaine Cowboys" was registered for film productions (registration number 012287496), but in 2021 the same trademark was refused for clothing (EUTM 018559785). See also: PWH Gevers, "Maakt onbeschaamd ook ongeschikt? Pleidooi voor terughoudendheid bij harmonisering en toepassing van de weigeringsgrond 'Strijd met openbare orde of goede zeden'" Benelux Merkencongres (2022).

76 EUTM 16 176 968, 12/12/2019, Case T683/18, *Cannabis Store Amsterdam*.

77 ibid para 76. EUIPO refused "Kritikal Bilbo" on grounds of conflict with public order and morality (R 1881/2015-1); "Weed" was also refused by the EUIPO on grounds of conflict with public order and morality (EUTM 016961732); EUIPO also found "Ibizaskunk" to be in conflict with public order and morality (EUTM 018097102).

78 Kist, Heemskerk (n 73) 17. However, it is possible to register a cannabis trademark in the EU. For example, the figurative mark "Cannabis Energy Drink" is validly registered as an EU trademark for energy drinks (EUTM 9784737).

79 Guidelines for Examining Absolute Grounds (n 59) 42.

denomination "Balaton" has been registered for Cannabis sativa L[80] and therefore is not suitable as a trademark for plant varieties (class 31). The denomination "Balaton" can, however, be registered for other classes, such as coffee (class 30).[81]

On the other hand, according to the Seed and Planting Material Act 2005 (SPMA), the proposed denomination of a variety should not be confusingly similar to an already existing trademark or tradename.[82] The applicant should waive their trademark rights to the name of the variety because the variety name is a generic designation and therefore cannot function as a trademark. Where the applicant fails to do so, the trademark application can be nullified on the grounds of being in conflict with public order.[83] In addition to the variety name for the new name (i.e., "Chuy" for Cannabis sativa L)[84] the trademark owner may also opt for a trademark (i.e., "Cannaflos"),[85] and introduce improved plant varieties under the same trademark.[86]

11.6 LIKELIHOOD OF CONFUSION

Exclusive trademark rights are regulated in Article 2.20(2) BCIP. This provision stipulates that the trademark owner has the right to prohibit the use of their trademark in the course of trade in relation to goods and services,[87] but also the right to prohibit the use of signs for purposes other than to distinguish goods or services.[88] The latter is not harmonised and is therefore excluded from the jurisdiction of the CJEU.[89]

In practice, the second infringement category, the prohibition on the confusing use of identical or similar signs for identical or similar goods or services, is invoked most frequently.[90] However, trademark infringement cases involving cannabis are rare. The likelihood of confusion must be assessed globally,

---

80 Registration number 20222086.

81 EUTM registration number 006858872.

82 See Art. 29 and Art. 27(5) SPMA.

83 Art. 2.2bis(1)(f) BCIP.

84 Application number 20190531.

85 EUTM registration number 018280583.

86 Art. 46(1) SPMA.

87 Art. 2.20(2)(a–c) BCIP. To be covered by the third infringement category, a trademark must be well known among a significant part of the Benelux public for which the goods and services are intended, which could be one of the Benelux countries (Case C-375/97 *Chevy* [1999] ECR I-5421).

88 Art. 2.20(2)(d) BCIP.

89 Case C-23/01 *Robelco v Robeco* [2002] ECR I-10913.

90 Geerts (n 59) 107.

considering all factors that are relevant to the case, such as whether there is a visual, aural, or conceptual similarity between the signs and the goods or services, including the distinctiveness of the trademark,[91] and how the trademark is used in practice.[92] In exceptional cases, a strong conceptual meaning of the sign or trademark may be sufficient to abolish the visual or aural similarity, such that there is no likelihood of confusion, not even where identical goods are concerned.[93]

In an opposition decision, the BOIP ruled that dried marijuana and cannabis for recreational use were similar to tobacco since the two goods had a similar purpose and method of use and could coincide in terms of the relevant public.[94] Although it is not necessary to mix marijuana with tobacco for consumption, the established practice strengthens the link between the two goods such that they could be designated as complementary. However, this does not extend to living cannabis plants because they are not directly suitable for consumption, and their nature, use, target audience, and distribution channels differ from those of tobacco products. Nutraceuticals – foods and dietary supplements with medicinal and health benefits – for medicinal use and cannabis oil for non-medicinal use are also not to be designated as similar to tobacco products.[95]

In a dispute between Henkel, holder of the wordmark "Substral", which was registered for a fertiliser, and defendant Canna, who used the sign "Substra Flores" to indicate their feed line intended for substrate cultivation, the District Court of The Hague ruled that the goods were also similar. Both signs were used to indicate fertilisers, and the fact that Canna's goods were intended specifically for cannabis growers did nothing to change this. The goods end up in the grow shops, and therefore the goods of the claimant ultimately reached the end users.[96]

Furthermore, the District Court found that the mark "Substral" was not purely descriptive, as the omission of the last letter(s) and the substitution of the letter "l" had moved it away from being merely descriptive and thus created a different word.[97] The trademark had become highly distinctive because of its long-term use on the market since 1947 and due to its significant market

[91] Case C-251/95 *Sabel v Puma* [1997] ECR I-6191.

[92] Case C-252/12 *Specsavers v Asda* [2013] ECLI:EU:C:2013:497.

[93] Case C-361/04 *P Picasso v Picaro* [2006] ECR I-643; Case C-328/18 *P EUIPO v Black Label* [2020] ECLI:EU:C:2020:156.

[94] BOIP, opposition decision 2014692 (n 56) para 55.

[95] ibid paras 52–54.

[96] District Court of The Hague, 25 October 2006, ECLI:NL:RBSGR:2006:BB2076 (Substral/Substra(flores)), para 4.7.

[97] ibid para 4.9, 4.10.

share. The signs were visually very similar.[98] Considering all this, the District Court ruled that a likelihood of confusion existed. The fact that the products of Canna were not offered in the same shops as the products of Henkel did not change this because the public could think that the goods had the same origin.[99]

The registration of a somewhat descriptive cannabis trademark does not always pay off. For example, in the Optima Formula case, the claimant registered the EU wordmark "CBN" for food supplements and pharmaceutical products (Class 5) and edible oils and fats (Class 29) made from hemp. The defendant, the operator Optima Formula, was engaged in the production and sale of cannabinoid products – concentrates of individual substances from cannabis – as well as food supplements and medicines, such as Optima CBN oil. The claimant argued that the defendant had infringed upon their EU wordmark. The District Court of Noord-Holland decided otherwise. It held that the trademark and sign differed greatly from a visual and aural perspective. A conceptual similarity did exist. Both signs referred to the main component, cannabinol, which is one of the active substances of the cannabis plant. The products of the defendants were consistently indicated as "Optima" followed by the name of the product concerned, in this case, the active component. Optima Formula was also obliged, on the basis of the Dutch Commodities Act (Warenwet)[100] to indicate all ingredients and active substances on the product or its packaging (this also applied to the claimant). According to the District Court, the indication could be seen as merely descriptive. Given the low distinctive character and the deviant visual presentation, the Court ruled that there was no infringement.[101]

11.7 LIMITATIONS

An important legal case on the concept of "due cause" has its origins in the Netherlands. This concerns a dispute between Henk de Vries, a highly influential cannabis operator in the Netherlands,[102] and the trademark owner Red Bull, well known for their energy drinks. The CJEU ruled that the Court of Appeal of Amsterdam had interpreted the due cause defence too strictly in this case. According to the CJEU, the due cause defence aims to strike a balance

---

98 ibid para 4.13.

99 ibid para 4.16.

100 Dutch Act of 28 December 1935 containing regulations regarding the quality and marking of commodities.

101 District Court of Noord-Holland, 19 June 2020, IEF 19297; ECLI:NL:RBNHO:2020:4409 (Optima Formula), para 4.9–4.10.

102 "The Bulldog" (*Wikipedia*) <https://nl.wikipedia.org/wiki/The_Bulldog>.

between the interests involved by considering third parties' interests in using this particular sign.[103] The CJEU held that the trademark owner is obliged to tolerate a similar sign if the third party's use is in good faith.[104] The use of the sign "The Bulldog" can be seen as a natural expansion of the assortment of the goods and services for which the sign already enjoyed a good reputation among its relevant public.[105]

The Court of Appeal of The Hague eventually decided after referral that there was no trademark infringement due to the lack of similarity between the signs. The conceptual differences between Red Bull and Bulldog were deemed to be so great as to completely cancel any aural and visual similarities. Therefore, the Court of Appeal of The Hague could not assess the likelihood of confusion and association and the due cause defence.[106]

In trademark law, humorous expressions about drugs can also provide a due cause defence. For example, in the Mercis and Bruna/Punt.nl case,[107] the Court of Appeal of Amsterdam ruled that it was permitted to make parodies of the respectable "Nijntje" by depicting it as a dope-smoking figure.

Considering the humoristic intention, the lack of competitive motives, the distance from the trademarks of the claimant, and the lack of likelihood of confusion, the Court of Appeal found that a due cause defence existed.[108] Furthermore, the Court of Appeal ruled that there was no copyright infringement because of a successful reliance on the exception of parody. The author of the work, Dick Bruna, did not want his work "Nijntje" to be associated with drugs, coarse language, aggression, and intolerance, and believed that the use of this sign would impair Nijntje's integrity and be disrespectful towards the child's world.[109] However, the parody was found to be compliant with what is reasonably permissible according to the rules of current social and economic life. The Court of Appeal concluded that it was not necessary that everybody should laugh at the parody.[110]

---

103 CJEU, 6 February 2014, C-65/12, ECLI:EU:C:2014:49 (Leidseplein Beheer/Red Bull), para 46.

104 ibid para 60.

105 ibid para 57.

106 Court of Appeal of The Hague, 14 March 2017, ECLI:NL:GHDHA:2017:561 (Red Bull/Leidseplein Beheer), paras 4.4, 5.1.

107 Court of Appeal of The Hague, 13 September 2011, ECLI:NL:GHAMS:2011:BS7825 (Mercis and Bruna/Punt.nl).

108 ibid para 4.19.

109 Court of Appeal of Amsterdam, 13 September 2011, ECLI:NL:GHAMS:2011:BS7825 (Mercis and Bruna/Punt.nl), para 4.15.

110 ibid paras 4.9, 4.13, 4.16.

11.8 PLANT VARIETIES

Recently, there has been a strong increase in the number of applications for plant variety rights on hemp in the Netherlands, due in part to the partial liberalisation of hemp cultivation.[111] Plant variety rights are regulated in the SPMA and can be granted for all crops belonging to the vegetable kingdom, including hemp.[112] Hemp can be divided into five types: (a) hemp for fibre or oilseed, seed propagated (excluding feminised) with a THC content lower than 0.3 per cent;[113] (b) hemp for fibre or oilseed, vegetatively propagated and with a THC-content lower than 0.3 per cent; (c) hemp other than for fibre or oilseed, vegetatively propagated and with a THC-content higher or lower than 0.3 per cent; (d) hemp other than for fibre or oilseed, seed propagated and with a THC-content higher or lower than 0.3 per cent; (e) hemp for fibre or oilseed, seed (feminised) propagated and with a THC-content lower than 0.3 per cent.[114]

11.9 ACQUISITION OF PLANT VARIETY RIGHTS

The granting of plant variety rights and the registration of a variety in the Dutch Variety Register take place through separate proceedings.[115] The substantial requirements are similar with the exception of the criterion of novelty that only applies to the granting of plant variety rights.[116] Only propagating material originating from varieties that are listed in the Dutch Variety Register may be traded. To be admitted to the Dutch Variety Register, the agricultural value must also be determined. The Board for Plant Varieties is responsible for performing the Value for Cultivation and Use (VCU) test.

Plant variety rights are acquired through an application submitted to the Board for Plant Varieties. The application includes a proposal for a name for the variety, a characteristic description of the variety, and a precise indication

---

[111] "Hennep" (*Raad voor Plantenrassen*) <https://www.raadvoorplantenrassen.nl/nl/actueel/themas/hennep/.>.

[112] The Netherlands is also a member of the UPOV Treaty (Union internationale pour la protection des obtentions végétales). The SPMA was adapted to the UPOV Convention in 1998, as amended in 1991. Furthermore, it is possible to obtain one plant variety right for the entire Union with a single application. National and community plant variety rights, however, cannot exist simultaneously (Art. 92 Community Plant Variety Rights Regulation).

[113] EU Regulation 1307/2013.

[114] See: Technical Protocol of Hemp from the CPVO (CPVO-TP/276/2).

[115] Art. 55 and Art. 35 SPMA respectively.

[116] Art. 49(2) SPMA. In the Netherlands, a "grace period" applies for one year before the sale or provision (four to six years abroad).

of the distinctive characteristics as outlined under Article 55(2) SPMA. The Board for Plant Varieties may request that a sufficient quantity of material of the variety be made available for the technical examination concerning the distinctiveness,[117] uniformity,[118] and stability[119] of the variety.[120] This technical examination is conducted by Naktuinbouw as per Article 49(7) SPMA requirements.[121] Following an assessment of formal and substantial requirements, the Board for Plant Varieties decides whether the plant variety right is granted and subsequently registers the plant variety under the given variety name and characteristic description.[122] The propagating material of the registered variety may be traded exclusively under this specific name.[123]

Plant variety rights are possible for all five types of hemp. Only hemp types with a low THC value and propagated by seed – types a and e specifically – may be registered in the Dutch Variety Register and therefore be traded freely. The technical examination (DUS)[124] and the VCU test take place in the open field. It is not possible to register hemp with a low THC value that is vegetatively propagated – type b – in the Dutch Variety Register hemp.[125] A permit is required to import and export this type of hemp.[126] The VCU examination is not possible; a DUS test can be conducted in the open field. Meanwhile, hemp used for other purposes than fibre or oilseed and that is vegetatively propagated – type c – or feminised seed – type d – with a THC content higher or lower than 0.3 per cent falls under the Opium Act. These types are used for the extraction of chemical compounds. The VCU test is also not possible for these types, which results in them not being listed in the Dutch Variety Register. The DUS test is performed in a greenhouse. Authorisation is required to possess,

---

117 Art. 49(4) SPMA.

118 Art. 49(5)jo. Art. 35(3) SPMA. Plants propagated by seed (such as hemp plants with a high THC content) differ more among themselves than plants categorised as vegetatively propagated varieties.

119 Art. 49(6)jo. Art. 35(4) SPMA.

120 Art. 1c SPMA.

121 Art. 19 SPMA states that legal persons under private law can be designated by a general administrative regulation as so-called inspection bodies. Article 2 of the Decree on the marketing of propagation material designates Naktuinbouw as the inspection institution for horticultural crops. Naktuinbouw is located in Roelofarendsveen.

122 Art. 25(3), Art 55–56 SPMA.

123 Art. 25(4), Art. 46(1) SPMA.

124 Distinctiveness, Uniformity, and Stability.

125 "Procedure landbouwgewassen incl. CGO" (*Raad voor Plantenrassen*) <https://www.raadvoorplantenrassen.nl/nl/kwekersrecht-en-toelating/procedure-landbouwgewassen/>

126 ibid.

propagate, and transport these types of hemp, because these types are in principle forbidden under the Opium Act. Naktuinbouw has a permit to test these types of hemp in a greenhouse. Before the plant material is sent for the DUS test, the breeder needs to show a permit for the import and export of hemp. It is only allowed to trade these hemp plants in a closed chain. The total revenue must be sold to the Ministry of Health, Welfare and Sport for regulated use.[127]

In light of the experiment with the closed coffeeshop chain, it can be expected that the number of applications for plant variety rights on hemp will further increase. Exemptions for the production and sale of cannabis based on the Opium Act will still be needed. Although it is not possible to register all five types of hemp in the Dutch Variety Register, since a registration means that the goods can be traded freely, the registration of plant variety rights is possible.

11.10 CONCLUSION

In the Netherlands, the use of cannabis is accepted. Possession of cannabis is illegal but exempt from criminal liability under certain circumstances. Growing cannabis for recreational use is also forbidden. This ambiguous approach can be seen in how intellectual property (IP) is used to protect cannabis in the Netherlands. Given the tolerance towards cannabis, trademark applications referring to cannabis products are, in principle, not refused on the grounds of public order and public morality.[128] Cannabis trademarks are more likely to be refused because of the absence of any distinctive character. Furthermore, it is possible to obtain a plant variety right on cannabis if the plant variety meets the DUS conditions. However, only hemp types with a low THC content, from which the cannabis is crushed from seed – types a and e – can be listed in the Dutch Variety Register and therefore traded freely. In light of the experiment with the closed coffeeshop chain, it can be expected that the use and sale of soft drugs will become increasingly accepted. After the experimental period, a report will be drawn up on the effects of the closed coffeeshop chain on public order, safety, nuisance, and public health. Based on this report,

---

127 ibid.

128 I searched the BIOP trademark register for trademark applications in the category "cannabis". Entering the word "cannabis" in the search field "goods and services" resulted in 96 international trademarks with validity in the EU and/or the Benelux, 1,447 EU trademarks, and 280 Benelux trademarks. Entering the word "cannabis" in the search field "verbal and figurative elements" and selecting the option "exact search term" resulted in 15 international trademarks with validity in the EU and/or the Benelux, 150 EU trademarks, and 21 Benelux trademarks (accessed on 17 March 2024).

the cabinet will decide how to proceed further.[129] If the results of the experiment are positive, it is likely that it will be extended to other municipalities in the Netherlands. This would lead to further legalisation and acceptance of cannabis and a further exploration of IP rights in relation to cannabis in general.

129 <https://www.rijksoverheid.nl/onderwerpen/experiment-gesloten-coffeeshopketen-wietexperiment/documenten/brochures/2019/04/11/spelregels-experiment-gesloten-coffeeshopketen>.

PART IV

Developmental, economic, and sociological analysis

12. Traditional knowledge, traditional cultural expressions and cannabis: an Indigenous rights-based access and benefit-sharing framework

Marcus Goffe

12.1 INTRODUCTION

There is a long history between Indigenous communities, traditional knowledge, and cannabis. Indigenous and other tribal, minority, and local communities suffered disproportionately under generations of prohibition and criminalisation of cannabis. Recent legal and policy trends across the globe towards cannabis decriminalisation "represent a break with an historical trajectory founded on dubious science and political imperatives".[1] Cannabis decriminalisation marks an "important first step in redressing past harms and presents Indigenous communities with new opportunities for greater political, economic, and cultural self-determination".[2]

As a result, many Indigenous communities are embracing the cannabis industry as an economic generator,[3] especially in a context where many generations of traditional growers have been victims of state persecution, including arrests and prosecutions, spraying of crops, and destruction of ecosystems and

[1] D Bewley-Taylor, T Blickman, M Jelsma, *The Rise and Decline of Cannabis Prohibition: The History of Cannabis in the UN Drug Control System and Options for Reform* (Transnational Institute 2014) 2.

[2] Koutouki, Lofts, "Cannabis, Reconciliation, and the Rights of Indigenous Peoples: Prospects and Challenges for Cannabis Legalization in Canada" [2019] Alberta Law Review 727.

[3] R Halseth, N Cappe, *Knowledge, Perspectives, and Use of Cannabis among Indigenous Populations in Canada in the Context of Cannabis Legalization: A Review of Literature* (National Collaborating Centre for Indigenous Health 2023) 27.

families.[4] It is therefore opportune to re-evaluate the cannabis-related rights of Indigenous Peoples and Local Communities (IPs & LCs), including the rights of communities to their genetic resources (GRs), traditional knowledge (TK), and traditional cultural expressions (TCEs), many of which form the bedrock of ancient cannabis culture and contemporary cannabis genetics.

This chapter explores the many layers of the legal relationship between indigenous rights and cannabis and the legal protection of TK and TCEs within the recently re-emergent cannabis industries, with particular emphasis on the global Rastafari community. The Rastafari community, as a distinct Indigenous/tribal/minority community, has had a long and unique spiritual and cultural relationship with cannabis and cannabis criminalisation over several generations. The chapter examines the cultural appropriation of Rastafari TCEs in cannabis-related goods and services globally within an Indigenous rights framework and, in that respect, assesses the intersection of Rastafari cannabis TK/TCEs and intellectual property (IP) laws related to trademarks, passing off, copyright, designs, geographical indications (GIs), and plant breeders' rights (PBRs). As the Rastafari case study shows, the rights of IPs & LCs in relation to cannabis must be reviewed within a decolonial, reparative justice context, bearing in mind the colonial history, stigmas, and prejudices of the past, and the need to repair the legacy of injustice by ensuring relevant national, regional, and international laws empower IPs & LCs through the legal recognition, protection, and enforcement of community rights, including moral and economic rights, over their cannabis-related GRs, TK, and TCEs.

12.2 CANNABIS-RELATED TK OF INDIGENOUS AND LOCAL COMMUNITIES

IPs & LCs across several continents have been using cannabis for generations and as a result, have developed cultivation, medicinal, spiritual, and smoking practices and traditions surrounding cannabis.[5] Some communities have long histories with cannabis, both as food and fibre, and for multiple uses, including ceremonially, recreationally, therapeutically, and medicinally. This also involves the cultivation and preservation of specific strains over time.[6] In particular, IPs & LCs have been "selecting and stewarding local landraces,

[4] T Kepe, "*Cannabis Sativa* and Rural Livelihoods in South Africa: Politics of Cultivation, Trade and Value in Pondoland" (2003) 20 Development Southern Africa 605.

[5] C Duvall, *The African Roots of Marijuana* (Duke University Press 2019) 8–10.

[6] Halseth, Cappe (n 3) 10.

cultivar and varieties of cannabis plants for centuries".[7] In each of those contexts, IPs & LCs hold TK related to the cannabis plant.

Landraces are strains that have been "preserved and isolated in remote regions around the world, providing the highest variety of different compounds, including many terpenoids and flavonoids which have never been scientifically studied".[8] Although often lower in tetrahydrocannabinol (THC), landraces may be higher in other cannabinoids, terpenes, or flavonoids or have unique combinations thereof that hold untapped therapeutic value.[9] Landraces therefore provide "a rich source of genetic material from which can be developed targeted medicines for different illnesses".[10] In the modern decriminalised environment, these cannabis landraces are often referred to as "The Holy Grail" given their genetic material.[11]

Heirloom strains are "typically open-pollinated cultivars that were grown prior to widespread use of hybridization".[12] Strain hunters and other bioprospectors, in their development of new cannabis strains, have globally sought out and relied heavily upon the genetic diversity of cannabis landraces and heirloom strains which embody the TK of IPs & LCs that have cultivated them over generations.[13] Many cannabis companies are today conducting research and developing heirloom strains from landrace varieties.[14] This has resulted in significant increases in cannabis-related patents in recent years since

---

[7] CS Duvall, "Drug Laws, Bioprospecting and the Agricultural Heritage of *Cannabis* in Africa" (2016) 20(1) Space & Polity 14, 11–12; Cannabis IP Trends, 18.

[8] A Feilding, "Jamaican Cannabis Landraces: History and Importance" *HuffPost* (7 December 2017) <https://www.huffpost.com/entry/jamaican-cannabis-landrac_b_9110156> accessed 3 August 2024.

[9] "Inclusive Development in the South African Cannabis Industry" (*Institute For Economic Justice*, 1 March 2023) <https://www.iej.org.za/inclusive-development-in-the-south-african-cannabis-industry/> accessed 3 August 2024.

[10] Feilding (n 8).

[11] ibid.

[12] G Kuepper, *Heirloom Vegetables, Genetic Diversity, and the Pursuit of Food Security* (Kerr Centre for Sustainable Agriculture 2008) 2 <http://kerrcenter.com/wp-content/uploads/2015/02/heirloom-report.pdf> accessed 3 August 2024.

[13] Koutouki, Lofts (n 2) 713.

[14] For example, Durban Poison, derived from a South African landrace variety, is now used as a key "heirloom" strain for multiple high-value branded cannabis varieties. See *Inclusive Development in the South African Cannabis Industry: Assessing the Challenges* (Institute for Economic Justice 2023) <https://www.iej.org.za/wp-content/uploads/2023/02/IEJ-CannabisReport-Feb2023.pdf> accessed 3 August 2024.

decriminalisation.[15] Undoubtedly therefore, "the present-day diversity of cannabis landraces is the result of human selection practices 'embedded in indigenous knowledge systems'".[16] Indeed, the contributions of modern cannabis breeders are built upon the contributions of those communities.[17] IPs & LCs are therefore "the traditional knowledge custodians and practitioners that provided the building blocks of medical cannabis knowledge to the medical cannabis researcher".[18]

Landrace varieties are therefore key Indigenous knowledge assets with immense potential commercial value, in light of the importance of new genetic material to the modern, global decriminalised cannabis industries.[19] Unfortunately however, "dominant interests have been able to define cannabis in ways that largely obscure and negate the role that these communities have played in the cultivation and protection of cannabis strains over many generations, along with the immense bodies of knowledge they have developed, stewarded, and imparted".[20] The contribution of IPs & LCs to the preservation of cannabis strains and culture has been and continues to be undermined within national and international cannabis law and policy.

The criminalisation of cannabis over the years has made it difficult for IPs & LCs to prove that particular cannabis-related TK is theirs.[21] At the same time, there is "a lack of Indigenous-based research on cannabis, which has resulted in prioritizing Western perspectives on substance use and associated harms over more holistic, relational, and strengths based Indigenous ways of knowing".[22] The cumulative effect of cannabis criminalisation and anti-Indigenous stigmatisation is the continued systematic difficulty experienced by IPs & LCs in preventing the misappropriation of their cannabis GRs and cannabis-related TK and challenges in having their cannabis products legally protected and commercially accepted. This is particularly egregious when considered within the context of the undeniably fundamental role of IPs & LCs in the existence and value of the global cannabis industries.

Indigenous knowledge, often considered by older Western standards as the common heritage of mankind, has resulted in the widespread "non-consensual use of genetic strains of cannabis (and associated traditional knowledge)

[15] J Wyse, G Luria, "Trends in Intellectual Property Rights Protection for Medical Cannabis and Related Products" (2021) 3 Journal of Cannabis Research.

[16] Koutouki, Lofts (n 2) 713; See also Duvall (n 7).

[17] Cannabis IP Trends (n 7) 18.

[18] ibid.

[19] Duvall, 2019.

[20] Koutouki, Lofts (n 2) 713.

[21] ibid.

[22] Halseth, Cappe (n 3) 38.

developed and cultivated by Indigenous Peoples over centuries".[23] Unfairly, "the benefits derived from these genetic resources and associated traditional knowledge are not being realized by the Indigenous and local communities themselves".[24] It is therefore important to protect landrace varieties as valuable Indigenous knowledge assets from the real and present threat of appropriation by entities in the cannabis and related biotechnological industries,[25] and to ensure that the benefits of the commercialisation of the cannabis-related TK and TCEs of IPs & LCs are fairly and equitably shared with these communities.

12.3 CHALLENGES OF IP TO PROTECT TK AND TCES

The tensions and intersections between IP, TK,[26] and TCEs,[27] are well documented today. It is widely recognised that the IP system is generally inadequate to protect TK for several reasons stemming from the different conceptual bases for protection between Indigenous peoples and "Western" societies.[28]

---

23 ibid 32.

24 Koutouki, Lofts (n 2) 713.

25 See Duvall (n 7); and A Singh, "Cannabis Biopiracy in the Era of Climate Chaos" (*Grow Opportunity*, 13 September 2022) <https://www.growopportunity.ca/cannabis-biopiracy-in-the-era-of-climate-chaos/> accessed 30 August 2024.

26 WIPO defines "Traditional knowledge" in its broad sense as including "the intellectual and intangible cultural heritage, practices and knowledge systems of traditional communities, including indigenous and local communities … as well as traditional cultural expressions, including distinctive signs and symbols associated with traditional knowledge". In a narrower sense, TK can be defined as "knowledge resulting from intellectual activity in a traditional context, and includes know-how, practices, skills, and innovations. Traditional knowledge can be found in a wide variety of contexts: agricultural knowledge; scientific knowledge; technical knowledge; ecological knowledge; medicinal knowledge, including related medicines and remedies; and biodiversity-related knowledge, etc". "Glossary" (*WIPO*) <https://www.wipo.int/tk/en/resources/glossary.html> accessed 3 August 2024.

27 WIPO defines "traditional cultural expressions" as "tangible and intangible forms in which traditional knowledge and cultures are expressed, communicated or manifested. Examples include traditional music, performances, narratives, names and symbols, designs and architectural forms", ibid.

28 The prevailing IP system's limitations in the protection affordable to TK and TCEs have been very well examined in the literature. See, for example S von Lewinski, "Traditional Knowledge and Folklore: A New Topic in the International Arena", in F Grosheide and J Brinkhof (eds), *Intellectual Property Law: Articles on Cultural Expressions and Indigenous Knowledge* (Molengrafica Series Intersentia 2002) 181–200.

National and international IP systems are based primarily on individual rights and largely driven by profit motives, while TK and TCEs are often held collectively and primarily premised on community rights, motivated by maintenance of community cultural tradition and identity.[29] IP rights are subject to specific exceptions and limitations, which may not in all instances be appropriate to recognise and protect the traditions of IPs & LCs. IP rights also expire and fall in the public domain thereafter, while TK and TCEs are maintained indefinitely by IPs & LCs. Additionally, IP rights do not protect TK holistically.[30] Undoubtedly, unrestricted and unregulated access to TCEs can and has caused damage to the cultural heritage and identity of IPs & LCs, as well as affected trade in authentic community crafts and other products.[31]

Commercial cannabis breeders may use Indigenous or local GRs and/or TK as a source of cannabis to produce hybrid and other strains, which may then be protected by plant patents or PBR. Additionally, cannabis cultivation or extraction methods or medical uses that can be patented by cannabis enterprises may have originated in a particular community or group of communities. The IP system and the patent and PBR systems in particular "work in favor of modern-day research in the developed world and offer little or no protection to the indigenous stakeholders".[32] While recognising that existing IP rights can be used to provide some recognition and protection for community TK and TCEs,[33] without recognition of the rights of communities in regard to the same, including the right to benefit-sharing to ensure just distributions of economic gains from landrace varieties, such rights can only provide limited, incomplete, and inadequate protection. Clearly, the IP system as currently structured is inadequate to protect the cannabis-related rights of IPs & LCs.

---

[29] See M Battiste and J [Sa'kej] Henderson, *Protecting Indigenous Knowledge and Heritage: A Global Challenge* (Purich Publishing Limited 2000) 145; C McManis and Y Teran, "Trends and Scenarios in the Legal Protection of Traditional Knowledge", in T Wong (ed.), 'Intellectual Property through the Lens of Human Development" in T Wong and G Dutfield (eds), *Intellectual Property and Human Development: Current Trends and Future Scenarios* (Cambridge University Press 2011) 139, 139–174.

[30] See, for example, M Blakeney, "Protecting the Cultural Expressions of Indigenous Peoples under Intellectual Property Law: The Australian Experience" in Grosheide, Brinkhof (n 28); McManis, Teran (n 29) 155; T Wong, C Fernandini, "Traditional Cultural Expressions: Preservation and Innovation" in Wong, Dutfield (n 29) 184–189.

[31] Wong, Fernandini (n 30) 182.

[32] Cannabis IP Trends (n 7) 18.

[33] The registration of GIs for landrace varieties and associated place names in particular has been proposed. See Inclusive Development (n 14).

12.4 INTERNATIONAL LAW PROTECTING COMMUNITY RIGHTS IN GRS AND ASSOCIATED TK

Although the international drug conventions that prohibit and regulate cannabis as an illicit drug provide exceptions for medicinal and scientific research, they do not recognise or include exceptions for the traditional or customary use of cannabis by IPs & LCs.[34] This is unsurprising in the context of international law's historical denial of recognition of Indigenous Peoples and their rights, which, until very recently, has not had any international IP law recognising and protecting TK. It is only more recently, with the advent of the Convention on Biological Diversity (CBD) in 1992 and in particular, its Nagoya Protocol on Access and Benefit Sharing in 2010, that the rights of IPs & LCs to their TK associated with GRs have been recognised in international law.

The CBD obliges contracting parties to respect, preserve, and maintain knowledge, innovations, and practices of IPs & LCs, requires the approval and involvement[35] of IPs & LCs in the promotion and use of their TK, and requires fair and equitable benefit sharing (F & EBS) with IPs & LCs in the event of utilisation of their TK.[36] The CBD has therefore been hailed as "a milestone in the evolution of rights and entitlements related to genetic resources and traditional knowledge",[37] and as a potentially significant instrument in the development of the rights of IPs & LCs.[38]

The Nagoya Protocol on Access to Genetic Resources and the Fair and Equitable Sharing of Benefits Arising from their Utilization to the Convention on Biological Diversity[39] aims to ensure that the benefits arising from the utilisation of genetic resources (GRs) are shared in a fair and equitable manner

---

[34] Single Convention on Narcotic Drugs, 1961, 30 March 1961, 520 UNTS 151 (entered into force 13 December 1964); Convention on Psychotropic Substances, 21 February 1971, 1019 UNTS 175 (entered into force 16 August 1976); United Nations Convention Against Illicit Traffic in Narcotic Drugs and Psychotropic Substances, 20 December 1988, 1582 UNTS 95 (entered into force 11 November 1990).

[35] Framed as "full and effective participation (F & EP)" by the author.

[36] CBD Art. 8(j).

[37] R Crookshanks, P Phillips, "A Comparative Analysis of Access and Benefits-sharing Systems" in T Bubela and ER Gold (eds), *Genetic Resources and Traditional Knowledge: Case Studies and Conflicting Interests* (Edward Elgar Publishing 2012) 74.

[38] J Gibson, *Community Resources: Intellectual Property, International Trade and Protection of Traditional Knowledge* (Ashgate Publishing 2005) 191–192.

[39] This is the full title of the Protocol.

with the sources of those resources. It requires the free, prior, and informed consent (FPIC) of IPs & LCs for access to their TK associated with GRs.[40] Further, any benefits acquired should be shared with the IPs & LCs that are holders of GRs where they have established rights to such resources.[41] The Protocol requires the sharing of benefits on mutually agreed terms (MATs).[42]

The Protocol obliges states to take into consideration customary laws, community protocols, and procedures of IPs & LCs. States are also encouraged to support IPs & LCs in their development of community protocols, minimum requirements for MATs, and model contractual clauses for benefit-sharing arising from the utilisation of TK associated with GRs.

The United Nations Declaration on the Rights of Indigenous Peoples (UNDRIP) also contains important provisions on the requirement for FPIC of Indigenous peoples. Under UNDRIP, "Indigenous Peoples have the right to maintain, control, protect and develop their cultural heritage, TK and TCEs, as well as the manifestations of their sciences, technologies and cultures, including human and genetic resources, seeds, medicines, knowledge of the properties of fauna and flora, oral traditions, literatures, designs, sports and traditional games and visual and performing arts".[43] They also have the right to maintain, control, protect, and develop their IP over such cultural heritage, TK, and TCEs.[44] According to the Declaration,

> States shall provide redress through effective mechanisms, which may include restitution, developed in conjunction with indigenous peoples, with respect to their cultural, intellectual, religious and spiritual property taken without their free, prior and informed consent or in violation of their laws, traditions and customs.[45]

The World Intellectual Property Organization (WIPO) Treaty on Intellectual Property, Genetic Resources and associated Traditional Knowledge, concluded on 24 May 2024, is the first WIPO Treaty that applies to GRs and TK, specifically protecting the TK of IPs & LCs.[46] The Treaty applies only to the patent system, unfortunately, and in that respect, its objectives are limited: (a) to enhance the efficacy, transparency, and quality of the patent system

---

40 Art 6(2).

41 Art. 5(2).

42 ibid.

43 Art. 31.

44 ibid.

45 Art. 11(2).

46 "WIPO Member States Adopt Historic New Treaty on Intellectual Property, Genetic Resources and Associated Traditional Knowledge" (*WIPO*, 24 May 2024) <https://www.wipo.int/pressroom/en/articles/2024/article_0007.html> accessed 3 August 2024.

with regard to GRs and associated TK; and (b) to prevent patents from being granted erroneously for inventions that are not novel or inventive with regard to GRs and associated TK.[47]

Upon entry into force, after 15 contracting parties have ratified or acceded to it,[48] the Treaty will establish a new international law requirement for patent applicants whose inventions are based on GRs and/or associated TK, to disclose the source of the GRs and/or associated TK.[49] Each contracting party is required to put in place appropriate, effective, and proportionate legal, administrative, and/or policy measures to address non-compliance. Each contracting party is also required to provide an opportunity to patent applicants to rectify their failure to disclose the information required, unless there has been fraudulent conduct or intent by the applicant. Although the Treaty does not prescribe specific sanctions and remedies for non-disclosure, contracting parties are precluded from revoking or invalidating the patent rights or rendering the same unenforceable solely on the basis of an applicant's failure to disclose the required information.[50] The Treaty is non-retroactive.[51] Further, it only applies to patents, GRs, and associated TK and not to other IP rights and other non-GR-associated TK or TCEs.[52] In that respect, the Treaty would not assist communities like the Rastafari, which have endured misappropriation of their TCEs in the global marketing of cannabis-related goods and services.

12.5 MISAPPROPRIATION OF CANNABIS-RELATED TCES: A RASTAFARI CASE STUDY

The Rastafari are perhaps the most globally recognised community in the Caribbean today. They have been described as a "cultural phenomenon" and one of the most powerful cultural forces in the world.[53] In many respects, the Rastafari community and its TCEs are at the heart of global cannabis culture.

---

47 *WIPO Treaty on Intellectual Property, Genetic Resources and Associated Traditional Knowledge*, Article 1 (WIPO) <https://www.wipo.int/edocs/mdocs/tk/en/gratk_dc/gratk_dc_7.pdf> accessed 3 August 2024.

48 ibid, Article 17.

49 ibid, Article 3.

50 ibid, Article 5.

51 ibid, Article 4.

52 WIPO (n 46).

53 NS Murrell, "The Rastafarian Movement, Introduction to the Rastafari Phenomenon" (*Global Exchange*) <http://www.globalexchange.org/countries/americas/jamaica/rasta.html> accessed 3 August 2024.

Rastafari is an Afro-descendant minority community; one that represents "[t]he most modern manifestation of African thought in Jamaica"[54] and a new pan-African ethnicity.[55] According to Murrell, "Rastafari is a modern Afro-Caribbean cultural phenomenon that combines concepts from African culture and the 'Caribbean experience' (social, historical, religious, and economic realities) with Judeo-Christian thought into a new sociopolitical and religious worldview".[56]

Today, Rastafari is recognised in Jamaica as an Indigenous Culture, but not as an Indigenous People entitled to Indigenous Rights. Nevertheless, whether classified as an Indigenous, tribal, or minority community, the Rastafari is a unique community and culture entitled to group rights, which group rights are, for the first time in post-colonial Jamaica, recognised in law by the Dangerous Drugs (Amendment) Act 2015, specifically in relation to ganja.[57]

Having first emerged in Jamaica in the 1920s, the Rastafari are considered Indigenous to Jamaica in the ordinary, non-legal sense of the word. However, applying the "pre-colonial continuity" definitions of Indigenous,[58] the Rastafari community does not qualify because the community did not exist prior to the colonisation of Jamaica. The Rastafari community has nevertheless consistently self-identified as descendants of Indigenous Africans forcibly displaced to Jamaica by slavery and colonisation.[59]

12.5.1 Status of the Rastafari under International Law

There is no internationally agreed definition of "Indigenous Peoples".[60] Indigenous Peoples are usually minorities, but minorities are not always

54 O Lewin, *Rock It Come Over: The Folk Music of Jamaica* (University of the West Indies Press, Jamaica 2000) 197.

55 T Martin, "African and Indian Consciousness" in B Brereton (ed.), *General History of the Caribbean, Volume V: The Caribbean in the Twentieth Century* (UNESCO Publishing 2004) 229, 224–281.

56 Murrell (n 53).

57 M Goffe, "The Rights of Maroons in the Emerging Ganja Industry in Jamaica" (2018) 67(1) Journal of Social and Economic Studies 85, 85–115.

58 M Goffe, "Protecting the Traditions of the Maroons and Ras Tafari: An Analysis of the Adequacy of the Intellectual Property Laws of Jamaica and Proposals for Reform" (2009) 6(3) SCRIPTed 575 <https://script-ed.org/wp-content/uploads/2016/07/6-3-Goffe.pdf> accessed 30 August 2024.

59 M Goffe, "Exploring Ras Tafari Culture" (2011) 2 World Intellectual Property Organization Magazine, April, 22, 22–24 <http://www.wipo.int/wipo_magazine/en/2011/02/article_0008.html> accessed 3 August 2024.

60 J Gilbert, *Indigenous Peoples' Land Rights under International Law: From Victims to Actors* (Transnational Publishers 2006) xvi.

Indigenous.[61] However, there are several criteria by which Indigenous Peoples can be identified and characterised. The classical concept of the term has historically been defined to refer to peoples who existed prior to invasion and colonisation by European and other Western powers between the fifteenth and nineteenth centuries (and the resultant establishment and imposition of foreign government and laws during that time).[62] This conceptualisation is exemplified by the ILO Convention No. 169 on Indigenous and Tribal Peoples in Independent Countries, which implicitly recognises "Indigenous Peoples" by their "descent from the populations which inhabited the country, or a geographical region to which the country belongs, at the time of conquest or colonisation or the establishment of present State boundaries".[63]

However, the ILO Convention No. 169 applies a purposive and inclusive approach to its definitions of protected communities.[64] The Convention applies not only to Indigenous Peoples but also to tribal peoples "whose social, cultural and economic conditions distinguish them from other sections of the national community, and whose status is regulated wholly or partially by their own customs or traditions or by special laws or regulations".[65] The principle of self-identification is recognised as fundamental to determining who qualifies as Indigenous and tribal peoples protected by ILO Convention No. 169.[66] Under ILO Convention No. 169, self-identification is the sole foundational criterion for indigenousness.

Applying the ILO Convention definition of tribal peoples, Rastafari is to be considered a tribal people because their social, cultural, and economic conditions distinguish them from other sections of the national community, and their status is regulated wholly or partially by their own customs or traditions, or by special laws or regulations.

The Rastafari community would also clearly qualify as a numerical and religious minority community in Jamaica and any other country where the

---

[61] P Justino and J Litchfield, *Economic Exclusion and Discrimination: The Experiences of Minorities and Indigenous Peoples* (Minority Rights Group International 2003) 4.

[62] Gilbert (n 60).

[63] ILO Convention No. 169 on Indigenous and Tribal Peoples in Independent Countries, Article 1.

[64] KN Bojosi, GK Wachira, "Protecting Indigenous Peoples in Africa: An Analysis of the Approach of the African Commission on Human and Peoples' Rights" (2006) 6 Afr. Hum. Rts. L.J. 382, 399; B Kingsbury, "'Indigenous Peoples' in International Law: A Constructivist Approach to the Asian Controversy" (1998) 92 Am. J. Int'l L. 414, 443.

[65] ILO Convention No. 169 (n 63).

[66] ibid Art. 1, in force since 5 September 1991.

extended community exists. In Jamaica, although not an ethnic minority, Rastafari is a religious minority, but in other jurisdictions where African ancestry is not the majority, they may be an ethnic minority as well. The community has a distinct set of traditions that have been passed down from generation to generation over the past 80 years. Rastafari is a community defined as "people sharing history, habits, customs, rituals, traditional knowledge, cultural expressions and other social practices",[67] and "whose sense of identity or connectedness emerges from a shared historical relationship that is rooted in the practice and transmission of, or engagement with, their intangible cultural heritage".[68]

12.5.2 Historical Link between Rastafari and Cannabis/the Basis for Rastafari Rights

12.5.2.1 Rastafari relationship to cannabis/ganja

In this section, cannabis is referred to as ganja because it is the term by which the grassroots and Rastafari in Jamaica refer to cannabis, and it is also the official term used for cannabis in the Dangerous Drugs Act of Jamaica up until the 2015 amendments.[69] Ganja is considered a religious sacrament by members of the Rastafari community.[70] It is used individually and collectively to facilitate reasoning,[71] and also ceremonially at worship celebrations, known as "nyahbinghi" or "grounations". For Rastafari, ganja is a way of life.[72] In addition to sacramental uses, Rastafari use ganja to make various by-products such as cakes, allspice, teas, tinctures, oils, tonics, tablets, wines, and cosmetics.[73]

---

67 S Chaudhuri, "Who is the 'Holder' of Intangible Cultural Heritage? Revisiting the Concept of Community from an Intangible Cultural Heritage Perspective", in T Kono (ed.), *Intangible Cultural Heritage and Intellectual Property: Communities, Cultural Diversity and Sustainable Development* (Intersentia 2009) 189–201, 191.

68 ibid.

69 The 2015 amendment differentiates between ganja, which is cannabis over 1 per cent THC, and hemp, which is cannabis not over 1 per cent THC.

70 K Bilby, "The Holy Herb: Notes on the Background of Cannabis in Jamaica" (1985) Rastafari Caribbean Quarterly Monograph, University of the West Indies, Jamaica 82–95, 82, 86.

71 A Kebede, JD Knottnerus, "Beyond the Pales of Babylon: The Ideational Components and Social Psychological Foundations of Rastafari" (1998) 41(3) Sociological Perspectives 499–517, 509.

72 Rastafari and Grassroots Ganja Association (RAGGA) Declaration (2021), on file with author. See M Goffe, "Rastafari Ganja Reparations: A Caribbean Decolonial Imperative" (2023) 69(3–4) Caribbean Quarterly 349–369.

73 ibid.

For Rastafari, ganja is given by Jah Rastafari for use in private personal and community collective life, not only as a sacrament, but for commercial, spiritual, economic, industrial, cultural, and medicinal/therapeutic healing of the nation; in other words, for the service of humanity. Rastafari enjoy a special sacred relationship with ganja as a sacrament, an innate part of Rastafari livity and culture.

Many Rastafari communities and thousands of community members were subject to targeting and criminal prosecution for ganja in Jamaica, the Caribbean, and across the world.[74] For the smoking of ganja, members of the Rastafari community have been distinctly targeted by law enforcement in Jamaica and other countries where Rastafari live.[75] From 1941 to 1954, one of the first Rastafari communities called Pinnacle in Jamaica was the subject of many raids by the police, who used the pretext of cannabis cultivation to invade, dismantle, disperse, and destroy the community repeatedly.[76] Each time the police raided Pinnacle, they would take away cash under the pretext that it was money earned from selling ganja.

During the heated years of Prohibition, Rastafari cannabis breeders particularly suffered, and Rastafari cultivation and breeding were forced underground, diminishing over time. However, with the growth in global popularity of Rastafari and reggae music, Rastafari became synonymous with global cannabis culture, especially smoking and lifestyle culture. This dynamic diffusion of local traditional ideology and culture into global popular culture in a relatively short period has been widely and repeatedly described as phenomenal.[77]

However, despite the immense popularity of Rastafari philosophy and culture, resulting in the sale of many Rastafari-themed cultural products and services globally, and the accumulation of wealth by a few well-known individual Rastafari such as Bob Marley through reggae, the Rastafari remain among the lowest socio-economic levels of Jamaican society.[78] At the same time,

---

[74] For a detailed account, see Office of the Public Defender, *An Investigation into the April 1963 Incident at Coral Gardens* (2015) <https://opd.gov.jm/wp-content/uploads/2020/09/Investigation-Into-The-April-1963-Incident-at-Coral-Gardens.pdf> accessed 3 August 2024, 13–23.

[75] See Goffe (n 72).

[76] Y Afari, *Overstanding Rastafari: Jamaica's Gift to the World* (Senya-Cum 2007) 48; IJ Tafari, "The Rastafari – Successors of Marcus Garvey" (1985) Rastafari Caribbean Quarterly Monograph, University of the West Indies, Jamaica 1–12, 3.

[77] See, for example, RJ Stewart, "Religion, Myths and Beliefs: Their Socio-political Roles" in B Brereton (n 55) 559–605, 560.

[78] V Pollard, *Dread Talk: The Language of the Rastafari* (McGill-Queen's University Press 2000) 21, 51.

Rastafari, and through Rastafari mainly, ganja has been infused and appropriated into global reggae culture, bringing with it the appropriation of Rastafari ganja culture, event and lifestyle branding, and the marketing of goods and services using Rastafari TK and TCEs.

12.5.3 Rastafari TK and TCEs

Rastafari TK and TCEs invariably reflect Rastafari ideology, spirituality, and symbolism, which are at the core of Rastafari identity and central to Rastafari physical and cultural survival. These include the Rastafari colour combination of red, gold, and green,[79] and the distinctive Imperial Ethiopian flag,[80] with the Lion of Judah centrepiece;[81] the iconic ungroomed dreadlocks of Rastafari, worn traditionally as an overt symbol of resistance and rebellion to colonial society and economy;[82] Rastafari language, called "Dread Talk" or "Iyaric" by researchers,[83] involving English words that have been altered by the use of the prefix "I", English words before which the sound "Y" is put, English words that are altered to reflect Rastafari ideology, such as "Downpress" meaning "Oppress", and words and concepts invented by Rastafari.[84]

Rastafari TK also includes the Ital Diet and Ital Livity, the words "ital" and "livity" being Rastafari words. An ital diet is a vegetarian diet consisting of vegetables, grains, peas, and fruits, with no meat and no salt. Livity involves "a philosophy of living harmoniously as well as collectively with nature".[85] This includes "'the practice of I-tal living' which is reflected in the Rastafarians' appearance, diet, use of herbs, process of reflection, modes of production, and aesthetic activity".[86]

The production of handicrafts, artwork, and smoking paraphernalia made from or otherwise depicting cannabis is almost always accompanied by distinctive Rastafari images, colours, and symbols. Rastafari TK also includes the

---

79 B Chevannes, *Betwixt and Between: Explorations in an African Caribbean Mindscape* (Ian Randle Publishers 2006) 200.

80 Lewin (n 54).

81 The flag is also officially used by the Crown Council of Ethiopia. The Rastafari community has adopted that flag as its own, and use of the flag today, both in Jamaica and internationally, is identified primarily with the Rastafari community.

82 Kebede, Knottnerus (n 71).

83 ibid.

84 Pollard (n 78) 103.

85 Kebede, Knottnerus (n 71) 503.

86 ibid quoting Johnson-Hill, *I-Sight the World of Rastafari: An Interpretive Sociological Account of Rastafarian Ethics* (The Scarecrow Press 1995) 25.

use of herbs, including but not limited to cannabis, and preparation and application of herbal remedies for the treatment of a range of medical conditions.

Rastafari TK and TCEs also permeate the art form of reggae. Rastafari gave the world reggae music.[87] Indeed, "Rastafarianism was to become the dominant ideology of Jamaican music in the mid-1970s".[88] As Pollard notes, "[b]y the time the lyrics of Reggae music reached the airwaves of the world, the language of Rastafari had become an integral part of its culture".[89] Through Rastafari influence, the locks, words, symbols, and colours of Rastafari became identified internationally with reggae, such that today, the colours of Rastafari are the colours of reggae.

12.5.4 Misrepresentation and Misappropriation of Rastafari TCEs

The Rastafari community has historically been marginalised and has had its cultural traditions misappropriated far and wide, in diverse forms, both nationally, regionally, and internationally, in print and electronic media, and therefore subjected to harm as a result. Such misappropriation is well documented.[90] Today, thousands of products and services are marketed and promoted using the Rastafari name, imagery, and TCEs without the consent of or any benefit accruing to the Rastafari community.

The unauthorised copying, reproduction, and association of Rastafari style of dress, talk, symbols, and imagery, raises serious issues with regard to the right of Rastafari as a community to safeguard the use and misuse of its culture. Not only does this risk harming the community, in that the community is often portrayed or represented inaccurately or in an objectified manner, but in relation to products which the Rastafari traditionally make and sell themselves, such as hats, tams, clothes, handicrafts, and other artistic works, the community members also suffer harm in the marketplace by having to compete with outsiders passing off their goods and services as Rastafari-made.

---

87 Martin (n 55) 224–281, 249.

88 S Barrow, P Dalton, *The Rough Guide to Reggae* (Rough Guides Ltd. 2004) 79.

89 Pollard (n 78) 97.

90 See, for example, Lewin (n 54); Pollard (n 78); B Chevannes, "New Approach to Ras Tafari" in B Chevannes (ed.), *Ras Tafari and Other African-Caribbean Worldviews* (Institute of Social Studies, The Hague, MacMillan Press 1995); E Brodber, JE Greene, *Reggae and Cultural Identity in Jamaica* (Institute of Social and Economic Research, University of the West Indies, Jamaica 1988); T Rommen, "Protestant Vibrations? Reggae, Ras Tafari, and Conscious Evangelicals" (2006) 25(2) Popular Music 235–263; Goffe (n 58).

This longstanding problem of misappropriation of Rastafari TK and TCEs has been significantly exacerbated by global cannabis culture and the Internet.

12.6 CULTURAL APPROPRIATION OF RASTAFARI IN CANNABIS GOODS AND SERVICES

Reggae music provided the soundtrack to the Rastafari articulation of the reverence for the holy herb. As reggae and Rastafari reggae pioneers like Bob Marley swept across Europe and the Americas in the 1970s, the identification of Rastafari and reggae with cannabis became internationally acknowledged. From that time until now, one of the clearest demonstrations of the pervasive and enduring popularity of Rastafari TCEs in relation to cannabis goods and services has been Amsterdam's coffeeshops. For decades, Rastafari and Rastafari-inspired words, colours, motifs, and imagery have been and continue to be popular choices among coffee shop owners for coffee shop names, logos, interior and exterior décor, as well as for smoking paraphernalia and cannabis strain names identified on cannabis menus.[91]

A recent search of several trademark registers shows the kind of usage of Rastafari TCEs in cannabis-related trademarks. The searches were done electronically in January 2024 of the trademark registers of Canada, the UK, and the EU. As the USPTO does not register cannabis-related trademarks due to the still illegal status of cannabis at the federal level, the US trademark register was not included. The searches were done in classes 5 and 34, where

---

91 See R Steves, "A Coffee Shop Conversation about Marijuana in Amsterdam" (*HeraldNet.com*, 11 April 2021) <https://www.heraldnet.com/life/a-coffee-shop-conversation-about-marijuana-in-amsterdam/> accessed 3 August 2024; "Buy Weed Online Canada" (*Weed Nations*, 23 September 2022) <https://weednations.ca/> accessed 3 August 2024; "Amsterdam Coffeeshop: First Timer's Guide with How-To's & Facts" (*IAmAileen*) <https://iamaileen.com/amsterdam-coffeeshop/> accessed 3 August 2024; E Moyer, "Reggae and Weed: Coffee Shop Encounter at Funky Munkey" (*Becoming Men*, 20 April 2017) <https://www.becoming-men.org/news/2017/4/20/reggae-and-weed-coffee-shop-encounter-at-funky-munkey> accessed 3 August 2024; "Coffeeshop Rasta Baby" (*Best Coffee Shop Guide*) <https://www.dutch-coffeeshops.com/coffeeshop-adresses/coffeeshops-amsterdam-3/coffeeshop-rasta-baby/> accessed 3 August 2024; P Hendrikkade, "Rasta Baby (Closed as of 2012) Coffeeshop Amsterdam" (*Coffeeshop Amsterdam*, 31 October 2014) <https://www.smokersguide.com/adressen/662/rasta_baby__closed_as_of_2012.html> accessed 3 August 2024; "'Coffeeshops': Amsterdam's Hazy, Dazy Cafés" (*Rick Steves*, 16 April 2024) <https://www.ricksteves.com/watch-read-listen/read/articles/amsterdams-coffeeshops> accessed 3 August 2024; "Coffeeshops in Amsterdam" (*AmsterdamSights.com*) <https://www.amsterdamsights.com/nightlife/coffeeshops.html> accessed 3 August 2024.

cannabis-related products tend to be registered, using search terms comprising Rastafari TCEs – "IRIE", "LIVITY", "ITAL", "RASTA", "GANJA", and "KAYA". The online searches were unable to search for the use of the Rastafari colours or other Rastafari symbols, imagery, and non-verbal TCEs.

The search of the UK trademarks register revealed several Rastafari TCEs included in trademark applications or registrations related to cannabis goods and services, including RR RASTA, rasta koala, GLOBAL RASTA, RASTA RAINBOW, IRIE, GANJA FARMER, GOURMET GANJA, KAYA, MY-KAYA, and KAYA EXTRACTS.[92] The search of the EU trademarks register revealed several Rastafari TCEs included in trademark applications or registrations, including ITAL for herbal products, IRIE for smoking products, IRIE for tobacco-free smoking products, RASTA for lighters and other smoking products, CANNABIS CHILLOUT, GANJA FARMER, and GANJAMAICA.[93] The search of the Canadian trademarks register revealed

---

[92] UK Intellectual Property Office <https://trademarks.ipo.gov.uk/ipo-tmtext> accessed 3 August 2024; "Trade Mark Number UK00918191271" (*UK Intellectual Property Office*) <https://trademarks.ipo.gov.uk/ipo-tmcase/page/Results/1/UK00918191271> accessed 3 August 2024; "Trade Mark Number UK00003542136" (*UK Intellectual Property Office*) <https://trademarks.ipo.gov.uk/ipo-tmcase/page/Results/1/UK00003542136> accessed 3 August 2024; "Trade Mark Number UK00003392417" (*UK Intellectual Property Office*) <https://trademarks.ipo.gov.uk/ipo-tmcase/page/Results/1/UK00003392417> accessed 3 August 2024; "Trade Mark Number UK00917962117" (*UK Intellectual Property Office*) <https://trademarks.ipo.gov.uk/ipo-tmcase/page/Results/1/UK00917962117> accessed 3 August 2024; "Trade Mark Number UK00918141836" (*UK Intellectual Property Office*) <https://trademarks.ipo.gov.uk/ipo-tmcase/page/Results/1/UK00918141836> accessed 3 August 2024; "Trade Mark Number UK00917939779" (*UK Intellectual Property Office*) <https://trademarks.ipo.gov.uk/ipo-tmcase/page/Results/1/UK00917939779> accessed 3 August 2024; "Trade Mark Number UK00801266622" (*UK Intellectual Property Office*) <https://trademarks.ipo.gov.uk/ipo-tmcase/page/Results/1/UK00801266622> accessed 3 August 2024; "Trade Mark Number UK00003379123" (*UK Intellectual Property Office*) <https://trademarks.ipo.gov.uk/ipo-tmcase/page/Results/1/UK00003379123> accessed 3 August 2024; "Trade Mark Number UK00003474484" (*UK Intellectual Property Office*) <https://trademarks.ipo.gov.uk/ipo-tmcase/page/Results/1/UK00003474484> accessed 3 August 2024.

[93] "ITAL 015323281" (*European Union Intellectual Property Office*) <https://euipo.europa.eu/eSearch/#details/trademarks/015323281> accessed 3 August 2024; "IRIE 018466454" (*European Union Intellectual Property Office*) <https://euipo.europa.eu/eSearch/#details/trademarks/018466454 > accessed 3 August 2024; "Rasta 1477994" (*European Union Intellectual Property Office*) <https://euipo.europa.eu/eSearch/#details/trademarks/W01477994> accessed 3 August 2024; "FA ENGINEERED NUTRITION CANNABIS CHILLOUT shot

several Rastafari TCEs included in trademark applications or registrations, including "LIVITY".[94] Details of these trademarks are included in Appendix 12.A1.

A Google search reveals much more misappropriation of Rastafari TCEs. In terms of cannabis businesses, GOURMET GANJA comes up. The trade name/trademark does not necessarily utilise any Rastafari TCEs, but the Facebook page for the business reveals the extent of usage of Rastafari TCEs.[95] A Google search for "Rasta Ganja products" brings up thousands of hits showing products with the image of the cannabis leaf, with the Rastafari colours or other Rastafari imagery of locks. These products include cannabis grinders, wrappers, lighters, ashtrays, cannabis lollipops, t-shirts, hoodies, stickers, pop sockets, iron-on patches, cigarette cases, tote bags, bag straps, belts, flags, key rings, bangles, bracelets, and other jewellery.[96] Indeed there is

---

018704747" (*European Union Intellectual Property Office*) <https://euipo.europa.eu/eSearch/#details/trademarks/018704747> accessed 3 August 2024; "GANJA FARMER 018141836" (*European Union Intellectual Property Office*) <https://euipo.europa.eu/eSearch/#details/trademarks/018141836> accessed 3 August 2024; "Ganjamaica 018192844" (*European Union Intellectual Property Office*) <https://euipo.europa.eu/eSearch/#details/trademarks/018192844> accessed 3 August 2024.

[94] "LIVITY 1970929" Canadian Trademarks Database (*Government of Canada*) <https://ised-isde.canada.ca/cipo/trademark-search/1970929?lang=eng&payload=%7B%22domIntlFilter%22%3A%221%22%2C%22searchfield1%22%3A%22nice_for_search%22%2C%22textfield1%22%3A%22%22%2C%22nicetextfield1%22%3A%5B%225%22%2C%2234%22%5D%2C%22extra%22%3A%5B%7B%22op%22%3A%22and%22%2C%22field%22%3A%22tm%22%2C%22text%22%3A%22livity%22%7D%5D%2C%22display%22%3A%22list%22%2C%22maxReturn%22%3A%22500%22%2C%22cipotextfield1%22%3Anull%7D&pageNum=0&pageLen=50> accessed 3 August 2024; "SACRED CANDY 1894657" Canadian Trademarks Database (*Government of Canada*) <https://ised-isde.canada.ca/cipo/trademark-search/1894657?lang=eng&payload=%7B%22domIntlFilter%22%3A%221%22%2C%22searchfield1%22%3A%22nice_for_search%22%2C%22textfield1%22%3A%22%22%2C%22nicetextfield1%22%3A%5B%225%22%2C%2234%22%5D%2C%22extra%22%3A%5B%7B%22op%22%3A%22and%22%2C%22field%22%3A%22tm%22%2C%22text%22%3A%22SACRed%22%7D%5D%2C%22display%22%3A%22list%22%2C%22maxReturn%22%3A%22500%22%2C%22cipotextfield1%22%3Anull%7D&pageNum=0&pageLen=50> accessed 3 August 2024.

[95] "Gourmet Ganja" (*Facebook*) <https://m.facebook.com/p/Gourmet-Ganja-100078653116008/?locale=zh_CN> accessed 3 August 2024.

[96] "Rasta Cannabis Leaf Rubber Silicone Wristband Bracelet Bangle Womens Mens Ladies" (*ELLU*) <https://www.ellu.com/products/rasta-cannabis-leaf-rubber-silicone-wristband-bracelet-bangle-womens-mens-ladies> accessed 3 August

an entire website named and dedicated to so-called "Rasta products" named "rasta-products.com",[97] which markets Rastafari-themed or Rastafari-styled products, including a "Rasta wholesale Rasta shop starting kit" marketed to persons "who want to open a Rasta shop and are looking for Rasta products to sell".[98]

It is those kinds of modern forms of commodification of Rastafari TCEs that have been described as "Ital chic", involving "reframing of Rastafari elements as fashionable … through the global recognition and validation of Rastafari and the international trends toward slow, natural, and ethical living".[99] This "ital chic" "combines environmental, ethical, and health concerns with a luxurious, chic sensibility … articulated principally through the indigenous practices, philosophy, and aesthetics associated with Rastafari".[100]

It is simultaneously recognised that the popularity of Rastafari TCEs "can be used beyond the limited sense of becoming natural to encompass a wider

---

2024; "Rasta Reggae Cannabis Leaf Patch Badge Iron/Sew On Hippie T Shirt Bag Jeans" (*ELLU*) <https://www.ellu.com/products/rasta-reggae-cannabis-leaf-patch-badge-iron-sew-on-hippie-t-shirt-bag-jeans?pr_prod_strat=e5_desc&pr_rec_id=c214cd4e8&pr_rec_pid=7178612229&pr_ref_pid=1992684997&pr_seq=uniform> accessed 3 August 2024; "Marijuana Rasta Flag – Cannabis Button Badge" (*BadgePig*) <https://badgepig.co.uk/products/marijuana-rasta-cannabis-flag-button-badge> accessed 3 August 2024; "Rasta Weed Stock Vectors & Vector Art" (*Alamy*) <https://www.alamy.com/stock-photo/rasta-weed.html?imgt=8&sortBy=relevant> accessed 3 August 2024; "Reggae Gear Rasta Weed Leaf Black Hoodie" (*Reggae Gear*) <https://reggaegear.co.za/product/reggae-gear-rasta-weed-leaf-black-hoodie/> accessed 3 August 2024; "Zippo Lighter Zippo Rasta Cannabis Design" (*Haddocks Lightershop*) <https://www.haddockslightershop.com/en/lighter-zippo-rasta-cannabis-design.html> accessed 3 August 2024; "Cannabis Lollipops – Rasta" (*Dr. Greenlove Amsterdam*) <https://drgreenlove.nl/product/cannabis-lollipops-rasta/> accessed 3 August 2024; "Plasma Lighter Rasta Cannabis Leaf" (*420Shop*) <https://420shop.nl/en/plasma-lighter-rasta-cannabis-leaf.html> accessed 3 August 2024.

[97] "Rasta Products" <https://www.rasta-products.com/> accessed 3 August 2024; "Patch Weed Leaf" (*RastaProducts.com*) <https://www.rasta-products.com/product/patch-weed-leaf/> accessed 3 August 2024; "50 Marijuana Leaf Hemp Rasta Pencil Case with Zip" (*RastaProducts.com*) <https://www.rasta-products.com/product/50-marijuana-leaf-hemp-rasta-pencil-case-with-zip/> accessed 3 August 2024.

[98] "Rasta Wholesale Rasta Shop Starting Kit" (*RastaProducts.com*) <https://www.rasta-products.com/product/rasta-wholesale-rasta-shop-starting-kit-1-of-all-our-products-at-wholesale-price/> accessed 3 August 2024.

[99] R Jaffe, "Ital Chic: Rastafari, Resistance, and the Politics of Consumption in Jamaica" (2010) 14(1) Small Axe 30–45, 33.

[100] ibid.

range of sentiments, such as rebelliousness or creativity",[101] which are also well-known Rastafari community attributes. Lewis rightly notes that "[t]he extended use of ital chic may simply be the presence of the Rastafarian red, gold and green tricolors in a clothing line, such as its popular display in Adidas' own copyrighted three stripe motif. Or it could be the employment of Rastafarian terms in the names and promotion of products".[102]

Unauthorised uses of Rastafari TK and TCEs appropriate the "auratic, affective, social worth ... " of Rastafari livity, ideology, culture, and symbols, for commercial profit with little or no benefit to the Rastafari community.[103] Such commercial exploitations "trade on the performative, aesthetic, and ideological productions of Rastafari and are therefore seen as infringements upon Rastafarian rights that offer neither compensation nor recognition".[104] Provided that the owners of the trademarks in Appendix 12.A1 are not Rastafari and/or not authorised by the Rastafari community to use those Rastafari TCEs, the registration and use of Rastafari TCEs in those trademarks could be argued to amount to an infringement of the collective moral and economic TK/TCE rights of the Rastafari community. This may therefore result in the passing-off of related products and services as being of Rastafari origin, or create a false connection with the Rastafari community and mislead the public in that regard.

The Rastafari community is therefore understandably very concerned about its IP rights and the loss of its cultural heritage and symbols as companies, especially from overseas, develop or sell Jamaican ganja products.[105] Principle 5 of the Jamaican Cannabis Licencing Authority (CLA) Guiding Principles states that "[t]he CLA recognizes the unique contribution and cultural and historical legacy of Rastafarians to the development of the industry and will work closely with their representatives and the Jamaica Intellectual Property Office (JIPO) in supporting the protection of their cultural identity as the

---

101 J Scott Lewis, "Sufferer's Market: Sufferation and Economic Ethics in Jamaica" (PhD thesis, London School of Economics and Political Science 2014) 180.

102 ibid.

103 J Scott Lewis, "Rights Indigeneity and the Market of Rastafari" (2017) 24 International Journal of Cultural Property 57–77, 67.

104 ibid.

105 S Davenport, B Pardo, *A Regulated Cannabis Industry for Jamaica* (BOTEC Analysis Corporation, 14 September 2015) 57 <https://www.cla.org.jm/wp-content/uploads/2023/06/BOTEC-Jamaica-Report.v1a.pdf> accessed 3 August 2024.

industry develops and grows".[106] That is as far as the CLA has gone to recognise Rastafari TK/TCEs rights and concerns. The CLA's pilot Alternative Development Programme (ADP) and proposed Transitional Permit for small traditional farmers and farming communities neither have nor will empower Rastafari or protect Rastafari TK and TCEs in the Jamaican cannabis industry.[107]

12.7 TK-PROTECTIVE MEASURES: JIPO PRACTICE NOTICES

In 1999, WIPO conducted a mission to Jamaica as part of WIPO's fact-finding mission to several regions of the world to assess the needs and expectations of Indigenous and local communities,[108] and hearkening to the cries of the Maroon and Rastafari communities. In April 2012, JIPO issued a Practice Notice recognising and protecting TK and TCEs of Indigenous and local communities, long before the amendments to the Dangerous Drugs Act were contemplated.[109]

Then, the 2012 Practice Notice outlined how JIPO approaches the interpretation of section 11(4) of the Trade Marks Act 1999, to protect TK and TCEs of Indigenous, traditional, or local communities in Jamaica.[110] It explained that all trademark applications received by JIPO will be assessed to determine whether they contain any elements of TK or TCEs of Jamaica or of any of the Indigenous, traditional, or local communities in Jamaica, including traditional words, signs, symbols, designs, imagery, colours, styles, or shapes, or their derivatives, and that if the mark is found to contain TK or TCEs of Jamaica or of any of the Indigenous, traditional, or local communities in Jamaica, the

---

[106] "Guiding Principles" (*Cannabis Licensing Authority Jamaica*, 9 May 2024) <https://www.cla.org.jm/guiding-principles/> accessed 3 August 2024.

[107] See critique of the ADP in Goffe (n 57) 114.

[108] *Intellectual Property Needs and Expectations of Traditional Knowledge Holders: WIPO Report on Fact-Finding Missions on Intellectual Property and Traditional Knowledge (1998–1999)* (WIPO 2001).

[109] "Practice Notice re: Traditional Knowledge and Traditional Cultural Expressions" (*Jamaica Intellectual Property Office*) <https://www.jipo.gov.jm/sites/default/files/PDF_Files/TM%20Practice%20Direction%20re%20TK%20TCEs%20final.pdf> accessed 3 August 2024.

[110] Section 11(4) of the Trade Marks Act of Jamaica provides that: "A trade mark is not registrable if – (a) it is contrary to public policy or to accepted principles of morality; (b) it is of such a nature as to deceive the public as to the nature, quality or geographical origin of the goods or services or otherwise; … (f) it is of such a nature as to – (i) disparage persons (living or dead) or institutions or beliefs; or (ii) falsely suggest a connection with such persons, institutions or beliefs."

application for registration may be refused or, where appropriate, accepted with a disclaimer or limitation.

In considering whether the mark falsely suggests a connection with a person, an institution, or belief under section 11(4)(f)(ii), it explained that the examiner will consider whether, as used on the goods or services in question, consumers could possibly view the mark as identifying or identifying with a particular community or as being clearly attributable to or associated with a particular community. In doing so, the examiner will consider whether (1) the mark is the same, similar to, or includes a word, sign, symbol, design, imagery, colour, style, or shape commonly used by or attributable to one of the relevant communities; (2) the mark identifies or identifies with a particular community, or the mark is such that a connection with a community could be reasonably inferred; and (3) the community that is referenced by the mark is not connected with the activities performed by the applicant under the mark. The Practice Notice also outlined that if it is found upon examination that a mark falsely suggests a connection with a particular community, then it may also be deemed to be of such a nature as to deceive the public as to the nature, quality, or geographical origin of the goods or services and may be refused on that basis also.

Subsequently, by virtue of a Revised Practice Notice dated 4 February 2015, the 2012 Practice Notice was extended to also apply to design and geographical indication registration applications received by JIPO. As a result, such applications are also examined to determine whether they contain protected TK or TCEs, including traditional words, signs, symbols, designs, imagery, colours, styles, or shapes, or their derivatives. Applications that contain protected TK or TCEs, including traditional words, signs, symbols, designs, imagery, colours, styles, or shapes, or their derivatives, will be refused unless the applicant shows that they are sufficiently connected to or have authorisation from the relevant source community.[111]

12.8 LIMITATIONS OF JIPO PRACTICE NOTICES: SNOOP LION TM OPPOSITION

In 2012, during a visit to the Nyahbinghi Rastafari community in Jamaica, well-known US rapper and cannabis icon Snoop Dogg was renamed Snoop Lion by legendary international Rastafari reggae icon Bunny Wailer. Shortly thereafter, Snoop (real name Calvin Broadus) adopted the moniker "Snoop Lion" and launched a new album and film titled "Reincarnated", in which he

---

[111] "Revised Practice Notice re: Traditional Knowledge and Traditional Cultural Expressions" (*Jamaica Intellectual Property Office*) <https://www.jipo.gov.jm/sites/default/files/PDF_Files/Revised_Practice_Notice_re_TK.pdf> accessed 3 August 2024.

documented his "conversion" to Rastafari in Jamaica and reincarnation of Bob Marley. In September 2012, he applied to JIPO to register the word mark "Snoop Lion", which comprised the words "snoop" and "lion" in black writing and nothing else. The classes applied for were classes 9, 25, and 41. The application for registration was opposed by a Rastafari community organisation on the bases, inter alia, that the applicant was not Rastafari and that he did not have the consent of the Rastafari community to register a trademark using a Rastafari TCE, the word "lion", and that the use of the word "lion" in the trademark was therefore likely to result in the passing-off of related products and services as being of Rastafari origin, create a false connection with the Rastafari community and mislead the public in that regard.[112]

Although the Registrar of Industrial Property acknowledged that "in the context of the average Jamaican consumer, it is not improbable that the 'lion' element of the mark will call to mind the Rastafari faith",[113] she found that the overall impression of the contested mark is a name which is distinctive of the persona of the applicant by virtue of the inclusion of the renowned "Snoop" component. The Registrar ruled that the "Snoop" element of the "SNOOP LION" mark is so strong and distinctive that it primarily calls to mind the Applicant and therefore could not be said to falsely suggest a connection with any Rastafari institution.[114]

The Registrar also ruled that, as the mark was being used solely by the Applicant and bears his name "Snoop", for which he is famous, even if the mark was conceptualised by members of the Rastafari community, the Applicant would be acting in legitimate self-interest in registering a mark whose goodwill belongs solely to him.[115] The Rastafari community's ground of opposition based on passing off was also rejected on the bases that the Opponent did not provide evidence of the existence of a goodwill or reputation in the "SNOOP LION" trademark or any other trademark, being used in connection with the trade of goods or services, or any earlier right by way of copyright or rights in designs which would prevent the registration of the "SNOOP LION" mark, pursuant to section 13(4)(b) of the Act.[116]

---

112 *In The Matter of Application No. 61,055 by Calvin Broadus to Register the Trade Mark Snoop Lion in Classes 9, 25 and 41*; and *In the Matter of Opposition No. 85/TM2013 by Ethio-Africa Diaspora Union Millennium Council.*

113 ibid, para 27. The lion in Rastafari TK is invariably linked to the person of HIM Emperor Haile Selassie I, the "Conquering Lion of Judah" and is one of the distinctive symbols and concepts used by the Rastafari community.

114 ibid para 50.

115 ibid para 45.

116 ibid paras 56–57.

Perhaps most interesting from a TK perspective was how the Registrar dealt with the ground of opposition based on JIPO's 2012 Practice Notice. The Registrar held that in order for the Practice Notice to be applied, the Opponent must prove that the contested mark contains TK or TCEs. The Registrar agreed with the Applicant that in the instance of a two-word trademark consisting only of "SNOOP" and "LION", to treat the word "lion" as a TCE would be too restrictive, as it would ignore the common meaning of the word and prevent its use by legitimate traders. The Registrar therefore ruled that the word "lion", without more, does not qualify as TK or a TCE,[117] and that the "SNOOP LION" mark was registrable.

The decision, delivered on 23 January 2019, highlights the many obstacles that face communities in trying to halt the misappropriation of their TK and TCEs within the trademark system and laws and exemplifies the need for *sui generis* legislation to effectively and comprehensively protect TK and TCEs. The decision makes the following conclusions inevitable. First, existing trademark laws will not protect non-unique TCEs/TCEs with shared or multiple meanings, especially where the mark is a simple word mark without any other distinctive TCEs. Second, the common law of passing off is inadequate to protect TK as communities are required to provide evidence of the existence of a goodwill or reputation in the trademark or any other trademark, being used in connection with the trade of goods or services, or any earlier right by way of copyright or rights in designs. Third, the overall impression of the mark may be perceived as satisfying the distinctiveness requirement and result in the mark being accepted, even if it incorporates TK or TCEs, if it includes a name or some other distinctive aspect of the mark or the applicant.

12.9 SOLUTIONS

In light of the foregoing challenges, as exemplified by the Rastafari case study, that face IPs & LCs in regard to the legal protection of their cannabis-related TK and TCEs, it is clear that IPs & LCs need to be recognised as GRs-TK-TCEs rightsholders equal with other IP right holders. It is also clear that they should have their GRs-TK-TCEs rights adequately and effectively protected within a *sui generis* national, regional, and international IP/GRs/TK/TCEs ABS framework that is consistent with international Indigenous rights standards (as outlined particularly in the UNDRIP, the CBD, the Nagoya Protocol, and the WIPO Treaty on Intellectual Property, Genetic Resources and Associated Traditional Knowledge) – a framework that should not be limited to patents

117 ibid para 61.

and should provide effective sanctions and remedies. Such a framework would feature the following principles:

1. The communities shall own and exercise their rights in TK and TCEs. The rights should vest in the IPs & LCs themselves, who may administer their rights themselves or authorise an agency to do so on their behalf.
2. The rights of IPs & LCs over their GRs, TK, and TCEs should be recognised within national legislation, including their rights to their cannabis-related GRs, TK, and TCEs and their rights to FPIC, F & EP, and F & EBS on MATs in respect of the access, use, or utilisation of the same by third parties.
3. There should be ABS legislation within national jurisdictions that regulate ABS regarding GRs, TK, and TCEs. Access to all GRs, TK, and TCEs including cannabis, must be regulated. The law and regulations must require BSAs. The ABS law(s) must provide for monetary and non-monetary benefit sharing for the state and/or relevant communities from access to GRs and TK.
4. Recognition of and respect for IPs & LCs' customary law, protocols, and practices, including regarding cannabis and IPLCs' use of IP, TK, TCE, ABS protocols, which may include use by communities of TMs including collective and certification trademarks, GIs, PBRs, or a combination thereof.
5. Patents, designs, trademarks, geographical indications, and plant breeders' rights laws within national jurisdictions should be amended to provide that an application for registration that reproduces, utilises, incorporates, or derives from cannabis-related GRs (including landraces and other varieties) and/or associated TK and/or TCEs of IPs & LCs must:
   (a) disclose the origin of the TK and/or TCEs used ("origin" to be defined as "country of origin" and/or "community of origin");
   (b) prove to the satisfaction of the Registrar that the applicant has obtained in writing the free, prior, informed consent of all IPs & LCs from which such cannabis-related GRs, TK, and/or TCEs originated or otherwise derived; and
   (c) prove to the satisfaction of the Registrar that the applicant has entered into fair and equitable benefit-sharing arrangements with the relevant IPs & LCs, on mutually agreed terms, in respect of their cannabis-related GRs and associated TK and/or TCEs utilised.
6. IPs & LCs should be expressly enabled within the law to oppose IP applications and apply for the invalidation or revocation/cancellation of IP applications on the basis of non-disclosure of origin, and the absence of FPIC, F & EBS, and MATs, in respect of the use of their cannabis-related

GRs, TK, and TCEs in IP applications. Copyright Acts like those of the US and Jamaica which permit copyright registration, should also be amended to allow IPs & LCs to challenge copyright registration of any work that uses their GRs, TK, and/or TCEs (including cannabis-related GRs, TK, and/or TCEs) without authorisation. The IPs & LCs should be able to prevent and/or challenge the registration of their traditional words as copyrights and their traditional signs, symbols, emblems, and logos, as trademarks, designs, or geographical indications by others.

7. There should be full and effective remedies for infringement of TK and TCE rights, including civil and criminal sanctions.

12.10 CONCLUSIONS

The rights of IPs & LCs in relation to cannabis must be reviewed within a decolonial context, bearing in mind the colonial history, stigmas, and prejudices of the past, and the need to repair the legacy of injustice meted out to such communities across the world, based on the false and discriminatory anti-cannabis regimes of the past.[118] Positioning relevant national, regional, and international laws to accomplish that objective must, of necessity, involve empowering IPs & LCs through the legal recognition, protection, and enforcement of community rights over their cannabis-related GRs, TK, and TCEs, as the Rastafari case study clearly shows.[119]

While it is absolutely important to amend existing IP laws to (a) prohibit access to, or registration of IP rights regarding TK and TCEs without (1) disclosure of origin; (2) free, prior, and informed consent (FPIC); and (3) fair and equitable benefit sharing (F & EBS) on mutually agreed terms; and (b) expressly allow communities to protect aspects of their TK via IP rights, there is undoubtedly a necessity for *sui generis* GRs-TK-TCEs laws to be implemented to recognise TK and TCEs as subjects of community rights, including cannabis-related TK and IP rights. This includes the rights of communities as TK holders and the right to regulate access to and benefit sharing in respect of GRs, TK, and TCEs, including cannabis-related GRs, TK, and TCEs.

---

118 This argument is expanded in relation to the Caribbean in Goffe (n 72).

119 See discussion of similar issues in the Canadian context in Health Canada, *Summary from "Engagement with First Nations, Inuit and Métis Peoples: The Cannabis Act and Its Impacts"* (Government of Canada 2023) 8–12; and in the South African context in A Bowman and K Lehmann-Grube, *Inclusive Development in the South African Cannabis Industry: Assessing the Challenges* (Institute for Economic Justice 2023) 52 <https://www.iej.org.za/wp-content/uploads/2023/02/IEJ-CannabisReport-Feb2023.pdf> accessed 15 August 2024.

Adopting a *sui generis* international legal instrument(s) to protect IPs & LCs' GRs, TK, and TCEs, as the WIPO IGC has been slowly but steadily working towards over two decades, is essential to facilitate international and cross-border protection of these newly recognised community rights.

While the passage in May 2024 of WIPO's first treaty on Intellectual Property, Genetic Resources, and associated Traditional Knowledge is timely, the treaty is not yet in force; it is limited in application only to patents, GRs, and associated TK and does not include other IP rights and non-GR-associated TK and TCEs.[120] In that respect, the existing treaty would not assist communities like the Rastafari, which continue to suffer misappropriation of their TCEs in the global marketing of cannabis-related goods and services.

It is only by implementing effective *sui generis* TK and TCEs laws or rules specific to the cannabis industry, within an access and benefit-sharing (ABS) framework, that cannabis-related GRs, TK, and TCEs of IPs & LCs like the Rastafari, as depicted in Appendix 12.A1, can be properly protected. Such laws and rules must be part of a larger reparatory justice revolution, nationally and internationally, to repair the harm done to IPs & LCs over many generations, including by the criminalisation of cannabis. Such measures should empower Indigenous communities within the cannabis-based industries via access to finance, equipment, and other corporate and administrative assistance and capacity building. An intellectual property-based ABS framework, that comprises national and international IP/GRs/TK/TCEs policies, principles, protocols, and procedures, to empower IPs & LCs and protect their GRs, TK, and TCEs, is therefore a fundamentally important component of Indigenous justice.

120 "WIPO Member States Adopt Historic New Treaty on Intellectual Property, Genetic Resources and Associated Traditional Knowledge" (*WIPO*, 24 May 2024) <https://www.wipo.int/pressroom/en/articles/2024/article_0007.html> accessed 15 August 2024.

APPENDIX

Table 12A.1 *Rastafari traditional and cultural expressions included in trademark applications and registrations*

TM name	TM type	TM no.	TM goods/services	Regn status
RR RASTA	figurative	00904121794 (UK)	Tobacco, smokers' articles, matches, cigarette cases and match holders, not of precious metal, pipe racks, fire stones, lighters for smokers, cigarette paper, pipe cleaners, tobacco pipes, tobacco pouches; Import, export, advertising and retailing in sales outlets and via global computer networks of smokers' articles of all kinds, office requisites, printing equipment and stationery, leatherware, side arms, articles for the hands and nails, giftware; organisation of exhibitions for commercial or advertising purposes, business management, business administration, office functions; Storage, distribution and transport of smokers' articles of all kinds, office requisites, printing equipment and stationery, leatherware, side arms, articles for the hands and nails, giftware; packaging and storage of goods	Regd (17 April 2008; renewed twice)[1]

[1] The proprietor is a legal entity in Spain. See "Trade Mark Number UK00904121794" (*UK Intellectual Property Office*) <https://trademarks.ipo.gov.uk/ipo-tmcase/page/Results/1/UK00904121794> accessed 19 August 2024.

TM name	TM type	TM no.	TM goods/services	Regn status
rasta koala	word	00918191271 (UK)	Homeopathic pharmaceuticals; Herbal teas for medicinal purposes; Chewing gum for medical purposes; Cough suppressants; Medicinal ointments; Analgesics; Sanitary preparations for medical purposes; Dietetic foods and substances adapted for medicinal or veterinary use; Dietary supplements for humans and animals; Adhesive plasters; Dressings, medical; Disinfectants for hygiene purposes; Food supplements, fortifying nutritional preparations; Protein and energy bars; Energy gels, tablets, pills, and energy bars for prophylactic purposes; Concentrates and syrups for medical purposes; energy gels for medical purposes; Tablets and pills for medical purposes; Pastries, cakes, tarts and biscuits (cookies); Edible ices; Sweetmeats (confectionery); Chocolates; Candy bars; Lollipops; Bubble gum; Tea; Coffee; Sugar; Grain-based chips; Tortilla chips; Chocolate chips; Muffins; Non-alcoholic beverages, including energy beverages; Beer, including flavoured beer; Articles for use with tobacco; Cigarettes, cigars, cigarillos and other ready-for-use smoking articles	Regd (16 October 2020)[2]

[2] The proprietor is a legal entity in Czechia named Rasta Koala s.r.o. See "Trade Mark Number UK00918191271" (*UK Intellectual Property Office*) <https://trademarks.ipo.gov.uk/ipo-tmcase/page/Results/1/UK00918191271> accessed 19 August 2024. From its website, Rasta Koala s.r.o. runs an online cannabis store selling a variety of cannabis products, including some Rasta-themed cannabis products, but judging from the absence of any reference to Rastafari on the website, it does not appear to be a Rastafari organisation. See "CBD and Hemp Products" (*RastaKoala*) <https://www.rastakoala.com/> accessed 19 August 2024.

TM name	TM type	TM no.	TM goods/services	Regn status
GLOBAL RASTA	word	00003542136 (UK)	Cannabis for medical purposes; Hand-held machines for making cigarettes; Hand-rolling tobacco; Herbal molasses [tobacco substitutes]; Herbs for smoking; Holders for electronic cigarettes; Holders of cigarettes of precious metal; Holders of cigars of precious metal; Hookah tobacco; Hookahs; Humidified cigar boxes; Humidifiers for cigars; Humidifiers for tobacco; Humidors; Leaf tobacco; Lighter flints; Lighters for smokers; Lighters for smokers [cigarette lighters] [not for automobiles]; Lighters not of precious metal [not for automobiles]; Lighters of precious metal; Liquefied gas cylinders for cigarette lighters; Liquid for electronic cigarettes; Liquid nicotine solutions for electronic cigarettes; Liquid nicotine solutions for use in electronic cigarettes; Liquid solutions for use in electronic cigarettes; Liquids for electronic cigarettes; Loose, rolling and pipe tobacco; Lighters for smokers; Food and drink catering	Regd (5 February 2021)[3]

[3] The proprietor is a UK-based individual. See "Trade Mark Number UK00003542136" (*UK Intellectual Property Office*) <https://trademarks.ipo.gov.uk/ipo-tmcase/page/Results/1/UK00003542136> accessed 19 August 2024.

TM name	TM type	TM no.	TM goods/services	Regn status
Rasta Rainbow	word	00003392417 (UK)	Plant nutrients; Protein and hemp oil, both derived from hemp for use in the manufacture of a wide variety of goods; Medicinal herbs; Pharmaceuticals and natural remedies; Smoking herbs for medical purposes; Tobacco substitutes for medical purposes; Tobacco-free cigarettes for medical purposes; Dietary and nutritional supplements; Hemp protein powder for use as a nutritional supplement; nutraceuticals for use as a dietary supplement; Topical creams, gels, salves, sprays, balms and ointments for analgesic purposes; Hemp & hemp-derived CBD products; CBD oils medical purposes; Herbal CBD medicine; Herbal CBD flowers for medicinal purposes; Herbs (Medicinal -); Herbs (Smoking -); CBD E-Liquids (Smoking -) medical purposes; Herbal sprays for medical use; Herbal teas for medicinal purposes; Medical marijuana and cannabis and derivatives thereof; hemp-based dietary supplements for general health and well-being, hemp-based protein powder, protein and fibre powder, meal replacement bars; Medicinal herbal extracts for medical purposes, namely medical cannabis and marijuana extracts; Medicinal herbal preparations, namely marijuana preparations including dried flower and marijuana derivatives that may be legally produced, namely liquids, oils, oral sprays, capsules; Medicinal cannabis oils; products for administering medical marijuana and cannabis, namely, buccal sprays, gel caps, and transdermal patches; Hemp-based beverages for medicinal and health purposes; Cannabis-based beverages for medicinal and health purposes; Hemp oil; hemp oil for culinary purposes;	Regd (6 September 2019)[4]

[4] The proprietor is a UK-based individual. See "Trade Mark Number UK00003392417" (*UK Intellectual Property Office*) <https://trademarks.ipo.gov.uk/ipo-tmcase/page/Results/1/UK00003392417> accessed 19 August 2024.

TM name	TM type	TM no.	TM goods/services	Regn status
			Edible oils and edible culinary oils; processed edible hemp seed; Herbs for smoking; Pipes; Articles for use with tobacco; Tobacco and tobacco products (including substitutes); Tobacco substitutes; Tobacco-free cigarettes, other than for medical purposes; Arranging and conducting educational and recreational events and meetings, including with the aim of sharing, developing and transferring knowledge in the field of cannabis and medicinal cannabis; Research in the field of cannabis and medicinal cannabis; Medical and pharmaceutical research, including in the field of cannabis and medicinal cannabis and the use of cannabis and medicinal cannabis; Consultancy relating to research and development in the field of cannabis and medicinal cannabis; Medical marijuana and cannabis dispensary services; Operation of a wellness centre for medical marijuana patients providing physician referral services; Clothing; footwear; headgear	

TM name	TM type	TM no.	TM goods/services	Regn status
irie	figurative	00917962117 (UK)	Tobacco-free cigarettes for medical purposes; nutritional supplements; analgesics; sedatives; psychotropics; pharmaceuticals; liquid herbal supplements; medicinal herbal preparations; Tinctures for medical purposes; medicinal infusions, oils and herbs; medicinal drinks; Medicated creams, powders and gels; Confectionery, chocolate, cakes, pastries, flavourings (other than essential oils), cereal bars; Infusions (not medicinal); Teas; Flavourings (other than essential oils) for beverages; Mineral and aerated waters and other non-alcoholic beverages; Preparations for making beverages; Essences for making beverages	Regd (5 February 2019)[5]
GANJA FARMER	figurative	00918141836 (UK)	Growing media, fertilizers and chemicals for use in agriculture, horticulture and forestry; Cosmetics; Cosmetics and cosmetic preparations; Soaps and gels; Body cleaning and beauty care preparations; Pharmaceuticals and natural remedies; Dietary supplements and dietetic preparations; Clothing; Footwear; Headgear; Seeds, bulbs, and seedlings for plant breeding; Dried flowers; Dried plants; Dried hemp flowers; Retail and wholesale services in relation to the above; Education and instruction services	Regd (27 February 2020)[6]

[5] The proprietor is a UK company. See "Trade Mark Number UK00917962117" (*UK Intellectual Property Office*) <https://trademarks.ipo.gov.uk/ipo-tmcase/page/Results/1/UK00917962117> accessed 19 August 2024.

[6] The proprietor is an individual from Poland. See "Trade Mark Number UK00918141836" (*UK Intellectual Property Office*) <https://trademarks.ipo.gov.uk/ipo-tmcase/page/Results/1/UK00918141836> accessed 19 August 2024.

TM name	TM type	TM no.	TM goods/services	Regn status
GOURMET GANJA	word	00917939779 (UK)	Natural plants; Natural edible plants [unprocessed]; Agricultural seeds; Seeds for planting; Seed germ for botanical purposes; Natural seeds; Crop seeds; Sowing seeds; Electronic cigarettes; Liquid solutions for use in electronic cigarettes; Flavourings, other than essential oils, for use in electronic cigarettes; Cartridges sold filled with chemical flavorings in liquid form for electronic cigarettes; Electronic cigarette liquid [e-liquid]; Articles for use with tobacco; Provision of social club services; Social club services for entertainment purposes; Production of music; Music performances; Organisation of live musical performances; Musical floor shows provided at performance venues	Regd (27 November 2018)[7]
KAYA	word	00801266622 (UK)	Smokers' articles, hookahs, hookah accessories, hookah hoses (included in this class), water pipe heads	Regd (3 August 2016)[8]
MY-KAYA	figurative	00003379123 (UK)	Medicinal oils; Hemp base mixed thread and yarn; Hemp thread and yarn; T-shirts	Regd (24 May 2019)[9]

[7] The proprietor is an individual from Spain. See "Trade Mark Number UK00917939779" (*UK Intellectual Property Office*) <https://trademarks.ipo.gov.uk/ipo-tmcase/page/Results/1/UK00917939779> accessed 19 August 2024.

[8] The proprietor is an individual from Germany. See "Trade Mark Number UK00801266622" (*UK Intellectual Property Office*) <https://trademarks.ipo.gov.uk/ipo-tmcase/page/Results/1/UK00801266622> accessed 19 August 2024.

[9] The proprietor is an individual UK resident. See "Trade Mark Number UK00003379123" (*UK Intellectual Property Office*) <https://trademarks.ipo.gov.uk/ipo-tmcase/page/Results/1/UK00003379123> accessed 19 August 2024.

TM name	TM type	TM no.	TM goods/services	Regn status
Kaya Extracts	figurative	00003474484 (UK)	CBD oils; CBD creams	Regd (9 August 2020)[10]
ITAL	figurative	015323281 (EU)	Herbs (Medicinal -); Medicinal herb infusions; Medicinal herb extracts; Liquid herbal supplements; Herbal tea for medicinal use; Herb teas for medicinal purposes. Processed herbs; Dried herbs; Culinary herbs; Herbal infusions; Herbal flavourings for making beverages; Herb teas, other than for medicinal purposes; Herbal preparations for making beverages; Herbal tea [other than for medicinal use]; Tea essences; Tea; Tea extracts; Tea for infusions; Herbal teas [infusions]; Processed herbs; Dried herbs; Culinary herbs; Herbal infusions; Herbal flavourings for making beverages; Herb teas, other than for medicinal purposes; Herbal preparations for making beverages; Herbal tea [other than for medicinal use]; Tea essences; Tea; Tea extracts; Tea for infusions; Herbal teas [infusions]	Regd (20 Feb. 2017)[11]

[10] The proprietor is a UK company. See "Trade Mark Number UK00003474484" (*UK Intellectual Property Office*) <https://trademarks.ipo.gov.uk/ipo-tmcase/page/Results/1/UK00003474484> accessed 19 August 2024.

[11] The proprietor is a UK company. See "ITAL 015323281" (*European Union Intellectual Property Office*) <https://euipo.europa.eu/eSearch/#details/trademarks/015323281> accessed 17 August 2024.

TM name	TM type	TM no.	TM goods/services	Regn status
IRIE	word	018466454 (EU)	Articles for use with tobacco; ashtrays, ashtrays for smokers, cigar cases, cigar lighters, cigarette lighters, cigarette rolling papers, cigarettes containing tobacco substitutes, electronic cigarettes, flavourings, other than essential oils, for tobacco, filter-tipped cigarettes, graters specially adapted for grating tobacco and herbs for smoking, hand-rolling tobacco, herbs for smoking, pipes, smokers' articles	Regd (25 Aug. 2021)[12]
irie	figurative	017962117 (EU)	Tobacco-free cigarettes for medical purposes; Nutritional supplements; Analgesics; Sedatives; Psychotropics; Pharmaceuticals; Liquid herbal supplements; Medicinal herbal preparations; Tinctures for medical purposes; Medicinal infusions, Oils and herbs; Medicinal drinks; Medicated creams, powders, and gels; Confectionery, chocolate, cakes, pastries, flavourings (other than essential oils), cereal bars; Infusions (not medicinal); Teas; Flavourings (other than essential oils) for beverages; Mineral and aerated waters and other non-alcoholic beverages; Preparations for making beverages; Essences for making beverages	Regd (5 Feb. 2019)[13]

[12] The proprietor is a company in Germany. See "IRIE 018466454" (*European Union Intellectual Property Office*) <https://euipo.europa.eu/eSearch/#details/trademarks/018466454> accessed 17 August 2024.

[13] The proprietor is a company in the UK, the same proprietor of UK Trade Mark Number UK00917962117 (n 5). See "irie 017962117" (*European Union Intellectual Property Office*) <https://euipo.europa.eu/eSearch/#details/trademarks/017962117> accessed 17 August 2024.

TM name	TM type	TM no.	TM goods/services	Regn status
RASTA	figurative	1477994 (EU)	Battery-powered lighters for smokers, cigar lighters, cigar lighters (gas containers for -), cigarette lighters, other than for use in motor vehicles, electrical cigarette lighters (smokers requisites), electronic cigarette lighters, flints for lighters, gas containers for cigar lighters, gas containers for cigarette lighters, lighters for smokers, non-electric lighters for smokers, pyrophoric lighters for smokers, table lighters	Removed from the Register, based on a successful opposition (11 Jan. 2019)[14]
RASTA	figurative	005134473 (EU)	Leather and imitations of leather, and goods made of these materials and not included in other classes; Bags, travelling bags, purses, not of precious metal, rucksacks, trunks, wallets, briefcases, saddlery, suitcases; Umbrellas, parasols, and walking sticks; Riding crops; Mineral and aerated waters and other non-alcoholic drinks; fruit drinks and fruit juices; syrups and other preparations for making beverages; Tobacco; smokers' articles; matches, cigarette cases, and matchboxes, not of precious metal, pipe holders, firestones, lighters for smokers, cigarette papers, pipe-cleaners, pipes, tobacco pouches	Regd 19 July 2007; Regn expired 13 Jun. 2016[15]

[14] This was an international application filed with WIPO via the Madrid Protocol. The proprietor was a company in New Zealand. See "Rasta 1477994" (*European Union Intellectual Property Office*) <https://euipo.europa.eu/eSearch/#details/trademarks/W01477994> accessed 17 August 2024.

[15] The registered proprietor is a legal entity in Spain. See "RASTA 005134473" (*European Union Intellectual Property Office*) <https://euipo.europa.eu/eSearch/#details/trademarks/005134473> accessed 17 August 2024.

TM name	TM type	TM no.	TM goods/services	Regn status
FA ENGINEERED NUTRITION CANNABIS CHILLOUT shot	figurative	018704747 (EU)	Dietary supplements for humans, food supplements, nutritional supplements, glucose dietary supplements, protein dietary supplements, dietary supplements containing caffeine, dietary supplements containing taurine, dietary and nutritional supplements, food supplements in liquid form, nutritional supplement food bars; Sports drinks, energy drinks, protein drinks, carbohydrate drinks, carbonated non-alcoholic drinks	Regd (15 Oct. 2022)[16]
GANJA FARMER	figurative	018141836 (EU)	Growing media, fertilizers and chemicals for use in agriculture, horticulture and forestry; Cosmetics, cosmetics and cosmetic preparations, soaps and gels, body cleaning and beauty care preparations; Pharmaceuticals and natural remedies; Dietary supplements and dietetic preparations; Clothing; Footwear; Headgear; Seeds, bulbs, and seedlings for plant breeding; Dried flowers; Dried plants; Dried hemp flowers; Retail and wholesale services related to the above	Regd (27/02/2020)[17]
GANJAMAICA	word	018192844 (EU)	e-cigarettes	Regd (27 May 2020)[18]

[16] The proprietor is a legal entity from Poland. See "FA ENGINEERED NUTRITION CANNABIS CHILLOUT shot 018704747" (*European Union Intellectual Property Office*) <https://euipo.europa.eu/eSearch/#details/trademarks/018704747> accessed 17 August 2024.

[17] The proprietor is an individual from Poland, the same proprietor of the GANJA FARMER Trade Mark 018141836 registered in the UK (n 93).

[18] The proprietor is an individual from Qatar. See "Ganjamaica 018192844" (*European Union Intellectual Property Office*) <https://euipo.europa.eu/eSearch/#details/trademarks/018192844> accessed 17 August 2024.

TM name	TM type	TM no.	TM goods/services	Regn status
LIVITY	word	1970929 (Canada)	Cannabis oil for cosmetic purposes; Body care products containing cannabinoids; Cannabis products and derivatives for medicinal purposes, cannabis products and derivatives for non-medicinal purposes; Drink products and food products containing cannabinoids; Retail sale, distribution, and wholesale of cannabis, cannabis related products, derivatives of cannabis and natural health products containing cannabis; Live cannabis plants; Cannabis seeds	Not regd[19]
RASTA	word	905038 (IR)	Tobacco; smokers' articles; matches; cigarettes; cigars	Regd (6 Nov. 2006)[20]

[19] Although this TM application was filed in 2019, it has not been registered because it has been preliminarily refused on the grounds, *inter alia*, that LIVITY is descriptive and non-distinctive, in light of the "Livity" cannabis strain attributed to Apothecary Genetics, and that "other traders should be able, in the ordinary course of their businesses, to use the same trademark in association with the same goods and services". See Examiner's First Report <https://www.ic.gc.ca/app/scr/opic-cipo/mc-tm/rd-dr/action/open/18074132/Examiner's%2520First%2520Report/PDF;jsessionid=0001-bvBIiyt0i4K91rruQyIz8Z:-2229HE> accessed 17 August 2024. Such strain names (which may or may not be registered as plant breeder's rights) and trademark registration applications are not examined and objectionable on the basis of the TK or TCEs of IPs & LCs and so, in this case, the only reason why this trademark application was preliminarily refused is because of the word "Livity" being deemed descriptive and non-distinctive and not because the word "Livity" is a Rastafari TCE.

[20] The proprietor of this mark is a Swiss company who registered the International Registration (IR) in France via the Madrid Protocol.

TM name	TM type	TM no.	TM goods/services	Regn status
RASTA ENERGY DRINK	figurative	1665065 (IR)	Energy drinks, energy drinks and sports drinks, including performance drinks enhanced with hemp extracted from mature stalks and sterilised seeds, isotonic beverages, protein-enriched sports beverages	Regd (22 March 2022)[21]

Note: A table consisting of Traditional and Cultural Expressions of the Rastafari community that have been included in trademark applications and registrations. It includes trademark names, type, the number registered, and the nature of the goods or services. For example, RR Rasta, is a figurative trademark, number 00904121794 in the UK registry, referring to items from smoking articles to giftware and packaging. This is one of the 21 examples included.
Source: TM registries indicated in the table (compiled by author)

[21] The proprietor is a company from Curacao who registered the International Registration (IR) in Austria, Benelux, Bonaire, St. Eustatius, and Saba via the Madrid Protocol. The mark was, however, refused registration in the US (on the basis of an earlier "RASTA" mark, without any reference to the Rastafari community) and Poland (with reference to the Rastafari religion's association with marijuana, but on the basis that it is contrary to public order and morality and illegal under the Counteracting Drug Addiction Law to advertise and promote narcotics). See "Contact Madrid" <https://madrid.wipo.int/documentaccess/documentAccess?docid=1692922601> and "Madrid Protocol" <https://madrid.wipo.int/documentaccess/documentAccess?docid=1640455101> both accessed 20 August 2024.

13. The economics of intellectual property protection for cannabis: challenges, opportunities and the evolution of patents

Cristiano Cantore

13.1 INTRODUCTION

Intellectual Property (IP) protection is crucial for promoting innovation and economic growth by granting creators exclusive rights, thereby incentivising research and development. This balance benefits both creators and the public through new knowledge dissemination. IP protection also creates a temporary monopoly, encouraging innovation but potentially creating entry barriers and stifling further innovation. Therefore, the economic approach to IP rights highlights the trade-off between their role in stimulating innovation and economic growth while considering potential market inefficiencies due to monopoly power. The variability of IP rights' impact across different industries and countries can be attributed to the allocation of resources for creating intellectual assets and the extent of protected knowledge utilised in production and consumption.

The cannabis industry presents unique challenges and opportunities for IP protection. As the industry evolves from a largely illegal market to a regulated and legitimate sector, the role of IP becomes increasingly prominent. Cannabis-related innovations span a wide range of products and processes, including cultivation techniques, medicinal formulations, recreational products, and consumption methods. Protecting these innovations through patents, trademarks, and trade secrets is essential for companies seeking to establish a competitive edge in a rapidly growing market.

The global medical cannabis market size reached US$31.8 billion in 2022, and it is expected to reach US$57.4 billion by 2028.[1] Unique economic challenges for IP in the cannabis industry include navigating a fragmented legal landscape and ensuring compliance across varying jurisdictions, which complicates the protection and enforcement of IP rights. Opportunities lie in differentiating products through branding and innovation, as well as leveraging IP for strategic partnerships and licencing to expand market reach.

Before examining the economics of IP protection in the cannabis industry, it is useful to compare it with the pharmaceutical industry. Both industries rely heavily on robust IP frameworks to protect their innovations and secure market advantages. Patents in both sectors are crucial for safeguarding new formulations, processes, and products, encouraging significant investments in research and development.

However, there are notable differences between the two industries. The pharmaceutical industry is characterised by well-established regulatory pathways and a clear legal landscape that facilitates patent protection and enforcement. In contrast, the cannabis industry faces a fragmented legal environment, with varying regulations across different jurisdictions complicating the patenting process. The pharmaceutical industry benefits from decades of accumulated research and a structured patent system, whereas the cannabis industry is still emerging from a history of prohibition, with much of its traditional knowledge unpatented and part of the public domain. Moreover, while both industries deal with bioactive compounds, the pharmaceutical sector often focusses on synthetic drugs with well-defined mechanisms of action, whereas the cannabis industry includes a broad spectrum of natural products and complex mixtures, presenting unique challenges in proving novelty and non-obviousness required for patent grants.

Given these differences, it is important to identify the challenges and opportunities of IP protection arising in the cannabis industry. This will be the starting point of the analysis in this chapter. Thereafter, the chapter discusses the economic relevance of IP in the industry. The chapter concludes by providing an analysis of the evolution of patent filings and grants in the industry across time, countries, and market concentration. This analysis will provide critical insights into how historical trends, geographical distributions, and regulatory changes have shaped the IP landscape in the cannabis sector. By comparing these dynamics with those in the pharmaceutical industry, we will

---

1 *Medical Cannabis Market: Global Industry Trends, Share, Size, Growth, Opportunity and Forecast 2023–2028* (*Research and Markets*, 2023) <https://www.asdreports.com/market-research-report-614472/medical-cannabis-market-global-industry-trends-share-size-growth-opportunity> accessed on 11 February 2024.

better understand the strategic importance of patents in driving innovation and securing competitive advantages in a rapidly evolving market.

13.2 IP PROTECTION OF CANNABIS, CHALLENGES AND OPPORTUNITIES

The cannabis industry presents a complex landscape for IP due to its unique legal circumstances and rapid market evolution. This section provides a brief overview of the multidimensional economic challenges and opportunities that IP rights entail in this growing sector.

13.2.1 Challenges

One of the primary challenges comes from the legal and regulatory complexities associated with cannabis, which remains illegal in several jurisdictions, including the US at the federal level. This illegality creates issues in securing and enforcing IP rights such as patents and trademarks. The legal ambiguity prevents businesses from protecting and capitalising on their IP assets, crucial for gaining a competitive edge and securing funding.[2] Moreover, the validity of cannabis-related patents frequently comes under scrutiny. The challenge involves demonstrating the novelty and non-obviousness of cannabis products, exacerbated by the plant's long history of informal use and cultivation.[3] The industry also faces market saturation and competition, making it difficult to establish distinct IP. This crowded marketplace diminishes the differentiation potential, diluting the value of IP assets.[4] Additionally, restrictions on cannabis research limit the development of new, patentable technologies and strains, decreasing opportunities for innovation and IP creation. Finally, the global divergence in IP laws complicates the protection and strategic management of IP across borders, impacting businesses looking to expand or operate in multiple countries.[5]

---

[2] *Cannabis Industry Report* (Ocean Tomo – JS Held 2023).

[3] S Keller, "*How Small Cannabis Businesses Can Survive the Hurdles of IP Protection*" (2020) 8Texas A&M Law Review 199 <https://doi.org/10.37419/LR.V8.I1.6>.

[4] R Bora, "*The Ultimate Guide to Intellectual Property Protection for Cannabis Businesses*" (2020) Cannabis Industry Journal <https://cannabisindustryjournal.com/feature_article/the-ultimate-guide-to-intellectual-property-protection-for-cannabis-businesses/>.

[5] J Wyse and G Luria, "Trends in Intellectual Property Rights Protection for Medical Cannabis and Related Products" (2021) Journal of Cannabis Research.

13.2.2 Opportunities

Despite these challenges, there are substantial economic opportunities for leveraging IP in the cannabis industry. Effective use of IP can differentiate a business in the marketplace. By developing unique strains, extraction methods, or product formulations, companies can establish a competitive advantage. Brand protection through trademarks helps in building recognition and loyalty, increasing long-term business valuation. Owning IP assets provides licencing opportunities, generating additional revenue streams. A robust IP portfolio makes cannabis businesses more attractive to investors by demonstrating a commitment to innovation and a strategy for long-term market presence.[6] Companies that secure their IP early can enjoy first-mover advantages, capturing significant market share before competitors.[7] Strategically managing IP in anticipation of legislative changes, such as potential federal legalisation in the US, can position businesses to capitalise on new market opportunities and adapt swiftly to legal changes, maximising their competitive edge.[8]

13.3 ECONOMIC IMPORTANCE OF INTELLECTUAL PROPERTY IN THE CANNABIS INDUSTRY

This section digs deeper into the critical role of IP in promoting innovation, enhancing market differentiation, and increasing profitability within the cannabis industry. It focusses on the role of IP in driving innovation and profitability in the cannabis industry and then discusses how IP assets contribute to market differentiation and brand development.

13.3.1 Role of IP in Driving Innovation and Profitability in the Cannabis Sector

As mentioned, IP is fundamental in driving innovation and profitability within the cannabis industry. By providing essential legal protections for new inventions such as unique cannabis strains and innovative cultivation techniques, IP rights encourage substantial research and development investments. These protections not only safeguard inventors from direct competition but also enhance a company's ability to maintain a competitive edge through market

---

6 Cannabis Industry Report (n 2).

7 JP Brown, ED Cohen, A Felix, "Economic Benefits and Social Costs of Legalizing Recreational Marijuana" (2023) Kansas City Fed Research Working Paper, 23–10.

8 E Auriol, A Mesnard, T Perrault, "Defeating Crime? An Economic Analysis of Cannabis Legalization Policies" (2019) CEPR Discussion Paper 13814.

differentiation and brand development. Strategic use of IP, including patents and trademarks, not only fortifies a company's market position but also significantly boosts its appeal to investors and potential partners. Moreover, IP is instrumental in enhancing market differentiation. Trademarks and branding are essential tools for cannabis businesses striving to distinguish themselves in a competitive environment. Effective branding, safeguarded by IP rights, allows companies to develop a distinct brand identity and consumer loyalty, which are vital in a market characterised by high product homogeneity. The strategic use of trademarks enables businesses to build and protect their brand names, logos, and even unique packaging,[9] making their products instantly recognisable and preferred by consumers.[10]

The value of IP assets extends beyond mere legal protection; they are crucial components that can significantly amplify a company's market value and profitability. For instance, patents allow firms to demand premium prices for their unique offerings. Similarly, trademarks boost brand equity, enhancing customer recognition and loyalty, which in turn drives sales and profitability. Ownership of IP rights also facilitates the formation of strategic alliances and licencing agreements. These arrangements are lucrative avenues for expanding market reach and exploring new business opportunities without the substantial costs associated with direct market entry. Licencing allows cannabis companies to generate revenue from their IP while partnering with others to broaden their operational scope.[11] To illustrate the significant economic value of IP assets in the cannabis industry, consider the example of Tokyo Smoke's partnership with Uber for home delivery of cannabis products. Tokyo Smoke leverages its strong brand equity and trademarks to enhance customer recognition and loyalty. By collaborating with Uber, they extend their market reach and operational scope without incurring substantial costs.

Another significant advantage of a robust IP portfolio is, as mentioned, its appeal to investors. In the rapidly evolving cannabis market, investors are particularly drawn to companies with a strong commitment to innovation and IP protection. A solid IP portfolio not only demonstrates a company's creativity and future growth potential but also its ability to sustain a long-term presence in the market.[12] Furthermore, in an industry where legal and regulatory frameworks are in constant flux, IP rights provide a semblance of security and a framework for navigating these changes. As more jurisdictions move towards

---

[9] Yet, in most jurisdictions, there are restrictions on the ability to populate the packaging with logos and other eye-catching elements. On these restrictions, see Chapter 6 in this volume, co-authored by Enrico Bonadio and Akshita Rohatgi.

[10] Bora (n 4).

[11] Wyse, Luria (n 5).

[12] Cannabis Industry Report (n 2).

legalisation, cannabis companies with established IP rights are well positioned to quickly capitalise on new markets and adapt to regulatory shifts, ensuring compliance and maintaining their competitive stance.

However, it is important to acknowledge the challenges investors face due to the current status quo of illegality. Some jurisdictions impose regulatory hurdles on investment and commerce, despite impressive IP portfolios. Additionally, certain regions have IP registration challenges, such as the refusal to register trademarks on grounds of immorality. These obstacles can impede the creation and protection of valuable IP assets, making it difficult for companies to fully capitalise on their innovations and for investors to gauge the long-term viability of their investments.

In summary, IP rights are legal tools that are fundamental to fostering innovation, securing competitive advantage, and enhancing profitability in the cannabis industry. They enable businesses to protect and monetise unique products and play a critical role in shaping the industry's growth and evolution.

13.3.2 How IP Assets Contribute to Market Differentiation and Brand Development

IP assets contribute significantly to market differentiation and brand development, which are particularly crucial in the competitive and rapidly evolving cannabis industry. Trademarks are vital for establishing a unique brand identity – a critical factor in a market where product differentiation is challenging. By securing trademarks for brand names, logos, and distinctive packaging, businesses create recognisable and memorable identities. This differentiation not only aids in distinguishing products from those of competitors but also builds consumer trust and loyalty. A strong brand identity, protected by trademarks, is indispensable for fostering customer recognition and preference, which directly impacts sales and market presence.

Patents grant cannabis companies exclusive rights to their innovations, such as new strains, cultivation methods, extraction processes, or product formulations. This exclusivity not only enhances market presence but also supports premium pricing strategies, thereby boosting profitability. Patented products are often perceived as higher quality or more desirable due to their unique characteristics and the research and development backing them, appealing to niche market segments. Trade secrets can include proprietary cultivation techniques, extraction methods, or specific product recipes. Maintaining these secrets provides businesses with a competitive edge by safeguarding methods or formulations that are not easily replicated by competitors. This form of IP protection is particularly relevant where unique product qualities or manufacturing processes directly influence product appeal and consumer satisfaction.[13]

Effective use of IP assets can significantly enhance brand equity. For instance, a well-recognised trademark can become synonymous with quality, reliability, or specific product attributes in the minds of consumers. This brand equity influences consumer buying decisions, driving market share and profitability. Moreover, a strong brand, supported by robust IP, is crucial in marketing and promotional strategies, further solidifying a company's position in a crowded market. In regions where regulatory compliance is a market differentiator, companies that effectively navigate complex legal landscapes and align their IP strategies accordingly can enhance their brand identity. Promoting compliance as part of their brand identity appeals to consumers who value legal and safety standards, providing an additional layer of differentiation.[14] To summarise, IP assets play a critical role in creating and maintaining market differentiation and brand development in the cannabis industry. They provide legal protection and competitive advantage, fostering a unique market identity that attracts and retains customers, ultimately contributing to the business's success and growth.

This section has explored how the cannabis industry's unique legal and economic landscape presents significant challenges and promising opportunities for IP protection. The sector's evolution from an illegal market to a regulated industry has highlighted the importance of IP in promoting innovation, market differentiation, and competitive advantage. Given these dynamics, the next section examines the evolution of patents in the cannabis industry across time, countries, and companies. Understanding the historical trends, geographical distribution, and market concentration of cannabis-related patent filings provides critical insights into the industry's growth patterns, regulatory impacts, and strategic manoeuvres by key players. This analysis, as explored in the next section, highlights how changes in legislation, technological advancements, and market forces have shaped the IP landscape, offering valuable perspectives on future developments and opportunities within the global cannabis market.

13.4 ANALYSIS OF EXISTING IP PATENTS IN CANNABIS

This section provides data analysis of the evolution of the landscape of patents in the cannabis industry.[15] It is based on searches using Google Patents

---

13 Keller (n 3).

14 Auriol et al. (n 8).

15 In doing so, we followed the approach of Wyse and Luria (n 5). Differently from them, however, we focus mostly on patents on medical applications, using a

for patents related to cannabis, focussing on patent classifications associated with medical applications and technologies for agricultural innovation.[16] The resulting data, depicted in Figure 13.1, outline the evolution of cannabis-related patent filings since the first filing in the database from 1974.[17]

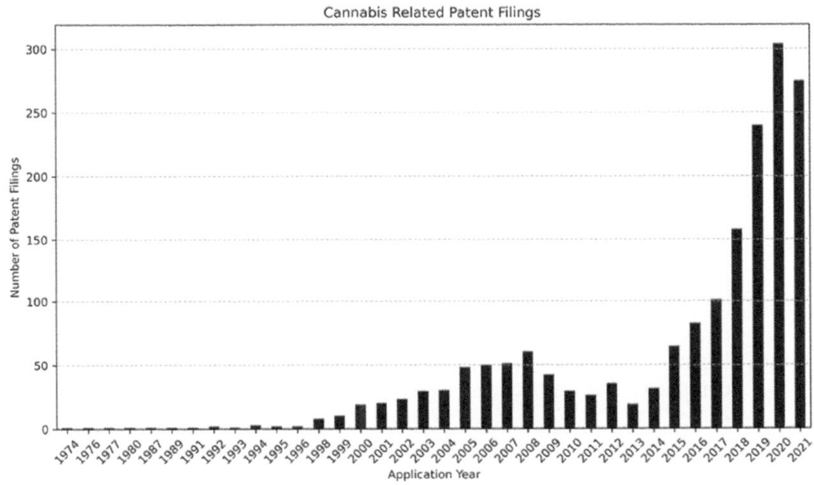

Source: Google Patents and author calculations.

Figure 13.1 Cannabis patent filings over time since 1974

---

different dataset, a longer data sample, and, importantly, analyse patent filings as well as patents granted.

16 The search was conducted on 11 February 2023. The keywords searched in the application title are: marijuana or cannabis* or tetrahydrocannabinol* or CBD or THC from 1 January 1800 to 31 December 2023. For patent applications, the data we show stops at the end of 2021. This is because patent applications are typically not published until 18 months following the filing date. Hence, the data for 2022 and 2023 are incomplete. Note that we are using here the raw number of patents, which might involve multiple counting in some instances if the applicant has filed the same application in more than one country. However, numbers are roughly in line with what was reported by Wyse and Luria (n 5) who use the PatSnap search engine instead.

17 Application filed by AG Schering on 3 July 1974 with the title "*7-Hydroxy-delta 8-tetrahydrocannabinols and microbiological production* thereof". See "Google Patents" https://patents.google.com/patent/US3897306A/en>.

13.4.1 Evolution of Cannabis-Related Patent Filings

The timeline of cannabis-related patent filings reveals an upward trajectory that highlights the growing sector of cannabis innovation. Initially, the frequency of filings was sparse, reflecting the early stages of recognition and exploration within the sector. However, as we see in Figure 13.1, there has been a significant and consistent increase in patent filings over time. It is useful to divide the sample into two periods: an initial phase running until 1999, followed by an acceleration phase.

- Initial Phase (1974–1999): There is minimal activity during this period, likely due to the stringent regulatory environments and the broader social stigma associated with cannabis. Early patents during this era were primarily experimental, focussing on limited medical applications and basic cultivation techniques.
- Acceleration Phase (2000–present): A marked increase in patent filings can be observed from the year 2000 onwards. This period correlates with significant legislative changes worldwide, where numerous jurisdictions began to recognise and legalise both medical and recreational cannabis use. This legislative shift has played a crucial role in driving patent filings, as more companies and researchers engage in cannabis-related innovations.

There are three broad categories of other possible factors, beyond legislative changes, influencing the surge in patent filings. These include:

- Technological Advancements: The advent of advanced biotechnological and agricultural innovations has provided new opportunities for patent filings. Innovations such as genetically modified strains, enhanced extraction methods, and optimised cultivation systems are notable examples that have attracted considerable IP focus.
- Therapeutic Potential: The growing body of research highlighting cannabis's therapeutic benefits has driven interest in securing IP rights related to medical cannabis. Patents in this category include novel formulations, drug delivery systems, and medical applications targeting specific health conditions.
- Market Formalisation and Competition: As the cannabis industry matures, the need for differentiation and competitive advantage has become more pronounced. Companies are increasingly relying on patents to secure exclusive rights to their innovations, protecting their market share against competitors, and establishing their standing in a rapidly evolving market.

The surge in patent activity signals an expanding frontier for cannabis-related IP, reflecting the industry's progression toward a more formalised and competitive marketplace. The steep rise in filings post-2000 suggests that the industry is poised for continued growth, driven by further technological advancements and potentially broader legislative reforms.

The next section analyses cannabis patent filing data by different types of applications from 2000 onwards.

13.4.2 Differentiation in Cannabis-Related Patent Filings: Agricultural Innovations versus Medical Applications

Figure 13.2 presents a detailed breakdown of cannabis-related patent filings, distinguishing between those aimed at agricultural innovations and those developed for medical applications. The data, categorised by Cooperative Patent Classification (CPC),[18] offer a revealing perspective on the divergent paths of innovation within the cannabis sector. The graph delineates a clear disparity in the volume and growth trends between patents filed for agricultural innovations versus those for medical purposes. Notably, the filings for medical applications have experienced an intense increase, particularly evident in the

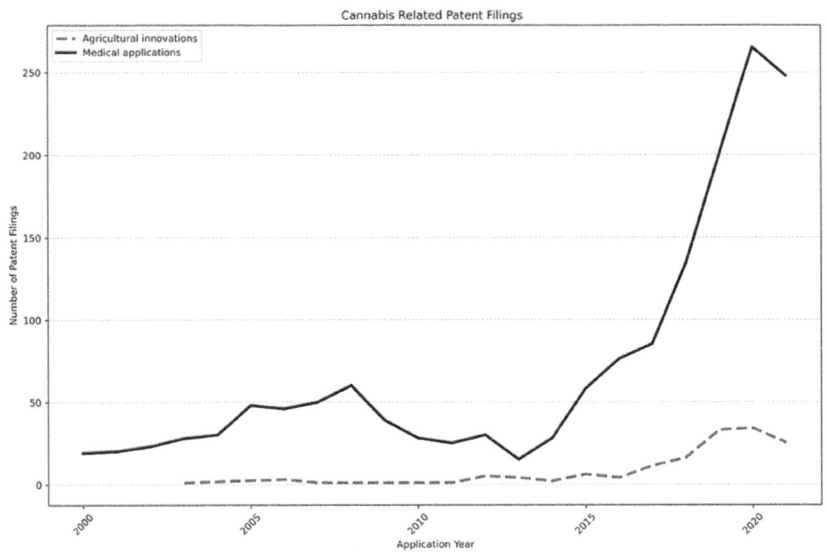

Source: Google Patents and author calculations.

Figure 13.2 Cannabis patent filings differentiated by applications

[18] Agricultural innovation includes patent filings with CPC equal to A01, C12N, C12M, and their subdomains. Medical applications include patent filings with CPC A61 and its subdomains.

last decade. This surge reflects a growing interest and substantial investment in the therapeutic potentials of cannabis, highlighting significant advances in medical research and drug development. This uptrend likely correlates with the increasing body of scientific evidence supporting the medicinal benefits of cannabis and cannabinoids. These benefits include treatment for chronic pain, epilepsy, and multiple sclerosis, among other conditions. The sharp rise in patent filings is indicative of a robust competitive environment where companies and research institutions are eager to secure IP rights for innovative treatments, formulations, and drug delivery systems. In contrast, patents for agricultural innovations have exhibited a more gradual increase. This trend suggests a steady, albeit slower, pace of technological advancements in cannabis cultivation and processing technologies. Key areas of innovation in this category include the genetic engineering of cannabis strains for increased yield or specific cannabinoid profiles, advancements in irrigation and lighting systems, and the development of new extraction techniques. While the growth is less pronounced than in the medical category, the consistent increase reflects ongoing improvements that aim to enhance efficiency, sustainability, and product quality in cannabis agriculture.

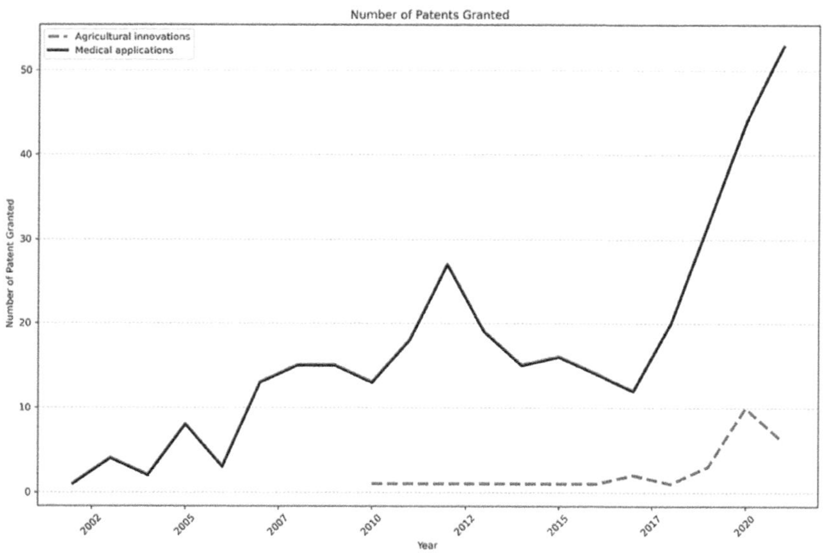

Source: Google Patents and author calculations.

Figure 13.3 *Cannabis patents granted differentiated by applications*

The stark difference in the growth rates of these two categories highlights the complex nature of development within the cannabis industry. Medical research, driven by the expanding legalisation of medical cannabis and the growing acceptance of its health benefits, appears to be a primary catalyst for IP generation. This focus on medical applications is aligning with consumer health interests and regulatory developments, pushing companies to invest heavily in this area.

On the other hand, the steadier growth of patents in agricultural innovations may reflect a more mature segment where incremental advancements continue to contribute to agricultural efficiency and product diversity. This area, though growing at a modest pace, is critical for supporting the scalability and sustainability of cannabis as an agricultural commodity.

Figure 13.3 shows a similar pattern by focussing on the number of patents granted instead of filings. This data illustrates not just the trends in patent filings, but more critically, the trends in patents that have successfully met the stringent criteria required for grant. It highlights not only the activity in patent filings but also the effectiveness and quality of the innovations being patented.

13.4.3 Geographical Trends in Medical Cannabis Patent Filings

As we turn our focus exclusively toward medical applications within the cannabis sector, we now try to understand the geographical distribution of patent filings. Figure 13.4 illustrates the global landscape of these filings, highlighting the predominant regions and their strategic significance in the industry.

The US emerges as the leader in medical cannabis patent filings, accounting for approximately 31.2 per cent of the total. This significant share underscores the US's essential role in the development of medical cannabis technologies and therapies. The robust IP framework, combined with advanced research facilities and a progressively evolving regulatory environment, makes the US a hotspot for innovation in medical cannabis. The large market size and substantial investment in healthcare and biotechnologies further fuel this dominance. Following the US, there is a substantial volume of filings for the World Intellectual Property Organization (WIPO) under the Patent Cooperation Treaty (PCT), representing 19.5 per cent of the total. The PCT route allows innovators to seek patent protection internationally for their inventions in a streamlined process across multiple countries. This high percentage reflects a strategic approach by companies and researchers to protect their innovations not just locally but on a global scale, indicating the international appeal and potential market for medical cannabis applications. The European Patent Office (EPO) accounts for 11.8 per cent of the filings, illustrating Europe's significant role in the medical cannabis landscape. The EPO provides a unified procedure that allows inventors to apply for patent protection in up to 44

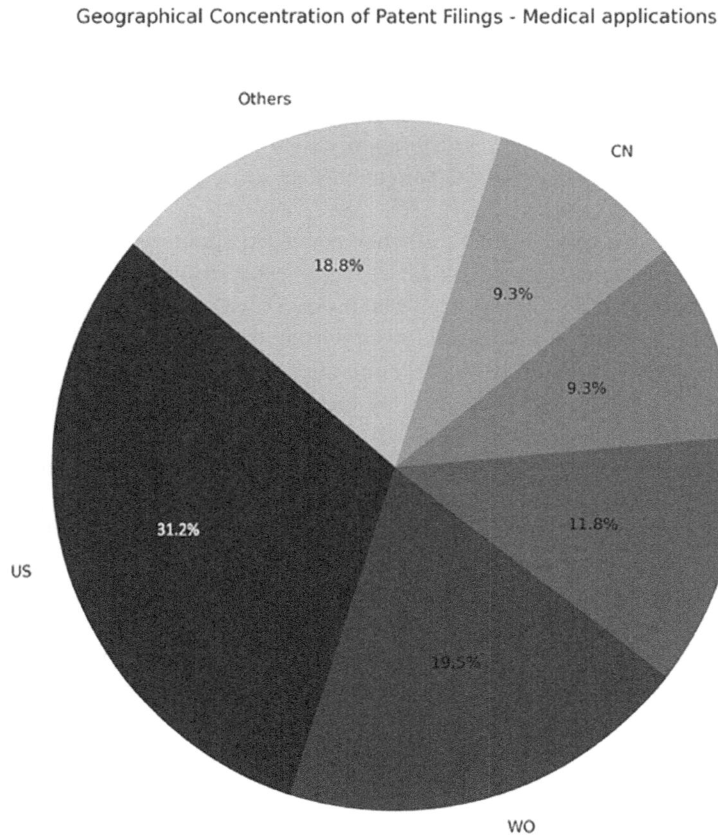

Source: Google Patents and author calculations.

Figure 13.4 Cannabis patent filings for medical applications by country of application

countries through a single application, making it an attractive option for entities looking to capture the European market.[19] Europe's complex regulatory framework and its gradual move towards more liberal medical cannabis policies contribute to its key position in global patent filings. China and Canada

[19] An EP patent application can lead to the grant of a patent in any of these European countries, subject to the patent being validated in each chosen country after the grant.

also represent notable shares of the filings, with 9.3 per cent each. China's growing biotechnology sector and increasing openness to medical cannabis research contribute to its rising figures. Meanwhile, Canada's established legal cannabis market and progressive research landscape make it a critical player in the sector. Both countries' strategic filings indicate their intent to establish and expand their presence in the global medical cannabis market. The remaining 18.8 per cent of the filings, grouped under "Others", encompass a variety of countries with emerging interests and developing frameworks in medical cannabis. This segment indicates a growing recognition of medical cannabis's potential benefits across diverse global regions, pointing to a broadening scope for international collaboration and market expansion.

This geographical distribution of patent filings highlights several strategic considerations. Companies should consider the regulatory environments and market potentials of these key regions when planning their global expansion and IP protection strategies. The concentration of filings in certain regions may suggest beneficial locations for conducting clinical trials, research collaborations, or partnerships. To mitigate risks associated with regulatory changes, companies may benefit from diversifying their patent filings across multiple jurisdictions.

This section considers the geographical and time dimensions together. Figure 13.5 offers a detailed view of the time-series dynamics in medical cannabis patent filings across the top patenting countries and regions. This data helps us understand how the global landscape of medical cannabis innovation has evolved over time and the strategic moves by entities involved in this sector. The data shows a significant variation in patent filings over the years, with noticeable trends emerging in several key regions. The US has demonstrated substantial fluctuations in patent filings, with a noticeable peak in recent years followed by a decline in 2020. This trend may reflect the regulatory environment in the US, where state-level legalisation advances against a backdrop of federal restrictions. PCT applications have shown a steady rise, particularly noticeable towards the late 2010s. This increase indicates a strategic turn by companies aiming for broader international market coverage, protecting their innovations in multiple jurisdictions simultaneously. Filings in the EPO have seen moderate fluctuations but remain an important part of the patent landscape, suggesting ongoing interest in securing a market presence across Europe, where medical cannabis policies are increasingly harmonising. Both China and Canada show growth in filings, reflecting their strengthening positions in global medical cannabis research and development. China's increase aligns with its rapid expansion in pharmaceutical innovations, while Canada's growth is supported by its advanced legal framework for cannabis. Countries like Australia (AU), South Korea (KR), Japan (JP), Spain (ES), and Great Britain (GB) display varied trends but generally lower and more stable filing numbers. These figures suggest a more cautious approach to cannabis-related IP in these regions, possibly due to differing regulatory landscapes.

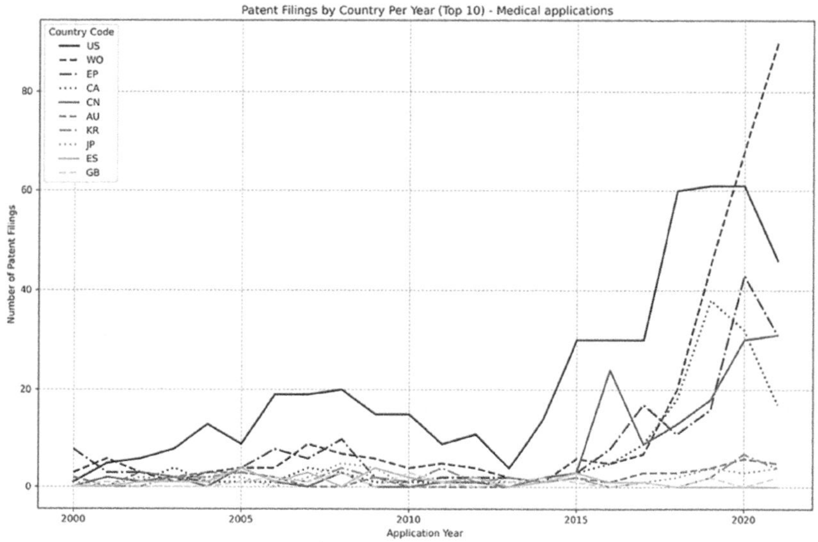

Source: Google Patents and author calculations.

Figure 13.5 *Cannabis patent filings for medical applications by country per year of application*

13.4.4 The Global Spread and Temporal Variations in Patent Filings Highlight Several Critical Points

The rise in PCT filings illustrates a clear move towards securing international IP protection, which is crucial in a competitive global market. Companies are increasingly aware of the need to protect their innovations not just locally but globally, to maximise their commercial potential. The fluctuations in national filings, especially the slowdown in 2020, may correlate with regulatory uncertainties or changes in the legal environment affecting cannabis research and commercialisation. The data indicates a diversification of innovation beyond traditional strongholds (US, EP) to emerging markets like China and established alternative markets like Canada, suggesting a more globally distributed innovation landscape.

In summary, the analysis of geographical trends in medical cannabis patent filings reveals a dynamic and strategically diversified global landscape. These trends underline the importance of strategic IP management and the need to stay adaptive to the rapidly changing global regulatory and commercial landscapes. Companies must consider not only where but also when to file patents, anticipating regulatory shifts and market developments.

13.4.5 Market Concentration of Patents in the Global Cannabis Industry

The global cannabis industry has witnessed a significant concentration of IP among a select few entities, as evidenced by the distribution of patent filings and grants. Analysing this concentration provides insight into the competitive dynamics and innovation leadership within the industry.

Figures 13.6 and 13.7 reveal a stark concentration of patent filings and grants among the top ten assignees in the cannabis sector. This concentration is indicative of the strategic importance that these entities place on securing IP rights as a means to solidify their market position and capitalise on emerging opportunities in cannabis-related medical applications. The data show

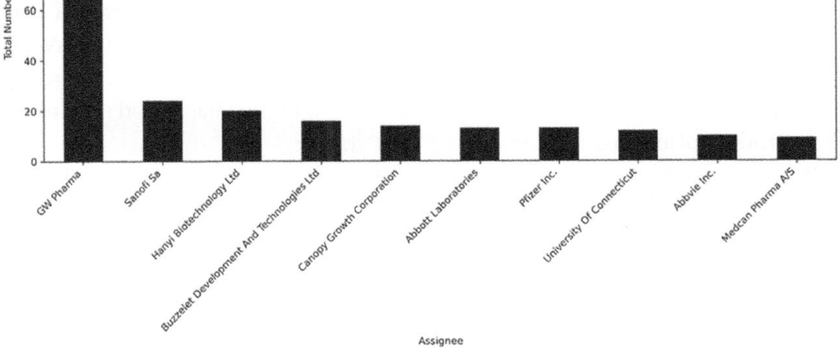

Source: Google Patents and author calculations.

Figure 13.6 Cannabis patent filings for medical applications by company

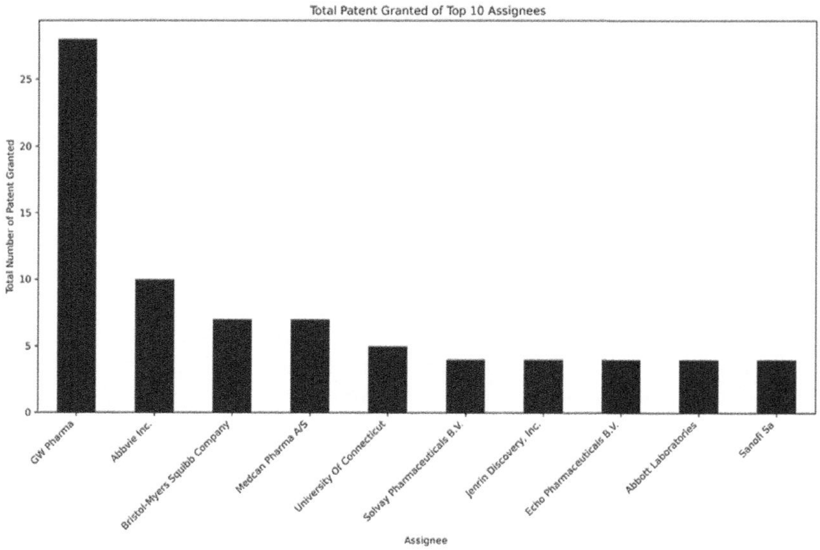

Source: Google Patents and author calculations.

Figure 13.7 *Cannabis patent granted for medical applications by company*

that a few companies dominate the landscape of patent filings. For instance, GW Pharmaceuticals appears as a clear leader, significantly outpacing other entities in the number of patent filings. This highlights their role as a major innovator and influencer in the sector, particularly in the development of cannabinoid-based therapeutics. Other notable entities such as Canopy Growth Corporation and Biotech Institute LLC also have substantial filings, reflecting their active engagement in broadening their technological bases and enhancing their product offerings.

When considering patents that have been granted, GW Pharmaceuticals again leads, which not only illustrates their success in filing patents but also their effectiveness in navigating the patent approval process. The presence of entities like Abbvie Inc. and the University of Connecticut highlights the involvement of both pharmaceutical companies and academic institutions in advancing cannabis research and securing proprietary technologies.

Figures 13.8 and 13.9 report the concentration ratios over time for both filings and grants. This analysis provides a deeper understanding of how control over cannabis-related IP has evolved since the beginning of the new century. The concentration of patent filings among the top assignees has shown fluctuations

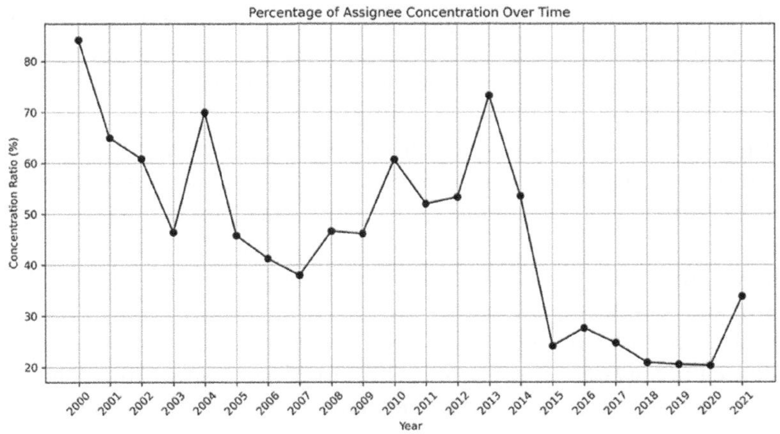

Source: Google Patents and author calculations.

Figure 13.8 *Concentration of cannabis patent filings for medical applications among the top ten filing companies*

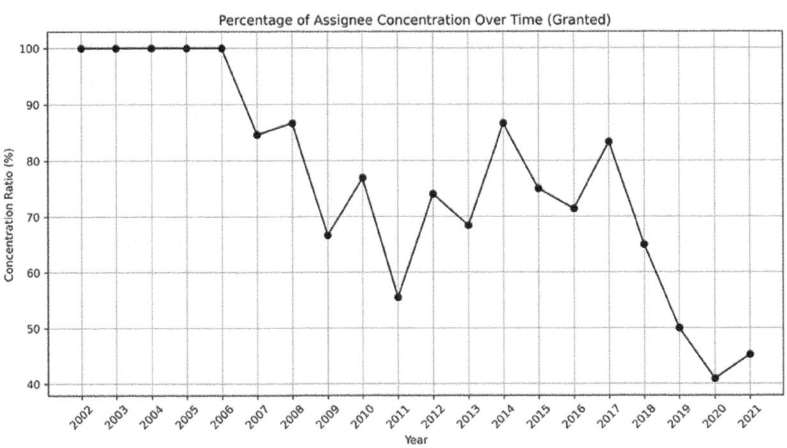

Source: Google Patents and author calculations.

Figure 13.9 *Concentration of cannabis patents granted for medical applications among the top ten granted companies*

over the years, with peaks indicating times when a few entities have dominated filings. For example, in the year 2000, over 80 per cent of patent filings for medical applications were concentrated in the top ten companies, and all patents granted were concentrated among these companies. The concentration of patent filings declined to less than 40 per cent in 2007 and peaked again at 75 per cent in 2013 before declining substantially after that year to reach its lowest in 2020 at 20 per cent. The concentration of patents granted shows a similar pattern with a lag of one or two years, which usually represents the time it takes for a patent to get approved. These fluctuations can be attributed to the varying pace of innovation, changes in regulatory landscapes, and the entry of new players into the market.

What is striking from Figure 13.8 is the substantial decline in patent filing concentration from 75 per cent in 2013 to 25 per cent in 2015. This can be attributed to several factors that may have influenced the cannabis industry during that period. First of all, this decline in concentration is related to regulatory changes (especially in the US) and the legalisation movement. Around 2013, several jurisdictions globally began to change their stance on cannabis, either moving towards legalisation or relaxing restrictions, particularly for medical use. For example, the US states of Colorado and Washington legalised cannabis for recreational use in late 2012, with laws taking effect in 2013.[20] These changes often open the market to new entrants and reduce the dominance of early pioneers who might have secured initial patents when the industry was less competitive. Second, as the legal landscape became more favourable, more companies and startups likely entered the cannabis market, leading to a broader distribution of patent filings across a larger number of entities. The entry of these new players could dilute the concentration of filings among previously dominant firms as innovation spreads across more companies. Third, by 2013, the cannabis industry had begun to mature in several key markets, with established players and new entrants contributing to a more competitive environment. As the industry matured, the initial rush to secure basic foundational patents subsided, leading to a decrease in concentration as more specialised and diverse innovations began to emerge. Fourth, with the advancement of cannabis-related technologies, there was likely an increase in patent filings covering a wider array of innovations, from cultivation methods to new medical formulations. This diversification in technology could have led to more companies being able to innovate independently, thus decreasing the concentration of patents among a few major players. Fifth, as companies began to recognise the global potential of cannabis, they might have started to

[20] On the US legal landscape, see Chapter 1 in this book, authored by Luke Zimmermann.

file patents in multiple jurisdictions outside their initial markets to protect their innovations internationally. This expansion into international markets could spread patent activity more evenly across different regions and companies. Finally, around this time, the financial landscape for cannabis investments might have shifted, with more venture capital and private equity flowing into the sector. Increased funding could support a broader range of companies in pursuing patent protections for their innovations, thereby decreasing the concentration ratio. Each of these factors likely played a role to varying degrees, contributing to the observed decrease in patent filing concentration in 2013. This shift reflects a dynamic period in the cannabis industry characterised by regulatory changes, market maturation, and increased competitive intensity.

The evolution of the market concentration of patents in the cannabis industry also carries several strategic implications. In the early 2000s, the cannabis industry exhibited a high level of market concentration in terms of patent filings and grants. This concentration is typical for emerging industries where a few pioneering entities dominate innovation. These entities often establish strong IP portfolios that act as significant barriers to entry for new competitors, effectively controlling major segments of the market. In such environments, the dominant firms enjoy substantial competitive advantages, including:

- Market Power and Pricing Control: Dominant firms can exert considerable influence over market prices and terms of trade within the industry.
- Innovation Leadership: They set technological and product standards and have the resources to sustain extensive research and development (R&D) activities.
- Strategic Partnerships and Influence: With robust patent portfolios, these companies are attractive partners for business collaborations and can shape regulatory and industry standards.

Over time, as observed with the decrease in patent concentration post-2013, the cannabis market has transitioned into a more competitive landscape. This shift is marked by a greater diversity of players obtaining patents, which suggests a democratisation of innovation within the industry. The implications of this more competitive market include:

- Lower Barriers to Entry: With more entities capable of innovating, new entrants find it easier to penetrate the market without facing overwhelming IP restrictions imposed by a few dominant players.
- Increased Innovation and Variety: A competitive market typically sees a surge in innovative activities as companies seek to differentiate themselves. This leads to a wider variety of products and services, driving rapid industry evolution.

- Collaborative Opportunities: As no single entity holds disproportionate control, there is more scope for collaborative efforts across different players, including cross-industry partnerships that can lead to breakthrough innovations.
- Market Resilience and Adaptability: A diverse array of companies contributing to the industry can enhance market resilience, enabling quicker adaptation to regulatory changes, consumer preferences, and technological disruptions.

Herein, it can be observed that the decrease in the concentration of patent filings and grants in the cannabis industry reflects its evolution from a market dominated by a few entities to a more dynamic and competitive sector. This transformation has important implications for business strategies, innovation pathways, and regulatory policies. Companies must now navigate a landscape where IP strategy involves not only securing patents but also engaging in alliances and adapting to a faster-paced innovation cycle. For new entrants, the diversified market presents more opportunities to establish a foothold without confronting a thick wall of existing patents. Stakeholders across the industry – whether investors, regulators, or companies themselves – must consider these changes in market dynamics when planning their strategies. The shift towards a more competitive environment promises a more robust and innovative cannabis industry, where collaboration and agility become key drivers of success. This evolution also encourages a healthier market structure that can better serve the needs of diverse consumers and respond adeptly to global market trends and regulatory shifts.

13.5 CONCLUSION

This chapter has explored the landscape of IP protection within the cannabis industry, focussing on patent trends across time, countries, and market concentration. As the cannabis sector transitions from an illegal market to a regulated and legitimate industry, the importance of IP protection becomes increasingly prominent.

We began by examining the economic approach to IP rights, emphasising the balance between incentivising innovation and ensuring public access to new knowledge and technologies. This balance is particularly pertinent in the cannabis industry, as opposed to the wider pharma industry, which faces unique challenges such as a fragmented legal landscape, intense market competition, and restrictions on research. Despite these challenges, we discussed how significant opportunities exist for businesses to differentiate their products, secure brand loyalty, and capitalise on strategic partnerships and licencing agreements.

Considering the complexity and unique characteristics of the cannabis industry discussed in the first part of the chapter, this contribution highlighted the need for a thorough understanding of patent trends across time, countries, and market concentration. This was the focus of the second part of this chapter. The analysis of cannabis-related patent filings showed a clear upward trend, divided into an initial phase of sparse activity and a subsequent acceleration phase driven by legislative changes, technological advancements, and increased recognition of cannabis's therapeutic potential. The geographical distribution of patent filings further highlighted the strategic significance of regions such as the US, Europe, China, and Canada in the global cannabis market. Finally, market concentration analysis revealed that while a few entities initially dominated the landscape, the industry has evolved into a more competitive environment with a broader distribution of innovation. This shift towards a diversified and dynamic market presents both challenges and opportunities for stakeholders, emphasising the need for adaptive strategies and collaborative efforts.

14. Post-colonial justice in the post-prohibitionist market: a political economy view on IP and cannabis

Bryan Khan

14.1 THE COLONIALITY OF PROHIBITION

14.1.1 Pre-Modern Era

The history of cannabis usage traces back not centuries, but millennia. Its use is recorded in ancient Chinese, Persian, Hindu, Greek, and Roman texts, often in a medical context. Cannabis is even believed to be one of the ingredients in the recipe for anointing oil, given to Moses by "the Lord" in the Old Testament.[1]

This is to just set the stage that cannabis usage has an incredibly long history, and surprisingly, so does discourse on cannabis prohibition. Around the tenth century, Muslim scholars supposedly debated whether cannabis use is consistent with the tenets of Islam, and whether it should be banned. Many texts on cannabis history claim official prohibition in 1378 by an Emir in a specific sub-region of Arabia, though this does not seem to stand up to research scrutiny.[2] A more verifiable historical reference for pre-modern prohibition is that in 1787, the King of the Kingdom of Merina (Madagascar) prohibited cannabis by threat of capital punishment, as he believed that smoking hemp took away the wit and senses of his courtiers.[3]

---

1 Exodus 30:22–23.

2 L Lewin, *Phantastica: A Classic Survey on the Use and Abuse of Mind-altering Plants* (Inner Traditions/Bear & Co. 1998) 89.

3 G Campbell, *David Griffiths and the Missionary "History of Madagascar"* (Brill 2012) 437.

14.1.2 Colonial Era

With the peak of European colonisation of the "New World" in the late nineteenth century, cannabis prohibitions were often used as a means to control colonial subjects. For example, in Guyana (at the time, British Guiana), the law "An Ordinance to Regulate the Sale of Opium and Bhang" was adopted by the British Colonial Government in 1861.[4] The reference here to "bhang" is a product made from cannabis leaves, or a cannabis-infused milk drink, consumed by some sects of the Hindu religion (and hence the Indian diaspora in the colonised New World) in traditional cultural, religious, and ceremonial contexts. On the relationship between colonialism and prohibition, it is important to understand that the issue is not just the legal control of substances. Rather, using the law as a tool to marginalise colonised peoples from their own traditions and cultural practices is a way to assert social and cultural hierarchies, reinforce the supremacy of the colonising power, and further processes of assimilation into colonial systems based on European norms and values.

Even outside of the framework of European colonialism, cannabis control was implemented in the nineteenth century as a means of social control over groups on the fringes of society within the Arab world, the Mediterranean, Brazil, and South Africa.[5] In the Arab world, for example, hashish was associated with the Sufis, a marginalised sector of Muslim society.[6] In Brazil, cannabis use was identified with Afro-Brazilian culture and folk medicine, and was even seen to represent a form of African cultural resistance to the white elites. An influential member of the Brazilian elite even presented a scientific paper in 1915 that described cannabis smoking as a "revenge of the defeated" by "savage blacks against the civilized white who had enslaved them".[7]

14.1.3 The Twentieth Century

In much of the Western world in the twentieth century, cannabis prohibition became institutionalised. South Africa was one of the first states to control cannabis, and nineteenth-century laws were aimed at prohibiting cannabis use and possession by Indian immigrants due to the perception that their consumption habits were a threat to white rule.[8] In fact, decades later, authorities

---

[4] *The Laws of British Guiana: A New and Revised Edition*, Vol V (Oxford University Press 1895).

[5] TNI, *The Rise and Decline of Cannabis Prohibition* (Transnational Institute and Global Drug Policy Observatory 2014) 2.

[6] ibid 9.

[7] ibid 10.

[8] ibid 9.

in South Africa – at that time politically independent but characterised by institutional colonialism and racism which would lead into the apartheid era – were responsible for first placing cannabis on the international drug control agenda in 1923. This was an action that should be understood as coming out of South Africa's long history of concerns about cannabis consumption amongst the Asian and African populations.[9]

In the US, the 1930s saw the demonisation of cannabis by newspaper industrialists with ties to the lumber and paper industries in an attempt to eliminate competition from the hemp industry. Sensationalised stories were published about "marijuana", in an attempt to demonise Mexican migrants in the US – an already racialised minority – in the context of the economic decline and social upheaval of the Great Depression. Cannabis products were eventually removed from the US Pharmacopoeia in 1942, even though hemp production was actively encouraged as part of the wartime effort to produce military supply inputs. This is yet another example of how the history of cannabis prohibition was directly rooted in the institutional use of regulation to further a racist agenda. The lasting legacy of this is evidenced by the fact that all over the Anglophone world, societies continue to use the word "marijuana" when referring to cannabis, despite this term's historically racist connotations.[10]

14.1.4 The UN Single Convention

Like historical colonialism, to understand cannabis prohibition we must consider the context of international relations, diplomacy, and competing (inter) national interests. A postcolonial view of cannabis prohibition would thus naturally align itself with a "pluralist" view of drug diplomacy, as it necessitates recognising the historical regulatory complexity of the issue, and the importance of pragmatic utility before expanding policies to the global level.[11] The watershed moment in drug diplomacy was the 1961 UN Single Convention on Narcotic Drugs. While previous international legal instruments on drug regulation existed, the Single Convention represented a regime change, and a shift from the previous regulatory focus towards an explicitly prohibitive approach.[12]

---

9 JH Mills, "The IHO as Actor: The Case of Cannabis and the Single Convention on Narcotic Drugs 1961" (2016) 13(1) Hygiea Internationalis 95, 101.

10 CARICOM Secretariat, *Report of the CARICOM Regional Commission on Marijuana 2018* (Caribbean Community Secretariat 2018) 8.

11 J Collins, "A Brief History of Cannabis and the Drug Conventions" (2020) 114 AJIL Unbound 279–284, 279.

12 D Bewley-Taylor, M Jelsma, "Regime Change: Re-visiting the 1961 Single Convention on Narcotic Drugs" (2012) 23(1) International Journal of Drug Policy

The Single Convention had the objective to terminate "quasi-medical" and traditional uses of opium, coca leaf, and cannabis – all plants cultivated and used historically in developing countries. Ultimately, the Convention banned cannabis cultivation, distribution, and use, as it introduced cannabis into the international drug regulation framework, categorising it in the strictest schedules. Schedule I includes cannabis, cannabis resin, extracts, and tinctures of cannabis – substances which might give rise to dependence, present a serious risk of abuse, and are subject to all of the Convention's control measures – while cannabis and cannabis resin are also listed in Schedule IV, namely substances with particularly harmful characteristics and extremely limited therapeutic value. On the matter of therapeutic value, an important driver of cannabis prohibition was reports produced by the World Health Organization (WHO), which were inputs into Convention negotiations. These reports were based largely on questionable evidence rather than rigid scientific inquiry.[13] Particularly, the extensive use of sensationalised and often misrepresented news clippings from South America underscores these reports' colonial and racist foundations, which influenced the position that cannabis had no useful medical purposes.

The international system for drug control was then further strengthened with the 1971 Convention on Psychotropic Substances and the 1988 Convention against Illicit Traffic in Narcotic Drugs and Psychotropic Substances. The 1988 Convention is relevant as it introduced a provision that dealt explicitly with "personal consumption contrary to the provisions" of the 1961 Convention, and codified possession as a criminal offence.

For general context, it is important here to keep in mind the global social and cultural climate of the 1960s, where youth-led counter-cultural movements were growing in Western countries, and independence movements were consolidating in the Global South. This context underscores that the coloniality of the international drug regulation framework was not just about power relationships between ethnic and social groups within nation-states, but also power relationships between territories of distinct developmental and independence statuses. In this regard, the system's inherently colonial foundations are apparent when one reflects on dominant Western attitudes toward different drugs. On this, it is notable that "Colonial cultural prejudices and Western pharmaceutical concepts have shaped the global drug control regime. They are still deeply embedded in misperceptions about "illegal" drugs and their comparative harmfulness".[14] In retrospect, one might thus reflect on how asymmetric

72–81, 72.

[13] Mills (n 9) 102.

[14] GCDP, *Global Commission on Drug Policy Report 2019* (2019) 10.

representations of interest might account for why an international convention on the control of alcohol never emerged.[15]

In encapsulating all of these perspectives, one of the most cogent commentaries on the coloniality of the international framework for drug regulation came from the Canadian Senate during policy discussions on cannabis reform, stating:

> We conclude from these observations that the international regime for the control of psychoactive substances, beyond any moral or even racist roots it may initially have had, is first and foremost a system that reflects the geopolitics of North-South relations in the 20th century. Indeed, the strictest controls were placed on organic substances – the coca bush, the poppy and the cannabis plant – which are often part of the ancestral traditions of the countries where these plants originate, whereas the North's cultural products, tobacco and alcohol, were ignored and the synthetic substances produced by the North's pharmaceutical industry were subject to regulation rather than prohibition.[16]

14.1.5 International Law as a Matrix of Power

What links the international frameworks for drug regulation and IP is that both are multilateral mechanisms within the larger system of international law and create positive obligations to enact related measures onto signatory nation-states. This system of international law is then a mechanism to create global order and, in many ways, maintain existing power structures through regulating the modalities of production and consumption.

Understanding the dynamics of international law again requires attention to the historical context in which they were adopted. A 1962 United Nations (UN) Office on Drugs and Crime note stated that "Cannabis drugs are also misused on the widest scale geographically, the areas of the world mostly concerned being Africa, north, south and central America, the Near East and the Middle East, the West Indies and the Indian-Pakistani sub-continent".[17] These were uncoincidentally the parts of the world in which independence and decolonisation were being negotiated, driven partially by the UN's 1960 Declaration on the Granting of Independence to Colonial Countries and Peoples. In the case of IP law, (formerly) colonised territories were previously incorporated into the international framework through the extra-territorial extension effects of key treaties drafted by European interests in the metropoles, without any

---

[15] TNI (n 5) 22.

[16] Senate of Canada, *Report of the Senate Special Committee on Illegal Drugs Summary* (September 2002).

[17] UN Office on Drugs and Crime, *The Cannabis Problem: A Note on the Problem and the History of International Action* (1962).

consideration for the dynamics of creativity and innovation in the colonial peripheries.[18]

As post-colonial states gained political independence and sovereignty, their emergence was within a pre-existing ecosystem of international law, which included the key treaties on both drug regulation and IP. Assimilation into the existing international order was inevitable in order to viably participate in the international legal system and the increasingly interconnected global economy. Deference to international legal obligations was thus a constraint on the process of decolonisation and self-determination. In the case of IP law, this assimilation and deference were more systematically institutionalised with the adoption of the Trade-Related Aspects of Intellectual Property Rights (TRIPS) Agreement, where developing (post-colonial) peoples again had little opportunity or capacity to participate in the development of legal norms, which were driven largely by state and private interests.[19]

Against this backdrop of the international legal system as a matrix of colonial power, we can draw several interesting parallels between the frameworks for cannabis prohibition and IP rights.

14.1.6 Power Asymmetries in International Institutions

First, it is key to understand both frameworks as being driven not just by institutional players, but specific key individuals with ideological interests. In the case of the TRIPS Agreement, the incorporation of IP norms into the multilateral system for international trade regulation under the GATT was a concerted project by US lobbyists who saw an opportunity to expand American neo-imperialist trade interests through legal harmonisation.[20] In terms of the Single Convention – including the scheduling of cannabis – the framing of drug regulation issues was due to the fact that pro-prohibition advocates held key positions in the relevant committees of the coordinating international institutions.

Furthermore, the very dynamics of international diplomacy are shaped by heterogeneity in states' negotiating capacities, expertise, and experience.

---

18 See generally: B Khan, *Intellectual Property, Development, and Inclusiveness: A Postcolonial Critique*. In C Sappa (ed.) *Research Handbook on Intellectual Property Rights and Inclusivity* (Edward Elgar Publishing 2024) 48–73.

19 RL Okediji, "The International Relations of Intellectual Property: Narratives of Developing Country Participation in the Global Intellectual Property System" (2003) 7 Sing. J. Int'l & Comp. L. 315, 317.

20 See generally: P Drahos, J Braithwaite, *Information Feudalism: Who Owns the Knowledge Economy* (Routledge 2002).

During the negotiations of the Single Convention, most country representatives had little experience with cannabis, any guiding statistics, or explicit instructions from their governments on the issue.[21] This very much parallels the realities of developing countries during the negotiation of the TRIPS Agreement, where many states lacked capacity and expertise in the complexities of IP law to meaningfully participate in deliberations. As such, while the dominant narrative of TRIPS is that developing countries accepted higher IP standards as a bargain in exchange for market access for primary commodities, narratives of coercion and/or ignorance still have an important place in the critical discourse.[22]

Even if post-colonial states now have a presence in discourse on current IP issues – or even had a presence during TRIPS negotiations – the reality is that this discourse is framed by pre-existing international agreements. In the case of IP law, the foundational international treaties – the Berne and Paris Conventions – were negotiated by European powers during the era of late-nineteenth-century colonialism, where the interests of colonised peoples were not represented, and laws could apply by extension to colonised territories.[23] These laws were then inherited by post-colonial states as part of their embedded legal systems as a starting point. Similarly, in the case of drug regulation, most post-colonial states could not be at the table, especially given that the precursors to the Single Convention occurred under the auspices of the (then) League of Nations before the emergence of the new global order – including decolonisation movements – that followed from the aftermath of World War II (WWII). The initial treaty basis for both the TRIPS Agreement and the Single Convention are thus found in agreements negotiated before the era of decolonisation.

In both drug and IP frameworks, the role of ideology in driving international law also interfaces with the politics of regulatory legitimisation. At the time of the early drug regulation debates, the relevant agencies were in their nascent stages, having just emerged as components of the post-war international architecture of the UN. From this perspective, the international prohibition of cannabis can be seen as a symptom of a wider project of empire-building and

---

21 TNI (n 5) 13–14.

22 PK Yu, "TRIPS and Its Discontents" (2006) 10 Marq. Intell. Prop. L. Rev. 369.

23 The marginalisation of colonial territories in the development of the international IP framework has also been highlighted in discourse on various other specific subject matter issues, such as the protection of country names. See: N Corthésy, *Intellectual Property Protection: Balancing Nation Brands and Geographic Commons in a Competitive Global Marketplace* (Ian Randle Publishers 2023) 65–66.

territory-claiming in the development of the post-war international order.[24] The decades that followed were defined by competing ideological and economic poles of power and influence. With the fall of the Soviet Union in 1991, the Cold War came to an end and Western liberal democracy ascended as the defining paradigm of international order within the onset of globalisation, in what political historians have now come to call the "End of History".[25] This new global order was influenced firmly by neoliberal economic ideology, which places laissez-faire market liberalisation and the strengthening of private property rights as unquestionable tenets of the law's functions. The strengthening and harmonisation of IP law under the TRIPS Agreement is a key outcome of this reconfiguration of international law in pursuit of institutionalising Anglo-American neoliberalism – again a form of regulatory legitimisation. We note here that neoliberal trade liberalisation was also linked directly to increased illicit cannabis cultivation. As free trade dismantled commodity agreements used to stabilise prices through quota systems, many agricultural producers in the Global South were displaced from global supply chains and were forced to pivot to illegal cannabis cultivation.[26]

As the flagbearer of neoliberal economic policy, the specific role of the US deserves some attention. In the US, the dynamics of cannabis regulation have always been conditioned by the complexities of how legislative power is delegated between the state and federal levels. In the early twentieth century, it appears that part of the US's strategy was to pursue international cannabis regulation in order to establish a domestic constitutional basis via international treaty for federal drug regulation.[27] In the post-war global order, as the US emerged as the new hegemonic power, it used its sphere of influence to export its policy agenda to the rest of the world. This allowed the US to be the driver of incorporating IP norms into the international trade law framework. Both developments reflect the use of hegemonic power to influence international law in pursuit of US domestic interests.

14.1.7 Legitimisation through Language

Back at the international level, another interesting parallel is how language and framing have been used to legitimise the law. As already noted, the Single Convention was based largely on faulty scientific evidence regarding the risks (and lack of benefits) of cannabis. This framing of drug regulation lends to a

---

24 Mills (n 9) 113.

25 F Fukuyama, *The End of History and the Last Man* (Penguin Books 2012).

26 M Jelsma, S Kay, D Bewley-Taylor, *Fair(er) Trade Options for the Cannabis Market* (Cannabis Innovate, Swansea University 2019) 11.

27 TNI (n 5) 17.

co-optation of scientific language, which attempts to legitimise cannabis prohibition. Since the adoption of the Single Convention, states have responded to international law with schedules and classification systems that are not evidence-based or rationally linked to the harms and benefits of substances, but rather based on political choices and benefits for policymakers.[28]

A similar process of legitimisation through the co-optation of language explains modern attitudes towards IP law. The framing of IP as a "right" and a form of "property" appeals to human rights perspectives, which imply IP is inherently self-justified and inalienable. The institutionalisation of this language shifts focus away from IP as a tool for regulating information flows and industrial organisation and is based on an inherently colonial and Eurocentric romanticisation of the individual author under personality rights philosophy. For both cannabis regulation and IP, understanding the rigidity of the international legal system must thus consider the role of language and the colonial implications of such.

Furthermore, both frameworks' rhetorical premises have failed to live up to empirical scrutiny. In the case of cannabis, it is the claims of usage as a gateway to "harder" drug use and criminality, while in the case of IP it is the unfulfilled promises of balanced economic development driven by technology transfer under the TRIPS Agreement.

14.1.8 National Policy Space

In all forms of regulation, a trade-off exists between maintaining a national policy space that can be adapted to the domestic context and responding to shared international challenges. What is important to understand is that the process of decolonisation and self-determination is inherently protective of this national policy space, as newly sovereign states need time and resources to define their development strategies and post-independence political orientations.

This is true for both IP as a tool in industrial policy and economic planning, as well as drug regulation, which is conditioned by the local social-cultural context. Unfortunately, from a political economy perspective, internationally harmonised IP norms can be antithetic to the relationship between sovereignty and economic development. Historically, hegemonic powers used liberal approaches to intangible property rights to develop industrial capacity and then later pivoted to restrictive rights in a strategy of nationalistic protectionism.[29] Post-colonial states that emerged into the pre-existing global order were denied these strategic industrial policy tools. While drug regulation might not

---

28 GCDP (n 14) 4.

29 See generally: HJ Chang, *Kicking Away the Ladder* (Anthem Press 2002).

have a similar relevance for historical economic growth, the legal status of cannabis certainly affects social and cultural relations within a multicultural post-colonial state. By being unable to regulate cannabis in accordance with the domestic cultural context, post-colonial states are denied a legal tool to promote solidarity and social cohesion, which are important institutions for inclusive development. Both cannabis prohibition and IP as a form of capital consolidation inherently reinforce class conflicts.

For much of the developing world, direct legal transplantation was the case for both cannabis regulation and IP law. For example, in the British West Indies, British drug laws were the model for drug regulation,[30] and the same applies for the IP laws inherited by newly independent states. Ironically, the principle of sovereignty was a concern raised by colonial powers in debates over the drafting of the Single Convention; it was the position of the UK in particular that a UN Agency should not determine the domestic affairs of a state, questioning the core political principles of the legal instrument.[31]

The strategic use of a post-colonial state's policy space is still conditioned by its complex position within the global order of international law. This is to say that post-colonial states – which historically tend to lack institutional and governance capacity due to size or development status – are not just recipients of legal transplants, but often implement legal norms through direct and literal transposition. This is to say that international law funnels a new mechanism for legal transposition which takes the place of colonial-era legal transplantation.

International IP treaties define minimum standards for protection in rigid terms, but frame public interest exceptions as "flexibilities" which are up to signatory states to craft, interpret, and implement. Similarly, in the 1961 Single Convention, full prohibition of cannabis is technically an option (though recommended), and prohibition is only required by a state "if in its opinion the prevailing conditions in its country render it the most appropriate means of protecting the public health and welfare". However, for less developed countries, it is often more politically feasible to implement rules based on international models and norms than to legislate exceptions that require justification based on welfare analysis. The entrenchment of international law into the national space for both drug regulation and IP thus disfavours small developing states that lack legislative drafting capacity, and adopt laws based on pre-constructed model legislation, which often focusses on treaty compliance without consideration of nuanced domestic social complexities.

This deference to treaty provisions and under-utilisation of permissible flexibilities is further reinforced by the role of international institutions

---

30 TNI (n 5) 16.

31 Mills (n 9) 111.

and agencies. In terms of drug regulation, an important role is played by the International Narcotics Control Board (INCB), an "independent and quasi-judicial monitoring body" for the implementation of the UN drug treaties. However, the INCB "has a history of promoting overly restrictive interpretations of the treaties, creating unwarranted impediments to policies widely recognized to fit comfortably within the treaty confines".[32]

In the case of the IP system, a similar monitoring body does not exist, as the World Trade Organization (WTO) only provides case-specific dispute resolution between Member States regarding compliance with the TRIPS Agreement. While several WTO disputes have occurred regarding TRIPS flexibilities, unless the material economic stakes are high, small developing states may be largely risk-averse in terms of pushing the limits of permissible flexibilities and facing the potential for trade retaliation or diplomatic tensions. While the World Intellectual Property Organization (WIPO) is also a key institution and forum for international discourse, it administers more than 25 IP treaties, of which only one focusses explicitly on specific and narrow limitations to IP rights.[33] Thus, while there is active international discourse on limitations, exceptions, and flexibilities, determinative constraints on IP rights are not a feature of the international IP treaty system itself.

Overall, both international drug regulation and IP law feature institutional mechanisms, which are independent of the international legal frameworks themselves, but create implicit pressure to limit the policy space of countries with less institutional, diplomatic, and implementation capacity.

While industrialised countries like Canada, which have undertaken major cannabis reforms, acknowledge their non-compliance with international law,[34] smaller less developed states are likely much more risk-averse to diplomatic pressures, especially where foreign aid and preferential treatment are tied to compliance with international law and drug cooperation. Differences in legislative capacity are also reflected in the latitude for creative interpretation by states with hegemonic geopolitical positions, which reinforces diplomatic power and influence over international policy discourse. Regarding cannabis regulation, the US has appealed to the drug treaties' recognition of constitutional limitations to argue that it is still compliant, as federal law still prohibits

---

32 J Walsh, M Jelsma, *Regulating Drugs: Resolving Conflicts with the UN Drug Control Treaty System* (2019) 1(3) Journal of Illicit Economies and Development 266–271.

33 Marrakesh Treaty to Facilitate Access to Published Works for Persons who are Blind, Visually Impaired or Otherwise Print Disabled 2013.

34 In discussing Bill C-45 (on cannabis drug reform) in 2018, the Canadian government explicitly recognised contravening obligations under the UN Drug Conventions.

cannabis despite state-level reforms.[35] Regarding IP, the US was not only a primary architect of TRIPS but has also notoriously been a driver of a maximalist approach to IP through the use of unilateral trade pressures outside of international multilateral law.[36] At the same time, the US has resisted pressures to reform its own laws where it has been deemed to be non-compliant with TRIPS.[37] Here the hegemonic state's ability to paradoxically enjoy the political and diplomatic latitude to creatively interpret the rules, while still reinforcing the rigidity of the multilateral legal order that serves its wider international interests, can be observed.

14.1.9 Inversions of Policy Positions

In tracking the early origins of international cannabis regulation, commentators note that the roles played by Egypt, South Africa, Italy, and Turkey are often overlooked, while the US did not play a leading role at all.[38] However, both the IP and cannabis regulation frameworks reflect evolving positions by diplomatic interests over time. To make a broad general statement, the historical paradigm of IP discourse is "developed countries promoting expansionism and developing countries resisting". Modern debates on IP policy now see these default positions inverted, with developed countries placing increased emphasis on nuanced limitations, and developing countries preoccupied with strengthening IP protection in pursuit of economic development.

While debates over cannabis regulation (and in particular medical uses) have always been contentious, inversions of policy approaches can also be observed. Within the UN system, countries in non-hegemonic regions such as Eastern Europe, Asia, and the Middle East have long been historically marginalised within the international drug regulation framework constructed during eras of reconstruction or decolonisation. However, many of these countries now oppose international drug reform and defend the integrity of the international system.[39] At the same time, many of the countries which originally supported the system now find that its rigidity is a difficult constraint that pits international compliance against domestic reform.

Both IP and drug regulation thus provide complementary insights into the complex interface between diplomacy, legal reform, and the role of international law in power relationships.

---

35 Walsh, Jelsma (n 32) 267.

36 See generally: Drahos, Braithwaite (n 20).

37 See, for example, WTO Dispute DS160.

38 Collins (n 11) 281.

39 GCDP, *Global Commission on Drug Policy Report 2021* (2021) 14.

14.1.10 Public Health Policy and Indian Advocacy

As already noted, the potential therapeutic applications of cannabis have always played a central role in debates over its regulation. Even a decade before the Single Convention, debates within meetings of the Commission on Narcotic Drugs (CND) noted that while prohibition of cannabis was supported by certain countries, resistance came from others who preferred regulatory control over prohibition, arguing that physicians should be free to choose between medicines.[40]

During negotiations on the Single Treaty, attempts were made to make cannabis the only "prohibited" substance on the premise that the WHO indicated that medical use of cannabis was obsolete and no longer justified. Strong objections were raised by India, which was barely a decade into its status as a post-colonial nation state, having become politically independent in 1947. India sought to defend the use of "bhang", the traditional preparation made from cannabis leaves with low psychoactive content.[41] As noted previously, bhang is used in traditional and religious ceremonies (partially due to associations between the Hindu deity Lord Shiva and cannabis), as well as within traditional medicine systems. In 1955, the Indian representative on the CND declared their opposition to the notion that cannabis had no medical application as "cannabis was used in both unani and ayurvedic systems of indigenous medicine, by which a very large proportion of the Indian population was treated".[42] In response to the US's argument that Asian therapeutic traditions should be dismissed as "quasi-medical uses", the Indian Government contested that these traditional medical systems "did not become quasi-medical merely because they were not Western systems".[43] The Indian Government succeeded in frustrating the cultural biases of Western medicine that defined the WHO at the time. However, one should be cautious in romanticising India's position as a defender of traditional knowledge, as this position was motivated by protecting the interests of "large firms which produced indigenous medicines".[44]

The histories of negotiating the TRIPS Agreement also reflect this narrative of India as an advocate for defending the policy space of the postcolonial world. During TRIPS negotiations, Indian representatives were key in raising concerns about the public health implications of extending mandatory patent

---

40 Mills (n 9) 97.
41 Bewley-Taylor, Jelsma (n 12) 77.
42 Mills (n 9) 103–104.
43 ibid.
44 Mills (n 9) 105.

protection to pharmaceuticals.[45] At least in the IP space, this international advocacy has been maintained consistently, as evidenced by India's key role in the Doha Declaration on Public Health and advocating for the TRIPS COVID-19 waiver. However, again, it is important to note that these positions are not just rooted in public policy, ethical, and cultural considerations, but also strategic economic factors. Indeed, India's historical opposition to pharmaceutical patent protection was tied to its position as a major producer and distributor of generic medicines. As such, both in the realms of cannabis regulation and IP rights, it is key to understand that policy positions can be motivated by economic and non-economic factors, which cannot be easily separated.

14.1.11 The Antibiotic Debate

Closely examining the history of the Single Convention, there is one specific incident in which the interface between cannabis, public health, and IP rights indirectly influenced negotiations. In the ongoing debate over cannabis prohibition, a 1959 draft resolution was tabled which momentarily went against the WHO's position that cannabis had no medical value and sought to investigate the potential antibiotic properties of cannabis. This resolution was drafted by Canada, the US, France, and the UK, but was also supported by Iran, India, the USSR, and China.[46] Ultimately, the response of the WHO was unfavourable, and further reports based on questionable scientific evidence were produced to reiterate the position that cannabis had no legitimate medical value.

This momentary deviation in attitudes is one of the first instances of the power of IP rights in medical cannabis debates. Once again, it is important here to understand the context of the world at the time. In the economic sphere, the major power centres of the world were in the midst of the post-war economic boom, civilian and industrial deployment of manufacturing technologies developed during the war, and full employment in the economy, including significant labour and capital investments in research. At the social level, the new social contract of the post-war Western world was one which sought to prioritise access to welfare and social services, including public health. At the political level, growing Cold War tensions were further driving major investments into science and technology in the two major poles of global political power. All of this created an environment extremely supportive of medical

45 For a discussion on India's role and positions in TRIPS negotiations, see: AV Ganesan, "Negotiating for India"; and J Watal, "Patents: An Indian Perspective" both in J Watal and A Taubman (eds) *The Making of the TRIPS Agreement* (World Trade Organization 2015).

46 Mills (n 9) 108.

research, which highlights why the potential for medical applications of cannabis was so attractive.

There was, however, an even more interesting historical factor at play. In 1928, penicillin was discovered in London, changing the course of modern medicine. Of course, the story of penicillin cannot be told without reference to IP rights. Penicillin was discovered by accident in 1928 after Alexander Fleming found that an isolated mould had an antibacterial effect on various pathogens, including staphylococci. The medical research team in the UK chose not to patent penicillin (debates over the patentability of the specific subject matter notwithstanding) as they viewed patenting such a life-saving drug to be unethical.[47] However, a collaboration between public and private actors in the US obtained patents on the process of penicillin production, leading to a situation where British stakeholders had to pay royalties for a breakthrough discovery made in the UK.

With this historical experience in mind, the discovery of antibiotics not only revolutionised modern medicine but also represented a new stream of research that could be extremely lucrative with the strategic use of IP rights. It is for these reasons that the potential for cannabis extracts to have antibiotic applications was an alluring pull factor that, at least momentarily, shifted the debates and affected diplomatic attitudes towards cannabis regulation in the late 1950s.

14.2 FRAGMENTED MARKETS, INNOVATION, AND TRADE

14.2.1 Market Boundaries and International Reform

During the colonial era, the legal extension of IP into the colonies served to facilitate commerce and regulate trade between colonial powers and the peripheries.[48] This was part of the larger project of power consolidation through international law. Similarly, colonial drug policy also served to define market boundaries and trade patterns, as European authorities extended their powers to control profitable monopolies in goods like opium, coca, and cannabis in their overseas territories. These colonial monopolies supplied Asian opium markets and North African cannabis markets in recognition of their traditional uses and also provided derived drug products to European medical markets.[49]

During the first half of the twentieth century, the international approach to drug regulation focussed on maintaining domestic policy flexibility with

47 R Gaynes, *The Discovery of Penicillin – New Insights after More Than 75 Years of Clinical Use.* (2017) 23(5) Emerging Infectious Diseases 849, 852.

48 Okediji (n 19) 324.

49 GCDP (n 14) 13.

control over international trade. This ensured that control over commercial trade was consolidated in the hands of colonial monopolies by mitigating diversion into illegal markets.[50] As European colonialism became less sustainable and decolonisation became increasingly inevitable, British, Dutch, and French colonial powers lost control over their legal monopolies in these commodities in former colonies in Asia and North Africa. This led to shifts in the positions of these colonial powers that previously resisted stricter prohibition rules. With the new post-war order of the mid-twentieth century, the balance of power then shifted and post-colonial states were less successful in resisting US pressures for a global drug prohibition regime than their former colonial rulers.[51]

While historical cannabis markets can be understood as based on political interests, future market developments are defined by the crop's different uses. More specifically, the constituent markets are for (a) an industrial product (hemp rope and cloth in particular), (b) a medical product (in traditional systems of medicine and modern innovative applications), and (c) a psychoactive substance (used in recreational settings, but also traditional contexts).[52] While industrial hemp was long used by European powers to build their colonial empires, the Single Convention restricted medical uses and prohibited recreational use.

Clearly, the issue of international cannabis reform is a complex matter. The most obvious options are comprehensive amendment or even a new drug regulation framework. This does not seem to be a realistic scenario as it requires consensus and navigating the complex diplomatic and geopolitical dimensions of the cannabis issue. There are, however, various potential paths forward that do not require wide consensus.

The option of unilateral action – such as late reservations, or denunciation and re-accession with new reservations – achieves state-level compliance but does not pave a path towards a liberalised international market. A more viable solution is to reschedule cannabis (requiring majority votes), which seems more likely given the partially favourable recommendations of the 2019 WHO review of cannabis.[53] However, the diplomatic and logistical constraints on the renegotiation process are still considerable. Another option discussed by many drug reform advocates is the possibility of "inter se modification" (as per

---

50 ibid 38.

51 ibid 15.

52 A regulatory problem for international trade is that different jurisdictions use different definitions for the threshold between hemp (legal industrial product) and cannabis (regulated drug). A standard definition is that hemp contains less than 0.3 per cent THC (tetrahydrocannabinol) based on dried biomass, but this is not internationally harmonised.

53 GCDP (n 14) 31.

Article 41 of the Vienna Convention on the Law of Treaties). This option would allow a subset of states to pursue reform without fundamentally disrupting the existing treaty regime, given the absence of consensus. This option is particularly attractive, as it would "open the possibility of international trade between regulated licit markets, enabling small farmers in traditional Southern producing countries to participate and diminishing the risk of a corporate capture of the emerging licit market".[54]

Despite the challenges of international reform, recent decades have seen remarkable legal developments at the national levels. Medical use of cannabis is now legal in several US states (starting with California in 1996), as well as many other countries, including some European states. A watershed development was the legalisation of recreational cannabis in Canada in 2018. A large number of other countries have also pursued decriminalisation and partial regulation. With these national legal efforts, booming domestic markets, and increasing corporate interest in the industry, it seems inevitable that the future may see liberalised international trade.

Our challenge is that the inevitably slow nature of international reform widens the gaps between the maturation of key national markets and the potential international market. Such gaps benefit countries which have liberalised their domestic markets earlier and have developed economic capacity in this space through innovation and IP assets. In other words, countries like the US, Canada, and the Netherlands stand to benefit from a strong first-mover advantage in international competition.

14.2.2 Market Transitions and Trade Positions

At this point, it is important to consider what recreational cannabis market liberalisation might mean in terms of economic development. The process of legalisation represents a discontinuity in markets, as cannabis moves from a strictly controlled substance to a tradable commercial commodity. As social norms, attitudes, and consumer preferences adjust to the post-legalisation landscape, the market for cannabis will evolve. However, the market is not emerging from typical organic processes that characterise most product lifecycles. Legalisation does not create a new market space from scratch, but rather legitimises a market space that has always existed. The legalisation process affects market equilibrium on both the demand and supply sides of the market, which can be described as four distinct processes: (i) existing (pre-legalisation) consumers adjust their preferences to adapt to the availability of new legal sources of supply, (ii) new (risk-averse) consumers enter the market based on

[54] Walsh, Jelsma (n 32) 269.

a strong preference for legal sources, (iii) existing illegal producers make strategic choices about pivoting into the legal supply chain, and (iv) new legal producers invest in the market. In all four processes, branding and product marketing play a key role, while technological innovation is important specifically for supply side processes. Overall, in contrast with this complex economic transition, the market goes from non-existent to partially developed in the eyes of the law, as the law is generally not designed to accommodate the pre-legalisation realities.

This transition does not represent any of the traditional categories of innovation in the Schumpeterian sense of economic theory. In this case, economic development driven by innovation is normally a phased process, whereby specific occurrences interact with the complex dynamics of competition and established economic patterns leading to new market structures. Rather, cannabis legalisation is more akin to a discontinuous shock than a gradual process, and there is simply little historical precedent for such a competition shock induced by exogenous legal factors.

Economic asymmetries in cannabis reform become apparent when one considers the role of international trade law. Large states with early-mover advantages seek to expand thriving domestic markets through exportation. Small developing states, on the other hand, may have a history and culture of domestic cannabis cultivation and may be navigating the complexities of domestic reform, but they need market access to benefit from the economies of scale necessary to be competitive in a liberalised market. These countries, however, are unable to trade due to current international prohibition despite domestic reforms.

Through the TRIPS Agreement, countries should not discriminate against each other's IP rights under the principles of most-favoured nation and national treatment. This supports cross-border commercial activity through foreign direct investment (FDI) in local cannabis markets, part of which is the registration of IP rights in foreign markets. As part of the WTO system, TRIPS implicitly acknowledges that the recognition of cross-border IP rights is inseparable from legal guarantees to market access. However, the simultaneous recognition of IP rights in cannabis products and lack of direct market access due to international prohibition breaks this linkage.[55]

National cannabis reform without international trade implies IP non-discrimination without free trade liberalisation. As part of the WTO framework, TRIPS harmonises minimum IP standards so that IP can serve as a catalyst

[55] We do, however, note that technically, international trade obligations on non-discrimination may still apply for cannabis, despite international prohibition. See: E Eliason, E Howse, "A Higher Authority: Canada's Cannabis Legalization in the Context of International Law" (2019) 40 MICH. J. INT'L L. 327.

to enhance international trade. Market opportunities drive the creation of IP through: (i) reputational effects which further drive investments in brands protected by trademarks, and (ii) creating surpluses which are reinvested into patent-producing research and development. When IP is created in commercially profitable markets, it is exported to emerging markets through the principles of TRIPS and international filing systems. Countries that legalise recreational cannabis earlier will thus have a first-mover advantage in both trademark reputation and innovation patents. This advantage is even more acute for industrialised states with established high innovation capacity and returns to research. This means that countries that legalise later will have a more difficult time competing as technology is monopolised and established brands have strong reputations.

The core idea of international trade is that countries should specialise in producing the goods in which they have a comparative advantage. Traditionally, this has meant that the Global North focusses on value-added goods, while the Global South focusses on primary commodities (such as agriculture). Cannabis markets represent a strategic opportunity for development, as they combine primary production with potential for localised high-value-added processing, and various downstream industrial and medical applications. Potential comparative advantage is, however, eroded because there is little international trade due to drug prohibition. Furthermore, while many small states in the Global South might still have a comparative advantage in traditional agricultural cultivation, they lack the corresponding experience in industrial scalability, processing, and distribution, which are necessary to compete in an internationally liberalised market.

For clarity, this chapter is not advocating for an internationally liberalised market as an imperative. Rather, it is highlighting that the cumulative effect of national cannabis reform trends, international drug prohibition, and TRIPS creates a regulatory disharmonisation in the international trade system. Assuming that an internationally liberalised market is inevitable at some point in the future, this disharmonisation amplifies concerns about equitable economic development in cannabis markets.

14.2.3 A Policy Agenda for Equity

Our discussions thus far underscore that future developments in the cannabis trade present challenges for both postcolonial justice and economic competitiveness. As profit-driven capital interests in the Global North compete aggressively to pre-emptively capture the emerging international market, states in the Global South need to reform laws, keeping in mind the importance of protecting small-scale farmers and traditional producers. The challenge for policymakers is now to "apply lessons learned from a history of colonialism and stigma as new markets are being designed that protect health, safety and autonomy".[56]

The misalignment between commercial realities and legal realities means that IP law needs to be very sensitive to the transition to legal markets. The typical processes of gradual innovation, creativity, and reputation building that underpin the IP system do not operate in the usual way. Proven knowledge on innovative production techniques may move from illegal to highly profitable, while branding and source-identification terminologies instantaneously go from illegal to commercially indispensable. Therefore, in pursuit of meaningful cannabis reform, established IP rules need to be utilised to both safeguard cultural assets from (mis)appropriation in the postcolonial world and correct for market-distorting first-mover advantages in the industrialised world.

The following section outlines three specific opportunities for IP law to be congruent with cannabis reform efforts.[57]

14.2.4 Safeguarding Cultural Practices against Appropriation

The first recommendation is that postcolonial states with histories of cannabis use should develop tools for the defensive protection of customs and cultural assets. More specifically, it is critical to prevent the registration of trademarks that misappropriate the state's local cultural norms, symbolism, and language as applied to cannabis goods and services.

This is critical as local cannabis culture is often associated with working-class peoples, and while cultural knowledge is widely diffused, it may not be known to the educated middle classes, who work with the IP system (including legal practitioners and IP examiners). This is to say that there is often a cultural knowledge gap between wider society and the gatekeepers of the IP system. Furthermore, while modern IP filing systems promote balance through opposition and nullification mechanisms, these procedures are usually designed to be used by competitors and are not suited for use by decentralised communities. Relatively short opposition times, which involve administrative fees, do not lend themselves to inclusivity for local communities within IP systems' examination and grant processes.

Part of domestic cannabis reform is often creating some regulatory authority empowered to oversee licensing and the sector's orderly development, and this competent national authority may also be tasked with policy advisory and market monitoring functions. As a part of these functions, the competent

---

[56] GCDP (n 39) 20.

[57] Needless to say, this is a non-exclusive list; see the other chapters of this book for further recommendations.

authority can monitor the national trademark, patent, and design registries for all IP applications related to cannabis commercialisation. It would be ideal to execute a memorandum of understanding between the national IP office and the competent authority to disclose and share information on cannabis-related IP filings, as is done in some jurisdictions for trademark applications which invoke Indigenous languages.[58] The idea is that the competent authority would be in an informed position to oppose or advise on IP filings which attempt to appropriate local cannabis culture or knowledge in a manner that would be detrimental to either historical justice or fair competition.

Concurrently, efforts should be made to systematically document a country's social and cultural norms surrounding cannabis usage. As illegal cannabis consumption may have a long history within a given society, unique social and cultural practices would have long developed among users before legalisation. These modern systems of norms need to be surveyed and documented, and may include unique local slang and terminology, methods of consumption, and other specific cultural practices. These efforts ensure that IP filings, including trademarks in particular, do not attempt to unfairly exploit local practices by giving a registrant an unjustified monopoly to the detriment of established social practices, cultural diversity, and healthy competition.

Connected with the trademark system, Geographical Indications (GI) also certainly provide strategic opportunities for postcolonial states to capitalise on cultural reputations in cannabis traditions.[59] However, GI protection itself can be rooted in issues of coloniality, and GI product specifications do not necessarily guarantee local ownership of key capital resources. Whether cannabis reforms can incorporate domestic ownership requirements is beyond the scope of this chapter, especially given the contentious issue of local content requirements in international trade law. Still, the IP system can be leveraged through the use of certification trademarks to differentiate and support locally owned (and ethical) cannabis companies. Under Article 20 TRIPS, mandatory co-use of a collective mark indicating non-local ownership, however, may not be permissible.

---

[58] For example, Sections 177–180 of the New Zealand Trade Marks Act 2002 provide for a Māori Trade Marks Advisory Committee, whose function is to advise on trademarks that include Māori texts or imagery. Australia is currently also exploring its various options for instituting an "Indigenous Advisory Panel" on IP issues.

[59] See Chapter 3 for an analysis of Geographical Indications and Cannabis.

14.2.5 Correction for Technological Asymmetries

Our second proposed recommended policy tool is to examine how the patent system might be used to mitigate the first-mover advantages of foreign corporations in cannabis innovation, which may potentially block domestic capacity development.

While early reform creates first-mover advantages, innovation head starts existed prior to the ongoing wave of cannabis commercialisation. The 1961 Single Convention obligates states to limit cannabis use to medical and scientific purposes and requires the establishment of national agencies to control the cultivation of crops so used. Investments in such research purposes and national agencies would require significant resources from developing countries dealing with issues of post-independence reconstruction and development strategies. Thus, while North-South relations are inherently defined by technological gaps facilitated by the IP system, these gaps were further reinforced by the Single Convention, specifically in medical cannabis research.

The question is now how the transition to legal markets should incorporate patent protection for industrial production, extraction processes, and medical applications. Here, perhaps some lessons may be learnt from the post-TRIPS phase of implementing pharmaceutical patents in countries which previously did not recognise such.

For pre-existing technologies, one approach is the "pipeline mechanism", which was controversially used by Brazil when implementing TRIPs-compliant patent law. It provides a transitional mechanism for the revalidation of patents granted in a foreign country, but which could not be domestically filed due to non-recognition of the subject matter under previous domestic law. Patents that benefit from this mechanism would usually be enforceable for their original term in the foreign country. The viability of this approach, however, is based on whether a country wishes to use the patent system to attract investment and technology transfer from established foreign companies; the alternative is to simply recognise the lack of novelty where the technology has been disclosed long before domestic cannabis reforms. In other words, this strategy depends on whether the strategic vision is for a craft-based industry (with a strong role for trademarks and GIs) or a commodity-based industry (with a strong role for patents).[60] Every state might be positioned differently in terms of its domestic market and potential participation in international supply chains.

For new technologies, an approach can involve drawing an analogy with the "mailbox" mechanism under TRIPs Article 70(8). Under this mechanism,

---

[60] J De Beer, A Gaffen, "Intellectual Property Rights in the Recreational Cannabis Market: Craft or Commodity" (2017) 50 UBCL Rev. 621.

a country accepts patent applications for non-protectable subject matter during the transition period, but the application is only examined after the new legislation has come into force, with the original priority date preserved. This approach can signal that a country is open to cannabis innovation but is only willing to provide protection after managing its transition to legal markets. Most importantly, it avoids the problem of restricting technological access during the legal domestic market's critical formative stages.

Both the pipeline and mailbox mechanisms only worked because the "patentability of specific subject matter" is a high-certainty determination. For cannabis-related innovations, pre-reform patent ineligibility is not necessarily so clear and might depend on a case-by-case interpretation of public order and morality exclusions as applied to regulated drugs. For the mailbox mechanism to be useful, the package of cannabis-reform policies may have to affirm that cannabis products and processes are not patentable due to illicit status but would be patentable after the transition period when domestic production capacity has been developed. This implies a counterintuitive, albeit temporary, strengthening of cannabis prohibition's IP dimensions in the process of reform. Some precedent for this radical approach can be found in Thailand, which passed reforms to permit medical cannabis in 2019. Public outrage followed when two foreign companies applied for key cannabis patents, and in response, Thailand adopted a legal order to refuse cannabis patent applications until the drug reforms came into effect.[61] However, this approach might be discordant in violating the spirit of the patent system and creates messy issues in evaluating priority dates. A possible improvement that has been proposed is a time-limited bar on post-reform patent enforcement, essentially amounting to a "limited-term subject matter eligibility exclusion for enforcement only".[62]

On a tangential note, discussions on cannabis patents should, of course also include the issue of plant breeding innovations. Most certainly, the international system for Plant Variety Protection (PVPs) provides opportunities for postcolonial states with traditions of unique strains and cross-breeding techniques. However, the international guidelines for assessing distinctiveness, uniformity, and stability – the substantive criteria for PVP protection – require applicants to supply at a minimum 50 young plants for vegetatively propagated varieties or 500 grams of seeds for seed-propagated varieties.[63] Additionally, the minimum duration of tests should normally be two independent growing cycles. PVP protection thus comes at high costs which favour industrial breeders who

---

[61] H Kellner, "Mitigating the Effects of Intellectual Property Colonialism on Budding Cannabis Markets" (2021) 28(1) Indiana Journal of Global Legal Studies 377–404, 390.

[62] ibid 396, 399.

[63] UPOV, *Testing Guidelines for Cannabis Sativa L.*, TG/276/1 Rev.

already benefit from scalability and established capital resources and is challenging for small-scale farmers. This is a constraint on the opportunities of the PVP system to give less developed states an alternative to trade in physical products by licencing protected cultivars. To resolve this challenge, postcolonial states may seek to provide institutional support for cannabis breeders in collaboration with local IP offices and cannabis authorities and create what essentially amounts to accelerator or incubator services, which reap economies of scale in breeding and PVP pre-testing infrastructure.

14.2.6 Future-proofing Traditional Knowledge

The third policy approach advocates for the protection of Traditional Knowledge (TK) in the trade for medical products.[64] Given current trends and legal realities, it is highly likely that the international market for medical cannabis will mature before an international recreational market emerges.

The conditions under which a medicinal herbal plant is cultivated can have major effects on the plant's active pharmaceutical ingredient. As such, many drug regulators adopt "Good Agricultural and Collection Practices" (GACP) guidelines for medicinal plants. GACP guidelines complement "Good Manufacturing Practice" (GMP) guidelines along the stages of herbal medicinal products' production chains. These guidelines can thus be an important regulatory tool for international trade in medicinal cannabis products.

As a reference point, the WHO has detailed GACP guidelines which can be used for formulating national guidelines.[65] Section 5.1.1 of these guidelines sets out guidance on "intellectual property rights and benefits-sharing", and allude to the complex issue of TK and genetic resources within the IP system:

> Agreements on the return of immediate and/or long-term benefits and compensation for the use of source medicinal plant materials must be discussed and concluded, in writing, prior to collection or cultivation. Contract cultivation of medicinal plants from propagation materials obtained from indigenous medicinal plants of a given country may carry varying degrees of property rights. The issue of rights of access to genetic resources is more complex, especially if the propagation materials have a long history as an item of international commerce, and are not indigenous to a given country.

Furthermore, it is recommended that "All agreements between the grower or collector, processor and purchaser, and intellectual property and benefit-sharing agreements should be recorded". The guidelines also note that future

---

64 See Chapter 12 for an analysis of Traditional Knowledge and Cannabis.

65 *WHO Guidelines on Good Agricultural and Collection Practices (GACP) for Medicinal Plants* (World Health Organization 2003).

research is needed on these complex issues and that countries are encouraged to establish national inventories of medicinal plants. The WHO-GACP guidelines thus create a link between drug regulation policy and the Nagoya Protocol of the Convention on Biological Diversity, which deals with the issues of access to genetic resources and benefit-sharing with local communities (ABS).

Unfortunately, ABS obligations are not generally incorporated into national-level GACP guidelines in major markets. In the EU, the Community Code on Medicinal Products sets out mandatory compliance with GMP guidelines, but GACP guidelines for herbal medicinal products are not strictly mandated.[66] However, the European Medicines Agency (EMA) quality guidelines for herbal medicinal products provide that GACP should be in place for the cultivation stages of production and requires that written GACP confirmation should be provided.[67] In any instance, EMA-GACP guidelines do not refer to IP or ABS compliance.[68] In the US, the Food and Drug Administration (FDA) recommends that in support of Phase 3 clinical studies of a botanical drug product, a drug sponsor should follow GACP principles in growing regions in order to ensure post-approval supply sufficiency and to assess quality and therapeutic consistency in raw materials.[69] These guidelines are, however, non-binding, and TK considerations are unlikely, given that the US has not ratified the Nagoya Protocol.

The opportunity here is that postcolonial states should incorporate medical regulation provisions into their international advocacy for the protection of TK within the IP space. Specifically, efforts might focus on lobbying import markets to adopt GACP guidelines which contain IP and ABS provisions. This would ensure that where herbal medicinal products are based on Indigenous resources over which postcolonial communities are the custodians, such communities are not excluded from the international value chain.

Admittedly, well-developed cannabis markets are already mature in terms of the wide availability of different cultivars with different cannabinoid and

---

[66] Consolidated text: *Directive 2001/83/EC of the European Parliament and of the Council of 6 November 2001 on the Community code relating to medicinal products for human use.*

[67] European Medicines Agency, *Guideline on Quality of Herbal Medicinal Products/Traditional Herbal Medicinal Products.* EMA/HMPC/CHMP/CVMP/201116/20051 Rev 3 (2022).

[68] European Medicines Agency, *Guideline on Good Agricultural and Collection Practice (GACP) for Starting Materials of Herbal Origin.* EMEA/HMPC/246816/2005.

[69] Food and Drug Administration, *Botanical Drug Development Guidance for Industry* (2016).

terpene compositions, which affect psychoactive and aromatic properties respectively. Both legal and illicit markets reflect well-developed traditions of innovation in strain breeding, and so dependence on specific Indigenous varieties is minimal. ABS provision in medical regulation might thus have little practical benefit for local communities with histories of cannabis cultivation.

Nevertheless, the goal is not just promoting historical and economic justice in relation to cannabis. Rather, the strategic interface between TK and cannabis can set a critical precedent for other regulated substances for which there are inevitably emerging global medical markets. There is immense commercial potential for medical applications of various "entheogens", that is, plants containing psychoactive substances used in traditional contexts, which are often endemic to the Global South. Current research into a variety of "ethnobotanics" is exploring the medical applications of different naturally occurring substances, which have been used for generations by Indigenous and local communities. For example, the ayahuasca plant, which is endemic to South America and known for its powerful hallucinogenic properties and use in Indigenous spiritual practices, has been subject to biopiracy concerns resulting from plant patents in the US.[70] Ayahuasca is now being explored for therapeutic applications for a range of substance abuse and mental health issues.

Many of these entheogens reflect policy histories that parallel cannabis. The issue of traditional uses of ethnobotanicals was raised in debates on expanding the Single Convention, specifically for psychedelic mushrooms containing psilocybin and peyote containing mescaline, which are now included in the schedules of the 1971 Convention.[71] The active compounds in the herbal stimulant khat – cathinone and cathine – are also under international regulatory control. Other herbal substances, such as kratom, are not under international control but fall within the national drug regulations of many states and may have commercial potential outside of their traditional cultural settings. At least one US state has laid out plans for regulated therapeutic use of psilocybin, in a development very reminiscent of cannabis reforms, which started with medical markets. Current scientific research is also examining potential uses of not only psilocybin but also dimethyltryptamine (DMT) and MDMA (the primary pharmacological ingredient in ecstasy) to treat trauma, depression, and other mental health disorders, in what is clearly a "contemporary psychedelic drug renaissance".[72]

While strengthening the links between drug reform and protecting TK as a form of quasi-IP through ABS provisions may not increase the competitiveness

---

[70] See generally: J Bosse, *Re-examining the "Wild" Story of the Ayahuasca Plant Patent* (2024) 2 Intellectual Property Quarterly 136–162.

[71] Bewley-Taylor, Jelsma (n 12) 79.

[72] GCDP (n 39) 19.

of cannabis producers in the Global South, it may at least set a critical precedent for future developments in ethnobotanical medical markets and signals an all-around gain for postcolonial justice.

14.3 CONCLUSION

It is clear that the historical legal framework for international drug regulation – and especially the inclusion of cannabis – is inherently colonial. This legal framework is rooted in social control over marginalised peoples, a misrepresentation of scientific evidence, and even racist ideologies. The legal framework for international IP also has roots in colonial power structures, though the prevalence of this basis seems less openly discussed.

Nevertheless, the histories of both international legal frameworks have a number of parallels, including power asymmetries in negotiations, the role of regulatory institutions and language framing, impacts on national policy spaces, shifting tides of national policy positions, and controversies around public health impacts. These parallels, however, are not unique to these two areas of international regulatory coordination. Rather, they both form part of the larger system of international law, which itself acts as a matrix of power that defines the political and economic relationships between the Global North and Global South.

What is unique about the interface between cannabis regulation and IP is that these power imbalances result in very specific market realities given trends in drug reform. What emerges is an unprecedented form of market development that creates specific benefits for large industrialised countries which have liberalised their cannabis markets, and are able to use the IP system to consolidate their first-mover advantages. The result is a legal and economic reality in which colonial injustice is reinforced, as developing states are unable to secure due comparative advantage in cannabis markets. It is thus imperative that postcolonial developing states approach cannabis reform with the dual goals in mind of promoting historical justice while creating equitable market structures for cannabis commercialisation.

As highlighted throughout this book, the IP system can play an important role in how cannabis is commercialised and how markets develop. What this chapter stresses, in particular, is that the IP system can be strategically utilised in plans to meet these objectives, specifically in the process of transitioning to liberalised markets. Herein, it has been suggested that important policy approaches might include documenting local cannabis practices to mitigate misappropriation, managing technological access in the transition period, and advocating for incorporating TK dimensions into medical regulations. Most certainly, further exploration will reveal a number of other ways in which IP law can be used to support equitable and just cannabis markets.

It is critical to note that IP is still just one part of the complex topic of cannabis reform. The regulatory design of licencing, labelling requirements, agricultural cooperative support, retroactive criminal justice, optimal taxation, labour standards, environmental sustainability, and an endless list of other policy concerns need to be crafted into a coherent drug reform strategy. Perhaps IP law might even have roles in these different concerns. At the international level, success in the global market may also require strategic coordination among key players in the Global South in order to compete with multinational capital interests, while still maintaining cannabis's historical role in social organisation and cultural diversity. A vision for an equitable and inclusive legal infrastructure to participate in the international Green Rush exists. Now, "build ting".

15. A history and social anthropology of the African origins of Jamaica's cannabis

Toby Leon Moorsom

15.1 INTRODUCTION

With the emergence of audio and visual media, Jamaica has gained a deep association with the cannabis plant, known colloquially as ganja. In fact, in North American popular culture, the association has become stereotype and cliché, in a manner which depoliticises, erases, and even mocks the Jamaican cultural context from which it emerged.[1] Exuberant politicians and investors talk about the brand value that Jamaica garners with hope it can be capitalised upon in international markets and tourism.[2] In the process, many appeal to notions of "authentic" Jamaican ganja as something that derives from cultivation methods, local strains, the land, plant breeding, and/or a specific manner of cultivation. The problem is, the material and cultural basis upon which one could make such a claim remain unacknowledged, and the associated genetic stock is at risk of extinction. This is a tragedy of the current moment in Jamaica's ganja history because it is likely that for a very long time, until the 1970s, there were traits of Jamaican ganja that were very specific, with it having a local (though always global) social history, as well as unique chemical,

1 DP Hope, "Gimme di Weed: Popular Music Constructions of Jamaican Identity", (2013) XIII(26) Revista Brasileira do Caribe, São Luis-MA, Brasil 341–368. IC Ramsay, "How Far Have We Come? A Comparison of Jamaican Representations in Cool Runnings and Luke Cage" (MA Dissertation, University of Texas at El Paso, Open Access Theses & Dissertations 2019) 2892.

2 "'It is Like Our Birthright' Wheatley says Jamaica must stake claim on" (*Jamaican Observer* 2018) <https://www.jamaicaobserver.com/2018/06/24/jamaica-must-stake-claim-on-local-marijuana-strains-says-wheatley/> accessed 26 March 2025.

molecular, and genetic profiles.[3] The degree to which such strains remain intact is an open question. A core facet of the intellectual content of Jamaica's original cannabis strains is that they derive from the African continent and are products of the collective labour of African peoples on the continent, in Jamaica, and in the Atlantic diaspora more broadly.

This chapter explores the historical specificity of Jamaica's cannabis and the ways its production and consumption have changed over time. First, the dominant historical narrative that ties the plant's history on the island with the arrival of East Indian indentured labourers post-emancipation, 1848, is challenged. Second, this contribution presents evidence suggesting it has a deeper history, linking it both culturally and materially to Africa. Third, this chapter argues that the preservation of the African plant in Jamaica throughout the colonial years was made possible by the fact it formed part of a wider ethnobotanical pharmacology maintained in Maroon territories in steep, inaccessible locations. Yet it was also likely linked to sub-dominant trade patterns in which Maroon production found local and international markets. The criminalisation of the plant served many functions, most of which relate to the devaluing of African labour to keep the wage rate on plantations low. Thus, it was linked to a deep historical process of demonisation and debasement of African knowledge and identity, to the past criminalisation of Obeah, to the suppression of labour resistance and lastly, to disrupt the appeal of the Rastafarian countercultural movement.

Regardless of its origins, in the early twentieth century, the plant's popularity rose alongside labour militancy and the simultaneous emergence of Rastafarianism. The two were interwoven but far from synonymous. On the latter, one must account for the dynamism and diversity of the Rastafarian religion, as well as its acephalous, non-hierarchical, and non-unified nature and its changing relationship with cannabis over time.[4] The process of listing ganja within the Dangerous Drugs Act, and the colonial government initiating a campaign of criminalisation, eradication, and enforcement was intimately tied with goals of managing labour and suppressing wages.[5] In this way, there is continuity with much earlier practices of fighting Maroon wars. In each

---

3 In the written record, Jamaican cannabis as a plant-drug is known as ganja. The terms will be used interchangeably, though one could make the case that ganja could be used to denote the specificity of cannabis grown in Jamaica.

4 R Goldson, "Ganja Struggles: Rastafari and the Contestation for Cannabis Rights in Jamaica" (2020) 55(4) Journal of Ecumenical Studies 569–594; AA Benard, "The Material Roots of Rastafarian Marijuana Symbolism" (2007) 18(1) *History and Anthropology*.

5 H Campbell, *Rasta and Resistance: From Marcus Garvey to Walter Rodney* (1st American edn., Africa World Press 1987) 94.

case, the goals were to suppress alternative livelihoods outside the plantation economy. During the Maroon wars, commencing upon British arrival in 1655, strategies of warfare involved targeted burning of their food crops and trying to gain control of territory, while, in response, Maroons burnt cane fields and pilfered food crops. In the post-emancipation era, the big planters wished to obstruct an independent peasantry and from at least as early as the 1950s, mining interests sought their removal ("downpression" in Rastafari terms). In all instances, there is evidence of Jamaican labouring classes creatively engaging in cultural resistance alongside strategies of emancipation from material impoverishment.[6] While Jamaican labourers were collaborating in strike action throughout the 1930s, they were also collaborating in ganja production, giving it wider collective meaning.[7] Consistent with Third World Approaches to International Law (TWAIL), it is evident the international legal framework built up around cannabis is one that served to entrench the structural inequalities of the slave-plantation economy long past the age of formal empire.[8]

Lastly, we consider charges of cultural appropriation and what, in genetic terms, has been defined as "bioprospecting". In liberal conceptions of capitalist property relations, appropriation can be understood as an attempt to extract intellectual property (IP) and possibly further cause "profound offence" to members of the affected culture, in part by distorting the cultural context it is extracted from and by trying to apply cultural practices in conditions markedly different from those they emerged within.[9] Bioprospecting involves finding genetic and molecular properties specific to strains that emerged within

---

[6] A Bakan, *Ideology and Class Conflict in Jamaica: The Politics and Ideology of Rebellion* (McGill-Queen's 1990) 86–89. GL Beckford, *Persistent Poverty: Underdevelopment in Plantation Economies of the Third World* (Oxford University Press 1972) 48. Beckford makes the comparison with Jamaican peasantry having the same impact as the Maroons.

[7] See Jamaica National Archives file 1B/5/77/562/1934, which details neighbourly cooperation in concealing crops and purposefully hiding crop ownership by planting on each other's land, offering deniability to the landholder.

[8] A Anghie, "Rethinking International Law: A TWAIL Retrospective" (2023) 34(1) The European Journal of International Law 7–112 <https://doi.org/10.1093/ejil/chad005>; R Kapur, "TWAIL and Alternative Visions: 'Talking About a Revolution': Afterword to the Foreword by Antony Anghie" (2023) 34(4) The European Journal of International Law 771–778 <https://doi.org/10.1093/ejil/chad054>.

[9] SE Merry, "Law, Culture, and Cultural Appropriation" (1988) 10(2) *Yale Journal of Law & the Humanities* 575–603, as quoted in W Crane, "Cultural Formation and Appropriation in the Era of Merchant Capitalism" (2018) 26(2) Historical Materialism: Research in Critical Marxist Theory 242–270 <https://doi.org/10.1163/1569206X-00001635>.

a relative degree of historical, geographic, cultural, and ecological isolation, leading to what plant biologists describe as one or more unique "land races".[10] Liberal notions of appropriation are complicated when considering Raymond Williams and Stuart Hall's theories of culture and resistance. Hall, drawing on Williams, counters essentialist claims about cultures, noting they are not discrete, ahistorical phenomena but in dialectical relationship to economic changes in modes of production. Most importantly, with the rise of capitalism, they have been deeply structured by class relations. For Williams and Hall, there are "high" and "low" cultures, though neither is fixed; they are always in contestation and informed by the precapitalist (e.g., feudal) forms that preceded them.[11] As Hall writes:

> The meaning of a cultural symbol is given in part by the social field into which it is incorporated, the practices with which it articulates and is made to resonate. What matters is not the intrinsic or historically fixed objects of culture, but the state of play in cultural relations: to put it bluntly … the class struggle in and over culture.[12]

Most rural Jamaicans grasp this in reference to cannabis, as is evident in the words of a prominent activist in support of legalisation since the 1970s, Ras Iyah V, as he states, "the majority of people who used ganja are working class people, which is why it was looked down upon".[13]

To accommodate the dynamism of culture, it is helpful to ground the analysis with reference to human labour accumulated from the past, in this case, congealed in genetic code and now a target of capitalist extraction and exploitation. While differing cultural practices around cannabis can exist within the realm of ideas, they are never separate from the labouring bodies that produce and consume the plant. As the cultures of production and consumption have shifted, and perhaps become more globalised, so too have the genetic stock and production methods.[14] Two additional Marxist concepts can help us examine changes in the production of the plant. These are the notion of alienation – which is a multi-faceted concept for Marx and coincides with processes of

---

[10] C Duvall, *The African Roots of Marijuana* (Duke University Press 2019) 212–222.

[11] Crane (n 9); S Hall, "Notes on Deconstructing 'The Popular'" in J Storey (ed.) *Cultural Theory and Popular Culture: A Reader* (Pearson/Prentice Hall 1998) 449.

[12] Hall (n 11).

[13] Interview, 9 February 2023.

[14] For this reason, many long-time Jamaican producers believe they can claim to produce authentically "Jamaican" cannabis, even though they have relied on imported, often hybrid seed stock.

"primitive accumulation"[15] whereby labour is separated from the means of production and capital (owners) extract (rob) value from non-capitalist spheres ("the commons") creating, in turn, propertyless labourers.[16] While capitalists may capture genetic content through biopiracy/bioprospecting, it coincides with larger processes of dispossession in which the rural producer is robbed of their livelihood and, in turn, subjected to multiple forms of alienation.[17] The prison is an obvious institution that robs someone of their personal autonomy, their connection to fellow labourers, family, and means of production (land, labour). Additionally, in its current iteration, through decriminalisation and legalisation of medical marijuana, the IP surrounding the plant must be questioned: IP refers to the expression of ideas, yet the historical usage is linked to the labouring bodies that first used the plant, not the capitalist class exploiting its commercial use today.

In this manner, the accumulated labour of past generations that has been archived in Jamaica's cannabis seed stock has been subjected to a historical process of dispossession, in which the small-scale producers whose fore-parents developed the seed stock have lost control of it, and capital accumulates mostly to those who have and maintain reliable genetics, namely seed and cloning stock.[18] International law has played a very large role in this process of dispossession and sits amidst an IP and property regime that systematically empowers global corporations who extract such genetic material from peoples in the "Global South" who themselves lack the legal and material capacity to protect and benefit from the product of their collective labour. In the Jamaican context, the terms of licensing for producers have played a significant role in

---

[15] The term "primary" or "original" better grasps what he intended in its original German "ursprünglich".

[16] W Bonefeld, "Capitalist Accumulation and Its Historical Foundation and Logical Premise: On Primitive Accumulation" (2023) 51(1) Critique 197–215 <https://doi.org/10.1080/03017605.2023.2267281>; K Marx, *Capital: A Critique of Political Economy Volume I*, Part VIII: Primitive Accumulation (1st edn., Progress Publishers 1887) 1.

[17] Separated from the creative labour process, from nature, the product of their labour, and their fellow labourers – whom they now meet in competition rather than through cooperative social bonds.

[18] A Klein, V Hanson, "Ganja Licencing in Jamaica: Learning Lessons and Setting Standards" (International Drug Policy Consortium, 24 April 2020); A Klein, R Marta, MA Emanuel, "Towards Social Justice and Economic Empowerment? Exploring Jamaica's Progress with Implementing Cannabis Law Reform" (2022) 43(11) Third World Quarterly 2693–2711; M Rychert, MA Emanuel, C Wilkins, "Foreign Investment in Emerging Legal Medicinal Cannabis Markets: the Jamaica Case Study" (2021) 17 Globalisation and Health 38.

preventing such benefits.[19] Capitalists are also internally divided, with larger, more globally connected producers today are capturing regional market share from those more deeply embedded in the rural economy of Jamaica.[20]

15.2 SCRUTINISING THE INDIAN ORIGIN STORY

It is widely claimed that cannabis arrived in Jamaica with Indian indentured labourers following emancipation in 1838. This is evident in the 2018 Report of the CARICOM Regional Commission on Marijuana: *Waiting to Exhale – Safeguarding our Future through Responsible Socio-Legal Policy*, which summed up the entire history of the plant prior to 1913 with one sentence. It states, "It was introduced during the post-emancipation period to the Caribbean countries of Guyana, Jamaica, and Trinidad and Tobago by East Indian indentured labourers".[21] This fact was recently described as "common sense" by an Indian diplomat to Jamaica.[22] This section argues that while this East Indian migration plays an important part of the story of Jamaica's cannabis history, it is very likely the plant arrived earlier and was imported by Africans, prior to 1838 and possibly even before 1655. This contribution presents material evidence that challenges this story and goes further to explore the anthropological links to patterns of use on the African continent. The historical specificity of Jamaica's cannabis almost certainly derives from the ingenuity of African cultivators transplanting and adapting African seed stock in the period between 1502 and 1848. The likely introduction of East Indian strains arriving with indentured labourers may have led to hybridisation of existing stock and could be responsible for the comparatively high THC content relative to the landraces in central Africa from which Jamaica's early stock derives.

Within the archival records, the earliest source supporting the claim that cannabis seeds had been transported by East Indian labourers is in a report by Chief Magistrate Christopher Hill in 1862, on the conditions of Indian

---

19 Klein, Hanson 2020 (n 18); Klein et al. 2022 (n 18).

20 I address this in § Moorsom, T.L. (2024) "Jamaican Ganja Farmers Face Extinction(s): Grassroots Activists Seek a 'Jamsterdam' Resuscitation", *The Journal of Peasant Studies*, DOI: 10.1080/03066150.2024.2424857

21 CARICOM Secretariat, *Report of the CARICOM Regional Commission on Marijuana 2018: Waiting to Exhale – Safeguarding our Future through Responsible Socio-Legal Policy on Marijuana* (Georgetown, Guyana 2018).

22 P Misra, "Rastafari: The Indian Connection" *Jamaica Gleaner* (26 March 2021) https://jamaica-gleaner.com/article/focus/20210326/prathit-misra-rastafari-indian-connection accessed 26 March 2025.

labourers on Jamaican plantations.[23] The report describes general living and working conditions, hours and rates of pay relative to other employees, housing, healthcare, and deductions for lodging, rations, and clothing, as well as provision grounds on many estates. In one specific case of the Tulluch Estate, he remarks that "Hindoo immigrants ...were carefully cultivating the Indian Hemp – Cannabis Indica, for the purpose of purchasing the powerful narcotic known as gunjah …".[24] In commenting on its effects, the magistrate cites James Johnson's *The Chemistry of Common Life* (1855), which also notes that "in Central and Tropical Africa it is almost everywhere known as a powerful medicine and desired indulgence". Outside of the quotation, he adds, "the Congo Africans use it in preference to tobacco. It is known to them by the name fuomo". It is not clear if this is in reference to those Congo Africans in Jamaica or if he is still drawing from the Johnson source. He adds that:

> The growing of Indian hemp is the only garden cultivation I have seen among the Hindoos. … Their indifference to gardening is a strong contrast to the Chinese immigrants, and to the Africans who are careful to plant ground provisions and farinaceous fruits.[25]

Based on this, it is demonstrated that both Indians and Africans grew and used cannabis, and that for the Indians, it was linked to religious practice. We can assume some Indians travelled with the seed, but we cannot exclude the possibility it was already present. In fact, based on the Hill report, it is not clear if it was practised widely by Indian immigrants because he describes conditions on dozens of plantations and singles out the Tulloch estate for this oddity.

It is next discussed in 1896 there are three references in the Gleaner newspaper. The first noting use by both populations and making the first claim Africans learned it from Indians. A plantation owner describes Indian labourers planting it outside their dwellings and notes its use is compatable with the work cycle. The government 'Protector of Immigrants', P.C. Cork, suggests the 'evils of ganja smoking are exaggerated' as its use has 'compensating advantages'. He also assumes 'the immigrants must have brought out the seeds with them from India'. Cork further notes the Jamaican government was waiting for 'the report of the Indian Commission' to determine the response 'we should take here', bringing weight to the claim that the term 'ganja' may have been

[23] National Archives (UK), Public Records Office, Kew, File C137/C368/C579914; Duvall (n 10) 149.

[24] National Archives (n 23) 223.

[25] ibid.

introduced from the top-down, as Bilby suggested in 1985. Aside from these citations, there is little evidence ganja was exclusively Indian.[26]

The earliest recorded arrests in association with it are of Black Jamaicans, in 1902 in Spanish Town, and 1907 in Morant Bay. By 1911, a presumably black clergyman was reported as gaining 'marvelous inspiration' from it and whose 'church was always packed'. By 1912, evangelical churches petitioned against its use, noting it was 'very largely used by West Indians and East Indians'. In 1913, when opium laws were being ammended to include cannabis, it was noted 'this vice is much indulged by East Indians and members of the lower classes'. The 1913 legal ammendment lists it as 'cannabis sativa', a taxonomical categorization defining it as a narrow leaf, tall growing plant, in comparison to the wide-leaf, short plants dominant on the Indian sub-continent. By this decade the Gleaner reports arrests of Africans and East Indians, although notably, Indian links were almost always in Kingston, with Kingston Pen being identified by a Sergeant Major as a place where 'very much ganja' was being grown.[27]

A *Jamaican Times* article initially published in 1929 and reprinted by *The Star* in March 1972 describes widespread cultivation among Jamaican peasants before any available police records in the (Jamaican) National Archives and Records Office. It also notes its trafficking to Panama and the United States (US). This is significant because it reveals widespread production and use pre-dating the rise of Rastafarianism, and that it was regionally traded. From at least as early as the late 1950s, *The Star* newspaper published a litany of sensationalist pieces about its cultivation and trade, of which many were published under the pseudonym "the Saint". None of these articles describe Indian involvement, though some describe production within the Maroon communities.

While newspapers may have popularised the Indian origin story, most assertions in academic literature rely upon repeated references to two limited studies based on cultural and linguistic associations. One derives from the British Colonial Government in a 1933 report to the League of Nations, while

---

[26] C Duvall 2019, The African Roots of Marijuana. Croydon: Duke University Press p. 149, National Archives UK, C137/C368/C579914, TL Moorsom "Jamaican Ganja Farmers Face Extinction(s): Grassroots Activists Seek a 'Jamsterdam' Resuscitation", The Journal of Peasant Studies, 2024. DOI: 10.1080/03066150.2024.2424857 p386, Bilby, K. 1985. "The Holy Herb: Notes on the Background of Cannabis in Jamaica." The Caribbean Quarterly Monograph (no volume number): 82–95. DOI: 10.1080/03066150.2024.2424857 p386, K Bilby, 1985. "The Holy Herb: Notes on the Background of Cannabis in Jamaica." The Caribbean Quarterly Monograph (no volume number): 82–95.

[27] This paragraph is a compressed version of one in Moorsom (2024) (n 20).

another is drawn from an otherwise excellent, wide-ranging study conducted in the early 1970s by Vera Rubin and Lambros Comitas, with funds from the National Institute of Mental Health, in Rockville, Maryland, US. Following its presentation to parliamentary committees, much of the report was published in serial form in the largest newspaper, the *Daily Gleaner*, between June and August 1972, and eventually as a monograph in 1975 titled *Ganja in Jamaica*. While it detailed widespread cultivation among rural Jamaicans, it describes the involvement of only one East Indian family in the area studied.[28] The Indian origin story is again repeated in *The Gleaner* in 1989 in an article on the "History of Ganja in Jamaica".[29] Again, no material evidence is offered; however, they do add that "At that time it was either brewed as a medicinal tea, or applied externally as an ointment", suggesting that smoking emerged thereafter. A few years later, one of Jamaica's most important historians also makes the Indian origin claim in her book devoted to the experiences of East Indians in Jamaica.[30] Yet Shepherd also fails to cite any supporting evidence, and the topic never arises in descriptions of culture and religious festivals, supporting the assertion of its use in such practices. In files of newspapers on East Indians in Jamaica in the National Library of Jamaica from 1900 to the present, there is not one reference to the smoking or growing of ganja, though elsewhere Mansingh and Mansingh have also noted its consumption among Indians.[31]

Aside from Shepherd and Mansingh, there is a relative dearth of academic study on the experiences of East Indian descendants in Jamaica. One significant PhD dissertation in Anthropology was published in 1969 by Ehrlich, under the supervision of the lauded and iconoclastic anthropologist Eric R. Wolf. It was based on research conducted from August 1966 to December 1967 among rural East Indian labourers in the sugarcane industry in Westmoreland, the portion of the country with the highest density of East Indian labourers at the time.

Ehrlich found there was little cultural integration between rural East Indian labourers and African Jamaicans, with animosities based on racist plantation work structures pervading social life in the village. Yet at the same time, there

---

[28] V Rubin, L. Comitas, "A Study of the Effects of Chronic Smoking of Cannabis in Jamaica" *The Gleaner* (24 June 1972) 3, 22, 23 (not all page numbers are visible).

[29] "History of Ganja in Jamaica" *The Gleaner* (4 October 1989).

[30] V Shepherd, *Transients to Settlers: The Experience of Indians in Jamaica, 1845–1950* (Peepal Tree 1994) 127.

[31] L Mansingh, A Ajai Mansingh, *Home Away from Home: 150 Years of Indian Presence in Jamaica, 1845–1995* (Ian Randle Publishers 1999); see also H Lee, *The First Rasta: Leonard Howell and the Rise of Rastafarianism* (Lawrence Hill Books 1999) 85.

were few remaining cultural distinctions between the groups, with Indians having been "completely absorbed into the mainstream of Jamaican rural life". Having been assimilated, he found "no clusters of activities around which the Indians can overtly exhibit their ethnicity".[32] What was notable about this community is that in the recent past, they had access to unused estate land in the Black River Morass, where they once grew rice, cane, and other crops, yet there is not one mention of them growing cannabis, though there is ample newspaper documentation of extensive production within the Morass throughout the following decade. After the sugar estate evicted them, they faced greater poverty and half the year without work. Yet, they never mention the growing of ganja as an alternative crop. As one informant explained: "Half of the year, you just ping-pong. You sit and talk a little, play some dominoes, drink, find a little day work, and just jump around from one thing to another – just ping-pong."[33] Furthermore, Ehrlich writes,

> While most of the villagers do have a square or two of land around their homes in which they have planted some of the local ground provisions – calilu, badu, yam, coco, okra, gunga peas, dasheen, and, other local foods – these gardens can hardly be thought of as income-producing units. The quantities of produce grown are too small to think of them as "crops".[34]

It is possible the author chose to omit any mention of ganja to protect informants, but this is unlikely given his methods involved false place names and pseudonyms. Regardless, there are two facts one can draw from this. The first is that in rural Westmoreland, an area considered the centre of contemporary cannabis cultivation, there were no discernible Indian influences assimilated among the wider working classes. On the level of crops, we know that Indians were agents in bringing rice cultivation, yet here they are described as absorbing the African and Taino staples.

The East Indian community in Westmoreland described by Ehrlich was apparently different from that in the parish of Clarendon, and from those urban East Indians in Kingston Pen; an area settled after 1920, consisting of Newland, Ackee Walk, Back-O-Wall, Grassyard, and Maranga Lane.[35] The Mansinghs

32 A Ehrlich, "East Indian Cane Workers in Jamaica" (PhD thesis, University of Michigan 1969) 121, citing J Hearn, "European Heritage and Asian Influence in Jamaica" in J Hearne and R Nettleford (eds) *Public Affairs in Jamaica: Our Heritage* (Vol. 1, The University of the West Indies, Department of Extra-Mural Studies, 1963) 7–34.

33 ibid 64.

34 ibid.

35 Chapter 3 considers whether it is better to have regional GIs such as "Westmoreland cannabis" rather than a nationwide "Jamaica cannabis".

describe Kingston Pen as becoming the "centre of Hinduism and Indian culture in Jamaica".[36] Many authors suggest East Indian cultural activities taking place in Clarendon could have influenced Leonard P. Howell, one of the founders of Rastafarian thought.[37] Howell would continue to be exposed to Indian, and particularly Hindu thought, even adopting a name derived from Hindi, Gungunguru Maragh, under which he published a foundational Rastafarian text, *The Promised Key*.[38] Hindu thought also certainly influenced Rastafarian adoption of vegetarianism, some spices, and most importantly a comprehension of metaphysics and cosmology that shows intimate exchange with people of Indian descent in Jamaica. There is also evidence Indian immigrants introduced post-harvest curing methods, picked up by other Jamaicans.[39] The Indian name for a small tubular smoking pipe, "chillum" has also been used to describe a Jamaican coconut pipe, though the latter is very different.

Although Back-O-Wall was within the area described by the Mansinghs, some Rastafari living there did not subscribe to the East Indian origin story. Ras Campbell, "chairman and principal speaker" at a well-attended meeting held by Ras Tafari Brethren United Front of Back-o-Wall, Western Kingston, on 5 June 1963, was cited by *The Star*:

> Rastafarians were entitled to their herb as they are nationals of Ethiopia and ganja is an important factor in their culture ... most of the fruit trees and other plants in Jamaica were brought from Africa which was also the continent of origin of ganja; yet, ... no ban was placed on the other plants.[40]

As important as these East Indian influences are in Jamaica, the prevailing evidence cannot explain the much richer documentation and actual material evidence of widespread cultivation among Jamaican peasantry and, most notably, in large quantities, among Maroon peoples, who in the earliest records were the primary producers. Overlooking this fact is an injustice that undermines

---

36 Mansingh and Mansingh (n 31) 79; Shepherd (n 30) 111, D Stewart, "Early Encounters in Colonial Jamaica: Hindu and Rastafari Divine Metaphysics" (2021) 32 *The Journal of Interreligious Studies* 51.

37 M Barnett, "Interrogating Leonard Howell as the 'First Rasta'" in C A Hutten et al. (eds) *Leonard Percival Howell and the Genesis of Rastafari* (Kingston, University of the West Indies Press 2015); RA Hill, *Dread History: Leonard P. Howell and Millenarian Visions in the Early Rastafarian Religion* (Chicago Research Associates School Times Publications/Frontline Distribution 2001); Lee (n 31) 84–86; Stewart (n 36).

38 Among his followers, Gungunguru would be colloquialised as "Gong", referring to his role as a "great teacher" or king.

39 Rubin, Comitas (n 28).

40 "Ganja said Factor in Rasta Culture" *The Star* (6 June 1963).

the ingenuity and ethnobotanical knowledge deriving from Africa, within which cannabis formed only a small part.

15.3 THE HIDDEN HISTORIES OF AFRICAN CANNABIS

A growing body of evidence suggests the seeds may have been transported to the island from the African continent, quite likely by Africans themselves. In fact, as our understanding of the early colonial period deepens, one can see so many opportunities for it to have landed prior to 1848; it would be unlikely if it had not. As a result, this chapter argues that the Indian influences in Jamaican cannabis history distort or overlay its deeper association with Africans, particularly those from Central African ancestry. Not only has there been a process of denial or erasure of the intellectual contributions of Africa, but there has also been further harm towards people deriving from Central Africa, whose histories were sublimated in narratives that valorise those arriving from West Africa. Resurrecting cannabis histories, to some degree, demands a re-examination of the role of Central African culture in the Caribbean to place it on the mantel alongside those from West Africa, while in turn doing the same for the under-recognised contributions of North Africans within Caribbean history.

Based on his observations of Kumina cultural practices in Jamaica, the anthropologist Kenneth Bilby suggested the plant may have arrived with African indentured labourers, post-emancipation, who were re-captives from Sierra Leone, taken first from Central Africa.[41] He suggests the adoption of the Indian term, "ganja" was likely an import by the British Administration, and noted local variants of "Diambo", a term used widely across Africa with local variations. Historical geographer Christopher Duvall agrees the term was likely imported to the Caribbean by the British.[42] His landmark book documents the use of the plant on the African continent from 2500 BCE in East Africa (for the Rasta giving some weight to the claim it grew on King Solomon's grave) and from at least 700 BCE in Southern Africa. In fact, Duvall provides convincing evidence cannabis use as a smoked drug was in fact an African innovation, with the coconut water pipe being widely dispersed across the southern half of the continent.[43] While identifiable groups arrived post-emancipation, Kumina

[41] K Bilby, "The Holy Herb: Notes on the Background of Cannabis in Jamaica" in R Nettleford, "Rastafari" *The Caribbean Quarterly*, Monograph, (University of West Indies Press 1985) 82–95.

[42] Duvall (n 10) 133.

[43] ibid 69.

songs and culture are still evident within the Windward Maroons, even if it holds less prominence than West African influences.[44]

Jamaican Rastafarians commonly use an innovation of the coconut or calabash pipe known as the "Steam Chalice" in sacrament and "reasoning sessions", which adds a vaporising chamber, an innovation that would merit IP protection. The name makes reference to the cup from which many Christians drink wine as analogy to the blood of Christ. Without a wine industry, it is logical Jamaicans would find an alternate valued commodity, especially so when it was commonplace for Central Africans to use the verb "to drink" in describing the act of smoking.[45] The steam chalice prevents the burning of the herb by adding a fired clay sieve over which charcoal is placed, similar to a Middle Eastern and North African hookah, except that in the latter, tobacco is burned, not vapourized. It is possible the North African hookah influenced pipes in East and Central Africa "either by way of the fifteenth century Zimbabwe and Swahili Coast trade with India, or by way of the later Arab slave and ivory trade".[46] They could have also arrived in Jamaica via early Moorish ancestry among Maroons.[47] Yet, this vaporising technology has also existed in Central Africa. For example, the Ovimbundu and the Bachokwe, from the area of present-day Angola, made use of it when smoking "hemp", by using a layer of large-grained sand or tin to prevent its burning.[48]

As noted above, sometimes the chalice is called a "chillum", the same name used for a much smaller Indian pipe associated with some Hindu practices. Warner-Lewis[49] and Bilby[50] note the commonalities between Myal and Rastafari use of cannabis in practices of worship with those of lower-caste Hindu practices, which both involve sitting around a central pipe. However, the African versions involve a water pipe, while the Hindus historically used a small clay pipe. Warner-Lewis sees stronger links to African use of hallucinogens and cannabis in religious activity, leading her to suspect the Indian

---

[44] K Bilby, *Music of the Maroons of Jamaica* (recorded and annotated by KM Bilby, Johns Hopkins, Folkway Records 1981) 5; B Carey, *The Maroon Story* (Agouti Press 1997); O Lewin, *Rock It Come Over: The Folk Music of Jamaica* (University of the West Indies Press 2000) 147–177, 215–253.

[45] M Warner-Lewis, *Central Africa in the Caribbean* (UWI Press 2003) 84.

[46] M Warner-Lewis, "African Continuities in the Rastafari Belief System" (1993) 39(3/4) Caribbean Quarterly 114.

[47] Ā Sulatānā, *Invisible yet Invincible: The Islamic Heritage of the Maroons and the Enslaved Africans in Jamaica* (Austin & Macauley 2012).

[48] Warner-Lewis (n 45) 84.

[49] Warner-Lewis (n 46) 114.

[50] Bilby (n 41).

influence may better be classified as "a reinforcement of subdominant trends in African cultural behaviour".

Figure 15.1 shows a contemporary Jamaican steam chalice, alongside a calabash pipe from Zambia of unknown date (purchased used in 2007), and a simple clay pipe of the Tonga people in Southern Zambia. The calabash pipe may also be of Tonga origin, though the author was told by the seller (when purchasing used, and possibly already antique, in 2008) it was from Zambia's Northwestern Province, where it may have derived from Lunda, Mbunda, or any other peoples bordering Zambia, Angola, and Congo DRC. Similar designs exist across the southern continent, including among the Makonde of Kenya, Tanzania, and Mozambique. Cultural practices vary, though the small Tonga pipe is used individually, while the more ornamental calabash pipe is more likely to be used collectively and ceremonially in a fashion comparable to the Jamaican Chalice. It is also more likely to be owned by someone with higher status. Among the Tonga of the Gwembe Valley, women make use of ornate calabash pipes for individual consumption. In central Africa, both tobacco and cannabis are consumed in the pipe, though many Christian denominations have created stigma around the use of the latter. Nevertheless, it remains common, especially among the elderly who may seek therapeutic effects.

The relative lack of documentary records that could corroborate the argument of African origins must be considered. As Duvall notes, for various reasons, the documentary record of its use in Africa "poorly reflects the plant's

Source: Toby Leon Moorsom, 2024.

Figure 15.1 *Photo of Jamaican steam chalice, a calabash pipe from Zambia, and a clay pipe from the Tonga people in Southern Zambia*

dispersal chronologically".[51] One, reason is the fact it tended to be used by the poorest, who also had reason to hide it (as was the case in Jamaica[52]). In the absence of such records, Duvall makes use of pollen evidence in archaeological artefacts, while also cataloguing and analysing an exhaustive linguistic data set and using archival data only for the years they become available late in the slaving period, after the 1840s for most locations. He finds variants of Diambo as early as the 1580s in Mozambique, where some of the earliest captives brought to Jamaica would have embarked, in a period when Portugal was responsible for transporting 75 per cent of those trafficked prior to 1641, had contracts with the Spanish King, and continued to supply the British well into their tenure as governors of the island.[53] Many Portuguese even migrated to Jamaica under the Spanish, after 1580.[54]

To be clear, Duvall argues that a narrow-leaf Cannabis *Indica* came to the Americas with enslaved people, and "to more locations and for a longer period of time than any other group of migrants".[55] Most of its dispersal to the Americas was with African captives from Central Africa after 1730, while its association with West African slaves occurred post-1800, the point at which it arrived from southern dispersal on land and with recaptives, some who would have been brought from Brazil, where the largest number of Central Africans disembarked, and where its documented use begins in 1749.[56] Many of the

---

51 ibid 127.

52 Rubin, Comitas (n 28).

53 According to UNESCO cataloguing, which misses large numbers of those transported on undocumented vessels, Duvall (n 10) 131 <https://slaveryandremembrance.org/>; on the latter, see (Knight, 170).

54 Knight (a slave trader) never acknowledges the presence of Africans in their numbers, yet notes their presence under the Spanish, and existing in rebellion, Carey (n 44) 38–50; J Knight, *The Natural, Moral, and Political History of Jamaica, and the Territories Thereon Depending: From the First Discovery of the Island by Christopher Columbus to the Year 1746* (JP Greene ed., University of Virginia Press 2021) 52–56.

55 Duvall (n 26) 125. Duvall argues the strain coming from Africa was actually an *Indica*, even though within Jamaica it has long been described as a *Sativa*, differing from the wide leaf varieties common within the Indian subcontinent. Duvall's term is supported by the taxonomy of geneticists as well: RC Clarke, MD Merlin, "Cannabis Domestication, Breeding History, Present-day Genetic Diversity, and Future Prospects" (2016) 35(5–6) Critical Reviews in Plant Sciences 293–327 <doi:10.1080/07352689.2016.1267498>; J Sawler, JM Stout, KM Gardner, D Hudson, J Vidmar, L Butler, JE Page, S Myles, "The Genetic Structure of Marijuana and Hemp" (2015) 10(8) PLoS One e0133292 <doi:10.1371/journal.pone.0133292> PMID: 26308334; PMCID: PMC4550350.

56 Duvall (n 26) 144–149.

medicinal plants valued by slaves travelled as weeds, alongside desired crops (such as maize), though Duvall does find a record of a slave departing from the area of Gabon, possessing cannabis seeds intended for transport from the mid -1850s.[57] There is widespread documentation of captive Africans transporting seeds, which Duvall points to with rice, pasture grasses, and medicinal ethnobotany being prominent.[58] Cannabis' links with the slave trade were extensive by the early 1800s, sometimes even being encouraged by slavers bringing captives from Angola because it was considered to "support the strength and condition" of the enslaved.[59] There are reasons, however, to consider a variety of routes through which it may have travelled, which include the possibility that at least some of Jamaica's ancestral plant genetics arrived prior to 1655, and at other times with non-enslaved Africans or enslaved Africans operating with significant levels of freedom within the regional and Atlantic world economies. Any gene stock travelling these routes could also have been cross-fertilised with industrial hemp being grown in Jamaica for supplying the shipping industry, with records in the British National Archives, dating from as early as 1709.[60] This might partly explain the high CBD percentages found in strains from Accompong in the *High Times* Cannabis cup of 2015.[61]

The historian Alfred Crosby is known for his work on the *Colombian Exchange* and *Ecological Imperialism*, in which he describes the spread of "neo-Europes", whereby imperial agents knowingly and unknowingly took with them a range of biota: feral animals, weeds, and pathogens.[62] For Crosby, "So successful was ... [the European colonist] that he accomplished what was probably the greatest biological revolution in the Americas since the end of the Pleistocene era".[63] Despite the triumphalist language, the credit for such successes, however, was attributable to unintended travellers that inadvertently "made possible the Europeanization of the whole lands". Such statements overlook the fact that for Crosby, Africans shared with Europeans a history of animal domestication, which led to the co-evolution of pathogens and immunity

57 ibid. 143.

58 ibid. 42, 148, 287.

59 ibid. 147.

60 British National Archives, ADM 106/639/88.

61 N Escondido, "Jamaican Cannabis Uncovered Part I: Quantifying & Analyzing Jamaican Strains" *High Times* (24 November 2015) 11, 20, 23 <https://hightimes.com/grow/jamaican-cannabis-uncovered-part-i-quantifying-analyzing-jamaican-strains/>.

62 A Crosby, *Ecological Imperialism: The Biological Expansion of Europe, 900–1900* (New edn, Cambridge University Press 2004) 149.

63 AW Crosby, *The Columbian Exchange: Biological and Cultural Consequences of 1492* (Greenwood Press 1972) 66; Crosby (n 62).

not shared by Native Americans and Polynesians. Yet Crosby does not offer the same triumphalist narrative to Africans surviving in the "New World". The Bantu, he claims, "have prospered because they survived military conquest, avoided the conquerors, or became their indispensable servants – and in the long run because they reproduced in greater numbers than the whites".[64] Challenging the passivity accorded to Africans in Crosby's account, historians are increasingly finding that despite the hostile conditions of the Atlantic world in the centuries of the slave trade, Africans did, nevertheless, have a great deal more agency than tends to be recognised. They too brought their own biological package and related ontological systems, in the form of a very wide variety of pharmacologically useful plants as well as commercial and food crops.[65]

In addition to linguistic and material evidence suggesting the cannabis plant travelled to the Americas with Africans, the plant's uses in Jamaica coincide with a broad pattern of consumption throughout Southern Africa among those employed in hard labour. Contrary to stereotypes of the plant promoting lethargy, the strains in Southern Africa were stimulants, being used like coffee to energise, suppress appetite, and provide analgesia during a break from hard labour. According to Duvall, it was a "labour enhancer" among culturally marginalised people who occupied hazardous environments of disease, malnutrition, dangerous work, poor housing, and psychological trauma.[66] For this reason, it was given as rations to labourers by some Portuguese plantation owners in Southern Africa, and there are records of it being given to slaves during transport to the coast. In the first 100 years of Portuguese engagement in Central Africa, this was their prominent source of slaves, as they allied with the Kongo and Ndongo Kingdoms. These slaves comprised the earliest labourers shipped to El Mina (Gold Coast), followed by the first sugar plantations in

---

[64] Crosby (n 62) 147.

[65] JA Carney, *Black Rice: The African Origins of Rice Cultivation in the Americas* (Harvard University Press 2001); JA Carney, RN Rosemoff, *In the Shadow of Slavery: Africa's Botanical Legacy in the Atlantic World* (University of California Press 2009); JJ Parsons, "Spread of African Pastures to the American Tropics" (1972) 25(1) Journal of Range Management 12–17; RA Voeks, *Sacred Leaves of Candomble: African Magic, Medicines and Religion in Brazil* (University of Texas Press 1997); RA Voeks, J Rashford (eds) *African Ethnobotany in the Americas* (Springer 2013). Within "ontological systems", one could of course add musical forms, as for example, FW Evans, *Congo Square: African Roots in New Orleans* (2011).

[66] Duvall (n 10) 160; CS Duvall, "Drug Laws, Bioprospecting and the Agricultural Heritage of Cannabis in Africa" (2016) 20(1) Space & Polity 10–25 <https://doi.org/10.1080/13562576.2016.1138674>.

Sao Tome, and then, after 1532, increasingly towards the Caribbean.[67] Trade from Benin would have also included the Bantu-speaking enslaved population that had a shared language structure, vocabulary, and some cultural practices with most peoples throughout the southern portion of the continent. These histories cannot inform claims of IP if they are not acknowledged. Furthermore, if products derived from Jamaican strains are used in a context in which IP indications function disproportionately in favour of Multinational Enterprises (MNEs) within the "Global North" and not in the service of those in the Global South[68] such as Jamaica, the global patenting system is structurally asymmetrical[69] and represents a form of erasure and violence against those whose labour brought the plant into the present: a form of dispossession.

15.4 HIDDEN HISTORIES OF CENTRAL AFRICANS IN THE CARIBBEAN AND THEIR WIDER IMPLICATIONS

Beyond the smoking of hemp, Warner-Lewis shows how Central African culture is deeply rooted in the Caribbean, despite being overshadowed by associated cultural linkages with West Africa. Central Africans comprised the greater part of the earliest slaves brought to the Caribbean, thus their cultural impacts in the Caribbean are the deepest. Often this is obfuscated by the fact that the British planter class became particularly fixated on the perceived benefits and risks of acquiring "Coromantee/Kromantee" slaves, brought from the Gold Coast, which in turn fed into a wider mythology of Jamaican

[67] C Ehret, *The Civilizations of Africa: A History to 1800* (University Press of Virginia 2002) 165–173; E Gilbert, JT Reynolds, *Africa in World History: From Prehistory to the Present* (3rd edn., Pearson 2012) 180–190; K Shillington, *History of Africa* (Rev 2nd edn., Palgrave-Macmillan 2005) 173.

[68] D Lea, The Expansion and Restructuring of Intellectual Property and Its Implications for the Developing World (2008) 11(1) *Ethical Theory and Moral Practice* 37–60 <https://doi.org/10.1007/s10677-007-9084-4>; Y Williams, "Intellectual Property Rights to Maximise Jamaica's Creations" *Jamaica Gleaner* (22 October 2023) <https://jamaica-gleaner.com/article/focus/20231022/yentyl-williams-intellectual-property-rights-maximise-jamaicas-creations> accessed 2 September 2024.

[69] Y Friedman, "Intellectual Property and Biotechnology Innovation: To Protect or Not Protect?" (2009) 15(4) Journal of Commercial Biotechnology 285–286 <https://doi.org/10.1057/jcb.2009.22>.

unruliness.[70] This reputation had, however, already existed from its earliest days.[71] Most of the earliest arrivals with the British had already been enslaved in Barbados and Suriname.[72] Dunn and Patterson cite a series of slave revolts in the late 1600s, which Patterson argues should be seen as part of one continuous war.[73] He cites three uprisings in particular that were understood to comprise predominantly slaves from the Gold Coast – mostly Ashanti and Dahomey, therefore arriving from expansionary warring empires resulting in many skilled soldiers being captured and sold.[74] It is true that between 1661 and 1760, British importation of slaves from the Gold Coast increased enormously. They came from a mix of ethnolinguistic groups, but when sold under the term Coromantee or Kromantyn, they fetched a higher price, causing some sellers to lie about their origins. As significant as the Coromantee influence was, they only represented 19 per cent of those imported in those years.[75] The disproportionate attention given to their members[76] can prevent us from understanding the divisions and exchanges within Maroon groups and cause us to miss the influences of others.[77]

---

70 V Brown, *Tacky's Revolt: The Story of an Atlantic Slave War* (Belknap Press 2020); E O'Neal, *Obeah, Race and Racism: Caribbean Witchcraft in the English Imagination* (University of the West Indies Press 2020); Warner-Lewis (n 45).

71 T Burnard, "Those Other English Colonies: The Historiography of Jamaica in the Time of James Knight" in Knight (n 54); RS Dunn, *Sugar and Slaves: The Rise of the Planter Class in the English West Indies, 1624–1713* (1st edn., Omohundro Institute of Early American History & Culture/The University of North Carolina Press/The University of West Indies Press 1972); RS Dunn, "'Dreadful Idlers' in the Cane Fields: The Slave Labor Pattern on a Jamaican Sugar Estate, 1762–1831" (1987) 17(4) The Journal of Interdisciplinary History 795–822 <https://doi.org/10.2307/204654>.

72 GW Bridges, *Annals of Jamaica* (1862); Dunn *Sugar and Slaves* (n 71) 157; M Curtin, *The Story of Westmoreland: A Jamaican Parish* (Self-published 2010) 10–36.

73 Dunn *Sugar and Slaves* (n 71) 161; O Patterson, "Maroon War Jamaica, 1655–1740" (1970) 19(3) Social and Economic Studies 289–322, 297–301.

74 Patterson (n 73) cites, in particular, 1673, Selby, St. Ann; 200 slaves, Clarendon, 1685, Grey, 150, St. Catherine, 1690; 400 Sutton, 1696, Herring, parish not stated, nor numbers, but they were believed to have joined the leeward group of rebels.

75 Brown (n 70) 99–107.

76 See, for example, R Mitchell, "The Maroons of Accompong" *Geographical Magazine* May (National Library of Jamaica 1950, other details unknown).

77 Patterson notes that at the beginning of the 1700s, the strategy of the original Maroon groups toward the new runaways shifted from one of rejection to one

Africans arriving from Central and Southern Africa brought familiarity and sometimes expertise with various technologies in use across Central and Southern Africa. Moreover, enslaved peoples of the early colonial period came from societies that had not yet become engulfed in extreme industrial warfare and impersonal capture. As Carey explains:

> All the evidence suggests that these first slaves and many of the others that followed, came from among the Bakongo or upper Angolan people, who were then Christians and with whom the Portuguese had already established a strong relationship. Many of these were educated Africans, knowledgeable in the sciences, in astronomy, and the crafts, for the Bakongo were well-known smiths and fluent in several languages – most definitely in Arabic (the language of culture and science) and quite possibly Portuguese as well as several native dialects which they would have needed for their extensive trading activities.[78]

Central Africans were also not materially inferior to the European societies commencing trade with them. Their metallurgy and textiles were superior, and Europeans did not then have firearms to provide an advantage in weaponry.[79] This also meant slaves were derived from smaller-scale, internal, and more localised disputes (rather than from rival empires). Thus, often they required long-distance transport from groups dispersed across the southern portion of the continent, with traders bringing them from as far as 2,500 miles inland on treks in which cannabis use was common.[80] There are many instances where purchasers dealt directly with kings and notables and sought those with particular skills. Skills in irrigation, plant biology, and medicinal ethnobotany would have been desirable, in the years before African medicine became associated with an ideologically derided obeah ("witchcraft"/African healer).[81] This was especially so among the earliest settlers in Jamaica, prior to the establishment of the sugar industry, as they had little capital, little experience working with crops such as indigo and yams, and needed to establish plots in hilly terrain or by draining wetlands.[82]

The Central African intellectual contributions in plantation development are richly documented,[83] yet IP protections were unevenly applied in the plantation economy system. Rather, they were extracted, taken abroad, and protected there, where they sometimes led to major innovations in industrial manufac-

of incorporation (n 73) 300.

78 Carey (n 44) 38.

79 Gilbert, Reynolds (n 67) 150, 180–182.

80 ibid 190.

81 Brown (n 70) 87–88; O'Neal (n 70) 102–130.

82 Dunn *Sugar and Slaves* (n 71) 168.

83 Warner-Lewis (n 45), 26–58.

turing.[84] European interest in African medicine was no doubt also influenced by the fact that those who tried to settle on the continent faced a mortality rate of 60 per cent per year.[85] Jamaican settlers and the enslaved also faced extraordinary mortality rates.[86] In the Caribbean, doctors were prescribing mercury pills to owners and slaves alike for almost any ailment – a substance causing dreadful harm.[87] As slaves in the early years were dying within six years of purchase, they were far more interested in the African pharmacopoeia than what the owners were providing, in a context where medicine was seen as an extension of the torturous carceral system that was systematically traumatising them.[88] In the early 18th century, according to O'Neal, "many Europeans were convinced that Africans and the indigenous peoples of the Americas had a vast knowledge of plant medicines and felt that more should be done to discover their secrets".[89] The later changes in attitudes toward African medicine and the role it played in colonial Jamaica become an important part of the story of cannabis, which contributed to the suppression of its history. As the slave trade intensified under British dominance and the abolitionist movement grew in power, colonial bigotries and lies about Africa were increasingly invoked, erasing African history and dehumanising Africans to justify its continuation.

These latter attitudes were more apparent in a narration from Maria Nugent, the wife of the Jamaican governor, written between 1801 and 1805, as she describes receiving the assistance of "an old black nurse [who] brought a cargo of herbs, and wished to try various charms to [expedite] the birth of the child ... But the [white] maids took all her herbs from her, and made her remove all the smoking apparatus she had prepared for my benefit".[90] It is possible the smoking implement described was to administer cannabis, as it has a recorded history of use in childbirth in Southern Africa, along with one record of its use for the same in 300 AD in Jerusalem.[91] Alternatively, it may have been a practice adopted from the Taino, as early records of Spanish settlers describe

---

84 A Graham, "Patents and Invention in Jamaica and the British Atlantic before 1857" (2020) 73(4) *The Economic History Review* 940–963 <https://doi.org/10.1111/ehr.12995>; JG Ortega, Machines, Modernity, and Sugar: The Greater Caribbean in a Global Context, 1812–50" (2014) 9(1) Journal of Global History 1–25 <doi:10.1017/S1740022813000478>.

85 Gilbert, Reynolds (n 67) 185.

86 Dunn (n 71) 164–165, 300–334.

87 Hall (n 11).

88 Dunn "Dreadful Idlers" (n 71).

89 O'Neal (n 70) 103.

90 ibid.

91 M Earlywine, *Understanding Marijuana: A New Look at the Scientific Evidence* (Oxford University Press 2003) 27.

them using ambient smoke from dried herbs as medicine (smudging).[92] It is doubtful, however, that such use would have demanded an "apparatus", while cannabis pipes derived from coconut or calabash could be described as such.

Opportunities for Africans to play a role in seed dispersal would have been greater in the early years of Jamaican settlement because they had greater levels of social mobility and spheres of freedom. Guasco shows that by the 1550s, following Sir Francis Drake's successful campaigns in the Americas, the English and Spanish saw that collaboration with marooned/non-enslaved Africans could be pivotal in capturing colonies.[93] Although free Africans faced the risk of being enslaved in the early colonial years, in the early 1700s, race was still not a fixed idea, ideologically or in practice.[94] In the 1730s, Knight, a slave trader and eventual planter-historian in Jamaica, according to Greene, "displayed no tendency to denigrate the mental capacities of the enslaved nor the integrity of their cultures, emphasizing instead their obvious aptitude for all kinds of work and social interaction, and making a serious effort to understand and appreciate their cultural diversity".[95] While Knight took for granted the legality of slavery in African societies, he recognised their "humanity and mental abilities to handle every sort of work or trade required", and later whose labour "accounted for virtually all of the produce and much of the technical and management skills associated with the island's economy" and its improvement.[96] In his time, there were also about 2,000 blacks and mulattoes living in Jamaica – not including the Maroon population – who had gained their freedom through "their fidelity, good services to their masters, ... [or] by distinguishing themselves" in battle against the French invasion of 1693 or during expeditions against the Maroons.[97] Unlike whites, they did not have access to the rule of law, but the point is that free Africans were not uncommon, and some were involved in trade.[98]

Central Africans also comprised a portion of the early buccaneering classes based out of Port Royal – a "cosmopolitan" place that acted for a time as "a haven for the persecuted",[99] or most importantly, in the north-eastern coastal

92 Knight (n 54).

93 M Guasco, "Free from the Tyrannous Spanyard'? Englishmen and Africans in Spain's Atlantic World" (2008) 29(1) Slavery & Abolition 1–22 <https://doi.org/10.1080/01440390701841018>.

94 Gilbert, Reynolds (n 67).

95 Greene in Knight (n 54) liv.

96 Knight (n 54).

97 Greene in Knight (n 54) 36.

98 Guasco (n 93).

99 Dunn *Sugar and Slaves* (n 71) 183–184.

areas, particularly in the vicinity of the Rio Grande.[100] It was not until the nineteenth century that freedoms for free Africans became more constrained, following a series of uprisings, with Tacky's revolt being the most impactful, and following which a law in 1824 required free blacks to be registered in their parishes.[101] At this point, the enslaved adopted feigned ignorance ("play fool fe catch wise") as a form of resistance and to avoid reprisals from fearful owners and overseers, while African knowledge was preserved in seclusion from whites and laws were passed against African cultural and religious expression.[102] It is important to recognise that for Africans, medicine, like other sciences, had not been ontologically separated from religious thought. Thus, religious leaders played important roles in maintaining African knowledge in medicine as well as playing an important role in generating political resistance to slavery.[103]

A key point here is that captivity for slaves was never total, with absenteeism from duty fluctuating alongside absenteeism of planters/owners, although its consequences could be grotesque and deadly. A case in point is the relative freedom of Africans in Jamaica as described in the famous diaries of Thomas Thistlewood, whose route toward land ownership involved him initially working as an overseer on plantations of the large, often absent, planter class. The ship he sails on in 1750 is boarded by a Black pilot to navigate it into port.[104] This pilot may have been free or enslaved, as it was customary for owners to hire out their workforce, as Thistlewood was to eventually do as a means of building the capital sufficient to purchase land. The fact is, many slaves had significant spheres of mobility to establish independent trading relations – in this case, with travellers on ships bringing slaves from the continent. Much earlier, in the 1680s, planters found "their indentured servants disappeared in the same direction" that English and Spanish colonies refused to go, in part because of the risks posed by buccaneers, although the avoidance was mutual.[105]

While the post-emancipation and post-colonial settings altered, the fundamental relationship between Jamaican agricultural producers of African descent and their knowledge remained. While they widened their spheres of mobility in the ensuing years and played a role in what some have described as "an experimental laboratory" for the invention and innovation of technologies that were vital to the modernisation of European industries, they never had

---

100 Carey (n 44).
101 O'Neal (n 70) 136.
102 Campbell (n 5) 22–25.
103 Brown (n 70); Campbell (n 5) 24–49; O'Neal (n 70) 2020.
104 Hall (n 11).
105 Dunn *Sugar and Slaves* (n 71) 150.

equal access to the law. Meanwhile, slave/plantation owners had the ability to take their innovations to Britain to be patented and increase the profits of industrial producers.[106]

Many of the runaways noted above became part of what Linebaugh and Rediker describe as "the many-headed hydra": the diverse and widespread yet interconnected resistance movements responding to the emerging capitalist order, colonialism, and the various forms of labour exploitation.[107] They did not have to be, however, as there were other routes through which economic market exchange took place regionally in the shadows of the wider "Atlantic World" economy, in which inter- and intra-imperial commerce has been erroneously seen as all-encompassing.[108] As Shepherd has shown, Indigenous long-distance trade and communication throughout the region pre-dated the "Atlantic world economy", and carried forth, primarily through production and exchanges by non-elite whites and free people of colour who were not wealthy enough to invest in the commonly exported commodities, which had, early in the process of colonial settlement, become monopolised by a small plantocracy. This encompassed a wider portion of internal and regional production and exchange than has been accounted for in histories to date. Cannabis could have been included in such trade, intentionally or not. Consider also the fact that on slave ships the rates of slave revolt were perhaps as high as a quarter,[109] while full mutiny occurred in at least 10 per cent.[110] A certain percentage of those succeeded, and those slaves could become buccaneers/pirates, maroons, or merchants and smugglers with the lines between them blurred. Wealthy West African traders were also involved in transatlantic trade, exporting a variety of commodities, including slaves. In the years after British abolition and the era of "legitimate commerce", some vessels surely were commissioned by such traders, though we have little record of them, let alone their cargo.[111]

---

106 Ortega (n 84); Graham (n 84) 943.

107 P Linebaugh, M Rediker, *The Many-Headed Hydra: Sailors, Slaves, Commoners, and the Hidden History of the Revolutionary Atlantic* (Beacon Press 2000).

108 VA Shepherd, "Unity and Disunity, Creolization and Marronage in the Atlantic World: Conceptualizing Atlantic Studies" (2004) 1(1) Atlantic Studies 49–65.

109 Gilbert, Reynolds (n 67) 163.

110 M Rediker, *The Slave Ship: A Human History* (Viking 2007).

111 Shillington (n 67) 234–235.

15.5 JAMAICAN MAROON TERRITORIES AS GENETIC RESERVOIR?

The third consequence of recognising the intellectual and cultural contributions of Central and Southern Africans in early Jamaican history is that we can see they were leading the earliest revolts, rebellions, and maroonage, and placed a deep cultural stamp within Jamaican maroon communities.[112] Escaped Africans were reported in the Caribbean as early as 1502, from the first Spanish expeditions.[113] Some had established free Black communities by the time the British arrived at war with the Spanish in 1660.[114] Campbell cites Curtin, claiming they mostly derived from the northern part of West Africa and from Angola, encompassing numerous tribal groups, though Kongo is just as likely to have been a port of embarkment with captives drawn from across the region.[115]

By 1655, there were at least three settled groups with known leaders, bolstered by 1,200 to 1,500 slaves who ran into the hills upon the Spanish surrender, to join existing groups.[116] Patterson, citing Colonial Office documents, says no less than half of the estimated 3,000 inhabitants upon arrival were Africans.[117] Spanish and British records indicate that for 155 years, the Spanish had been highly dependent on the production of free Africans/Maroons.[118] Carey has provided the richest and most reasoned examination of the political economy of Jamaica under the Spanish. She documents Taino agricultural surpluses being shipped to Cuba and other Spanish colonies. She shows how some Taino "intermingled" and even "integrated into Spanish society and culture up to 1530", though after this time, policies toward them became more severe.[119]

> Despite the cruelties that had formerly been meted out to the Taino, not every Taino found the Spaniards intolerable. There was undoubtably a social intermingling of the various ethnic entities existing in Jamaica at that time, namely the swarthy

---

112 Warner-Lewis (n 45) 58–70.

113 EK Agorsah, "Archaeology and the Maroon Heritage in Jamaica" (1995) 24(2) Jamaica Journal 1–9; R Price, *Maroon Societies: Rebel Slave Communities in the Americas* (2nd edn., Johns Hopkins University Press 1979).

114 MC Campbell, *The Maroons of Jamaica, 1655–1796: A History of Resistance, Collaboration & Betrayal* (Bergin & Garvey 1988); Carey (n 44) 91; B Edwards, "The History of The West Indies, Vol. 1" (1907 Appendix 2) in Price (n 113) 522–535, 537–545; Warner-Lewis (n 45) 69; Knight (n 54).

115 ibid 16.

116 Campbell (n 114) 22; Edwards (n 114).

117 Patterson (n 73).

118 Campbell (n 114) Knight (n 54); Carey (n 44).

119 Carey (n 44) 57.

> Spaniards, who had themselves descended from a Moorish-European-mix, the Taino people, and of course, the new blacks.[120]

She also considers the diversity of roles Africans were playing, despite their limited accounts. Most importantly, she argues there was a large population of African herdsmen, managing at one point a massive number of cattle, horses, and hogs, bringing their skills from Central and North Africa and re-establishing familial structures (as the Spanish encouraged gender parity for social reproduction), in a context where herding was not a Taino practice. Carey also hypothesises that Taino and Africans would have worked together in various spheres, but most importantly, in gold mining. All three economic roles – cropping, herding, and mining – converged in the Rio Grande Valley of Portland. Furthermore, she cites evidence that Taino villages still existed in the latter sixteenth century, with their densest concentration in the Rio Grande. She argues that in this context, intermarriages occurred between African herder men and Taino homesteader wives, providing a social base from which the Leeward Maroons emerged. Similar processes also took place in St Thomas, though there are no known sites of mining activity.

While leeward Maroons survived historically through ecologically minded, land-based livelihoods rooted in place, they were simultaneously highly cosmopolitan. They were comprised of Arabic-speaking Muslims,[121] and Sephardic Jews from the Iberian Peninsula and North Africa, Africans from the South, Central, West, and Sahel along with smatterings of joiners from various parts of Europe and the British Isles. Some were also, for a time, relatively wealthy, as Carey explains:

> There is evidence from the Maroon's oral history and elsewhere to suggest that in Spanish times, and continuing to the early eighteenth century period, many of the Maroons were maritime traders and merchants who operated from the bases in the Rio Grande Valley, and along the northeast coast of the island. The present-day Maroons speak of the great wealth owned by the Nanny Town Maroons in silver plate, gold bullion and other valuable goods. Slaves who would be interviewed one hundred years later would describe the Maroons' wealth in gold, at a time when there was no opportunity for Maroons to earn the same.[122]

Carey argues that the invention of jerk pork on the north-east coast, particularly in Boston Bay, is a product of Maroon cosmopolitanism. It was particularly

---

120 ibid 62.

121 The term "Moors" is often used in the literature, though it is an "exonym", a categorisation not necessarily accepted by those it defines. The term has changed meaning over time, so it is not always a helpful moniker.

122 Carey (n 44) 70.

important for the French buccaneer trade carrying on outside of English and Spanish dominated routes, playing a crucial role in the Maroon economy, and forming cultural exchanges between Taino, Carib, Africans, Arab Muslims, and Jews and a cosmopolitan working class.[123]

Much of what has been said of the influence of Central Africans in Early Jamaica can also be true of the influence of Moors from North Africa, who Sulatānā believes were also working as herdsmen.[124] The influence of "Moorish Muslim mariners and the enslaved Moors" has been under-accounted for and overshadowed in Christian-dominant imperial record-keeping. Some went clandestinely or altered names to escape persecution under King Ferdinand.[125] They, and Muslims from across North and West Africa, were also brought for their skills in agricultural science, military skills, and strategies of defence and security. Windmills, for example, were a westward transmission from Iberian culture originally derived from Muslim Spain, allowing Moors to run millstones and to raise water for irrigation, as they were involved in establishing the earliest sugar plantations and even the Hope Aqueduct in Kingston, which still carries water from the River Hope to the Mona Reservoir for domestic use.[126]

In Jamaica today, the dominant political class continues to deny Maroon indigeneity, in part because doing so would pressure adherence to the United Nations Declaration on the Rights of Indigenous Peoples and jeopardise their interest in mining territories claimed by Maroons, namely Cockpit country.[127] Lackey Espeut offers arguments in support of such claims, repeating findings of a study from 1938 that described Taino origin claims by a Maroon Colonel

123 ibid.

124 Sulatānā (n 47).

125 Curtin (n 72) 10–11. Carey (n 44) posits that Maroon may have actually derived from "Marranose", that is, Jews, rather than the commonly referred to Cimarron.

126 Sulatānā (n 47) 192.

127 R Connell, *The Political Ecology of Maroon Autonomy: Land, Resource Extraction and Political Change in 21st Century Jamaica and Suriname* (UC Berkeley, PhD Thesis 2017) <https://journals.openedition.org/echogeo/17599>; R Connell, "Maroon Ecology: Land, Sovereignty, and Environmental Justice" (2020) 25(2) The Journal of Latin American and Caribbean Anthropology 218–235 <https://doi.org/10.1111/jlca.12496>. For a legal overview of the challenges in accepting claims on indigeneity in Jamaica based on international law, see M Goffe, "The Rights of the Maroons in the Emerging Ganja Industry in Jamaica" (2018) 67(1) Social and Economic Studies 85–115, 103–109 <http://www.jstor.org/stable/45174652>.

from Accompong as "myth-making".[128] His intervention reveals lazy scholarship since archeologists, anthropologists, and historians long ago found hard data proving that in the Maroon experience, African and Taino peoples produced children together, with the Taino passing on Indigenous knowledge to their Maroon offspring. Archaeological work with the University of the West Indies (UWI) in the early 1990s showed that the oldest Maroon town, of what became known as the "leeward maroons", was in fact first a township populated by Taino peoples (Nannytown), with an overlap of Africans, suggesting the first Maroons were in fact Taino.[129] Furthermore, a genetic study published in 2015, using the DNA of 400 people within the territory of the Accompong Maroons, concluded "the genetic data in the current study lend support to the idea that Africans and Taino people both held formative roles in the emergence of Accompong Town Maroons".[130] The genetic diversity of Accompong was not dramatically different from the surrounding areas, which is largely attributed to the fact that Maroons produced children throughout the Island.[131] In response, some mistakenly make the claim that therefore all Jamaicans are in some way Maroon. This is false because the claim to indigeneity also depends upon the maintenance of place-based cultural practices tied to land, generally, though not exclusively, lacking private title. The gradual encroachment upon territory by extending private title has been one assimilationist strategy of the colonial and post-independence state to weaken Maroon autonomy.

The merging of Taino and African peoples is important in this argument because the Taino were seafaring and had familial relations among the islands, through which they travelled regularly,[132] while oral history sources show continued cultural linkages.[133] A monograph in 1938, *The Maroons of Jamaica*,

---

[128] JJ Williams, *The Maroons of Jamaica* (Boston College Press 1938; Espeut, 2021). See also, newspaper clipping from unknown source in National Library of Jamaica in 1938, filed under "Maroons Pre-1900", detailing the release of Joseph Williams' 1938 monograph *The Maroons of Jamaica*.

[129] Agorsah 1993 (n 113), 2007.

[130] N Madrilejo, H Lombard, J Benn Torres "Origins of marronage: Mitochondrial lineages of Jamaica's Accompong Town Maroons" (2015) 27 American Journal of Human Biology 432–437 <https://doi-org.proxy.queensu.ca/10.1002/ajhb.22656>.

[131] Post-1739, slave owners encouraged such relations – forced or otherwise – between Maroon and their slaves because they saw them as being strong "stock", in the same manner they would cattle.

[132] H Beckles, V Shepherd, *Liberties Lost: Caribbean Indigenous Societies and Slave Systems* (Cambridge University Press 2004) 13.

[133] See, for example, Mama G and the Indigenous Women's Circle, but also *The Kromanti Language of the Jamaican Maroons (Final Edit)* (Caribbean Indigenous and Endangered Languages website, the Jamaican Language Unit/

describes a legend of the Moore Town Maroons as having been "maritime people".[134] There is evidence of clay pipes being widely used among slave populations in the Caribbean, turning up in excavations and in Maroon settlements.[135] We know from studies of Central Africans in the Caribbean that smoking was widely practised by both men and women, irrespective of tobacco or hemp.[136] Thus, cannabis genetics likely entered Jamaica via multiple routes at different times. It is also possible African strains were crossed with East Indian strains post-1838, and/or both strains were crossed with hemp.[137]

A rich PhD thesis in Botany from 2011, by Summer Austin Ragosta at the University of Hawai`i at Mānoa, supports the claim that cannabis was part of a wider Maroons ethnobotany.[138] During her fieldwork among the Charlestown Maroons, she catalogued medicinal uses of over 160 plants, with cannabis among them. The Maroons of Scott's Hall claim the extent of their knowledge of medicinal plants extends to over 300 species. Though little commercial cannabis is presently grown in Scott's Hall, it continues to be grown for personal consumption.[139] The idea that Maroon ethnobotany includes cannabis and has a history of regional exchange is also consistent with the written and oral history of the Indigenous Women's Circle in Jamaica, and Gaama Gloria "MaMa G" Simms, first female queen of the Maroons of Suriname, Trinidad and Tobago and keeper of oral history.[140] Mama G explained her mother called it "Guinea Weed", making the point for it to not be confused with "Guinea Hen Weed", another medicinal plant important to Maroons.[141]

Unit for Caribbean Language Research, University of the West Indies, Mona, and UNESCO) <https://www.youtube.com/watch?v=TBKoDaR12UQ>.

134 While the cited source has not been located by the author, this derives from a review of the book in a newspaper cutting with an incomplete reference and only dated by the archivist as "1938". It is titled "First History of the Maroons" and describes the content of the monograph by Williams (n 128). Filed in the National Library of Jamaica, "Maroons Pre-1900s".

135 Beckles, Shepherd (n 132) 87.

136 Warner-Lewis (n 45).

137 Klein et al. (n 18), British National Archives (n 60).

138 SA Ragosta, "Historical Influences on the Development of Indigenous Jamaican Maroon Ethnomedicine: Comparisons with West African and Arawak Ethnopharmacopia" (PhD dissertation, University of Hawai`i at Mānoa 2011).

139 Interview with Deputy Colonel Jone Williams (along with Colonel Lloyd Lattibeaudiere and Secretary Jaqueline Phillips), 1 December 2022.

140 GG "Mama G" Simms, "Maroon Indigenous Women Circle, Jamaica: Historical Recurrences from Indigenous Women's Perspectives" (2018) 19(2) *Journal of International Women's Studies*.

141 Personal conversation, Friday 24 June 2022, during the Annual Charlestown Maroon Conference.

15.6 JAMAICAN MAROONS AND GANJA IN THE EARLY TWENTIETH CENTURY

Colonial archives corroborate evidence of the African origins of Jamaican cannabis. The 1933 report to the League of Nations stated, "the tree has spread nearly over the whole Island, the extreme western parishes – St. James, Hanover and Westmoreland – being the only ones that appear to be free from it".[142] This was a time when one source already claimed it was trafficked to Panama, along with Jamaican workers during its construction between 1904 and 1914.[143] On 22 October 1936, an Inspector General of the Jamaica Constabulary wrote to the Colonial Secretary in Kingston, noting that "Most of the Ganja is grown in the mountainous country and the Buff Bay district which is difficult to access".[144] It is repeatedly described as a tree in police records, consistent with the strains from Southern Africa considered to be "sativa". In 1913, when opium laws were being ammended to include cannabis, it was listed as "cannabis sativa".[145] In recent years, plant biologists dispute the common taxonomy, but the important distinction is that strains from Southern Africa were tall, narrow-leaf varieties, rather than the short, wide-leaf ones common in India – and thus categorised as "indica" – a strain only found by police to be growing in Jamaica as late as September 1989 (though multiple growers in their senior years describe it arriving in the 1970s, which gives a clear example of the ways official state records significantly lag, as Duvall notes of many earlier records).[146] As noted above, this commonly accepted taxonomy is not scientifically sound; however, the Jamaican Constabulary Force was correct that short, wide-leaf plants derived from landraces of the Indian subcontinent were a new importation.[147]

Another report from 10 June 1940 describes the trade in ganja in four mountainous parishes – Trelawney, St Thomas, Portland, St Catherine – home to significant Maroon communities. In this report, a Resident Magistrate for Spanish Town, St Catherine, writes that:

---

142 Jamaica National Archives and Records, File 1B/5/77/330.

143 *The Star* (March 1972, reprint from 1929).

144 Jamaica National Archives and Records, File 1B/5/77/562/1934.

145 Moorsom, 2024, 396 (n 20), Gleaner, "Will Amend Law on Ganja." 1913, Nov 7 p13, Jamaica National Archives, 1970, Daily Gleaner. 1989. "Ganja Growers Turn to New Type of Plant." September 26

146 "Ganja Growers Turn to New Type of Plant" *Daily Gleaner* (26 September 1989); Duvall (n 10) 127.

147 Clarke, Merlin (n 55); Sawler et al. (n 55).

> during the past twelve years during which I have been performing the duties of a resident Magistrate in this Island, I have observed, particularly in the last seven years a considerable increase in the traffic in Ganja – In Trelawney, St. Thomas, Portland, St. Catherine, parishes in which I have had actual experience, the growing of the weed is very extensively (sic) practiced in the less accessible uplands where the police do not visit regularly, and I regret to say Crown Bailiffs (of Crown Lands) and District Constables apparently connive with the cultivators ...[148]

Had the crop arrived with East Indians, and been deeply embedded in their culture, an explanation would be needed as to why Portland, and Buff Bay in particular, would be cited as a centre of the industry in the 1930s. Nowhere do police records make any mention of East Indians being involved in the production, trade, or consumption. In the early twentieth century, a significant number of East Indians were employed labouring on banana plantations in the vicinity of Buff Bay, yet the surrounding uplands were the territory of the Charlestown Maroons, along with a significantly larger population of free Black peasants.[149] Meanwhile, the constabulary force claimed most of the production was destined for consumption in Kingston, rather than for those rural East Indian labourers.[150]

By 1921, close to 73 per cent of the East Indian working population remained agricultural labourers.[151] Some had gained small plots in a settlement programme that ended in 1906, ten acres or one additional acre for every child. A total of 1,204 acres was allocated "primarily in St. Catherine and St. Thomas, then St. James and Clarendon [with] a very small number in St. Elizabeth", while none were in Portland.[152] In fact, Shepherd notes that the slow pace of land acquisition prevented a quick and complete break with the estates and plantations. The primary reason for this was that most remained very poor. A very small number of high-caste Indians bought large plots. However, between 1879 and 1939 the total acreage owned by Indians in Jamaica decreased rather than increased.[153] In 1914, two East Indians in Kingston Pen were charged with growing it, and the arresting officer noted much was grown in the area.[154] Thus, we can be confident that East Indians would only have played a minor role in the ganja produced at the turn of the century. In describing their crop

148 Jamaica National Archives (n 142).

149 See Moorsom, (n 20) that discusses how the plant, growers, and techniques have been systematically "underdeveloped" in these communities.

150 Jamaica National Archives (n 142).

151 Shepherd (n 30) 119.

152 ibid 120–123.

153 ibid 124.

154 Moorsom (n 20) 396; Gleaner (Kingston Daily). 1914. "East Indians Punished for Growing Ganja." March 13, 10.

production, Shepherd claims they grew the plant but offers no material evidence or sources for this assertion.[155] There is some evidence East Indians did grow ganja in the Kingston Pen area, although little evidence of them growing it elsewhere.

If African descendants adopted the practice of smoking it from the East Indian arrivals, there is a logical problem of how they first obtained it, and furthermore, how it was rapidly acclimatised to grow in the parish with the most hostile, damp conditions and farthest away from concentrations of East Indians,[156] who supposedly brought the plant for their own consumption. The earlier cited 1929 article, the 1933 UN, and police reports tell us the production and trade in ganja were widespread, increasing in scope and, to some extent, international. Leonard Howell arrived back in the country from Panama and Harlem, New York, in 1933 and only gained minor attention in St Thomas by 1934. Ganja's mass use in Jamaica predates the rise of Rastafarianism by at least two decades, at least as far as formal doctrine is concerned. Consistent with the plant's African history, its use was associated with harsh labour conditions. Punishments for its use increased alongside labour militancy during the depression of the 1930s, which coincided with a renaissance in racial consciousness and pride in Black, African identity.[157]

It is likely that the territories of the Leeward Maroons, and particularly Buff Bay, were described as the core of production in the 1930s because the plant had a history dating back to activities on the north-east coast in the sixteenth and seventeenth centuries. This was the Rio Grande and cosmopolitan north-east coast Carey describes, within which there is rich evidence of Central African culture, as well as cannabis use. Another aspect of this puzzling history is that if it was grown widely among Portland Maroons, it would still need to be explained how it became less prominent in their culture as the plant's production moved west. The role of cannabis within the Rastafari movement has been dynamic and gained greater importance as it expanded and became more integrated into commercial cultural production.[158] At the same time, Maroon

155 Shepherd (n 30) 127, 130. There is a puzzling inconsistency in Shepherd's narration because earlier cited data on land grant allocations shows none in Portland, and yet later she writes that "Deeds up to 1940 indicated that more land was owned by Indians in St. Thomas, St. Mary and Portland than [any] other parishes combined", suggesting "a high concentration on banana farming in those parishes" where they sold their crop to agents, including the United Fruit Company.

156 Ehrlich (n 32).

157 Campbell (n 5) 39–65.

158 Benard (n 4).

culture has shifted, partly due to their embrace of Christian churches,[159] and perhaps by seeking the respect of governments, leading people to abandon aspects of their African cultures in favour of parts that more easily qualify for culture and tourism grants.[160] Through much of the past two centuries, Maroons have had an ambivalent relationship with governments, both desiring independence and simultaneously seeking their respect and collaboration. Drawing on the martial culture that helped them survive, many joined police and military forces in Jamaica and in the UK, US, and Canada. Yet, elders today have explained that in their youth in the 1950s, they learnt to be ashamed of their Maroon identities, partly because of the mercenary role some played for the colonial government in suppressing slave and working-class rebellions, but also because they were impoverished, continually encroached upon, and faced repression and high outmigration.[161] Maroons of Moore Town (in the Rio Grande Valley) protested in November 1946, that members of the Jamaica Constabulary had "stormed their town … recklessly beat up unoffending old people and children, threw away their Abeng (cow horn instrument) smashed their drums and threw them in the river".[162] One might interpret that, in some respects, the campaign against ganja was an extension of this form of cultural desecration. That said, it would be a mistake to say Maroons in Portland abandoned it. In fact, the administration of former Colonel Frank Lumsden played a prominent role in advocating for changes to the Dangerous Drugs Act (DDA) in 2015 and argued for language safeguarding the rights of Indigenous Maroon communities in the industry and creating a framework that allowed them greater participation in the industry.[163]

In Accompong, the 1956 Mann-O-Rowe case exemplifies how the Jamaican state showed its historic contempt toward the principles of the 1739 treaty and the rights of Maroons to produce cannabis. The case of Mann Octavius Rowe, as reported in the *Daily Gleaner*, " … arises out of a raid by the police, led by Superintendent James Ricketts, on January 23, this year[.] They are said to have found 3,1/2 bags of ganja weighing 75lbs, and [a] match box containing

---

[159] Kopytoff, B. K. 1987. Religious Change among the Jamaican Maroons: The Ascendance of the Christian God within a Traditional Cosmology. *Journal of Social History*, *20*(3), 463–484. http://www.jstor.org/stable/3788108

[160] Such as those from The National Heritage Trust, the Minister of Culture, Entertainment and Sport, and the Tourism Enhancement Funds.

[161] Scott's Hall, 26 October 2023, Charlestown 24 June 2022, and Charlestown 23 June 2024.

[162] "Maroons Resentful over Quaco's Fate" *Kingston Gleaner* (12 November 1946) 1.

[163] Goffe (n 127). See also Chapter 12 of this volume by Marcus Goffe.

ganja seeds in Rowe's room", along with "certain banned books".[164] To this, Rowe had "admitted that the ganja was in his room but said that he had it there for medicinal purposes. He also admitted the possession of the books". In court, it was argued that the Jamaican constabulary force did not have jurisdiction because their Treaty, signed in 1738, meant that aside from the crime of murder, Maroons had the right to be tried by their own community.[165] The judges in a court of appeals eventually ruled against him in the case, citing nine "statutes subsequent" to the Treaty between 1741 and 1855 through which the government had assumed control of the land and that the "myth" of Maroon control remained only because some commissioners had "failed to divide up the land at Accompong as at other places". Rowe was sentenced to six months in jail with additional time for the banned literature.

Much about this case is fascinating, but most notable is the fact that Rowe was to become a notable figure in Accompong, if he were not already at that time. He would go on to become Secretary of State, and just over a decade later he ran for the position of Colonel, coming in second place quite respectably. He later described himself as a member of the largest family in Accompong, in his words "considered like a 'Royal Family'", tracing on his paternal side lineage with Queen Nanny eight generations down the line.[166] He was last recorded by Besson at the healthy age of "nearly 95" in 1999. Here, a respected Maroon figure was arrested with 75 pounds in 1956, presumably grown on his ten acres of hereditary land, or potentially, further in the bush. It is hard to believe his claim that it was for medicinal purposes, though the trustworthiness of the full story is questionable. It is theoretically possible that he planned to make herbal tonics, which had international markets. In the 1930s, Leonard Howell may have been selling such tonics in Harlem.[167] The important fact is that as far as his Maroon community was concerned, Rowe's ganja production was clearly acceptable. It is also consistent with the findings of Rubin and Comitas who found habitual cannabis production and consumption deeply integrated into the agricultural work cycle in rural communities, for whom "for the great majority, it is an agricultural sideline which fits well with their established style of life and for some, it provides additional income".[168] This is

[164] "Are Maroons Exempt from Jamaica Law? No, Says R.M." *Daily Gleaner* (13 March 1956).

[165] "Maroon Loses Ganja Appeal" *Daily Gleaner* (26 June 1956).

[166] J Besson, *Transformations of Freedom in the Land of the Maroons: Creolization in the Cockpits, Jamaica* (Ian Randle 2016) 113–121.

[167] Lee (n 31) 33–34.

[168] V Rubin, C Lambros, *Ganja in Jamaica* (Mouton 1975); Klein et al. (n 18).

generally true of much of rural Africa.[169] Herein, it has been shown that there are no such equivalent historical Indian records. Yet, there is potent evidence of African usage of ganja, albeit ground and crushed, across several historical and anthropological sources. The origin story of Jamaican cannabis and its African roots adds not only a new area to be researched, but also a new basis upon which the IP system that seeks to protect owners' rights must be questioned in today's post-colonial epoch.

15.7 CONCLUSION

The criminalisation of the cannabis plant in Jamaica was linked to demonisation and debasement of African identity, including the criminalisation of Obeah, the suppression of labour resistance, and to Rastafarianism. The implications of the argument here are that if the gene stock of Jamaican cannabis arrived with Africans, then issues of reparatory justice should be considered in plans to profit from it, including the protections sought using IP laws. Currently, this gene stock is disappearing, as producers increasingly resort to imported, hybridised varieties which are then subject to open pollination. Thus, after so much suffering because of this plant, Jamaicans, and especially Maroon peoples, are gradually being dispossessed of their inheritance despite increasing interest in the commodity.

Key policy positions should be taken to address several issues. The first is to ensure that crop destruction is halted while a genetic survey is conducted to determine what strains are present and whether any have been conserved from the era of "longtime" ganja (plants that took up to nine months to mature and were passed down from earlier times). Given that Maroons of Moore Town, Charlestown, and Accompong clearly played important roles in transmitting the seed into the present, they should be involved in the practice of gene collecting in their territories and should have some level of ownership over any remaining seed stock. This would invoke further consideration of plant varieties.[170] Second, with their involvement, a seed bank and preservation farm could be created, which could help protect the integrity of ancient strains, if they do still exist. Some Rastafari have been conserving the original strains, and others are trying to revive old strains by breeding from feral seed stock found in remote locations, making efforts to breed out traits introduced by open-pollinated hybrids. Third, genetic mapping of these strains can help us

---

169 C Duvall, "A Brief Agricultural History of Cannabis in Africa, from Prehistory to Canna-colony" (2019) 48(48) EchoGéo <https:/doi.org/10.4000/echogeo.17599>.

170 For a discussion of plant varieties, see Chapter 7 of this volume by Larry Sandell.

put together pieces of Jamaica's history that remain mysteries, potentially revealing the extraordinary achievements of their ancestors. Thereafter, the community can choose the IP protection most suitable for them.

Coming back to the discussion of culture and resistance in the theoretical framework provided by Williams and Hall, the dual impacts of repression and commercialisation on Maroon and Rastafarian cultures of cannabis in the Jamaican context must be considered. The impacts on systems of cannabis production and plant genetics are complicated, but coincide with forms of development and under-development. Most importantly, there is a turn toward the importation of fast-maturing hybrid seeds and the increasing use of cloning. Given the dynamic variables on the cultural, legal-juridical, biological, and production factors, the idea of authenticity in the plant, a system of production, and cultural practices around it is highly problematic. Hence it ought to be asked, who has the right to claim authenticity when culture is not static? What is the relationship between culture and power, especially when the culture has relative and reflexive structuration within the confines of global capitalist relations of production?[171] In answering these questions, one must recognise that the foundations of Jamaica's original strains are African, and Maroons have played a crucial role in keeping them alive over hundreds of years, supporting the continuation of consumption patterns common among the poorest of working-class people coping with multigenerational traumas.

These should also be considered when assessing changes in ganja culture following the 2015 amendment to the DDA 2015, particularly as they relate to the sale of legal recreational and medicinal use. The process of decriminalisation and legalisation coincides with new forms of retail that present the plant in new ways, to some degree linked to the science of the plant and others towards the sciences and arts associated with marketing and branding.[172] The latter involves the psychology of manipulation – suggestion and enticement – possible within the confines of the law, or its interpretation and enforcement. These changes have accelerated pre-existing trends in breeding and methods of production, which impact patterns of rural life and agricultural production (e.g., cloning, 3+ crop cycles, drying methods), and consumption, with rising THC levels. The former craft product "gom" (finger hash) is being displaced by increased uses of oils and concentrates. For example, young people are adding liquid nicotine to their joints, vaping pens are introduced, some with the additions of flavours or terpene profiles intentially more appealing to children. In this discussion, the continued relevance or application of the concept of alienation should be considered when teasing out the nature of changes in the

[171] See also Chapter 14 of this volume by Bryan Khan.
[172] See Part I of this volume on "Branding".

industry, and what the "Frankfurt school" thinker, Walter Benjamin, described as "aura" in the "Work of Art in the Age of Mechanical Reproduction".[173] Considering Jamaican cannabis as a work of art and cultural resistance, this chapter concludes with the consideration of whether it is possible for the Jamaican cannabis industry to progress *without* smallholder, Rastafari, and Maroon producers being further estranged from the product and production of the plant their forebears fought for. A historically aware approach, as advanced in this chapter and by TWAIL scholars, would argue for more than simply recognition of the past achievements of Maroon and Rastafari producers, but also for material benefit in the future industry.[174]

ACKNOWLEDGEMENTS

This chapter was produced by research conducted with the support of the Social Sciences and Humanities Research Council Postdoctoral fellowship number: 756-2021-0343 under the supervision of Dr Daniel Tubb in the Department of Anthropology, University of New Brunswick, and was given ethics approval under file number REB #2021-111. I am especially grateful for the help of Adolphus Depass at the National Library of Jamaica, whose dedicated work over many years has assisted greatly in accessing relevant documents. I am also grateful for the far-reaching support of Karine Girard, who, in addition to freeing up some of my labour time, edited work at various stages of this project.

[173] W Benjamin, *Illuminations: Essays and Reflections* (Schocken 1968).

[174] Elsewhere I argue that this is only possible through the formation of a democratically controlled marketing board, possibly within the umbrella of the Jamaican Agricultural Commodities Regulatory Authority, but not beholden to it, and only in a context that recognises particular rights of Maroon and Rastafari producers, Moorsom (n 20).

Epilogue to *Intellectual Property and Cannabis*

Andrea Zappalaglio

The contributions that compose the present book provide a nuanced picture of how difficult it is to adapt the paradigm of law, specifically of Intellectual Property (IP) Law, as well as the social sciences, to one of the most complex and controversial products on the planet: cannabis. Put simply, the relationship between law, social sciences in general, and cannabis is a real mess.

This complexity stems from different factors, the key being the many faces and lives of this iconic member of the family *Cannabaceae*. What is cannabis? A traditional cultural expression, a flowering plant of religious importance, a national symbol of Jamaica, a source of molecules for therapeutic use? Or, is it a dangerous drug, often used by music and movie stars as a distinctive item calculated to spark controversy? According to the descriptions provided in the scientific literature, media, and popular culture, cannabis is all of the above. Cannabis is a truly *multidimensional good.*

Unsurprisingly, this complex background leads to further complications when the paradigm of IP Law is applied to it. This area of law protects, in its essence, intangible assets of different kinds: cultural goods, such as art and music (copyright); the distinctive character of signs used in the course of trade (trademarks); new and non-obvious industrial inventions (patents), and so on. The IP family is very diverse and inhomogeneous. Thus, its interaction with cannabis is necessarily complicated and variable.

Indeed, the contributors to this volume provide plenty of examples of the complexity of this scenario. For instance, it is shown that while patents provide protection to a growing number of cannabis-based products, trademarks still deny protection to this good and the imagery related to it, such as its iconic leaf, on the basis of morality and public order public clauses. Similarly, while the Law of Passing Off protects the goodwill associated with the business of artists and stars who associate themselves with cannabis, the use or association of a copyright work with marijuana can be considered "prejudicial to the honour or reputation" of the artist who owns such a right.

This contradictory scenario is, in turn, nothing but a symptom of a larger problem: IP is often incapable, because of its very design, of providing a satisfactory answer to systems that are too complex and multifaceted. This issue is by no means unique to the study area investigated in this work. However, this is a perfect case study. In fact, cannabis can be at the same time a source of innovation, a powerful driver for business, and a symbol of tradition, culture, and spirituality. It is fair to say that there is no single legal tool that can provide a satisfactory answer to all the dimensions embodied in a product as complex as this.

Speaking about the multidimensional nature of this good, the heated debates concerning the legalisation of cannabis and the related political discussions must not divert attention from what can be considered one of the most important points in this analysis. That is, cannabis is by no means just a business and/or an icon to exhibit for marketing purposes. Cannabis is a fundamental symbol of Jamaica, its culture, its producers, and their historical roots.

This is why it is important to prevent the genericization of the "product cannabis". In other words, *Jamaican* cannabis must not be trivialised as merely "something to smoke", but protected as a source of specific place-based know-how as well as an essential component of the – too often diluted and tarnished – "brand Jamaica". Indeed, this book puts forward a number of strong arguments as to why this must be the case, showing how much this product represents emancipation from colonial and post-colonial politics, fights for civil rights and against racism, and more. In this regard, some IP rights, such as Geographical Indications, Collective Marks, and *sui generis* provisions, more or less modelled upon IP logic, can potentially contribute to providing an answer, even if only indirect and partial.

This brings my reflections to a final point: Can IP Law and law, in general, support cannabis and its importance for innovation, tradition, medicine, culture, etc., rather than merely criminalise it? The answer is probably yes, *as long as* expectations are kept within reasonable boundaries. In particular, it must not be forgotten that cannabis is not just a multidimensional good but also global in nature. In this sense, it is really a symbol of the worldwide success of Jamaican culture.

This means that a complete and coherent harmonisation of the legal provisions on cannabis, although desirable, is unlikely. This means that, among other things, it is destined to remain perfectly legal in some countries, while being merely tolerated or totally illegal in others. This occurs even in the same regions. For instance, in the EU, Cannabis is legal in Germany but criminalised in neighbouring France. This scenario will undoubtedly make conducting business in this area harder and riskier and, even worse, hinder innovation based on cannabis and its molecules. Efforts should be made to prevent or at least limit these unreasonable adverse effects related to the regulation of this product. Moreover, it is equally important to ensure the protection of cannabis as a traditional cultural expression, with its related symbolic and identity value, preserving its uniqueness from genericisation and trivialisation.

This volume provides a wealth of suggestions on how this can be done, while at the same time, reminding the academic community of the importance of reflecting on the unique challenges linked to unique, multidimensional products.

Index